Jerry F. Hough

# The Struggle
# for the Third World
## Soviet Debates and American Options

The Brookings Institution

*Washington, D.C.*

*Library of Congress Cataloging-in-Publication Data*

Hough, Jerry F., 1935–
  The struggle for the third world.

  Includes index.
  1. Developing countries—Foreign relations—Soviet
Union.     2. Soviet Union—Foreign relations—Developing
countries.     3. World politics—1945–
I. Title.
D888.S65H68     1985     327.470172'4     84-45856
ISBN 0-8157-3746-7
ISBN 0-8157-3745-9 (pbk.)

987654321

THE BROOKINGS INSTITUTION is an independent organization devoted to nonpartisan research, education, and publication in economics, government, foreign policy, and the social sciences generally. Its principal purposes are to aid in the development of sound public policies and to promote public understanding of issues of national importance.

The Institution was founded on December 8, 1927, to merge the activities of the Institute for Government Research, founded in 1916, the Institute of Economics, founded in 1922, and the Robert Brookings Graduate School of Economics and Government, founded in 1924.

The Board of Trustees is responsible for the general administration of the Institution, while the immediate direction of the policies, program, and staff is vested in the President, assisted by an advisory committee of the officers and staff. The by-laws of the Institution state: "It is the function of the Trustees to make possible the conduct of scientific research, and publication, under the most favorable conditions, and to safeguard the independence of the research staff in the pursuit of their studies and in the publication of the results of such studies. It is not a part of their function to determine, control, or influence the conduct of particular investigations or the conclusions reached."

The President bears final responsibility for the decision to publish a manuscript as a Brookings book. In reaching his judgment on the competence, accuracy, and objectivity of each study, the President is advised by the director of the appropriate research program and weighs the views of a panel of expert outside readers who report to him in confidence on the quality of the work. Publication of a work signifies that it is deemed a competent treatment worthy of public consideration but does not imply endorsement of conclusions or recommendations.

The Institution maintains its position of neutrality on issues of public policy in order to safeguard the intellectual freedom of the staff. Hence interpretations or conclusions in Brookings publications should be understood to be solely those of the authors and should not be attributed to the Institution, to its trustees, officers, or other staff members, or to the organizations that support its research.

iii

names.

↑ 63, 233, 235, 237-38
240, 248, 284-86
276

# Foreword

FOR THE PAST twenty-five years, most crises in Soviet-American relations have occurred because of events in the third world—in Vietnam, Iran, Angola, Nicaragua. Confrontations over third world countries seem destined to continue as the superpowers attempt to extend their influence and achieve at least symbolic economic and political victories. Objectively seen, the Soviet Union has not achieved much success in the competition for world influence, but American images of a decisive, ideologically monolithic, determined foe persist nonetheless. Given that much of the world is naturally turbulent and that U.S.-Soviet interactions can make any world issue very dangerous, it seems important that more reflective judgments be applied.

The major purpose of Jerry F. Hough's study is to contribute to a more sophisticated understanding of Soviet attitudes toward the third world, and of their behavior there and how to cope with it. Because official Soviet policy directives are unavailable and activities in third world countries are subject to contradictory interpretations, the author turns to scholarly discussions of third world issues published in Soviet books and journals. Reviewing debates that have occurred over half a century and probing beneath the elliptical narrative required by censorship—the esoteric subject matter, the stylized jargon—Hough discerns internal attitudes toward Soviet policy that are varied, sometimes uncertain in their implied recommendations, and often contentious. He argues that the Soviet Union is grappling with many of the same dilemmas the United States confronts and is reassessing the validity of its traditional goals and analyses. As Americans understand this, he believes that we will be in a better position to understand the world that we seek to shape and the influence we can reasonably hope to achieve.

Jerry F. Hough is professor of political and policy sciences at Duke University and an associated staff member of the Brookings Institution. He would like to acknowledge the helpfulness of Karen Dawisha, Franklin Griffiths, and John Steinbruner, who read the manuscript and whose com-

v

ments he deeply appreciates. He also thanks James Schneider, who edited the manuscript; Christine Potts, who verified its factual accuracy; and Nancy Brauer, who coordinated the project. Further acknowledgments appear in the author's preface.

Brookings gratefully acknowledges the financial support provided by the Ford Foundation throughout the project's duration and by the John D. and Catherine T. MacArthur Foundation during its final phases.

The author wishes to note that the International Research and Exchange Board supported four exchange trips to the Soviet Union between 1977 and 1983 in connection with this project and also brought Soviet scholars to the United States. Carly Rogers of the board kept the author informed about Soviet visitors and arranged meetings.

The views expressed here are solely those of the author and should not be ascribed to the persons or organizations whose assistance is acknowledged or to the trustees, officers, or staff members of the Brookings Institution.

BRUCE K. MACLAURY
*President*

*January 1986*
*Washington, D.C.*

# Author's Preface

FOR A BOOK so many years in the making, those who have contributed details or ideas may not only be too numerous to mention, but perhaps too numerous even to recall. Nevertheless, two broad groups, at least, deserve special citation. First, in the 1960s and early 1970s many scholars wrote books and especially dissertations on the growing Soviet literature about the outside world. Written as censorship was just being loosened and before much contact was permitted with Soviet scholars, this literature contains many excellent insights, but also much analysis that has not stood the test of time as more access has been possible and more information available. I thought it would be misleading to refer the reader uncritically to such works without pointing to differences in interpretation, but it would also be churlish to quarrel with this pioneering work.

The compromise I have made has been to leave much of this early literature uncited, but it is an uneasy compromise. In the aggregate this literature is an indispensable aid to the serious scholar studying this period. Its contribution to this book has been substantial—far more so than is indicated in the footnotes—and real thanks should be expressed to those who began opening the door to a new type of analysis about the Soviet Union at a time when the difficulties were very great.

The second group whose help is not adequately acknowledged in the footnotes are the Soviet scholars. I have met some 200 of them during the past eight years, including a great many of those whose work is cited in the footnotes. Most have been more than willing to discuss and explain their work and that of other scholars, to provide bibliographic leads, and in some cases even to read sections and chapters of the manuscript and provide comments. A number—"conservative" as well as "liberal"— have been as forthcoming in discussing Soviet scholarly debates as Western colleagues would be in discussing theirs. It is unfortunate that these scholars in particular cannot be named, but the rules of the scholarly exchange dictate that all conversations be off the record.

Still, Soviet scholars as a group have made an enormous contribution to this book. They have contributed greatly to an understanding of the complexity of the Soviet polity and even of the degree of freedom within it that would not be suspected from the Western totalitarian model of the Soviet Union or from those Soviet spokesmen who strengthen the totalitarian image in the West by themselves presenting a misleading narrow view of the Soviet Union. These latter have done great harm to their country in international relations, and the author is especially grateful to those others who have had the courage to trust a foreigner writing about very sensitive subjects because they thought a more realistic understanding of the Soviet Union abroad was worth the personal risk. I have, of course, made my own judgments about the Soviet debates and especially about the policy inferences to be drawn from them; Soviet scholars bear no responsibility for the errors in the book. I hope the help they have provided is only a foretaste of the relationship between American and Soviet scholars that will become increasingly open and civilized—and that will be an important part of breaking down the dangerously simplified stereotypes that exist on both sides.

J.F.H.

# Contents

ix

CHAPTER ONE

# Introduction

THE CENTRAL problem in Soviet-American relations is clearly the nuclear relationship, for only in this realm do the two superpowers have the ability to destroy each other. The key geopolitical problem has long been considered the alignment of Europe, because imbalances in that alignment have touched off two wars in this century. Yet since the building of the Berlin Wall in 1961, the major crises in Soviet-American relations have occurred in the third world: Cuba, Vietnam, the Middle East, and Afghanistan. Even lesser third world events have provoked a temporary sense of crisis in the United States, although they carried no real threat of U.S.-Soviet confrontation. Only the specialist remembers Patrice Lumumba's revolutionary activities in the Congo in the early 1960s or the American invasion of the Dominican Republic in 1965. More recently it has become a cliché that events of similar magnitude—Soviet-backed Cuban activities in Angola, for instance—have seriously compromised détente.

There are several reasons for the disparity between our sense of the importance of Europe or the nuclear balance and the degree to which events in the third world have been the center of attention in the U.S.-Soviet relationship. Basically, the issues of Europe and nuclear balance have become less significant than traditional geopolitical analysis would indicate. This analysis was developed in the prenuclear age when the number of troops and the deployment of weapons had clear-cut meanings and when the formation of alliances and the acquisition of allies had a calculable effect. In the nuclear era, alliances have often become less important for the safety of the superpowers. Indeed, in a nuclear age, as Robert Tucker rightly points out, "allies cannot improve one's core security, [but] they may threaten it, since the prospect of using nuclear weapons is most likely to arise as a result of threats to their security."[1] Conquering Western Europe would not serve Soviet interests; it would merely deprive the USSR of a source of advanced technology and present it with headaches analogous to those caused by Solidarity in Poland. As for nuclear balance, no foreseeable weapons program on either side can really upset it. The real problem has become how to structure nuclear forces so as to reduce the sense of anxiety on both sides.

Some of the factors in international relations that have increased in importance since World War II are associated more with the third world than with Europe. Dependence on Middle East petroleum is only the most dramatic example of a more general Western reliance on the supply of third world raw materials. Moreover, many in both the United States and the Soviet Union see the two countries as locked in a struggle over values in which the ideological threat, especially in developing countries, seems as great as or maybe greater than any military threat.

Basically, however, the U.S. problem with the third world is anxiety about the unknown, about symbols, and about ambiguous goals. Although Western Europe has been very stable and the Soviet Union has remained willing to intervene militarily to preserve stability in Eastern Europe, the third world has seemed strange, fragile, and explosive. A coup based on a single brigade brought Gamal Abdel Nasser to power, and his death brought another drastic reorientation in Egypt's foreign policy and economic life. Communists in Afghanistan attempted to seize power in a desperate response to the arrest of their leaders, and their effort happened to work. The defeat of Chad's 2,500-man army in the remote Saharan desert by an army not much larger left its 3.5 million people virtually defenseless. Even a little foreign involvement can affect civil wars between such small forces. Thus the temptation to intervene covertly or with proxies is strong, and the temptation to believe that the intervention of an adversary or his proxies is having a decisive impact is even stronger.

Anxiety about events in the third world is intensified by an awareness that, aside from a handful of specialists, we do not understand the forces at work there. Islamic fundamentalism in Iran and sectarian conflicts in Lebanon represent values and intensities of feeling beyond our experience. And we have learned from bitter experience the dangers of thinking we do understand. Neither American doves nor hawks, for instance, compre-

---

1. "The Nuclear Debate," *Foreign Affairs*, vol. 63 (Fall 1984), p. 30. Tucker also points out that our commitment to Western Europe is more a commitment to values than to safety—as it was in leading to intervention in World War I and World War II.

hended that a major reason for the communist success in Vietnam was that the revolution was directed not only against the Western foreigner but also against the "foreign" Chinese middle class that dominated South Vietnamese cities and was being supported by the United States. Americans instinctively feel that if they do not understand a situation, then anything—even something worse than the oil boycott or the seizure of hostages in Iran—can happen.

The anxiety is also intensified by Americans' sense that the will of the United States is being tested in the third world in a way that goes beyond the issues immediately involved. In this nuclear era, deterrence rests on logically irreconcilable bases. To refuse to threaten nuclear retaliation would be to invite nuclear blackmail by an opponent, but the actual use of nuclear weapons would likely lead to such horrible results that such use would be irrational. A reliable deterrent essentially rests, however, on the sense of the opponent that one will ultimately meet a commitment, even if it is irrational to do so. Tests of will between the United States and the Soviet Union in a nuclear context are obviously too dangerous, yet U.S. and Soviet leaders want to demonstrate to themselves and to others that they cannot be pushed around, that they have the will to meet commitments. Countries that have little strategic or economic significance in themselves thus become symbols of the most profound questions of national defense because they provide the only seemingly safe arena in which each side can judge the other's resolve and intentions.

And finally, the anxiety is intensified because the United States has never seriously faced up to the question of the kind of Soviet restraint in the third world that it can reasonably expect to promote. Much of the discussion of a "code of détente" implicitly assumes that the United States should be free to engage in a range of overt and covert military, economic, and political actions to influence the third world—including detailed efforts to influence the composition of the Lebanese and El Salvadoran governments—while the Soviet Union should withdraw altogether from efforts to influence third world developments.

The list of cases in which the United States has established double standards for third world superpower behavior is a long one indeed. It is simply asserted as self-evident that sovereign Nicaragua—1,000 miles from U.S. shores—cannot be allowed to accept Soviet MiG-21s, while the United States must be able to send the equivalent of much more advanced MiG-29s to Pakistan, which virtually borders on the Soviet Union. America's use of France as a proxy in African activities is taken for granted—in fact, the only complaint was about French reluctance to intervene in Chad—but the Soviet Union has no right to use Cuba as its proxy in Africa. The United States has every right to send armed forces to rescue hostages in Iran, but imagine the reaction if the Soviet Union would send a naval armada to the Caribbean and then send helicopters to rescue Soviet hostages in Mexico City.

Expectations of a code of détente in which the Soviet Union withdraws from the third world are simply unrealistic as long as it has any image of itself as a superpower. There must be a vague unconscious sense that we are trying to achieve the impossible, that the rules of the game we are trying to enforce are inherently unstable over the long term, and that some day the Soviet Union is going to insist on its right either, for example, to send MiG-21s to Nicaragua or to exclude advanced American weapons from Pakistan or even Turkey.

It is scarcely an original idea that U.S. insecurity about its third world policy has been counterproductive both at home and abroad. Usually, this insecurity is referred to as a post-Vietnam syndrome, but public insecurity predated U.S. entry into the Vietnam War and was a major reason for that entry. American leaders knew that Vietnam might well be a quagmire—everyone remembered France's humiliating withdrawal—but they feared the domestic political consequences if South Vietnam fell.

Those who think that American insecurity over the third world began with the defeat in Vietnam should review the reactions of the American press of the late 1950s and early 1960s. They bear striking similarities to the reactions of the late 1970s and early 1980s. In the late 1950s the talk was of a missile gap rather than a window of vulnerability. The launching of Sputnik and then Yuri Gagarin into space produced fears that technological advances would enable the Soviet Union to outstrip the progress of the United States and that the Soviet economic model would become an irresistable lure for developing countries. Henry Kissinger was making his reputation with a book on the problems of using nuclear weapons in Europe and the need to reassure Europeans about the reliability of the American nuclear umbrella. But as in the 1970s and 1980s, attention was focused primarily on the third world. Fidel Castro's victory precipitated a major crisis in the Caribbean. Africa was in turmoil: Ghana, Guinea, and Mali were in the Soviet camp, Patrice Lumumba was leading radical forces in the Belgian Congo, and the revolt in Algeria was destroying the stability of the French political system. Guerrilla action simmered in Vietnam, and communist influence was increasing in Indonesia. Nasser seemed a Soviet proxy who was trying to dominate the Middle East. When John F. Kennedy stated in his inaugural address that "a new generation, born in this century, has come to power," he was talking about Ronald Reagan's generation (the two presidents were only six years apart in age), and Kennedy and Reagan both campaigned on the same major themes of the Soviet threat and the need to correct American weakness.

American fears were clearly overreactions. Although Vietnam went communist and Cuba remained so, Indonesia and Egypt are now friendly to the United States. With the exception of other parts of Indochina, the countries of East and Southeast Asia that were thought to be dominoes actually prospered as moderates after the fall of Vietnam. Algeria served as a mediator in the hostage crisis in Iran; Zaire (the old Belgian Congo) has sent troops to support the United States in Chad. And as for the fear of Soviet technological superiority and attractiveness for the third world, few other concerns of 1960 seem so anachronistic.

There are, to be sure, other countries of concern today, but on balance the Soviet position in the third world is no better than it was a quarter of a century ago. Indeed, in fundamental terms it is worse. Radical revolutions have been occurring only in such preindustrial countries as Afghanistan, Yemen, Ethiopia, Angola, and Nicaragua. The politics of industrializing third world countries—Taiwan, Indonesia, Iran, Egypt, Brazil, and Mexico—have been moving to the center or the right. Radical countries such as China and Mozambique have also had a tendency to move to the right in recent years.

The reason has been that the Soviet economic system has not proved a strong model for economic growth and has lost out to the Western and Japanese models. The system has also prevented the Soviet Union from developing the kind of ability to export technology that has been achieved by South Korea, Hong Kong, and Brazil—let alone Japan.

From the perspective of twenty-five years, the constant sense of tension and crisis with respect to the third world has been costly as well as exaggerated. In particular, given the basic similarities in the third world in 1960 and 1985—and, indeed, the favorable direction of the trends—the United States has paid too high a domestic price for its insecurity. Political leaders hope that a dramatic posture in foreign affairs—some might say dramatic posturing—will project an image of strong leadership, but in practice the inability to control events contributes far more to an image of weakness. The popular sense of constant Soviet threat and of constant American weakness is one of the reasons that the United States has had six presidents in the last quarter century.

The Reagan administration has helped reduce the level of American insecurity, but it has done so in a very dubious manner. By exaggerating dangers in cases like Grenada, it created a mood of triumph when American policy and actions succeeded, but the exaggeration has also created grounds for real panic if something goes wrong somewhere in the world. The administration has intensified America's sense of a Manichean struggle of good and evil between the Soviet Union and the United States that will plague its successors—and maybe itself—because someday something surely will go wrong.

A new realism about the third world, about the Soviet role there, and about the very nature of international relations is vital. By failing to develop realistic expectations and rules of the game, the United States is setting the stage for a dangerous and unnecessary crisis sometime in the future. Because of its failure to realize that the influence of the Soviet Union has been in decline in the third world, the United States has not understood the necessity for applying one of the major lessons of the Cuban missile crisis: an adversary who is willing to retreat and make concessions must be given some face-saving way of doing it. (This becomes particularly true in dealing with a young leader such as Mikhail Gorbachev.) Because it has not understood that the Western economic system has been the decisive element in defeating the Soviet Union in the third world, the United States has exaggerated the importance of military force and neglected the importance of interest rates and the value of the dollar as elements of national security. Americans have not paid as high a price for mistakes as they might have because they have faced an ailing and sluggish Soviet leadership over the last decade, but over the next decade the challenge is likely to be much more vigorous.

The major purpose of this study is to contribute to a more sophisticated understanding of Soviet behavior in the third world and of how to cope with it. It does this not by looking at the steps the Soviet Union has taken in these countries but at Soviet debates about third world issues.

The problem with examining actual Soviet actions as a key to understanding is that they will always support alternative interpretations. Was the invasion of Afghanistan an attempt to avoid the loss of an ally or an aggressive thrust toward the Persian Gulf? Was the Soviet provision of powerful antiaircraft missiles to Syria an effort to protect it against potential Israeli aggression (and to save face after the Israeli decimation of older Soviet missiles) or an encouragement of Syrian expansionism? Was the agreement to have Cuban troops in Africa an attempt to use détente as a cover to take over southern Africa or a response to previous covert action by the United States and the Republic of South Africa? The list could go on endlessly, and there is no way to demonstrate the correctness of either answer. In practice, Soviet decisions often entail a weighing of offensive and defensive arguments, with a combination of both behind each option.[2]

Examining Soviet debates as a way of understanding Soviet foreign policy also has pitfalls, of course, and obviously such analyses should not be used alone. Yet understanding the debates enables one to see how options are formulated, how arguments are linked, and how risks and opportunities are being assessed. Such knowledge is normally far more important than understanding goals because most countries share similar goals. The crucial issue in foreign policy is what various governments consider the best ways to achieve their goals and the extent of their willingness to pay a price and to incur a risk to achieve them.

It is particularly important for Americans to understand Soviet debates because we have often assumed that they do not exist. Americans have a strong tendency either to make a priori judgments about Soviet perceptions or to consider formal Marxist-Leninist doctrine (as we understand it) the key to policy decisions. We discuss the impact of ideology on Soviet foreign policy as if it were a monolithic construct that creates a drive to communize the world, that provides mental blinders causing Soviet leaders to misperceive the outside world, that represents outworn dogma that has been replaced by a new realism and pragmatism, or perhaps that serves as a mask for traditional Russian national drives. In fact, there is no coherent, uniformly agreed-upon Marxist-Leninist ideology. As will be discussed in the next chapter, Marxism contains both normative values and descriptive analyses, and there are major inconsistencies both between the values and the analyses and within them.

In practice both Soviet official doctrine and the views of most Soviet specialists on the third world have changed greatly over the last forty

2. Among the factors that argued for Soviet intervention in Afghanistan, for instance, were the defensive fear of losing an ally and the expansionist thought that airbases there might be useful in some unspecified future. Among the factors that weighed against invasion were the defensive fear that being tied down there might limit the ability to handle another threat (for example, the rising unrest in Poland that presaged Solidarity) and the expansionist fear that the invasion would frighten or antagonize forces in Iran that might be on the verge of giving the Soviet Union a great victory.

years. To some extent this evolution has resulted from changes in Soviet leadership, especially the death of Stalin. To a greater degree, however, the changes have occurred in response to such unexpected events as Nasser's radical military coup, Castro's development from "bourgeois nationalism" to socialism, the overthrow of radical regimes in Africa, and the success of Islamic fundamentalism in Iran. The fact that foreign investment in the third world turned out to be crucial for economic growth rather than incompatible with it also had an enormous impact on Soviet thinking.

But we should not consider the evolution of perceptions simply as a learning process on the part of leaders or officials of the international department of the Central Committee. Nor should we consider it simply as the result of the replacement of dogmatic officials by realistic ones. The changes result from continuing debate as well as from events. Perspectives among Soviet specialists on the third world differ as widely as those of their Western counterparts, and not surprisingly so since Soviet specialists are familiar with the Western literature and with the differing interpretations made within the third world itself. They thrash out these issues among themselves, and it is these ongoing debates with which outside events interact.

The debates that have arisen concern the most fundamental problems of Soviet ideology and foreign policy. Does the old insistence that all societies move through five stages of history—primitive-communal, slaveholding, feudal, capitalist, and socialist—make any sense, especially in the third world? Was Marx right that capitalism is the natural consequence of feudalism (which would mean that the third world will follow the path taken by Western Europe) or was Lenin correct that a country might easily skip the capitalist stage of development? Is American foreign policy in the Middle East part of a conscious desire to encircle the Soviet Union (using Israel as a proxy) or does it reflect various less threatening domestic pressures? Should Soviet news coverage of Ayatollah Khomeini's Iran have been as favorable as it was, and is the Islamic revolution likely to spread? Are third world governments the tool of their capitalists (or feudal class if they are preindustrial) or do they try to mediate among the classes? The list can be extended, as we shall see.

In a sense the subject of the book is the imposition of Stalinist orthodoxy in the realm of foreign policy and the breakup of this orthodoxy since his death. Separate chapters cover debates on the preindustrial evolution of society (on whether all societies evolve from the primitive-communal through the next three stages); on patterns of economic development (on whether "capitalist" development in the third world and especially foreign investment leads to dependent, deformed growth or is necessary for rapid growth); on political development and revolutionary strategy, especially the ambiguity in Marxism-Leninism on whether Russian political development was the exception or the rule; and on foreign relations in the third world. In addition, the book examines several relevant broader debates on the nature of Western economies in the 1950s, on the relationship of the state to the business class in the West, and on the general Soviet theory of international relations and the Soviet foreign policy relationship with the West.

The study is built on eight years of reading and rereading Soviet books and articles and of talking with some 200 Soviet scholars who have taken part in the debates. It also draws from a growing Western literature over the past twenty years on the Soviet institutes and Soviet perceptions of the outside world. While much of this literature focuses on "the" Soviet perception of this or that question or the evolution in the official image, much has also explored differences of opinion.[3]

The strength of this book lies, I hope, in its attempt to be comprehensive in its coverage of the regions of the world and the aspects of development and policy that are the subjects of the debates. The book also concentrates on the changing focus of the debates since World War II. In this way the inherent political and foreign policy issues become more visible than they would in separate studies of individual debates. Moreover, covering a forty-year time span allows easier understanding of certain concepts and allusions in contemporary discussions that no longer have to be explicated to a Soviet audience. Such coverage also makes it much easier to understand past debates that were obscure to Western authors at the time because of tighter censorship, greater difficulty in meeting Soviet scholars, and the absence of later Soviet written descriptions of the debates.

The book makes no effort to evaluate the accuracy of Soviet scholars' perceptions, analyses, and predictions. After thirty years of studying the Soviet Union, I have a clear sense of the difficulties in evaluating the relationship of the Politburo to the Soviet economic elite, the degree to which the Soviet economy is in crisis, and the strength of the political forces pushing for change. It would be presumptuous to adopt a Zeus-like

---

3. The literature is too voluminous to cite here, but special mention should be made of the seminal work of Franklyn Griffiths, "Images, Politics, and Learning in Soviet Behavior toward the United States" (Ph.D. dissertation, Columbia University, 1972). Many other works are cited in the footnotes of the chapters that follow.

role and to say that one Soviet specialist who knows far more about, say, Latin America than I do is a dogmatist or has ideological blinders or misperceptions, while another, who also knows far more about Latin America than I do, is realistic, has developed a sophisticated perception, or the like. As a conservative Soviet scholar correctly warned me, just because a perception has changed or become more Western in character does not guarantee its accuracy; it only means that it is fashionable.

Those who make policy decisions or give policy advice must make judgments about which specialist seems most convincing, and such judgments are implicit in the concluding chapter. In the analytical heart of the book, however, the aim has been to analyze the evolution of the various debates as objectively as possible. I have tried to translate the substance of the debates not only from Russian into English but from Soviet Marxism into American English. I have also tried to probe the policy implications—usually but not always the intentional policy implications—of esoteric formulations, specific quotations from Lenin, or historical references.

If the primary goal of the book is to illuminate Soviet patterns of thought, the secondary goal is to contribute to an understanding of what the United States should do in its policy toward the Soviet Union and the third world. Part of this contribution, paradoxically, may come through improving the average reader's understanding of the complexity of the third world. Those who have had little systematic exposure to the relevant literature may well share my unexpected experience while working on this book: I learned more about the third world in the last eight years than about the Soviet Union as I read the debates.

This is not to say that Soviet scholars have captured the "truth" about the third world. Instead, in looking at the Soviet debates we are reminded that even scholars coming from a rather rigid ideological system have discovered there is no "truth" about it. The issues dividing them also divide Western specialists. The uncertainties that bedevil them involve questions Americans should not answer with rash confidence.

This is particularly important for us to understand. Prevailing opinions about the third world in American political circles are often far more Stalinist than current Soviet official doctrine, let alone the opinions of the most prestigious Soviet scholars. Stalin believed that the world was divided into two sharply defined camps and that a country's economic system determined its foreign policy. A country with a capitalist system, even one like in India that claimed to be neutral, had to be pro-American; a country with a socialist system had to be pro-Soviet; and a country on the socialist path inevitably had to follow through to Soviet-model socialism. Soviet scholars have now rejected such a view, as have American specialists on the third world, but in an unacknowledged manner it permeates much of American public thinking. If a country calls itself Marxist-Leninist, too many assume that it is inexorably on the Soviet path and is undeviatingly pro-Soviet. Americans reflect too little about precisely what it is that really worries them in the third world and about the best techniques to reduce that worry. The possibility of weaning a radical country from a foreign policy sympathetic to the Soviet Union or of moderating its internal policy through economic incentives rather than economic ostracism is often neglected.

Only as we begin to make the distinctions that are being made in the Soviet debates can we begin to sort out the various goals in U.S. foreign policy toward the third world and be able to make sound decisions on how to achieve them. That Nicaragua calls itself Marxist-Leninist and supports Soviet foreign policy should be the beginning of the debate in the United States, not the end. U.S. debates should center on the possibility of Finlandizing Nicaragua, on what types of investment and loan programs could strengthen its regime and what kind could increase dependence, on whether a major power such as Mexico with whom we have coinciding interests could neutralize the country with greater ease than could the United States. That these questions are not really part of the public discussion is evidence of how truncated American debates, and often American thinking, usually is.

The United States and the Soviet Union have had only forty years' experience as superpowers. Leaders such as President Reagan and Foreign Minister Andrei Gromyko were already in their late twenties when other powers were making the crucial foreign policy decisions in the late 1930s. They were in their mid-thirties when atomic weapons were first exploded. The novelty of the role of superpower for each country, as well as the novelty of atomic weapons and the difficulty of assimilating their enormous significance for old geopolitical concepts, has made the U.S.-Soviet relationship very difficult to handle for the Reagan-Gromyko generation and those that preceded it. If in the 1980s we move toward a more mature understanding of the nature of international relations in the nuclear age, perhaps some of the irrational elements in the U.S.-Soviet conflict over the last forty years can be overcome.

I hope that this book will make a contribution to that process. At a minimum it will demonstrate that the Soviet Union does not have a rigid ideology determining its goals or perceptions, for the ideology has become a medium of debate, with room for many competing perceptions. It will also demonstrate that many people in the Soviet foreign policy establishment have developed serious doubts about the prospects for third world revolutions in the foreseeable future and therefore about the advisability of incurring heavy costs or throwing away other strategies in an attempt to further such revolutions. Instead, a growing number of Soviet analysts advocate increasing geopolitical relations with large moderate states such as India. They deemphasize concentrating on relations with small, radical countries.

As we see the Soviet Union groping with many of the same dilemmas that the United States confronts and pondering the validity of traditional goals and analyses, we will be in a better position to begin thinking about the world that we would like to shape. Americans must realize that although the third world is complex and beyond control of any nation, the natural state of affairs in international relations is that all nations—including, of course, the United States—will attempt to expand their influence. The United States need not panic in the face of competition, for it has the cards to win. It need not treat the Soviet Union as an unspeakable pariah for simply trying to seize opportunities and expand its influence. Instead, Americans must give more thought to distinguishing between normal and abnormal expansionism, between acceptable and unacceptable behavior, for only then will the United States be in a position to see what influence it can reasonably hope to achieve.

If we hope that either détente or military buildup, either a policy of confrontation or one of accommodation, will end Soviet attempts to expand its influence, we are going to be badly disappointed. The same will be true if we insist on unconditional Soviet surrender. Leaders who hold out any such unreasonable hopes to the American people will eventually convince the public that they are weak or reckless or both. They will also lose the opportunity to avoid unnecessary risks, to defend important interests, and perhaps to channel Soviet behavior in more acceptable directions.

# CHAPTER TWO

# Understanding the Soviet Debates

MANY in the West assume that Soviet media operate under very strict censorship and that no significant criticism of the Soviet system, of Soviet policy, and especially of Soviet foreign policy can appear. They would react with skepticism to any assertion that Soviet journals and books contain either advocacy of major changes in what have long been considered fundamentals in the Soviet ideology or that they include debates on such matters as policy in the Middle East and Latin America.

There is some truth in this view. Certainly the Soviet media do operate under strict censorship. Only institutions of the government and the Communist party or organizations strictly subordinated to them, such as the trade unions and the Academy of Sciences, are permitted to publish anything, and that includes mimeographed leaflets and pamphlets. Editors are appointed by higher authorities, and significant ones must have their appointments confirmed by the Central Committee apparatus or even the Politburo (it is said that such posts are in the Central Committee's *nomenklatura*, the list of posts requiring confirmation before personnel action can be taken). At least in social studies and political journals, editors must be members of the Communist party and hence subject to party discipline. The editorial boards of journals covering the outside world normally also include one or two fairly high officials in the international department of the Central Committee. In addition, a scholarly book published by the Academy of Sciences must be approved by the scholarly council of the institute sponsoring it and must also have a "responsible" editor, a scholar who is generally sympathetic with the author's point of view but who vouches for the book's general soundness.

Even these institutions must submit all books and issues of periodicals to the official state censor, Glavlit, and receive its sanction. In practice, Glavlit exercises relatively little control over the Soviet debates about the outside world. It checks to ensure that numerous types of concrete information, primarily military or economic, are not included in the manuscript, but it is not responsible for ideological or political rectitude in the social sciences or in the news. That censorship is exercised primarily by the editorial boards of newspapers, journals, and publishing houses.

Those who are skeptical about the extent of debate in the Soviet media are also correct in emphasizing the limitations imposed. The kind of direct attack on the policies of a political leader that is common in the United States—that indeed seems necessary if the critic is to get maximum press attention—would be unthinkable in the Soviet media. It is forbidden directly to criticize the general secretary, the Politburo, or the Ministry of Foreign Affairs in print on any issue. Anyone writing about political affairs in Soviet newspapers, journals, and books must say that the Soviet leaders and party are following a policy devoted to peace, détente, disarmament, and justice throughout the world and to the support of the national liberation movements abroad, although not through the military exportation of revolution. In addition, Soviet authors cannot normally make detailed proposals on policies the Soviet Union should follow toward a specific country or in specific negotiations.

Restrictions on the Soviet media are then very real, but their power should not be exaggerated. Communication does not require everyday language. Diplomatic notes are cautious and understated and avoid personal criticism of leaders, but their meaning will be clear to the experienced reader if the writer so intends. The language of American political science can seem opaque and clotted with jargon to the outsider, but vigorous debates can be conducted with it. Similarly, even though Mikhail Gorbachev cannot be criticized by name and authors frequently must use Marxist-Leninist terminology, communication does take place in the Soviet Union. The very existence of censorship means that sophisticated readers are sensitive to nuances and esoteric communication, that they read between the lines in a way that is not as necessary in an open society.

Similarly, the impossibility of debating the details of foreign policy in the media should not lead us to assume that broader statements cannot be made. The Soviet press contains no information on Soviet military aid to Nicaragua and El Salvador, but the journal on Latin America carries debates—rather free-swinging debates—on whether the Soviet Union should bet on the Nicaraguan government and El Salvadoran rebels. In terms of our understanding of the evolution of Soviet thinking, these general debates are important, perhaps even more important than debates on details would be.

Even the strictest censorship, therefore, has limits, and an almost infinite variety of techniques can be used for elliptical communication. Censorship cannot block all of them if the media is to carry any information at all. And the impetus to discuss, analyze, and debate is always there. In almost all countries with censorship—and certainly in the Soviet Union—intellectuals have a tendency to give status not to those among them who live in fear but to those who operate at the limits of the controls. Even under Joseph Stalin, Soviet scholars identified themselves as members of the intelligentsia, descendants of the Russian nineteenth century intellectuals who opposed the tsarist repression and tried to get around it in a variety of ways. In 1949 a Soviet author was able to remind his readers that the nonsocialist Russian revolutionary who was most glorified in the Stalin era, Nikolai Chernyshevsky, had been one of the boldest in using discussions of history and current analysis of foreign countries as implicit commentary on Russia and its policy:

Despite the strictness of the censorship, he brilliantly utilized the legal press, resorting to the most diverse ruses to circumvent the vigilance of the tsarist censors. . . . Chernyshevsky did not want to—and could not—turn the magazine into a bureaucratic journal of official instructions and directives from the government. Halfway measures were alien to him. He tried to take advantage of the mass of legal opportunities that were permitted by the tsarist government.[1]

It is not difficult to believe that these words were intended to have a contemporary meaning.

Debate also emerges in the Soviet media in spite of censorship because the post-Stalin Soviet leadership wants it. Members of the first generation of revolutionary Soviet leaders sometimes had a sense of ideological certainty about the world that led them to think of debate as unnecessary, although even Stalin established institutional arrangements to try to ensure that he received the diversity of views held by middle-level officials.[2] Recent leaders have been more open about their lack of certainty. Leonid

1. N. Makeev, "N. G. Chernyshevsky—redaktor 'Voennogo sbornika,' " *Voprosy istorii*, no. 4 (April 1949), pp. 65, 81.
2. See the discussion in Jerry F. Hough, "The Historical Legacy in Soviet Weapons Development," in Jiri Valenta and William C. Potter, eds., *Soviet Decisionmaking for National Security* (London: Allen and Unwin, 1984), pp. 87–115.

Brezhnev asserted that "a party and state leader . . . cannot consider himself the sole and indisputable authority in all areas of human activity." Complex problems are solvable, he said, only by "collective reason," and hence "it is necessary to listen to specialists and scholars, and, moreover, not only of one orientation or school."[3] Yuri Andropov repeatedly acknowledged that he was uncertain what to do about economic reform, even phrasing his uncertainty in terms of a lack of understanding of the basic laws of socialism.[4]

A realization that sophisticated policy requires expert advice has corollaries that Stalin never absorbed or else feared. He understood the need for mechanisms to ensure that major differences of opinion among experts reached him. However, the experts themselves have imperfect understanding, and they are continually called upon to explain phenomena that their previous analyses suggested were impossible or highly improbable (for example, Fidel Castro's evolution toward socialism and the success of the Ayatollah Khomeini). If experts are not encouraged to study the unknown and to rethink the known, if they cannot draw upon each other's work and challenge each other's interpretations, the quality of their analysis and advice will suffer.

### The Rules of the Game

Soviet debates on foreign policy and international relations have always been more tightly controlled than those on most domestic policy issues. Soviet leaders have worried that criticism of their foreign policy at home would weaken their position abroad, and they have been insensitive to the greater danger that their censorship policy would strengthen the image abroad of the Soviet Union as a monolithic and inhuman threat led by impersonal representatives of an alien ideology with no domestic restraints on an aggressive policy. Yet because scholars and journalists who must publish for a living may want to work at the edges of censorship and because the leadership itself has an interest in the exchange of ideas and information, implicit rules of the game for the debaters have evolved. Unfortunately, these rules are complex and vary from time to time and from issue to issue.

3. *Tselina* (Moscow: Politizdat, 1978), p. 21.
4. *Pravda*, June 16, 1983.

The first rule is that debates on international relations cannot discuss Soviet policy directly; they must do so indirectly through analyses of the outside world or the foreign policy of other countries.[5] This phenomenon is not limited to the Soviet Union. American debates on Vietnam often focused on whether we were dealing with a civil war or aggression from the north, while those on policy toward the Soviet Union often center on the degree of Soviet aggressiveness. In the United States, of course, the conclusion need not be unstated, but few doubted the policy conclusion when an American insisted that Vietnam was involved in a civil war.

The second rule is that certain givens must always be accepted: the United States is fundamentally aggressive and the Soviet Union always peace loving; if the Western governments do anything favorable, it is because they have been forced to by internal or external necessity; Western governments always exploit the third world, although they are restrained by fear that the latter will become communist; Western systems are doomed to collapse; and, of course, Lenin and Gorbachev are always right, except that in a few cases Lenin was right for his time but things have changed somewhat since then.

Once these givens are understood, one can see how Soviet authors play off them. If the threat posed by the United States is described as limited by some factor, that implies it is less ominous and accommodation is possible. (Statements about the changing correlation of forces in favor of socialism, while often frightening to Americans, are most often an attempt to make a case in favor of détente.)[6] If the American threat is described as relentless and the result of the inner workings of the capitalist system or of American historical tradition, that implies the Soviet Union must hang tough. If the immediate preconditions for revolution are said not to be present in a third world country, then by implication the local communists should collaborate with more moderate forces in the short run.

A third rule of the game is that the Marxist-Leninist framework of analysis must never be challenged. Occasionally specific propositions advanced by Marx and Lenin can be described as outmoded or (in Marx's

---

5. This was first discussed fully in Franklyn Griffiths, "Images, Politics, and Learning in Soviet Behavior toward the United States" (Ph.D. dissertation, Columbia University, 1972).

6. For a book that is based on an insufficient understanding of the logic of the debates and often reverses the positions of Soviet scholars, see John Lenczowski, *Soviet Perceptions of U.S. Foreign Policy: A Study of Ideology, Power, and Consensus* (Cornell University Press, 1982).

case) based on insufficient information, but the far more prevalent practice is for the writer to assert that he is in accordance with Marx and Lenin—indeed, to cite quotations from Marx's and particularly Lenin's work to support the analysis being made. This requirement, however, is not as constraining as one might assume. Marx wrote for forty years and Lenin for thirty, and a different thirty years at that. The events and circumstances to which they reacted were very different. Moreover, they wrote scholarly works, matter-of-fact journalistic articles, serious tactical analyses, and pure revolutionary propaganda. In such copious and diverse material it is possible to find a quotation to support almost anything.

Beyond this, Marxism-Leninism contains fundamental ambiguities. At the simplest level there is a difference between normative judgments and the perceptions and analysis provided. In the original Marxist analysis the bourgeoisie were described as tragic heroic figures who conquered nature and built the industrial base for human paradise but who, independent of their will or their ability to prevent it, were driven by imperatives of the market to actions that eventually were to destroy their system and themselves as a class.[7] Yet the normative judgments about the bourgeoisie had no touch of tragedy or pity. They were treated as a loathesome group of bloodsucking parasites whom the workers (and everyone else) should not only oppose but hate. Carl Schurz recalled "the cutting disdain with which [Marx] pronounced the word 'bourgeois.' [For him it represented] the deepest mental and moral degeneracy."[8] Lenin also strongly resisted significant cooperation with the bourgeois parties, and the middle-class parties, and the liberals, let alone the idea that the overthrow of the tsar should be followed by the establishment of a bourgeois capitalist system.

Thus many of the values of Marxism-Leninism are separable from its perceptions about the world. A Soviet specialist can conclude that nuclear weapons and the rise of the Soviet Union as a superpower made Lenin's analysis about the inevitability of wars between capitalist states invalid for the modern world, but he can still retain the old feelings of revulsion toward capitalism and the determination to treat the West as a moral

---

7. There are few more ringing tributes to the achievements of early capitalism than in *The Communist Manifesto*. "The bourgeoisie, during its rule of scarce one hundred years, has created more massive and more colossal productive forces than have all preceding generations together. Subjection of nature's forces to man, machinery, application of chemistry to industry and agriculture, steam navigation, railways, electric telegraphs, clearing of whole continents for cultivation, canalization of rivers." See Karl Marx and Friedrich Engels, *The Communist Manifesto* (New York Labor News, 1948), p. 14.

8. *The Reminiscences of Carl Schurz* (McClure, 1907), vol. 1, p. 140.

pariah. Or he can accept many of Marx's and Lenin's basic class and economic analyses of state and society, decide that they were unduly utopian in their predictions about the disappearance of classes and the state under communism, and lose the feeling of moral absolutism in condemning capitalist society. Indeed, instead of being perceived as degenerate, the Western capitalist societies could be seen as having interesting devices—representative institutions and market mechanisms, for example—that socialism might adopt in part to control economic bureaucrats.

The normative values of Marxism and the empirical analysis of Marxism-Leninism are also ambiguous within themselves. In its image of the ultimate future, Marxism-Leninism enshrines and glorifies the classic Western values—individual freedom, development of the human personality, equality of the individual, participation in society, and so forth. The thrust of the Marxist argument was that the existence of classes and private property prevented the ideals of Western civilization from being realized, and only their removal would allow realization of the utopian goal. In this sense Marxism represented Westernization—in fact the greatest Western influence on Russia. Yet for a Russian (or a citizen of the third world), a rejection of capitalism in this century often really stemmed from a xenophobic rejection of the West and its institutions. This attitude was clearly expressed in the proud assertion of a leading theorist of the late Stalin period that Russia had decided "not to dogmatically borrow the achievements of Western European civilization, not to assimilate them 'in the manner of India,' but to create a more advanced social structure that better answered the interests of the masses than Western European civilization."[9] In a real sense the Iranian shah and the Russian tsars were following rapid industrialization and Westernization programs, and the revolutions that overthrew these leaders had far more similarities than appear on the surface.

The analytical aspects of Marxism-Leninism are no less contradictory than the normative aspects. For example, Marx described the socialist revolution as the natural result of forces produced only in the last stages of capitalism when its potential for economic and technological advance had been exhausted. Lenin, however, argued that the capitalist revolution occurring at the end of the feudal stage in Russia could "grow over" into the socialist stage before capitalism had really developed very far. Likewise, Marx and Lenin treated the bourgeois state as a direct tool of the ruling

9. M. Iovchuk, "Klassiki russkoi filosofii XIX veka," *Bol'shevik*, no. 12 (June 1944), p. 26, and see pp. 27–28.

class, but Lenin demanded that foreign communist parties support Soviet foreign policy as a condition for joining the Communist International, a demand that implied action of the masses could influence the foreign policy of the bourgeois state. For foreign policy itself the ideology suggested on one hand that the bourgeoisie of the different capitalist countries were drawn together by their class hatred of the proletarian Soviet Union and on the other hand that these countries were so antagonistic that they would be driven to war by the economic "contradictions" and competition among them. And so it goes on, issue after issue.

Over the years, Soviet leaders have tried to impose their definitions of the elements of Marxism-Leninism that constitute the "real" ideology, but these official definitions have varied widely. Stalin imposed the notion of a five-stage process of historical development in the third world (primitive-communal, slaveholding, feudal, capitalist, and socialist) that was not even part of the Marxist debates of the 1920s. Many of his definitions were rejected as dogmatic after his death, usually in the name of a return to Leninism. (In many books and articles it was easy to find where the most radical ideas were being expressed: one simply looked for the places where the number of footnotes citing Lenin increased sharply.) It was, however, a return to a Leninism that Lenin sometimes would not have recognized—except perhaps as the views of his opponents—and on some crucial questions such as the inevitability of war between capitalist states, Lenin's views have been repudiated altogether.

In recent years, ideology has become much more ambiguous—no doubt deliberately so. The major documents, such as the Central Committee reports to party congresses, have come to be drafted by committees, with each of the members making certain that the language is ambiguous enough for him to live with. As will be seen, many of the most central ideas are open to challenge and debate. In the more propagandistic treatments for the broad public, the ideology can be a summary of generally accepted clichés, but for those in the intellectual establishment, broadly defined, it becomes the medium of discourse.

## The Forms of the Debates

Soviet debates on foreign relations take many forms, and the participants in them use a variety of techniques. In some cases a debate may be clearly labeled as such. A journal may carry a roundtable, a conference report, or the like. It may have a special section for articles presenting controversial points of view. These sections may have such titles as "The Tribune of the Economist and International Specialist," "Exchange of Opinions," or "Discussions and Disputes." At other times the editor attaches a note that an article is published for purposes of discussion or that it contains controversial (*diskussionyi*) propositions, and he may specifically call for articles that respond to it. The editors of *Izvestiia* published a note in 1983 in which they stated, "under the rubrics 'Opinion of a Political Observer' and 'Problems and Thoughts,' *Izvestiia* publishes articles dedicated to actual questions of international life. Opening these formats to all-sided discussion of this or that problem, the editorial board does not necessarily share completely the opinion expressed by the author."[10]

These debates, even those openly labeled as such, may be conducted in jargon or elliptical language, but sometimes the policy implications are obvious. For example, when the journal *Latin America* carried a discussion on whether Nicaragua should follow the Cuban path to socialism, the reader was left in little doubt about the meaning of the different positions.[11] Expressions of differences in near-term economic forecasts in the journal of the Institute of World Economics and International Relations (IMEMO) frequently have clear implications for Soviet trade policy, particularly in discussions of trends in commodity prices.[12]

Basically the same type of debate occurs when authors criticize each other directly, as they often do. Increasingly, articles are explicitly aimed at an opposing position, and the better books now frequently contain surveys of the literature that outline the range of positions taken. At a more general level, the author may criticize a group of opponents. Thus Marshal Nikolai Ogarkov, head of the general staff, criticized the press as a whole for underestimating the danger of war and a number of unnamed persons for thinking that any peace was a good one.[13] Although book reviews in scholarly journals may often be bland summaries, they can attack a posi-

10. *Izvestiia*, October 26, 1983.

11. Compare K. L. Maidanik, "Kliuchevoi vopros—edinstvo," *Latinskaia Amerika*, no. 2 (February 1980), pp. 41–50, with A. F. Shul'govsky, "Eksperiment bol'shoi istoricheskoi vazhnosti," no. 3 (March 1980), pp. 5–12, and B. I. Koval', "Revoliutsiia—dlitel'nyi istoricheskii protsess," no. 3 (March 1980), pp. 12–18.

12. See, for example, "Mirovye tseny: dolgovremennye tendentsii i novye iavleniia," *Mirovaia ekonomika i mezhdunarodnye otnosheniia*, no. 6 (June 1978), pp. 83–104. (Hereafter *MEiMO*.)

13. "Na strazhe mirnogo truda," *Kommunist*, no. 10 (July 1981), pp. 90–91.

tion frontally or at least indicate the points over which there are disagreements.

In a second form of debate—especially on more sensitive questions—a controversial position is presented in a straightforward manner without any indication that it is controversial or that another position is being attacked. A collection of essays on the Soviet-Chinese Revolution of 1925–27, for instance, alternated articles written from nonorthodox perspectives with traditional ones but gave the reader no hint that the articles were contradictory.[14] This form of debate is used with particular frequency in discussions of Soviet-American relations, in which acknowledged differences of opinion are only rarely permitted. The journal of the Institute of the USA and Canada, for example, carried articles by key institute scholars from July to November 1981, none of which suggested that they were part of a debate, but they expressed starkly different pictures of American foreign policy and, by implication, of the prospects for détente.

The first article, by Henry [G.A.] Trofimenko, head of the foreign policy department of the institute, described the postulates of American foreign policy in the most negative of terms: reliance on military force, playing with messianism, neocolonialism, a high degree of ideologization of foreign policy, hegemonism, a geopolitical approach, technical fetishism, and last and surely least, the two-party system.[15] In earlier articles, Trofimenko had repeatedly asserted that the United States has a first-strike strategy, which is a real threat to the Soviet Union.[16]

Three issues later, Andrei Kokoshin, head of the domestic politics department and a strong proponent of détente with the United States, analyzed American foreign policy in terms of the impact of public opinion and of divisions within the American bourgeoisie. He argued that the seizure of the hostages in Iran increased chauvinism in American opinion and affected tens of millions of people. These assertations clearly implied that American opinion could change and could have a decisive effect on events. His long section on American reactions to events in the third world makes little sense unless it was intended to raise (in an extremely tentative manner) the question of whether a change in Soviet policy in the third world might have an effect on American policy. A footnote attacking

14. L. P. Deliusin, ed., *Revoliutsiia 1925–1927 gg. v Kitae* (Moscow: Nauka, 1978).

15. "Osnovnye postulaty vneshnei politiki SShA i sud'by razriadki," *SShA: ekonomika, politika, ideologiia*, no. 7 (July 1981), pp. 3–14.

16. "Strategicheskie metaniia Vashingtona," *SShA*, no. 12 (December 1980), pp. 53–59.

Khomeini severely for his internal policy was surely an attack on the Soviet propaganda line at the time, which had treated him as a leader of the Iranian national liberation movement but had said little about his internal policy.[17]

In November, Vitalii Zhurkin, the leading deputy director of the institute, was more cautious than Kokoshin but moved in the same direction, at least on the general question of American policy. After describing various American aggressive actions, he emphasized factors he thought limited the American threat: the inability of the United States to achieve military superiority and upset the military balance, the restraining influence of the allies, and the inability of the American economy to sustain the Reagan buildup.[18]

A third form of debate discusses policy questions through ideological or historical surrogates and labels. Any serious ideological or terminological debate, no matter how abstract on the surface, seems always to have a practical policy meaning if only it is properly understood. Indeed, the more abstract the debate, the more sensitive the real issue is likely to be.

The list of surrogate subjects seems limitless. Discussion of the nature of the Western state and its relationship to the bourgeoisie has typically been the favorite medium for a discussion of foreign policy posture.[19] Assertions that the American state is "subordinated" (or "completely subordinated") to the "monopolistic bourgeoisie" (big business) have much more hard-line foreign policy implications than the assertion that the two are "coalesced" (*srashchennyi*). To say that the state is responsible to the bourgeoisie as a whole has fewer ominous overtones than the contention that it is a tool of the "monopolies" or "Wall Street" (big financial capital). To say that a radical third world regime is a "revolutionary democratic dictatorship of the people" is a very positive evaluation, but to call a regime a "revolutionary democratic petty-bourgeois dictatorship" is to raise grave doubts about its long-run revolutionary prospects.

Historical interpretation has often served a similar function. If the most radical Russian revolutionaries of the nineteenth century were said to cooperate with the moderate reformers of the times, if Lenin cooperated with other parties or wanted a multiparty coalition in November 1917, that

17. "Gruppirovki amerikanskoi burzhuaz'ii i vneshnepoliticheskii kurs," *SShA*, no. 10 (October 1981), pp. 3–14.

18. "Respublikanskaia administratsiia i formirovanie voenno-politicheskoi strategii," *SShA*, no. 11 (November 1981), pp. 4–16.

19. This point was first analyzed in Griffiths, "Images, Politics and Learning in Soviet Behavior," pp. 235–62.

legitimizes such cooperation at the present. If they were implacable foes of compromisers or "reformism," then compromise is little better today. If one emphasizes the Marxist roots of Leninism, that reminds the reader of the Western roots of the revolution (as one Soviet citizen told me with scorn, Marx was "nobody but a German Jew"); if one emphasizes the Russian roots (notably Chernyshevsky), that suggests that Russia owes little to the West and still has little to gain from it.[20]

Similarly, after the Soviet invasion of Afghanistan, an article written by an international relations specialist, not a historian, and describing America's progressively deeper and unanticipated entrapment in the quagmire of Vietnam surely was a warning about a similar danger for the Soviet Union.[21] An increasing number of articles about the Soviet suppression of the Basmachi (mountain rebels in central Asia) in the 1920s just as surely was a way in which other authors said that Afghan rebels could be easily handled.[22]

An event such as the Genoa conference of 1922, which resulted in the Rapallo Treaty with Germany but the failure of economic negotiations with England and France, can be discussed in a variety of ways.[23] In the late Stalin period the treaty was generally ignored because it involved some cooperation. Those who now want broad cooperation with the West can cite Lenin's more general calls for flexibility at the conference, while those who would like to split the United States and Western Europe can emphasize the Rapallo agreement.[24] Those who generally favor good relations with the West but do not want to make major concessions can cite Lenin's adamant rejection of the advice of his top foreign policy advisers to win economic cooperation by recognition of the debts owed to foreign individuals.[25]

20. For a discussion of this issue at the end of World War II, see Jerry F. Hough, "Debates about the Postwar World," in Susan J. Linz, ed., *The Impact of World War II on the Soviet Union* (Rowman and Allenheld, 1985).

21. A. G. Arbatov, "V tupike politiki sily," *Voprosy istorii*, no. 9 (September 1981), pp. 104–18.

22. *Literaturnaia gazeta*, January 20, 1982.

23. This example is discussed at length in Franklyn Griffiths, *Genoa Plus 51: Changing Soviet Objectives in Europe*, Wellesey Paper 4 (Canadian Institute of International Affairs, 1973).

24. Compare the positions of B. E. Shtein and Evgeny Choussudovsky with that of Iurii Zhukov, discussed in Griffiths, *Genoa Plus 51*, pp. 26, 35, 42–43.

25. This is the argument in A. O. Chubar'ian, *V. I. Lenin i formirovanie sovetskoi vneshnei politiki* (Moscow: Nauka, 1972), pp. 12, 236–37, 247–48.

A fourth form of debate involves criticism of an idea or practice in a foreign context as a way of criticizing a domestic opponent. Articles condemning revisionism abroad have normally been written by conservatives while those attacking dogmatism or left radicals abroad are normally written by less orthodox thinkers. In 1974 three leading Latin American specialists who doubted the possibility of successful revolution in the major Latin American countries asserted that "left radicals absolutize the tendency for foreign monopolistic capital to be strengthened in Latin America."[26] One of their leading protagonists directed his first fire at a *New York Times* editorial that had blamed Salvador Allende's overthrow on his decision to push beyond the original nationalization of foreign firms. The latter author suggested this was an understandable view for "liberal-reformist circles."[27] Clearly, neither was talking to leftist radicals abroad or to the *New York Times* editorial writers.

By the same token, some of the criticism of American military spending and its deleterious economic impact, as well as criticism of many American strategic concepts, is surely directed at the Soviet military. A Soviet military intellectual complained in 1976 about the treatment of the relationship between the military and science in the Soviet Union: "Unfortunately one meets a one-sided approach to this complex problem in our literature. It consists in emphasizing that military needs hinder the development of science or cause its lopsided development."[28] Because no one in the Soviet Union can publish such an attack on the Soviet military, it is clear that the complaint was being made about authors who purportedly were writing about the West.

A final form of debate might be termed the "false denial." Sometimes an author may present an argument only to denounce it, but the argument is so fresh to the reader or so well presented that one suspects the author's real purpose was to ensure that it received circulation. This technique is particularly easy to document in the early 1960s when restraints on the expression of unorthodox ideas were tighter. A number of scholars who wrote articles in which the arguments did not seem to correspond with the conclusion later wrote other articles that reversed the conclusion in whole

26. B. I. Koval', S. I. Semenov, and A. F. Shul'govsky, *Revoliutsionnye protsessy v Latinskoi Amerike* (Moscow: Nauka, 1974), p. 298.

27. K. L. Maidanik, "Vokrug urokov Chili," *Latinskaia Amerika*, no. 5 (September–October 1974), p. 114.

28. V. M. Bondarenko, *Sovremennaia nauka i razvitie voennogo dela* (Moscow: Voenizdat, 1976), p. 49.

or in part.[29] The practice still seems to be going on, but it is necessary to wait for confirmation.


## Deciphering the Debates

A Westerner reading the Soviet debates faces many difficulties in understanding them fully. The first obstacle is the deep-seated assumption from the past that no significant debates can take place in the Soviet media, especially on foreign policy. While an increasing number of Westerners have learned to look for debates and to write about them, the normal practice is still to describe "the" Soviet view. Worst of all, analysts rely primarily on *International Affairs*, which is translated into English and which is basically the organ of the hard-liners. In the process a variety of positions may be merged into an uneasy and misleading whole.

Once the search for the debates begins, many problems remain. In some cases everything seems completely clear. A debate in 1979 in the journal *Latinskaia Amerika* about the sincerity of President Jimmy Carter's human rights program, for example, only needed to be translated from Russian into English to be perfectly intelligible to any educated American.[30] But a criticism of the Soviet military in the guise of a criticism of the American military, let alone a denunciation of a view as a means of getting it in print, could not have been published if its meaning were indisputable.

As a consequence, Western readers face many pitfalls in understanding the debates and the issues in them. The greatest dangers, of course, arise in interpreting the criticism of foreign ideas and experience, let alone possible false denials. If those responsible for censorship in the broadest sense of that term cannot be certain that a criticism of the American military is really a criticism of the Soviet military or that a condemnation of the immoralism of President Carter's policy in Iran is really a condemnation of the immoralism of Soviet policy there, then we too cannot be certain.[31]

29. See S. M. Menshikov, "Poslevoennyi tsikl i perspektivy kapitalisticheskoi ekonomiki, *MEiMO*, no. 9 (September 1961), pp. 53–67.

30. "Administratsiia Kartera i Latinskaia Amerika, (kruglyi stol)," *Latinskaia Amerika*, no. 4 (July–August 1979), pp. 100–60.

31. For a very strange article that combined a strong attack on Khomeini with an assertion that Carter immorally provoked the hostage crisis and that was entitled "Moral Principles in Politics and Politics in the Region of Morality," see R. Ul'ianovsky, "Moral'nye printsipy v politike i politika v oblasti morali," *Literaturnaia gazeta*, June 22, 1983.

Even free-swinging debates are often carried on in Marxist jargon. The connotations of labeling left-wing regimes in Africa "petty bourgeois" may be absolutely clear to all likely Soviet readers and certainly to editors and censors, and nothing illegitimate may be occurring from anyone's point of view. Yet Americans who have had no immersion in the Marxist tradition may find the arguments meaningless at first glance. As already noted, it is necessary to translate from Marxism to American English.

The translation of Marxist and semi-Marxist categories and catchwords, however, also has perils. When a word or phrase becomes enshrined in party documents and the speeches of the leader (for example, "developed socialism" for the Soviet Union of the Brezhnev period or "noncapitalist path of development" or "revolutionary democratic" regimes for radical third world countries), it is usually universally accepted, but then people try to define it in a way that is congenial to their own position. Or if there is a broad official definition of the concept, as is normally the case, scholars choose several aspects of the definition to emphasize for the same purpose. Hence it is the variation in the definition or in the emphasis that constitutes an important part of the debate, not just which word to choose.

Indeed, it is in the proposal of new definitions of old concepts that some of the most unorthodox ideas are advanced. For example, "the national liberation revolution" (and the "national liberation movement" that promoted it) was always said to have two phases—an anticolonial achievement of political independence and then a socialist revolution as the only means to obtain economic independence from the West. One of the major ways in which skepticism about the near-term triumph of socialism in the third world was first expressed was to say that there was no necessary second phase in the national liberation revolution, that the socialist revolution was a separate process.

A second danger in translating Marxist phraseology is the tendency to overgeneralize a scholar's position from one or two catchwords. It *is* often possible to identify the general camp in which a scholar is located by his use of a few sensitive words, but this process is not automatic. At the simplest level, scholars in all countries try to hoist opponents on their own petards. Soviet scholars can quote opponents' statements to support their own views,[32] and they may try to reverse accusations as a debating tool.

32. For example, I. I. Kuz'minov, the most traditional of scholars in the 1950s and 1960s on the question of the subordination of the capitalist state to the monopolies, quoted Otto Kuusinen to support his position, but that did not mean the two men were allied. Instead, Kuusinen was one of the most unorthodox of officials, as Kuz'minov himself

For example, dogmatism was a favorite charge against the conservatives in the 1950s and the 1960s. The conservatives in turn sometimes said that to believe the third world must go through a long capitalist phase as Europe had was a dogmatic reading of Marx's writings on stages of history. The same technique was also used against the Chinese in the second half of the 1950s.[33]

The problem goes beyond one of the technique of argument. Views can be multidimensional and, logically at least, they can be combined in different ways. When Viktor Tiagunenko, the leading third world specialist of IMEMO for over fifteen years, died in 1975, he was praised by his colleagues as "a creative Marxist, a scholarly innovator . . . an enemy of doctrinaire attitudes and dogmatism."[34] His opponents called him a dogmatist.[35] Both evaluations were essentially correct. Tiagunenko was perhaps the leading force in revising doctrine to emphasize the possibility of a communist revolution under forces other than the Communist party, but he also retained a belief that the national liberation movement must and would have two stages—that nationalism would push the third world to socialism.

Presumably almost any theory can lead to different policy conclusions, depending on the other theories with which it is combined.[36] To say that the correlation of forces has come to favor socialism at the expense of capitalism can lead to the argument that the United States is not as threatening as once thought and that détente is possible, or it can lead to the conclusion that the Soviet Union can and should push forward vigorously.

---

pointed out in noting that Kuusinen could "scarcely be accused of dogmatism." See "K voprosu o nauchnoi polemike," in I. I. Kuz'minov and others, eds., *Metodologicheskie problemy politicheskoi ekonomii* (Moscow: Mysl', 1965), p. 265.

33. The Chinese charged that Soviet courtship of the bourgeoisie in the third world was nonrevolutionary and revisionist. Soviet writers began to praise the Chinese for their accommodation of their domestic bourgeoisie. In a classic case of false denial, they raised the charge that the Chinese policy was Bukharin-like, only to say that it could not be so since the Chinese said that it was not.

34. G. I. Mirsky and V. V. Rymalov, "Pamiati V. L. Tiagunenko," *Narody Azii i Afriki*, no. 5 (1975), p. 247.

35. N. A. Simoniia, "O kharaktere natsional'no-osvoboditel'nikh revoliutsii," *Narody Azii i Afriki*, no. 6 (1966), p. 13.

36. A scholar in the debates on Latin America noted that "people assert . . . that the theory of dependent capitalism answers the needs of the development of the anti-imperialist struggle, while the conception of middle-level capitalism implies a reconciliation with it," but he objected that "revolutionary or nonrevolutionary conclusions can be drawn from either theory." See V. L. Sheinis in *Latinskaia Amerika*, no. 2 (March–April 1979), p. 130.

To say that radical but noncommunist regimes in the third world are likely to evolve toward communism can lead to the conclusion that the Soviet Union need not invest so much economic and political capital on them or to the conclusion that the Soviet Union should give more emphasis to communist revolutionary forces.

In addition, if one thinks that the possibility of a devastating war is strong or the need for Western industrial investment in the Soviet Union is inexorable, then one may not follow a strong policy in the third world even if one is optimistic about chances there. If one thinks that the United States is making a third world conflict into a test of Soviet will and ability to stand up to pressure, then one may feel that the credibility of Soviet commitment to allies or even Soviet nuclear deterrence is at stake and may make a stand even if in general terms one would prefer not to.

There is, however, a natural tendency for people to adopt views that are psychologically consistent or that build the strongest case for a policy they prefer. Moreover, they are never totally confident about the accuracy of their assumptions. Thus among Americans, opinions about the Soviet Union, the causes of crises in the third world, and the proper American response are not combined in equal proportions in the variety of ways that would be predicted logically; instead two main clusters of opinions emerge.[37] One opinion states that the Soviet Union is expansionist, that this expansionism is the cause of third world instability, and that the United States should be confrontational; the other opinion favors the reverse of these three positions. In the Soviet Union too there has been a similar tendency. Nevertheless, one can never assume that this grouping is inevitable. If one sees one-half of the opinions that are psychologically comfortable, the scholar need not invariably hold the other half.

Another danger in deciphering Marxist categories and catchwords is to assume that the same "dictionary" is valid for all times and circumstances. In practice, things change. In the 1940s and 1950s, for example, the rigidity of the censorship drove many who were interested in policy into writing about such a subject as the Russian revolutionary movement because it was one of the few available ways of arguing about the relationship with the West. As the restrictions on discussion became less severe, policy-oriented scholars could move on to less obscure methods of de-

37. See the discussion of Robert Jervis and Jerry F. Hough in Robert E. Osgood, ed., *Containment, Soviet Behavior, and Grand Strategy*, Institute of International Studies, Policy Paper 16 (University of California, Berkeley, 1981), pp. 50–53, 56–58.

bate.[38] At the same time, many historians became increasingly determined to depoliticize their profession.[39] While a fair amount of historical work on traditionally sensitive subjects has continued to be written with an eye toward political implications, much has reflected professional interests, and one must be much more cautious than in the past in assuming that an aesopian meaning is intended.

Even more important, the terms of the debate also evolve over time. What may be a radical position at one time may later become conventional, while what had been conventional may fall out of favor. These changes are important indicators and reflections of changes in policy and in elite thinking. On an individual level, however, it is highly dangerous to draw conclusions from the fact that a scholar repeats a phrase or analysis that is conventional at the time. To determine whether the scholar is making a political point, the article or book must be judged against the conventional background to see what is unusual in content or emphasis. As a consequence, a phrase that may have important policy implications when it is uttered before it comes into favor may mean absolutely nothing when it is repeated a few years later after it has become conventional. By contrast, an old phrase that used to connote nothing about an individual's views may acquire great meaning when it is used after it has become passé.

Other types of context must also be taken into account. Even unorthodox scholars who speak abroad or at a conference at which foreigners are present tend to become spokesmen for more orthodox positions. In broader, more propagandistic settings at home, they may also become more conventional,[40] and there are also cases in which they choose to do so for tactical reasons.[41]

38. For example, Fedor Burlatsky's first book was on the political views of N. A. Dobroliubova, a nineteenth century Russian revolutionary; see *Politicheskie vzgliady N. A. Dobroliubova* (Moscow: Gosiurizdat, 1954). It was clear from reviews and discussions at the time that broader political issues were involved. Subsequently, Burlatsky, who (as the footnotes of this book indicate) remained an active and controversial participant in the debates, no longer felt compelled to use this kind of historical media.

39. N. M. Druzhinin, *Vospominaniia i mysli istorika* (Moscow: Nauka, 1967), pp. 80–88, 108–14.

40. See Griffiths, "Images, Politics, and Learning in Soviet Behavior," pp. 226–27.

41. In the case mentioned in footnote 32, Otto Kuusinen led the author's group of a textbook, *The Basis of Marxism-Leninism*, which adopted an unexpectedly conservative definition of the relation of the state and big business in the West. When asked about this later, members of the group said that the main purpose of the text was to introduce changes in doctrine relevant to domestic policy and that they decided to be fairly orthodox on foreign questions to reduce the controversy.

Another danger in deciphering the debates is to fail to distinguish one that has foreign policy implications from one that really is part of the domestic debates. Criticisms of China in particular have often varied from author to author in a way that must have been intended to make a domestic point: progressive scholars concentrated on Mao Zedong's dictatorial methods and the consequences of one-man rule, while conservatives emphasized the post-Mao deviations in economic policy as unacceptable.[42] A long and abstract argument about the Marxist theory of land rent that centered on the high levels of investment in Western agriculture really was addressing the need for more investment in Soviet agriculture.[43] The growing emphasis upon the need for caution in nationalizing trade and small industry in the third world, coupled with praise for the New Economic Policy (NEP) of the Soviet Union in the 1920s as a model for the third world, must sometimes have bespoken a belief that this would also be a good model for the Soviet Union of the 1980s.[44]

A final danger in analyzing the debates would be either to exaggerate or minimize the differences of opinion within the Soviet foreign policy establishment. To a large extent the situation in the Soviet Union in this respect is similar to that in the United States. There are major differences between the views and policy advice of, for example, a Marshall Shulman and a Richard Pipes. Yet, especially from the perspective of the Soviet Union, they have many assumptions and attitudes in common. The meaningful debate in the United States on the proper posture toward the Soviet Union takes place within a framework of agreement that on the one hand certain American interests must be defended even to the point of war and on the other hand some actions should not be taken because of the risk that they might cause nuclear war. Shulman would not think of abandoning NATO nor Pipes of sending troops to support Solidarity in Poland.

So it is in the Soviet Union. The number of citizens who, like Andrei Sakharov, want (let alone advocate) an increase in the number of Ameri-

42. Compare F. M. Burlatsky, *Mao tsedun i ego nasledniki* (Moscow: Mezhdunarodnye otnosheniia, 1979), with V. I. Lazarev, *Klassovaia bor'ba v KNR* (Moscow: Politizdat, 1981), pp. 12, 20, 311–16. For an excellent book that explores the domestic implications of Soviet debates on China, see Gilbert Rozman, *A Mirror for Socialism: Soviet Criticisms of China* (Princeton University Press, 1985).

43. The debate began with G. Shmelev, "Sovremennyi kapitalizm i absoliutnaia renta," *MEiMO*, no. 1 (January 1966), pp. 88–98, and continued intermittently in the journal through "Eshche raz ob absoliutnoi rente," no. 12 (December 1968), pp. 73–82.

44. See, for example, L. I. Reisner, *Razvivaiushchiesia strany: ocherk teorii ekonomicheskogo rosta* (Moscow: Nauka, 1976), pp. 73–104, 320–24.

can rockets aimed at the Soviet Union is as small as the number of Americans who want an increase in the number of Soviet rockets aimed at the United States. Members of the Soviet foreign policy establishment may disagree with this or that policy of their government—sometimes strenuously—but they all feel that the Soviet Union has certain interests it must defend and that it has a right to be treated with dignity and equality. Nearly all support strong action when important interests or Soviet dignity are challenged. All feel some attraction to human rights as a Marxist would define them. Even those who would not sacrifice other goals to support the rebels in El Salvador still feel that socialist victories in Central America would be a step forward in the struggle for human justice, and they would rejoice at such victories.

This complexity of values must always be kept in mind when we read Soviet debates. Often Soviet scholars begin by acknowledging their acceptance of some proposition in official doctrine as well as the validity of some of their opponent's points. Then comes the "but" or the "however." It would be a grave mistake to go through articles to find some common sentence and then conclude that all Soviet scholars think alike. It would be equally wrong to look at the discussion after the "however" and forget the common assumptions.

Basically there are only two solutions to the problem of overcoming these difficulties and avoiding these dangers. The first indispensable step is to read and read and then reread. Most important, one must look at the exchanges in the reports of conferences and roundtables, at the surveys of literature both in separate articles and books and in the opening pages of articles and books (the Soviets call these surveys historiography), at the critical articles, and at the book reviews. The surveys of the literature frequently present not only the two or three main positions, but also the phrases or interpretations of phrases that convey the positions. In the critical articles and book reviews, scholars often pick out the most offending and therefore the most sensitive phrases in their opponents' work and point out their concrete implications. In the process the meaning of the catchwords and of the Marxist jargon gradually becomes clear.

Reading the debates cannot be limited to a brief period. Implications of concepts are often much more evident as they are first explained and criticized than when they come to be taken for granted. Concepts also change their meaning over time or are used differently by different scholars, but this too can never be understood without a clear perception of the historical background against which the changes occur. Indeed, it is necessary to go back at least as far as the debates of the 1940s to become aware of the full context of the discussions of the post-Stalin period. In the Stalin years, scholars had to be particularly careful and subtle in their arguments, but the denunciations of unacceptable views were particularly harsh and blunt. When the condemned words and phrases began reappearing in the mid-1950s, their meaning was clear. Reading decades of debates is also vital in order to gain a sense of the major participants as persons. The general foreign policy perspectives and postures of individuals tend to remain stable over the years. The young participants in the debates of the 1950s who favored détente are still usually fighting that same battle in the 1980s. One of the scholars who has been most outspoken in advocating a position favoring immediate revolution—his opponents have labeled him the "Che Guevara of the Soviet Union"—recalls in private how enthusiastically he contributed kopecks to the drive to support the Spanish Civil War in the 1930s when he was a child.

Such a familiarity with the positions of actual individuals is important for several reasons. When individuals whose general posture is known express themselves in different contexts, the reader has a better chance to see which arguments and style of argumentation are associated with which position. When those favoring détente consistently emphasize that the correlation of forces has changed in favor of socialism and in contexts that promote détente, it becomes clear that such an argument often is not made to legitimize confrontation but to reduce the sense of American threat and to make the case that the Soviet Union can relax its military program.

By the same token, shifts in the method of argumentation by known individuals often show a great deal about the changing political climate. In 1973 anyone skeptical about the success of the arms control process could do no more than express caution that a SALT II agreement would be fairly difficult to reach, but in the early 1980s he could contend that the United States was following a first-strike strategy.[45] Those who have thought that an improvement in relations with the United States is possible and indispensable could cite a range of arguments in the mid-1970s, but now they are largely driven to suggesting that the problems are the fault of the Reagan administration, thereby implying that relations could improve with a change in administration.

---

45. M. A. Mil'shtein and L. S. Semeiko, "Organichenie strategicheskikh vooruzhenii: problemy i perspektivy," *SShA*, no. 12 (December 1973), pp. 3–12; and Mil'shtein, "K voprosy o neprimenenii pervym iadernogo oruzhiia," *ibid.*, no. 3 (March 1983), pp. 20, 24.

This methodology is not foolproof. Some people do change their views. Henry Trofimenko, whose assertions about the messianism, hegemonism, and ideologization of American foreign policy have already been quoted, used to be one of the most optimistic scholars writing about American foreign policy.[46] One can imagine that he is now playing an extremely deep game in which he really is criticizing Soviet foreign policy for the faults that he attributes to American policy, but the more likely explanation is that he has become disillusioned and has made a pilgrimage to the right.

If reading and rereading is the first secret of deciphering the Soviet debates, a second is extensive contact with the participants. Scholarly exchanges allow the chance to visit the Soviet institutes and talk with scholars, and they provide Soviet scholars with the opportunity to come to the United States where they can be met. Conferences, other exchange visits, and tourist visas expand these opportunities.

As noted above, Soviet scholars abroad make formal presentations that are seldom revealing, and if they are asked a general question, they will usually give a general answer. If, however, a Westerner has read their work and the debates in which they take a part, specific questions about the meaning of obscure specific points will often lead to full explanations. Questions asked in jargonized Marxism in Russian will produce franker answers in jargonized Marxism than questions asked in American English that require answers in non-Marxist Americanese. Soviet scholars will explain not only their positions but those of their opponents. (Of course, as in the United States, one should not necessarily assume that the opponent's views will be described fairly, and it is necessary to talk with representatives of all sides in a debate.) Current policy implications of an esoteric formulation is a very sensitive issue, but some scholars will answer questions about older debates and thus illuminate current ones.

This book has benefited not only from reading the debates but also through meetings with some 200 Soviet scholars over a seven-year period. These personal contacts have eliminated innumerable errors and illuminated many questions discussed in this book. They have not, of course, guaranteed that all the interpretations are correct. In all countries, debates are very messy affairs. Everyone says that everyone else's concepts are confused and ambiguous; everyone claims that his views are being misrep-

---

46. Compare his "Realizm i vneshniaia politika SShA," *MEiMO*, no. 3 (March 1960), pp. 29–42, with the more sober analysis by S. Men'shikov, "Diskussiia o vneshnei politike v SShA," *MEiMO*, no. 4 (April 1960), pp. 102–14.

resented by his opponents and that his opponents in turn do not understand the unspoken assumptions of their own work. Scholars are, in fact, often ambivalent or simply cautious about committing themselves. An American cannot summarize American scholarly debates about the Soviet Union without being controversial, and the problem is more difficult in dealing with a foreign culture. At a minimum it is virtually certain that this book has made the Soviet debates too clear and the contending positions too neat.

## Conclusion

If many nuances have been missed in this book, the essential fact still remains: there are major debates in the Soviet Union, they touch on the most fundamental questions, and they are meant to be relevant to policy. The essential questions also remain: What is the real impact of the debates on Soviet foreign policy? What is their implication for policymakers in the West? It is to these latter questions that we will return in the last chapter. There are certain reasons to believe that the debates provide clues about the direction of Soviet foreign policy and its motivation, but the strength of these clues needs to be discussed after the debates have been examined.

At a minimum, however, a simple understanding of the fact and complexity of the debates can be vital in breaking up some of the stereotypes that have so shackled American foreign policy toward the Soviet Union. The dogmatic Soviet image of the United States, which has led to so many serious foreign policy errors, centered on a united American ruling class that was inexorably driven to an aggressive foreign policy by the logic of its system. It is only as the complexities of the United States and its policies have been understood—and this still is far from a completed process—that the Soviet Union has been able to move toward a more sophisticated policy. The Korean airline incident shows that Soviet policy is never going to become really sophisticated until the leadership or their advisers develop a much better understanding of Western psychology. In the United States too, we have often had an image of a united Soviet ruling group inexorably driven to an aggressive foreign policy by the logic of its system. It is only as we begin to understand the complexity of the Soviet Union that we too will be able to move toward a more sophisticated policy.

# CHAPTER THREE

# Patterns of Historical Development

THE THIRD WORLD has posed special problems of understanding for the Soviet Union. The lack of familiarity with third world cultures that was found in Europe and the United States was even greater in Russia. Except for limited contact in the late nineteenth century with peoples in central Asia, Russia did not even have the kind of exposure to the third world that the West received through the ownership of colonies. In the early twentieth century the Bolsheviks focused their attention on Europe, and their postrevolutionary experience did little to improve their understanding. They became deeply involved in China in the 1920s (generally displaying a singular lack of comprehension of what was going on), but Joseph Stalin seemed stung by the defeat of the Chinese Revolution in 1927 and retreated from further involvement in the third world.[1] After 1931 he generally cut off open discussion of China and of the nature of the third world society and in 1937–38 killed many who had developed some expertise on China in the 1920s.

To some extent, isolation from the third world was not the product of Soviet choice alone. Much of Asia and Africa remained under colonial rule and was permitted no diplomatic representation. Moreover, the colonial powers had little interest in permitting Soviet scholars or other communist "agitators" to wander around their colonies: the first Soviet scholar set foot in tropical Africa only in 1957. And although Latin American countries were not colonies, they generally refused to have diplomatic re-

---

1. See the discussion in Conrad Brandt, *Stalin's Failure in China, 1924–1927* (Harvard University Press, 1958).

lations with the Soviet Union except for a brief period around World War II.

The Soviet Union was able to establish diplomatic relations with former colonies in Asia after the war, but again Stalin retreated into isolation. He declared that political independence was a sham as long as a country was noncommunist and that the former colonies were subordinated to the United States even if they declared their neutrality. Little effort was made to study the postcolonial situations. As Anastas Mikoian, a leading Politburo member, complained about the Institute of Oriental Studies in 1956, "if the entire East has awakened during our time, then this institute still dozes until the present day."[2] *Pravda* and *Izvestiia* had no correspondents in the third world at the time of Stalin's death, and Soviet libraries received little third world material. The Soviet Union received no newspaper at all from Kenya, for instance, despite the importance of the Mau-Mau revolt.[3]

When Nikita Khrushchev actively began to court neutral third world countries in 1955, the Soviet leadership began to develop the needed expertise. The Institute of Oriental Studies was expanded, with emphasis given to seeking specialists on current affairs; the Institute of Africa and the Institute of Latin America were created in 1960 and 1961 respectively.[4] By 1964, *Izvestiia* had at least six correspondents in the third world and *Pravda* at least eight.

The Soviet intellectual community faced two related problems. Basic factual knowledge had to be gathered about countries that had hardly been analyzed in Soviet literature outside of tendentious discussions of communist parties, working class movements, and Western policy in the third world. The intellectual community also needed to break away from the rigid categories of analysis imposed by Stalin in the postwar period. This was especially crucial in understanding the preindustrial course of development in those countries, for the "feudalism" that Stalinist ideology described was, to an overwhelming extent, the socioeconomic form of organization in the rural countryside that constituted over 80 percent of the third world.

2. *Pravda*, February 18, 1956.
3. Book review by G. A. Nersesov in *Sovetskaia etnografiia*, no. 5 (1957), p. 197.
4. The decision to organize the Institute of Africa was made on October 2, 1959; see Oded Eran, *Mezhdunarodniki: an assessment of professional expertise in the making of Soviet foreign policy* (Ramat Gan, Israel: Turtledove Publishers, 1979), p. 89. This book provides a good history of the institutes.

## The Stalinist Orthodoxy

Westerners concerned about the evolution of Soviet foreign policy often have one major question, which they express in different ways. Has the Soviet Union become a "normal" great power? Have Soviet leaders abandoned their Marxist-Leninist ideology? Do they now see the world "realistically" rather than distorted through Marxist lenses?

In the discussions that flow from these questions, little attention is given to the character of the ideology under consideration. Marx and Lenin are seldom read, and then usually their shorter, more propagandistic works. What Westerners have in mind when they speak of Marxism-Leninism is generally that version of it that became codified in the late Stalinist period and survived in substantial part in the simplified textbooks of the post-Stalin period.

For the foreign policy specialist this is the correct focus because most recent Soviet leaders and foreign policymakers have probably read little more of Lenin or Marx than we have. Most learned the ideology from textbooks and had it reinforced by patriotic speeches and simplified articles that they had to read. They internalized the Stalinist version of Marxism-Leninism, and they have either continued to believe or have moved away from it.

Nevertheless, in discussing various positions in scholarly debates, one must take care in defining Marxism-Leninism; otherwise one may fall into the trap of believing that an unorthodox scholar has repudiated the doctrine when in fact he has resurrected views of Marx and Lenin that Stalin found it useful to hide or distort. Least of all should one attempt to impose labels. A scholar who deviates from Stalinist orthodoxy on one question may be quite orthodox on another.

The Marxism-Leninism that emerged from the Stalin period certainly had a great many differences from the doctrine as it was perceived in the 1920s when many had a very clear sense of the works because they had continually discussed them in the years before the revolution. For example, T. D. Lysenko's theory of the transmission of acquired characteristics, which many Westerners considered "ideological," was not the one that most participants in the debates of the 1920s considered the correct Marxist position,[5] and this pattern was frequently repeated. The nonparty Konstantin Stanislavsky became posthumously enthroned in drama rather than his Marxist opponent, Vsevolod Meyerhold, and the anti-Bolshevik

5. David Joravsky, *The Lysenko Affair* (Harvard University Press, 1970), p. 232.

Ivan Pavlov was transformed after his death into the epitome of Marxist psychology.[6] (Lysenko himself neither then nor later was a member of the Communist party.)

The correct Marxist-Leninist view of the outside world was the subject of intense debate in the 1920s. Because no one thought a socialist regime could survive in Russia if the revolution did not spread to Western Europe, there literally was no Marxist orthodoxy about relations between capitalist and socialist countries. Lenin himself had only a few years to try to adjust his thinking to the new situation. In welcoming foreign investment, in participating in the Genoa conference and concluding the Rapallo Treaty with Germany, he gave signs that he might move toward an analysis of the world situation very different than the one that became codified under Stalin. This is, of course, by no means certain, but it does indicate that the nature of the correct Marxist-Leninist view was subject to debate.

The complexities of ideology in conceptions of the third world begin with debates over one of the seemingly simple tenets of Marxism, the stages of history. As formalized in the Stalin period, the ideology emphasized the existence of five discrete stages or formations (*formatsiia*): primitive-communal, slaveholding, feudal, capitalist, and communist. A formation has been defined as "a social system that has as its base a historically defined means of production. Over the economic base is raised a complex system of superstructures: a political system, ideology, and so forth."[7] Lenin emphasized that a formation was "a special organism that has special laws of its birth, functioning, and transition to a higher form— a transformation into another social organism." In the late Stalin period, ideology stated that the development of third world countries also had to obey these laws.[8]

6. Sheila Fitzpatrick, "Culture and Politics under Stalin: A Reappraisal," *Slavic Review*, vol. 35 (June 1976), pp. 222–27.

7. E. M. Zhukov, "Diskussiia," in V. I. Shunkov, ed., *Perekhod ot feodalizma k kapitalizmu v Rossii: Materialy vsesoiuznoi diskussii* (Moscow: Nauka, 1969), p. 107.

8. V. I. Lenin, *Polnoe sobranie sochineniia* (Moscow: Politizdat, 1958), vol. 1, pp. 165–68, 429. Paradoxically, at the same time that the scholars studying the third world had to find the five-stage pattern of history in their countries, other historians had to deny that Russia had a slaveholding stage. The period in Russian history that could be most convincingly labeled as slaveholding was Kievan Russia from the ninth to the eleventh century. But Western Europe was already feudal by this time, and to assert that Russia was slaveholding in this period might make it seem more backward than Western Europe. That was then less permissible than ideological inconsistency. For an explicit discussion of Russian backwardness, see V. Dovzhenok and M. Braichevsky, "O vremeni slozheniia feodalizma v drevnei Rusi," *Voprosy istorii*, no. 8 (August 1950), p. 60.

Yet in Soviet Marxist discussions of the 1920s many of these assumptions were absent or at least controversial. In 1931 a scholar who spoke about the type of formation that existed in Asia was told, "the concept of a formation is not a Marxist concept. The classics of Marxism did not contain it. It was introduced into circulation by Bogdanov, Stepanov, and also Rozhkov."[9] Another scholar recalled that the concept was not introduced into discussions until 1924.[10]

Whatever language was used, the notion that Asian countries usually had a five-stage pattern of historical development was completely absent from the literature. Virtually all Marxist scholars assumed that Asia had not had a slaveholding stage and had featured a form of society very different from that found in European history. Like Marx himself, Soviet scholars of the 1920s often had the sense that Western scholarship, Marxist or non-Marxist, had only begun to explore the history of land relationships in ancient and medieval Asia. They were often uncertain about the best conceptualizations to use and, as a result, discussion tended to be volatile, with individual participants frequently changing their positions.

At the end of the decade a number of scholars returned to a line of analysis that Marx had advanced for a time, that Asia had had a special Asiatic mode of production. This mode was described variously, but its central characteristic was that land in Asian peasant society was owned by the state or perhaps the peasant commune rather than by landlords.[11]

From Stalin's point of view, discussions of the historical evolution of Asia had two problems. First, the liveliest participants in the discussion were not academic scholars but communists who had become directly or indirectly involved in the Chinese Revolution and who had developed their ideas in the context of fierce policy debates. Especially because everyone's knowledge was skimpy, conceptual arguments often had a close relationship to policy advocacy. Those who contended that China had some special Asiatic mode of production were also usually arguing that China was still ripe for revolution.[12] (The essence of the argument was that because China had no landlords, Chiang Kai-shek had no strong class base and thus could easily be overthrown.) Stalin had no interest in or belief in a

9. S. M. Dubrovsky in Shunkov, *Perekhod ot feodalizma k kapitalizmu v Rossii*, p. 141.

10. V. N. Nikiforov, *Sovetskie istoriki o problemakh Kitaia* (Moscow: Nauka, 1970), p. 204.

11. Ibid., pp. 204–05, 210–40.

12. Richard C. Thornton, *The Comintern and the Chinese Communists, 1928–1931* (University of Washington Press, 1969), pp. 3–29.

communist revolution in China after 1927, and he did not like implicit criticism of his policy.

The theory of an Asiatic mode of production also had disturbing domestic connotations. The theory featured not only the absence of landlords but also the presence of a strong bureaucracy and an oriental despot; in most versions their power derived from the state's economic role in organizing and operating irrigation systems. The thought might occur to someone that, like the Asia of the theory, socialist Russia also had no propertied class but had a state that was initiating a major economic program, a bureaucracy that was growing as a consequence, and a leader who spoke Russian with a heavy "Asiatic" accent. There had been a long-standing discussion of whether Russia was Asiatic,[13] and one of the participants in the discussions of the 1920s, Karl Wittfogel, was later in emigration to argue explicitly that the discussion applied to the Soviet Union.[14] Stalin must have suspected that people were implicitly criticizing his rule, and with a particularly annoying criticism because Leon Trotsky had been contending that the bureaucracy led by Stalin had throttled the Bolshevik Revolution.

In 1931 Vasilii Struve, a nonparty specialist on ancient Egypt, proposed for the first time that the five-stage model be applied to the Orient as well as the West.[15] This proposal was soon introduced into college textbooks, but many leading scholars resisted. Only when a collective world history was begun in the early 1950s were nearly all of them brought into line. The world history was organized by historical stage, with the first volume on the primitive-communal and early slaveholding, the second on slaveholding, the third on early feudalism, and so forth. Specialists on each area of the world had to write a section for each volume, and this meant that each of the specialists on Asia had to find a slaveholding stage.

If the Stalinist rigidities about historical stages had been limited to an insistence on a universal five-step (*piatichlennaia*) pattern, scholars of ancient history might have been disconcerted, but those working on the contemporary third world would have been little bothered. The problem for contemporary analysis was that almost all precapitalist societies of

13. Joseph Schiebel, "Aziatchina: The Controversies Concerning the Nature of Russian Society and the Organization of the Bolshevik Party" (Ph.D. dissertation, University of Washington, 1972).

14. *Oriental Despotism: A Comparative Study of Total Power* (Yale University Press, 1957).

15. Nikiforov, *Sovetskie istoriki o problemakh Kitaia*, p. 248–53.

recent centuries were classified as feudal, and in a simplified version of historical materialism published in 1938 in *Pravda*, Stalin defined feudalism in specific terms: "Under the feudal order, the bases of productive relations are the ownership by the feudal lord of the means of production and partial ownership of the productive workers—the serfs whom the lord cannot kill but whom he can buy and sell."[16] This popularized definition was not immediately binding on sophisticated scholars, and in the 1940s they argued whether "noneconomic compulsion" or only the ownership of land by feudal landlords was a key feature of feudalism.[17] If noneconomic (that is, political) compulsion were recognized as a key part of the definition, then it was possible to recognize the centrality of the village commune. If the essence of feudalism had to be landlord ownership, then obviously land in the precapitalist East had to be owned by landlords.

In 1952 Stalin emphatically associated himself with the latter position.[18] The reason for this action is not totally clear. As the director of the Institute of Oriental Studies asserted in 1962, "the study of eastern countries perhaps proved to be in an even more difficult position than other branches of history [under Stalin]. Considering himself to be an unquestionable authority on oriental history, Stalin imposed his opinions and views in this realm."[19] In addition, however, the issue of noneconomic compulsion had been important in the debates on Russian history, and domestic considerations may also have been at work. Perhaps if noneconomic compulsion were recognized as part of the definition of feudalism, then one could raise the possibility that collective farms were a form of feudal exploitation.

Whatever their ultimate cause, Stalin's definitions of feudalism created enormous problems for those trying to investigate contemporary develop-

16. "O dialekticheskom i istoricheskom materializme," *Pravda,* September 12, 1938. Reprinted in Robert H. McNeal, ed., *I. V. Stalin: Sochineniia* (Stanford, Calif.: Hoover Institution on War, Revolution, and Peace, 1967), vol. 1, p. 314.

17. The thesis was put most strongly in a series of articles by Boris Porshnev in *Izvestiia Akademii Nauk SSSR, seriia istorii, filosofii:* "Sovremmenyi etap marksistsko-leninskogo ucheniia o roli mass v burzhuaznykh revoliutsiiakh," no. 6 (1948); "Istoriia srednikh vekov i ukazanie tovarishcha Stalinia ob 'osnovnoi cherte' feodalnogo obshchestva," no. 6 (1949); "Formy i puti krest'ianskoi bor'by protiv feodal'noi ekspluatatsii," no. 3 (1950); and "Sushchnost' feodal'nogo gosudarstva," no. 5 (1950). For a denunciation of Porshnev, see "Za voinstvuiushchii materializm v obshchestvennoi nauke," *Kommunist,* no. 2 (1953), p. 10.

18. "Ekonomicheskie problemy sotsializma v SSSR," *Bol'shevik,* no. 18 (September 1952), p. 22.

19. *Vsesoiuznoe soveshchanie o merakh uluchsheniia podgotovki nauchno-pedagogicheskikh kadrov po istoricheskim naukam, 18-21 dekabria 1962 g.* (Moscow: Nauka, 1964), pp. 414-15.

ments in the third world. The difficulties were particularly great for the Africanists. Obviously it could not be said that Africa was at the classless, nonexploitive, primitive-communal stage, for a number of areas had had significant governments centuries before. Because the state was said to be the tool of class domination and its very existence to be the product of the desire to maintain such dominance, classes must by definition have existed even then. There was no evidence that current African systems were slaveholding (or most past ones for that matter), and tropical Africa certainly was precapitalist. The only alternative was that Africa was feudal, but there were no typical landlords except on the Western-owned plantations. Scholars were driven to describe the tribal chief as a kind of landlord or semifeudal lord.[20] The consequences were not enlightening.

There were also major rigidities in Stalinist orthodoxy about the transition from feudalism to capitalism. Because the laws of history were universal, it followed that capitalism did not arise in the West because of some chance factor such as the Protestant ethic or the discovery of the New World, but because of the inner workings of the laws of feudalism. If this were true, then feudalism in Asia should also have produced capitalism on its own, and scholars were encouraged to seek precolonial beginnings of capitalism there as well. (This tendency was strengthened by the desire to push the origins of capitalism in Russia as far back in time as possible so that the country would not seem backward in comparison with Western Europe.)[21] Questions about the class structure and driving forces of the transition period in the third world were also answered in a highly schematic manner, with concepts such as "bourgeoisie," "workers," and "peasants" being used in their Western sense.

Despite Stalin's power, he was not able to bring published debate about the third world (or other parts of the world) under complete control, and the agreement on universal laws of history in the third world often became a façade behind which a great deal of disagreement was hidden.[22] Scholars

20. I. I. Potekhin, "Stalinskaia teoriia kolonial'noi revoliutsii i natsional'no-osvoboditel'noe dvizhenie v tropicheskoi i iuzhnoi Afrike," *Sovetskaia etnografiia*, no. 1 (1950), p. 28.

21. Shunkov, ed., *Perekhod ot feodalizma k kapitalizmu v Rossii*, p. 8. See the exchange between N. P. Dolinin and A. L. Shapiro, pp. 176, 185, for some of the emotion in the issue.

22. The game was not limited to the third world. "By the early 1930s, Soviet historians had almost universally agreed that Kievan Rus' was feudal, [but] the period since then has produced a tremendous variation of opinions about the specific elements of Kievan feudalism." See Thomas S. Noonan, "Fifty Years of Soviet Scholarship on Kievan History: A Recent Soviet Assessment," *Russian History*, vol. 7, pt. 3 (1980), p. 337.

avoided theoretical articles and generalizations and concentrated on detailed work that bowed in the direction of the orthodox conclusions while
often undermining them. As a scholar expressed it in 1966, "until quite
recently, the view was dominant in Soviet historical science that any
concrete ancient Eastern society could only be slaveholding and nothing
else. As a result, investigators, having established that there were very few
slaves in the concrete ancient Eastern society that they studied, that they
did not play any noticeable role in its economy, and that some other forms
of exploitation clearly existed, then hurried . . . to proclaim that it was
slaveholding."[23] Indeed, during the preparation of the multivolume world
history there were open discussions on a number of these subjects.
Scholars of ancient history concentrated on the nature of the producers in
specific ancient civilizations at specific periods—were they really slaves or
not? Historians of Russia focused on dating the feudal period—which
meant, in practice, discussing criteria for defining the nature of feudalism
and the nature of the transition both into it and away from it.[24]

## The Reemergence of the Asiatic Mode of Production

After Stalin's death, scholars were slow to challenge the five-stage
pattern of development frontally. Even aside from other considerations,
the first two volumes of the world history (the ones on the slaveholding
systems, which remained the most controversial) were not published until
1955 and 1956 respectively, and it would have been awkward to repudiate
a project to which nearly all major scholars had so recently contributed.
Typically, the entry on Vasilii Struve in the new edition of the *Great Soviet
Encyclopedia,* which was signed to press on April 21, 1956, stated flatly
that he had proved that the first system in the East with classes was the
slaveholding one.[25]

The attacks on the old orthodoxy began with criticisms of the simplified
textbook generalizations about the nature of the slaveholding and feudal
societies of the East. In particular, writers began gingerly criticizing the

23. Iu. I. Semenov, "Sovetskie istoriki o stanovlenii klassovogo obshchestva v drevnem Kitae," *Narody Azii i Afriki,* no. 1 (1966), p. 161.

24. Almost every issue of the major historical journal, *Voprosy istorii,* carried at least
one article on this subject from November 1949 through February 1951.

25. *Bol'shaia sovetskaia entsiklopediia,* 2d ed. (Moscow: Izdatel'stvo "Bol'shaia sovetskaia entsiklopediia," 1956), vol. 41, p. 147.

lack of scholarship on the village commune and the free peasants who continued to live in it in the slave period, as well as the variety of landowning relationships that existed in it later.[26] Conclusions were not drawn, but the implications were clear. Authoritative statements soon began to appear on the need to pay more attention to individual variations in the development of historical stages (*formatsiia*).[27]

The old concept of an Asiatic mode of production was not formally espoused until 1961—and then in a specialized monograph[28]—but almost immediately there were hints for the initiated about a stirring beneath the surface. Eugen Varga's first post-Stalin book, signed to press on August 8, 1953, was more explicit. Varga labeled China as feudal in the period before Western penetration, but he added that it did not have the classical feudalism of the Middle Ages in Europe. Not only was there a different landlord-peasant relationship but also a strong central authority whose economic basis was irrigation.[29] Similarly, in 1956 the leading journal on oriental studies published a nine-page review of a major book by one of the country's leading orientalists that criticized the author: "Ignoring the question of state ownership of land, the author thus passes over one of the basic positions of Karl Marx on the East—the state-feudal ownership of land in the East."[30] In 1957, Leonid Vasil'ev, a young Ph.D. candidate, argued even more directly the thesis that collective-communal forms of property existed in China 2,000 years ago, and exploitation by the ruling class was exercised "only with the help and through the means of an extremely durable and far-flung state and administrative apparatus."[31] He declined to take on "the responsibility of giving another or new label" to this system, but anyone with any experience could recall that a new label was not needed. As the major historiographer on Soviet oriental studies later noted, "the whole course of [Vasil'ev's] discussion led to the conclu-

26. G. A. Melikishvili and G. F. Il'in in *Vestnik drevnei istorii*, no. 2 (1953), pp. 84, 90. This issue was sent to the press on July 10, 1953.

27. "Uchebnoe posobie po istoricheskomu materializmu," *Kommunist*, no. 1 (January 1955), p. 123.

28. L. S. Vasil'ev, *Agrarnye otnosheniia i obshchina v drevnem Kitae* (Moscow: Izdatel'stvo vostochnoi literatury, 1961).

29. *Osnovnye voprosy ekonomiki i politiki imperializma (posle vtoroi mirovoi voiny)* (Moscow: Gospolitizdat, 1953), pp. 389, 391.

30. A. Z. Arabadzhan's review of I. M. Reisner, *Razvitie feodalizma i obrazovanie gosudarstva u afgantsev* in *Sovetskoe vostokovedenie*, no. 6 (1956), p. 146.

31. "Agrarnye otnosheniia v Kitae v nachale I tysiacheletiia do N.E.," *Vestnik drevnei istorii*, no. 2 (1957), pp. 109, 129–30. For Vasil'ev's biography, see S. D. Miliband, *Bio-bibliograficheskii slovar' sovetskikh vostokovedov* (Moscow: Nauka, 1975), pp. 107–08.

sion that there was a special Asiatic formation in ancient China."[32] The editors of the major journal *Herald of Ancient History* signaled their attitude by choosing Vasil'ev as the reviewer for the China section of the first two volumes of the world history, but again he was very cautious.[33]

Nearly all the hints of theoretical modification of the five-stage pattern came from scholars who worked on Asia, but in many respects the fastest evolution of views was occurring among the Africanists. They had consisted of three diverse groups: ethnographers who had concentrated their attention on ethnic and language questions, analysts of the policies of the various Western powers toward Africa, and historians of the working class, working class movements, and the communist party in Africa. None of these groups was really working on economic, social, and political conditions in the contemporary African countryside. The categories of analysis that Stalin had forced them to use were singularly ill suited to the task.

Beginning in 1957, however, these scholars began to visit Africa, and Khrushchev's interest in the more radical African regimes (especially Ghana and Guinea) meant that a rapidly increasing number of people were recruited into the field. The contact with Africa was enough by itself to shatter many simplified notions. Thus when the leading Africanist, Ivan Potekhin, visited Ghana, he "always heard it categorically denied that feudalism existed in Ghana," and this concept became progressively more difficult to defend. By 1960 he had put the tribal commune so much to the fore of his analysis that he was suggesting Africa could use it to bypass the capitalist stage altogether and proceed directly to socialism.[34]

The question of the Asiatic mode of production was a matter of interest to the Asian specialists, and it is not clear why they approached it with such extreme caution in the late 1950s. Of course, a central point of the old orthodoxy was at stake, but some East Germans and Hungarians were advancing the concept and even more important dogmas were being challenged, some (for example, Lenin's theory of imperialism) by Nikita Khrushchev himself.[35]

One reason for Soviet caution may have continued to be the domestic

32. V. N. Nikiforov, *Vostok i vsemirnaia istoriia* (Moscow: Nauka, 1975), p. 6.

33. *Vestnik drevnei istorii*, no. 3 (1957), pp. 192–93.

34. *Afrika smotrit v budushchee* (Moscow: Izdatel'stvo vostochnoi literatury, 1960), pp. 20–27.

35. For the East German and Hungarian arguments, see Nikiforov, *Vostok i vsemirnaia istoriia*, pp. 6–8.

implications. At a time when Stalin was being attacked and some wanted to extend the attack to the system he had built, the regime may still have had reservations about permitting a theory positing a repressive state in a society without private ownership of property. A more important reason must have been sensitivity about the feelings of the Chinese. The Asiatic mode of production had entered Soviet literature in a debate about China, and Mao Zedong strongly disapproved of the theory. Because he was already upset about so many important policy questions, it probably seemed pointless to offend him on such a theoretical matter.

In the mid-1960s the restrictions against theorizing about the stages of history were substantially reduced, probably in large part because the conflict with China had come into the open. Just as the Asiatic mode of production had been the last subject of a free-swinging debate in the 1930s before Stalin repressed it, so it became the first subject of serious debate when the restrictions were lifted. Indeed, the continuity went even further. In the 1920s Eugen Varga had been a leading spokesman for the view that China had a strong bureaucracy based on state ownership of land and irrigation. In 1964, just before his death, he openly repeated his old thesis.[36] Shortly afterwards, Vasilii Struve, the original proponent of a universal slaveholding stage in Asia, reversed himself and also espoused the theory of an Asiatic mode of production. His theses, along with those of two French supporters, were published in the leading journal of oriental studies.[37]

In the discussion that followed, the supporters of the Asiatic mode turned out to be diverse. Varga's conception was narrowly limited to societies based on irrigation; he did not consider that Asian countries with sufficient rainfall had an Asiatic mode. Another scholar saw the system as a special cabal that involved a mixture of slaveholding and feudalism.[38] For many, the Asiatic mode was actually a society based on a village commune that had basic control of the land, a universal or near-universal stage through which all Western and Eastern countries had passed.[39] For

36. *Ocherki po problemam politekonomii kapitalizma* (Moscow: Politizdat, 1964), pp. 358–82.

37. V. V. Struve, "Poniatie 'aziatskii sposob proizvodstva,'" *Narody Azii i Afriki,* no. 1 (1965), pp. 104–09. The translations of the French articles are in pp. 101–04 of this issue.

38. Iu. I. Semenov, "Problema sotsial'no-ekonomicheskogo stroia Drevnego Vostoka," *Narody Azii i Afriki,* no. 4 (1965), pp. 76–79.

39. The first to emphasize the peasant commune was N. B. Ter-Akopian, "Razvitie vzgliadov K. Marksa i F. Engel'sa na aziatskii sposob proizvodstva i zemledel'cheskuiu obshchinu," *Narody Azii i Afriki,* no. 2 (1965), pp. 74–88, and no. 3 (1965), pp. 70–85.

some, the Asiatic mode was found only in antiquity; for others it could extend until the capitalist period in countries where landlords had not acquired a dominant position. (The most thoroughgoing spokesman for the latter point of view, Igor Andreev, specifically emphasized the existence of the Asiatic mode in contemporary tropical Africa.)[40]

The discussion of the Asiatic mode of production raged for several years in the leading journals and then subsided somewhat. Some in the West believed the discussion had been instigated by the Soviet leadership as a subtle attack on China, a way of charging that Mao's regime was not socialist but was rather an oriental despotism rooted in Chinese history. The Soviet leadership had then supposedly suppressed the debate for polit-ical reasons, perhaps once again because of its domestic connotations.[41] While the discussion of the Asiatic mode surely included articles aimed at the Chinese regime,[42] it was primarily the result of scholarly interest, an interest that became less prominent but that hardly disappeared.[43]

Most Soviet scholars rejected the theory of the Asiatic mode of produc-tion, at least if presented in fairly universal terms, for the same reason that they resisted the rigid form of the five-stage model of history: national experiences were too diverse to fit within it. Even a single country such as China had different patterns of land ownership in different regions, and the patterns varied within each region from time to time. Those who found the old categories a straitjacket did not want to exchange them for another. In addition, to the extent that the Asiatic mode was an implicit criticism of the Chinese political system, many historians had no desire to liberate themselves from thirty years of one type of politically motivated restraints only to have their scholarship turned into a political weapon in another crusade.

40. V. V. Krylov and I. L. Andreev in *Obshchee i osobennoe v istoricheskom razvitii stran Vostoka: Materialy diskussii ob obshchestvennykh formatsiiakh na Vostoke (Aziatskii sposob proizvodstva)* (Moscow: Nauka, 1966), pp. 93–94, 194–96. See also Andreev, "Spetsifika nekapitalisticheskogo razvitiia narodov, ne zavershivikh protsessa skladyvaniia klassov," *Voprosy istorii*, no. 9 (September 1970), pp. 56–73.

41. Robert Michael Gates, "Soviet Sinology: An Untapped Source for Kremlin Views and Disputes Relating to Contemporary Events in China" (Ph.D. dissertation, Georgetown University, 1974), pp. 67, 194.

42. L. S. Perelomov, "O roli ideologii v stanovlenii despoticheskogo gosudarstva v drevnem Kitae," *Narody Azii i Afriki*, no. 3 (1967), pp. 62–73.

43. The debate was so substantial that several long books and articles were written to summarize it, and each included long bibliographies for those interested in following the question. In particular, see V. N. Nikiforov, *Vostok i vsemirnaia istoriia*, 2d ed. (Moscow: Nauka, 1977), pp. 320–25; and N. S. Illarionov, "Problema formatsionnoi prinadlezhnosti afro-aziatskikh obshchestv (sovetskaia literatura 1976–1980 gg.)," *Narody Azii i Afriki*, no. 5 (1982), pp. 158–68.

## Rethinking the Five Stages of History

The major importance of the discussion of the Asiatic mode was its indirect impact. In one of the first collective discussions, held in 1965 in the Institute of History, the attention of the participants "from the beginning was directed not so much at the problem of the Asiatic mode of production as at the wide circle of questions connected with it. . . . The problem of the Asiatic mode of production only provided a background."[44] From this perspective there was actually little slackening of the movement toward developing and expressing concepts Stalin would have found abhorrent. Even supporters of the five-stage theory acknowledged "a certain lack of correspondence between the traditional ideas about the slaveholding system and feudalism . . . and the accumulated factual material on the history of Asia, Africa, and America."[45] They asserted that "it is necessary to think about a widening and a rethinking [pereosmyslennost'] of the concepts being used."[46] Others took a stronger position. In 1960 two scholars suggested that "it was not an anomaly" if primitive-communal societies evolved to feudalism rather than to slaveholding, and in 1966 two others suggested that there were three possible paths away from the primitive-communal stage: slaveholding (antiquity), feudalism, and the Asiatic mode.[47] As early as 1970 a scholar asserted that no one defends the idea that every single society is to be understood in terms of passage through a succession of five stages of history, each more progressive than the other.[48]

The slaveholding stage became the focus of special questioning. Many scholars directly denied that their particular country had had such a stage, and some argued that it never existed anywhere, not even in Rome (the latter admitted that Rome had slaves, but asserted that those working the

44. O. A. Afanas'ev, "Obsuzhdenie v Institute istorii AN SSSR problemy 'aziatskii sposob proizvodstva,'" *Sovetskaia etnografiia,* no. 6 (November–December 1965), p. 124.

45. Iu. V. Kachanovsky, *Rabovladenie, feodalizm, ili Aziatskii sposob proizvodstva?* (Moscow: Nauka, 1971), pp. 16–17. See pp. 17–18 for a series of quotations to this effect from scholars of the older generation.

46. A. A. Guber in A. I. Pavlovskaia and S. L. Utchenko, "Nauchnaia zhizn'," *Vestnik drevnei istorii,* no. 1 (1966), p. 149.

47. M. N. Meiman and S. D. Skazkin, "K voprosu o neposredstvennom perekhode k feodalizmu na osnove razlozheniia pervobytno-obshchinnogo sposoba proizvodstva," *Voprosy istorii,* no. 1 (January 1960), p. 83; and L. S. Vasil'ev and I. A. Stuchevsky, "Tri modeli vozniknoveniia i evoliutsii dokapitalisticheskikh obshchestv," *Voprosy istorii,* no. 5 (May 1966), p. 90.

48. Kachanovsky, *Rabovladenie, feodalizm, ili aziatskii sposob proizvodstva?* p. 97.

main means of production—land—were not slaves).[49] Even defenders of the five-stage theory recognized that Asia bore little resemblance to Stalinist concepts about the slaveholding stage in the Greco-Roman world and that, indeed, the concepts had to be qualified when applied to Greece and Rome.[50]

Similarly, discussions beginning in the mid-1960s also shattered the Stalinist conception that the essence of feudalism was always landlord ownership of land.[51] Some contended that ownership was not even a usual feature,[52] but at a minimum the question clearly was open to doubt. This set the stage for a serious consideration of the nature of land relationships in particular countries and also the nature of the village commune. It led to serious debates about the history of each of the countries of Asia. Did, for example, India have feudalism in the centuries just prior to colonization?[53]

Many scholars did not limit themselves to emendations but suggested that the five-stage theory was totally inappropriate for the precapitalist period. At times they did so implicitly by proposing new systems of grouping or defining precapitalist societies that were radically different from the old categories. One proposed that such societies be divided into three groups: animal raising, agriculture with irrigation, and agriculture without irrigation.[54] Another strongly emphasized the importance of the distinction between personal and impersonal relations in a way reminiscent of the analysis of Max Weber.[55]

The old conception of two precapitalist types of class society is said still to be widespread, but it was reported in 1983 that "the conception of a single [precapitalist] stage is becoming all the more popular in its different

49. Iu. M. Kobishchanov in *Obshchee i osobennoe v istoricheskom razvitii stran Vostoka*, p. 45.

50. Kachanovsky, *Rabovladenie, feodalizm, ili Aziatskii sposob proizvodstva?*, pp. 146–47.

51. L. V. Danilova, "Diskussionnye problemy teorii dokapitalisticheskikh obshchestv," in L. V. Danilova, ed., *Problemy istorii dokapitalisticheskikh obshchestv* (Moscow: Nauka, 1968), pp. 50–51.

52. See the discussion by Iu. M. Kobishchanov, L. S. Vasil'ev, and I. A. Stuchevsky in *Obshchee i osobennoe v istoricheskom razvitii stran Vostoka*, pp. 44, 119, 132.

53. For assertions that India was feudal, see K. Z. Ashrafian, "Problemy razvitiia feodalizma v Indii," *Narody Azii i Afriki*, no. 4 (1969), pp. 68–79. For a survey of the literature and for the argument that India was not feudal, see M. K. Kudriavtsev, "Kontseptsiia indiiskogo feodalizma v sovetskoi istoriografii," *Narody Azii i Afriki*, no. 1 (1970), pp. 72–84.

54. L. A. Sedov, "O sotsial'no-ekonomicheskikh tipakh razvitiia," in *Obshchee i osobennoe v istoricheskom razvitii stran Vostoka*, p. 49.

55. A. Ia. Gurevich, "K diskussii o dokapitalisticheskikh obshchestvennykh formatsiiakh: formatsiia i uklad," *Voprosy filosofii*, no. 2 (1968), pp. 127–29.

variants."[56] For example, a Leningrad historian talked about "ancient society, where the ruling class was the whole citizenry [*grazhdanskoe naselenie*]," and hinted that the line between ancient (slaveholding) and medieval (feudal) society might be blurred.[57] Vasilii P. Iliushechkin has argued that there is one general estate-class [*soslovno-klassovoi*] stage between the primitive-communal and the capitalist, which is based on what he calls the "rental mode of production."[58] As will be discussed shortly, the Vasil'ev who first cautiously raised the question of the Asiatic mode in 1957 now speaks of a "state [*gosudarstvennyi*] mode of production" in most of the world, while Iurii Semenov speaks of a "politarny" society in most of preindustrial Asia.[59] The leading specialist of the Institute of Africa on the preindustrial period, Iurii M. Kobishchanov, has also discussed a single precapitalist stage after the formation of classes, but he labeled it "feudal."[60] Obviously, however, a specialist on Africa will never apply the word "feudalism" to that continent's historical development if he defines it strictly according to the Western European experience. In practice, Kobishchanov spoke of a variety of "types of feudal society": nomadic-patriarchal, caste feudalism, clan dominated, multistructural in the cities, and so forth.[61]

Increasingly in the second half of the 1970s and the early 1980s, Soviet scholars adopted the label "traditional society" for precapitalist society, using it in ways that would be familiar to Western scholars.[62] This did not

56. V. P. Ilin, "Teoretiko-metodologicheskie problemy obshchestvennogo razvitiia," *Narody Azii i Afriki*, no. 2 (1983), pp. 131–32.

57. V. A. Iakobson, "Nekotorye problemy issledovaniia gosudarstva prava drevnego Vostoka," *Narody Azii i Afriki*, no. 2 (1983), p. 89.

58. Ilin, "Teoretiko-metodologicheskie problemy," pp. 127–28, 131. Also see V. P. Iliushechkin, "Obshchee i osobennoe v razvitii doburzhuaznykh klassovykh obshchestv," in V. P. Iliushechkin, ed., *Sotsial'naia i sotsial'no-ekonomicheskaia istoriia Kitaia* (Moscow: Nauka, 1979), pp. 5–24.

59. Iu I. Semenov in "Gosudarstvo pravo na drevnem Vostoke," *Narody Azii i Afriki*, no. 2 (1984), pp. 103–04. This concept is not clear; it is described in an article in a book that seems not to be available in the United States: "Ob odnom iz tipov traditsionnykh sotsial'nykh struktur Afriki, Azii," in Iu. G. Aleksandrov, ed., *Gosudarstvo i agrarnaia evoliutsiia v razvivaiushchikhsia stranakh Azii i Afriki* (Moscow: Nauka, 1980).

60. Ilin, "Teoretiko-metodologicheskie problemy," p. 131.

61. F. B. Borisov, "Obsuzhdenie problem tipologii razvitogo feodalizma v stranakh Vostoka," *Narody Azii i Afriki*, no. 2 (1977), pp. 74–75.

62. As early as 1975 a book was published on the Soviet historiography of traditional institutions in the historical development of the peoples of the East. The first article, written by E. M. Medvedev, was "The Study by Soviet Historians of the Problems of the Formation of Traditional Society in India." See L. R. Polonskaia, ed., *Sovremennaia istoriografiia stran zarubezhnogo Vostoka: Rol' traditsionnykh institutov v istoricheskom razvitii narodov Vostoka* (Moscow: Nauka, 1975), pp. 3–31.

necessarily mean an abandonment of the old concepts of slaveholding and feudal stages. For example, one of the strongest supporters of the five-stage theory, Vladimir Nikiforov, states that he himself sometimes uses the word "traditional" and that traditional society had a slaveholding and feudal stage. Nevertheless, for most scholars "traditional society" clearly implies a preindustrial society in which commonalities are more important than differences between the stages of history as formerly defined. One scholar made this point explicitly: "there is a significant group of countries with a preponderance of precapitalist and even prefeudal forms of social life. This is a traditional-colonial society, which cannot be called either feudal or slaveholding or primitive-communal."[63]

Most of those who merged the slaveholding and the feudal stages in their conceptualization have distinguished between the East and the West. Adherents to the theory of the Asiatic mode of production are still found,[64] but the most striking formulation of the distinction between East and West has been advanced by Leonid Vasil'ev. Actually, for Vasil'ev the normal pattern of historical development was that found outside Western Europe. In his view, evolution away from the classless primitive-communal society did not begin with the development of private property and of different classes based on their relationship to property; rather, the state arose from the "chiefdom protostate," which in turn emerged from the institution of tribal chief. The key step was "the institutionalization of power and the legitimization of the status of the political leader."[65] Those who managed to acquire political power then used it to acquire property—indeed, to develop the concept of property rights.

With political authority preceding property, Vasil'ev saw the state as an institution (or a system of institutions) that was the main driving force [sub'ekt] of economic relations, rather than the reverse:

63. L. M. Entin, *Politicheskie sistemy razvivaiushchikhsia stran* (Moscow: Mezhdunarodnye otnosheniia, 1978), p. 85.

64. Ilin, "Teoretiko–metodologicheskie problemy," p. 131. For an article by such an adherent, see R. M. Nureev, "Problema 'aziatskogo sposoba proizvodstva' v sovetskoi literatury," in N. A. Tsagalov, ed., *Razvitie politicheskoi ekonomii v SSSR i ee aktual'nye zadachi na sovremennom etape* (Moscow: Izdatel'stvo Moskovskogo universiteta, 1981), pp. 259–70.

65. L. S. Vasil'ev, *Problemy genezisa kitaiskogo gosudarstva* (Moscow: Nauka, 1983), p. 28. For a full discussion of Vasil'ev's views of the origins of political power, see his "Stanovlenie politicheskoi administratsii (ot lokal'noi gruppy okhotnikov i sobiratelei k protogosudarstvu-chifdom)," *Narody Azii i Afriki,* no. 1 (1980), pp. 172–86, and "Protogosudarstvo-chifdom kak politicheskaia struktura," ibid., no. 6 (1981), pp. 159–75.

[In all areas except Western Europe] private property as it emerged encountered an extremely strict [political] structure that had been formed long ago and that usually saw sources of accumulation of riches not connected with the "power-property" [*vlast'-sobstvennost'*] . . . as subversive of the interests of the state as a centralized structure. . . . The state in non-European precapitalist structures always strove to limit this [private] sector by controlling it, by sporadic confiscation of the property of the extremely wealthy, etc. . . . Private property as such, although it arose at a certain stage of the development of the state and even flourished at times . . . did not in the final analysis become a structure-forming force in society.[66]

In Vasil'ev's view, the consequence of this situation was that a state [*gosudarstvenny*] mode of production became the dominant one in most of the world. He goes on to note, "the essence of this model lies in the active role of the state (in the person of the ruler, the top ruling circles, and the administrative apparatus) in the organization of production and the redistribution of excess product."

Although Vasil'ev's state mode of production had much in common with the Asiatic mode (indeed, he argued that "Marx had this in mind when he introduced the concept of an 'Asiatic mode of production'"), he did not see it as a deviation from the natural laws of historical development. Rather, "the exception is the development of Europe from antiquity to the present time, while the rest of the world is the norm. . . ." Europe was a peculiar mutation that, like the Cro-Magnon biological mutation, proved to be successful.[67]

Most of the attacks on the old theory of five stages of history dealt with preindustrial or precapitalist society. In 1983 a major book coedited by Ivan Ivanov, deputy director of IMEMO in charge of the third world, went even further. Ivanov not only served as editor but also wrote the introduction, in which he called for focus upon "macroformations." He pointed to three such macroformations: "the primary (primitive-communal), the secondary (the private-property one), and the highest, Communism."[68] The secondary or private-property macroformation obviously included the capitalist stage as well as the slaveholding and feudal stages (or whatever replacement was proposed for them).

If a single formation lasted from the first introduction of classes to the successful socialist revolution, not much was left of presocialist stages of history. In fact, little basis was left for a comparative analysis of different

66. Vasil'ev, *Problemy genezisa kitaiskogo gosudarstva*, p. 55.
67. Ibid., pp. 55–56.
68. I. V. Aleshina, I. D. Ivanov, and V. L. Sheinis, eds., *Razvivaiushchiesia strany v sovremennom mire: edinstvo i mnogoobrazie* (Moscow: Nauka, 1983), p. 8.

societies in virtually all of recorded history. The IMEMO volume did recognize this problem, and it suggested three criteria for distinguishing between societies: structure, age, and character of evolution. These categories had relatively little relationship to economic criteria, and the book emphasized the point by focusing on "two different sociohistorical types of society"—the one in Western Europe and the one in the developing countries. The differences between the two were not, however, attributed to the dependence of the latter on the former nor to a later development of capitalism. Instead, the differences "began to be formed at the dawn of mankind."[69]

Paradoxically, by the mid-1980s the argument that both the East and West had a "Middle Ages society" that belonged to a single type of feudal formation was an argument for which one scholar felt it "necessary to give a justification."[70] Indeed, this scholar, Nodari Simoniia, insisted on the basic similarity in order to make a point that was far removed from the Stalin orthodoxy—namely, that the East was on the same path of capitalist development that Western Europe had experienced in the late eighteenth and early nineteenth centuries.

## The Multistructural Society

While the debates about preindustrial society have major practical and theoretical significance for Soviet views of the third world, the discussions of the Marxist theory of historical development with the greatest policy relevance are those that deal with the transition to industrial society, with what traditionally was called the transition from feudalism to capitalism to socialism. Basically, the discussion of this subject is synonymous with the discussion of the nature of contemporary economic and political development in the third world and is subject matter for a number of chapters. Nevertheless, one development in the analysis of contemporary society should be discussed in a chapter on the evolution of Soviet thinking on stages of history. This is the concept of a multistructural (*mnogoukladny*) society, for in many respects it has represented the most important attack upon the old rigidities.

The attempt to define the character of society on the basis of its mode of

69. Ibid., pp. 13–14.
70. L. I. Reisner and N. A. Simoniia, eds., *Evoliutsiia vostochnykh obshchestv: sintez traditsionnogo i sovremennogo mira* (Moscow: Nauka, 1984), p. 30.

production, even if one is nonorthodox and speaks of an Asiatic or rental mode, tends to imply that it has a specific mode of production. Indeed, in a simplified version of historical materialism written for *Pravda*, Stalin could assert that "in the primitive-communal system exists one mode of production, in slavery exists another mode of production, in feudalism a third mode of production."[71] Yet even during the Stalin era, scholars recognized that societies could be complex in periods of transition. Capitalist modes of production began developing in feudal society well before they led to the revolution that brought the bourgeoisie to power. After the bourgeois revolution, remnants of the feudal system continued to exist for a long time. This meant that a society could have several modes of production: the dominant one that defined the character of society and one or two subordinate ones associated with a rising or declining class. This subordinate mode of production and the relations associated with it is called an *uklad* in Russian, usually translated as "structure" and translated in this book as "substructure."

As long as one spoke only about one substructure in a society (in the third world, a developing capitalist substructure within the feudal system), no enormous ideological problem developed; but even here difficulties were possible. As a critical review in the Central Committee's theoretical journal, *Bol'shevik,* noted in 1952, if the period of the formation of a substructure is a process that extends over several centuries, the concept of a qualitative change that occurs in the movement of one stage of history to another is wiped out.[72]

Several times after the revolution, however, Lenin referred to a number of presocialist substructures that still existed in Russia. In these discussions he went well beyond a simple statement about capitalist remnants to list "at least" four substructures in addition to the socialist one: patriarchal (either nomads or peasants producing for themselves rather than the market), small-scale commodity production (peasants producing largely for the market, usually grain), private capitalism, and state capitalism (nationalized industries).[73] A society with such a number of substructures came to be described as multistructural (*mnogoukladnyi*).

If there were at least four presocialist substructures in 1918, it obvi-

---

71. "O dialekticheskom i istoricheskom materializme," in McNeal, ed., *I. V. Stalin: Sochineniia,* vol. 1, p. 307.

72. L. Maksimov, "O zhurnale *Voprosy Istorii," Bol'shevik,* no. 13 (July 1952), p. 67.

73. *Polnoe sobranie sochineniia* (Moscow: Politizdat, 1962–63), vol. 36, pp. 295–96, and vol. 43, p. 158.

ously followed that they had existed before the revolution, but Lenin himself never wrote of substructures in feudalism or capitalism.[74] During the Stalin period, scholars sometimes wrote about the multistructural character of the new people's democracies in Eastern Europe and Asia, but they too did not extend the analysis to prerevolutionary Russia or to the third world (or perhaps they simply were not permitted to do so).[75]

In the 1950s and early 1960s several senior scholars, including Rostislav Ul'ianovsky, deputy director of the Institute of Oriental Studies, referred to the multistructural character of third world societies. Because these men were scarcely radical and used the term very casually, one suspects that they were employing a term that was familiar to them from discussions of the 1930s.[76] In the 1960s the first explicit advocacy of multistructural analysis seems to have been made by historians of nineteenth century Russia. In 1961 one commented on Lenin's "teachings about the competition of socioeconomic substructures." Two years later another was quietly insisting that prerevolutionary Russia had a multistructural character, and by 1965 a collective report to a major conference asserted that this fact had great significance for an understanding of Russian history.[77]

At the same time, scholars were beginning to write about the complexity of the class structure in the contemporary third world, and a seminal 1962 article attributed that complexity to the peculiarities of the historical development there:

> The class structures of society in the underdeveloped countries of Asia, Africa, and Latin America are extraordinarily complex, for they bear the imprint of different epochs. . . . Many of these countries did not have a developed slaveholding system or a developed feudal system, let alone a high degree of development of capitalist relationships. . . . As a result, socioeconomic relationships that are

74. N. L. Rubinstein, "O melkotovarnom proizvodstve i razvitii kapitalizma v Rossii XIX v.," *Istoriia SSSR,* no. 4 (July–August 1962), p. 66. Rubinstein opposed analyzing prerevolutionary Russia as multistructural, but no one has ever challenged such an assertion about Lenin.

75. P. K. Figurnov, "Perekhodnyi period kapitalizma k sotsializmu v europeiskikh stranakh narodnoi demokratii," *Voprosy filosofii,* no. 1 (1950), p. 85.

76. V. A. Maslennikov in "Diskussiia ob ekonomicheskom razvitii kolonial'nykh i zavisimykh stran v epokhu imperializma," *Sovetskoe vostokovedenie,* no. 4 (1955), p. 139; and R. A. Ul'ianovsky, "Agrarnye reformy v stranakh Blizhnego i Srednego Vostoka, Indii, i iugo-vostochnoi Azii," *Narody Azii i Afriki,* no. 1 (1961), p. 13.

77. R. G. Ryndziunsky, "O melkotovarnom uklade v Rossii XIX veka," *Istoriia SSSR,* no. 2 (March–April 1961), p. 50; A. M. Anfimov, "O melkom tovarnom proizvodstve v sel'skom khoziaistve poreformennoi Rossii," *Istoriia SSSR,* no. 2 (March–April 1963), p. 141; and Shunkov, ed., *Perekhod ot feodalizma k kapitalizmu v Rossii,* p. 41.

different in their historical significance and essence formed layer upon layer on each other, "coexisting" together for centuries and only slowly being subjected to change.[78]

Nevertheless, references to substructures and multistructural societies only gradually entered the Soviet literature on the third world. Not until 1965 did an Azerbaidzhani professor, G. A. Dadashev, propose that a new section on the process of development be added to political economy courses in the universities because of the differences between the third world and the West:

> The distinctiveness of production relations in the social structure of these countries finds its direct expression in the multistructural character of their econo-mies and in the features of the substructures themselves. . . . They include the tribal substructure, which is preserved in a series of Arabian countries and even more in the countries of black Africa; the patriarchal-natural (peasant economy); the small-scale commodity substructure; the landlord economy; private capital-ism; the colonial capitalist sector; the national monopoly capital (for example, in India); the state sector; and so forth. . . . It often is not easy to define which of these economic substructures is the predominant one or which precisely of the modes of production is the ruling one.[79]

At the end of the 1960s, the late Aleksei Levkovsky, an important scholar at the Institute of Oriental Studies, took this line of analysis, refined it, and placed it at the center of his conceptualization of the third world. Levkovsky maintained that the multistructural character of the third world was "the most important specific fact about production relations" there and that it is "a special kind of multistructureness that has no parallel in Western history."[80]

Several features of Levkovsky's work distinguished it from earlier dis-cussions. First, like Dadashev but unlike most other scholars, he spoke not of one capitalist substructure but of three: a small-business and trader substructure, a developed capitalist one, and a foreign capitalist one. He also referred to the small-scale commodity substructure in the countryside and the state-capitalist substructure, both of which could be labeled as

78. R. Avakov and G. Mirsky, "O klassovoi strukture v slaborazvitykh stranakh," *Mirovaia ekonomika i mezhdunarodnye otnosheniia,* no. 4 (April 1962), pp. 68–69. (Here-after *MEiMO.*)

79. "Marksistskaia politicheskaia ekonomiia i razvivaiushchiesia strany," *MEiMO,* no. 2 (February 1965), pp. 87–88.

80. "O mnogoobrazii tret'ego mira," *Aziia i Afrika segodnia,* no. 1 (January 1969), p. 6. This was Levkovsky's first major article on the subject and was followed by seven more in the next two years of the journal. See also "Spetsifika i granitsy kapitalizma v perekhodnom obshchestve 'Tret'ego mira,' " *MEiMO,* no. 1 (January 1974), p. 114.

capitalist. Second, while Ul'ianovsky had asserted in 1961 that capitalism is "the leading economic substructure even in the least developed" of third world countries,[81] Levkovsky contended that these countries seldom had a leading substructure. "Leading" did not necessarily mean numerical predominance (Ul'ianovsky acknowledged that more people were occupied in natural and small-scale commodity peasant production in countries where capitalism was the leading substructure). Instead, "leading" referred to the substructure that determined the superstructure or soon would. Levkovsky's denial that there was a leading substructure implied that third world countries were not in one of the traditional formations or stages of history but were in transition. Indeed, he specifically declared, "multistructureness as a qualitatively independent social phenomenon disappears with the victory of a definite mode of production—that is, at the moment . . . that a new formation has arisen. . . . It is incorrect in principle to transfer these concepts beyond the boundaries of the transition period."[82]

Levkovsky's definition of a multistructural society as purely transitional could have been made relatively noncontroversial. Eastern European countries in 1945 had long been treated as passing through a special transition stage, and few scholars had difficulty in dealing with much of tropical Africa in transitional terms. Levkovsky, however, argued that the transition would be persistent and prolonged. Having stated that the word "multistructural" should be applied only to countries in transition, he still called India a multistructural society. India was the one underdeveloped country in Asia that everyone had long considered capitalist.[83] It was by no means clear that Levkovsky even believed Brazil and Mexico to have ceased being multistructural and to have become capitalist.

Levkovsky certainly asserted that the eventual outcome of third world development would be socialism. Indeed, his insistence that the capitalist substructure had almost never become the leading one provided a strong theoretical base for the argument that the future of the third world was open and that many of these countries would move from the transition stage directly to socialism. Nevertheless, if the third world as a whole was generally going to remain in transition until it reached or passed the level

81. "Agrarnye reformy v stranakh Blizhnego i Srednego Vostoka, Indii, i iugo-vostochnoi Azii," p. 13.

82. "Spetsifika i granitsy kapitalizma v perekhodnom obshchestve 'tret'ego mira,' " p. 113. The order of the sentences has been reversed.

83. In 1961 Levkovsky himself had spoken of the leading capitalist substructure there. See *MEiMO*, no. 2 (February 1961), p. 155.

of economic development of Mexico, it was going to be between formations for a long time. Except for those countries that became socialist, the
concept of a formation as defined in the Stalin period was not going to be
relevant for third world analysis for an entire professional life.

Levkovsky did not limit himself to making a provocative point in passing and then letting the attentive reader draw the theoretical implications.
He wrote and edited eight books between 1970 and 1981 and explicitly
emphasized the most explosive implications of his analysis—that a society
without a dominant class could not have a government that was subordinated to a dominant class.[84]

While the word "multistructural" has become almost universally accepted as a way of describing the socioeconomic complexity of the third
world, Levkovsky's treatment of it has, of course, been highly controversial. Indeed, there is no unanimity among the innovative theorists. An
equally provocative and respected scholar, Nodari Simoniia, a friend and
colleague at the Institute of Oriental Studies, thinks that Levkovsky's
analysis, while essentially correct in a static sense, is far too general to be
useful in predicting the future course of development:

> It is not enough simply to postulate the common character of these countries,
> expressed in the presence of a multistructural base. By only specifying the transi-
> tional character of any society, the multistructural concept still says nothing about
> the chief trend or direction of the given transition. One multistructural society can
> be distinguished from another by where the transition began, by where it is
> headed, and how it occurred. Only the singling out of the leading trend will
> provide the key to understanding the internal contents of the socioeconomic and
> political development of this or that liberated country and make it possible to
> group them scientifically by corresponding types and variants.[85]

Simoniia thinks that for all the complexity of the third world countries the
major ones are firmly on the capitalist path.

Other critics are concerned not about the generality in the concept of a
multistructural society but about what they see as its heretical character. In
1973 Sergei Trapeznikov, head of the science and education department
of the Central Committee, attacked the use of multistructural analysis
instead of stage of history. He began with a threatening discussion of the
need for "partyness" in the social sciences and with a reference to "apolo-

84. For Levkovsky's bibliography, see "Spisok osnovnykh nauchnykh trudov doktora
ekonomicheskikh nauk, Professora A. I. Levkovskogo," *Narody Azii i Afriki*, no. 5 (1984),
pp. 198–99.

85. *Strany Vostoka: puti razvitiia* (Moscow: Nauka, 1975), pp. 170–71. Another innovative thinker, Viktor Sheinis, made the same point a few years later.

gists of capitalism" who attack the Marxist-Leninist concept of stage of history.[86] Rostislav Ul'ianovsky, one of the deputy heads for the third world in the international department of the Central Committee, capped a strong personal attack on Levkovsky with the charge that he was replacing the concept of class with that of substructure.[87]

On these issues, as on those of the patterns of precapitalist development, most scholars take an intermediate position. They use the term "multistructural" freely, but they do not accept Levkovsky's insistence that the concept be limited to periods of transition. Instead, they often speak of multistructural societies with a leading or ruling substructure, thereby trying to have the best of both worlds.

## The Impact of Tradition and Culture

For all its controversial nature, multistructural analysis has rested solidly on one part of the Stalinist orthodoxy. In this orthodoxy, cultural, spiritual, political, and ideological factors have been considered part of a superstructure that expresses the interests of the ruling class in control of the economic base. By beginning with the insistence that the economic base was complex in periods of transition, multistructural analysis was simply drawing the orthodox conclusion that the superstructure would also be variegated.

In a way a more radical break with Stalinist views has been represented by an increasing tendency over the past two decades to see elements of the superstructure as influential in their own right. This process began in the Khrushchev era, but it was relatively slow to develop at first. The reluctance to challenge the five-stage theory of historical development kept the focus on the economic base, and even the original theories of an Asiatic mode of production did, after all, begin with an analysis of a mode of production. In addition, as will be discussed in the next chapter, the belief remained strong that Western investment and capitalist production relations would put such a strong brake on economic development that this

86. "Sovetskaia istoricheskaia nauka i perspektivy ee razvitiia," *Kommunist*, no. 11 (July 1973), p. 83.

87. A. U. Roslavlev, "O klassovom podkhode k problemam osvobodivshikhsia stran," *Rabochii klass i sovremennyi mir*, no. 6 (1974), p. 103. Roslavlev is Ul'ianovsky's pseudonym. See "Spisok osnovnykh nauchnykh rabot Professora R. A. Ul'ianovskogo," *Narody Azii i Afriki*, no. 2 (1964), p. 231, for an indication of this.

economic factor would be a driving force in third world politics. And, finally, those reading the Western literature of the time found a view of modernization that in its way also emphasized universal laws of development and that saw traditional society undergoing rapid transformation produced by industrialization.

A number of events in the mid-1960s led to an increasing emphasis on the role of historical and cultural factors in third world developments. Khrushchev had been leading an active campaign against religion at home and this had made it difficult to discuss religion in the third world objectively. With Khrushchev's overthrow, it became possible to hold conferences to discuss the subject.[88] Liudmila Polonskaia, a scholar who became the leading specialist on the subject, asserted in 1966 that religious, philosophical, and sociological concepts are not always directly connected with the interests of a particular class and that religious traditions continue to have "an essential influence" in their own right.[89]

The recognition in the mid-1960s that the split with China was likely to be long-lasting also was important. Chinese developments demanded explanation, and they could not be attributed to the communist system of rule. Many sinologists in the Soviet Union, as in the West, began to interpret Chinese deviations in terms of the influence of China's past. Certainly the purpose of some of those writing about an Asiatic mode of production was to imply a contemporary impact of the past, and the same was true of those looking at early Chinese philosophy. Fedor Burlatsky, a leading intellectual who interpreted China for a broader audience, wrote that "previously we thought little about the past of China and the influence it can exert on the present and the future of the country," and suggested that this was a mistake: "The history of a people is not divided into pieces, but is continuous in its intermittent way, united through its ups and downs. Even such a sharp break as the Chinese Revolution, which embraced all sides of the social life of the country and penetrated into all corners of Chinese society, cannot be considered independent of its preceding history, the level of its economic, social, and political development, the

88. See A. B. Belen'ky, "Religiia i sovremennaia obshchestvennaia mysl' narodov zarubezhnogo Vostoka (diskussiia v INA AN SSSR)," *Narody Azii i Afriki,* no. 4 (1966), pp. 264–70.

89. L. R. Polonskaia and A. D. Litman, "Vliianie religii na obshchestvennuiu mysl' narodov Vostoka," *Narody Azii i Afriki,* no. 4 (1966), pp. 10, 15. When she began writing about Afghan tribes, Polonskaia used her married name, Gordon, then switched to Gordon-Polonskaia, and finally to her maiden name Polonskaia. Her work can be found under all three names.

traditional culture and national psychology, the way of life, customs, and habits of a many-million mass of people." Burlatsky added the warning that some phenomena observed in China "have accompanied and accompany the revolutionary movement in the whole world, especially in backward countries."[90]

And finally, events in the third world were having a sobering effect on the optimism of both Western and Soviet scholars about the possibility of rapid change there. In Africa in particular, the overthrow of radical regimes in Ghana and Mali opened the way to the recognition and description of precolonial traditions that still had great force. Vladimir Iordansky wrote at length about the exotic features of African life in a way that conveyed a clear sense of their persistence and importance.[91] Roza Ismagilova, the top specialist in the Institute of Africa on ethnic questions, evolved from a person who scoffed at the importance of ethnic factors to one who asserted in 1970 that "the role of traditional tribal institutions, morals, ceremonies, and customs . . . is extraordinarily strong, even in our days."[92]

Yet in the early Brezhnev period this growing recognition of the importance of historical influences remained peripheral to the major lines of analysis. Such factors were usually seen as survivals either to be used or overcome. The debates on religion faced more tactical questions such as whether religion (notably Islam) would be used by radical regimes or, more practically, how the Soviet Union should react to radicals who established Islamic socialist regimes.

In the second half of the 1970s the emphasis upon traditional factors took on a quantitatively and qualitatively different character. As far as can be judged, a very important event in this development was a theoretical seminar held in April 1975 to discuss a paper by East German Africanist Klaus Ernst. Ernst emphasized the need to focus on problems associated with traditional society, traditional structures, traditional relations, and traditional institutions.[93] When objections were raised that such concepts

90. *Lenin, gosudarstvo, politika* (Moscow: Nauka, 1970), pp. 485–86.

91. "Sotsial'nye dlvigi v gorodakh Tropicheskoi Afriki," *MEiMO,* no. 10 (1967), pp. 68–83, and "Tropicheskaia Afrika: vnutriobshchinnye protivorechiia," *MEiMO,* no. 9 (1968), pp. 49–59.

92. "Etnicheskii sostav naseleniia Tangan'iki," *Sovetskaia etnografiia,* no. 3 (1956), pp. 97–103, and E. N. Galich, "Tropicheskaia Afrika: natsional'nalnoe edinstvo i etnicheskii faktor," *MEiMO,* no. 3 (1970), p. 68.

93. E. N. Galich, "Diskussiia v Institute vostokovedeniia AN SSSR o roli obshchiny i perspektivakh ee evoliutsii v razvivaiushchikhsia stranakh," *Sovetskaia etnografiia,* no. 6 (1975), p. 161.

were not proper, a leading Soviet scholar pointed to places in *Das Kapital* where Marx had talked about traditional relations.[94]

Interest in the social role of tradition was greatly heightened by the victory of the Iranian revolution in 1979. Before then, Soviet scholars had argued about the stability of the shah's regime and the future course of the country's development, but everyone essentially assumed that the shah would lead the country to capitalism and that capitalist relations would lead to his overthrow either by a "bourgeois" or radical revolution. The Khomeini revolution was first described as antiimperialist and anti-monarchical (or even democratic, with emphasis on the anti-Americanism, antiauthoritarianism, and radical egalitarianism among the left wing students leading the demonstrations). When it turned out that the mullahs not only won but had a "backward" fundamentalist program that seemed supported by most of the population, Soviet scholars had basic questions to answer. And because the Soviet Union contained so many Moslem citizens, they felt an urgency in finding answers that was absent in American scholarship.

The extent that the evolution in views has reached is illustrated by a 1983 review of a book written by Evgenii Primakov, the director of the Institute of Oriental Studies. Primakov emphasized the Islamic revolution and its implications, but the reviewers, Viktor Sheinis, the leading comparativist of IMEMO, and Anatolii El'ianov, one of its most important third world economists, argued that he should have gone further:

> The burst of neotraditionalism showed how dangerous it is to underestimate the role of sociocultural factors in the development of Eastern societies, and how one-sided is any attribution of such movements exclusively to class interests and class units. Religion not only provides popular forms for the expression of class and political interests (p. 79 of the book) but in concentrated form itself expresses the interests of a definite sociocultural community. . . . The formula, "basically progressive in content, but backward in form," does not work. Millions of people are mobilized under the banner of a reactionary utopia.[95]

For the experienced reader the review must have come as a shock. The Institute of Oriental Studies had been criticized by IMEMO for two decades for overestimating historical factors and ignoring the "international" ones. Now two IMEMO scholars were accusing the institute's director of the opposite sin.

In general the period from 1975 to 1985 witnessed "an extremely rapid growth of publications dedicated to cultures and civilizations, to tradi-

94. Ibid., p. 164.
95. *Narody Azii i Afriki*, no. 2 (1983), pp. 181–82.

tional and contemporary values."[96] For the first time, serious attempts were made to study what the historical tradition really was, both in the pre-colonial and colonial periods. Titles such as "Communal Institutions of the Ashanti in the Precolonial Period," "British Colonial Practice in Nigeria," and "Traditional Political Culture and Colonial Society in Countries of Africa" began to appear along with such general studies as "Traditions and the Cultural-Historical Process" and "Politics and Traditions in Developing Countries."[97]

Even the language and labels describing third world developments often changed—a fact of great significance, for labels can be decisive in shaping an understanding of what is central and what is peripheral in social development. In 1977 an introductory (and presumably noncontroversial) statement about a discussion that had taken place on "traditional cultures and modernization in developing countries" asserted that these countries "can scarcely be studied and described without a 'social anatomy' of such a unique phenomenon as the 'traditional culture.'"[98] Sheinis and El'ianov, it may have been noted, wrote of a "definite sociocultural community," while an ethnographer wrote of "economic-cultural types of traditional society," referring to differences between societies with different uses of animals and ways of cultivating land.[99] Vladimir Khoros applied the label "populist" (*Narodnik*) to men such as Kwame Nkrumah in Ghana and Ne Win in Burma who led countries of "socialist orientation" (the Narodniki had been the Marxists' main enemies in the revolutionary movement in Russia in the late nineteenth century). Khoros cited a previously suppressed quotation of Lenin that Russia "stands on the border of the civilized countries."[100]

The 1983 summary IMEMO volume coedited by Ivan Ivanov, deputy

96. L. Reisner, "'Tsvilizatsia' i 'formatsiia' v obshchestvakh Vostoka i Zapada," *Aziia i Afrika segodnia,* no. 6 (1984), p. 22.

97. V. A. Popov, "Obshchinnye instituty ashantitsev v predkolonial'nyi period," *Narody Azii i Afriki,* no. 3 (1981), pp. 51–61; E. A. Glushchenko, "Britanskaia kolonizatsionnaia praktika v Nigerii," ibid., no. 5 (1981), pp. 26–38; L. E. Kubbel', "Traditsionnaia politicheskaia kul'tura i kolonial'noe obshchestvo v stranakh Afriki," ibid., no. 6, 1981, pp. 26–37; A. I. Pershits, "Traditsii i kul'turno-istoricheskii protsess," ibid., no. 4 (1981), pp. 69–84; and V. Khoros, "Politika i traditsii v razvivaiushchikhsia stranakh," *Aziia i Afrika segodnia,* no. 1 (1981), pp. 28–31, 43.

98. L. Reisner, "'Tsvilizatsiia' i 'formatsiia' v obshchestvakh Vostoka i Zapada," p. 22.

99. Nikiforov, *Vostok i vsemirnaia istoriia,* p. 4.

100. V. Khoros, "V. I. Lenin i revoliutsionnoe dvizhenie narodov Vostoka," *Aziia i Afrika segodnia,* no. 7 (1984), pp. 2–3.

director in charge of the third world, strongly emphasized "the spiritual-cultural peculiarity" of different societies and the impact of "traditions, conventions, and innumerable taboos directly on production." He noted that "taken together, these enumerated elements of the individuality of the analyzed sociohistorical type of society were deposited in a specific *social-genetic 'code'* of their development. It is as if this 'code' absorbed in itself the stable instruments of heredity of each stage of history of the given societies, passed through each change in their evolution, and influenced the whole course of social development."[101]

None of this is totally incompatible with former analyses of historical development. The argument that traditional and cultural influences play a major role in the present is scarcely an idea that would have been foreign either to Marx or Lenin, both of whom had a sense of uncivilized Asia and of a distinct historical tradition in Russia that was semi-Asiatic. It is quite possible to reconcile the concepts of separate "civilizations" and of "historically formed diversity of traditional relations in different regions" with the concept of stages of history, but very different impressions of what is important in historical development are created by the new emphases and the new language.

## The Concept of Stage of History

The discussion of most of the issues raised with respect to the influence of cultural factors really belongs to subsequent chapters on contemporary economics and political development. What is important in this chapter are the implications of the new analyses for the Soviet understanding of the course of historical development.

First, of course, the emphasis upon culture and tradition raises fundamental questions about the driving forces of history. The more culture, religion, and ideology are considered independent forces rather than simply part of a superstructure derivative of the class and economic relationships of a society, the less one is speaking of a thoroughgoing economic determinism. And this in turn raises the question of whether other parts of the superstructure—notably the political institutions—also simply reflect the interests and desires of the ruling class. And, in fact, by 1984 it was

---

101. Aleshina and others, *Razvivaiushchiesia strany v sovremennom mire: edinstvo i mnogoobrazie*, p. 16.

reported that "practically all orientalist scholars agree that politics has undoubted primacy over economics in the oriental countries in the period of their independent development."[102]

Second, the attack on the five-stage pattern of historical development, the multistructural analysis of Levkovsky, and the emphasis on the impact of culture and tradition all raised fundamental questions about the concept of stage of history as it had been understood in the Stalin period. If a slaveholding and feudal stage is not universal, if the concepts are so loose and general as to have little meaning, let alone if all private-property societies are in a single stage, then the meaningfulness of history as a succession of stages may be called into question. This is particularly true if the Western development, based on strong concepts of private property and strong owning classes, was a chance mutation rather than the natural product of social forces.

Similarly, if one speaks of a prolonged transition from one stage to another in which many substructures persist, this at a minimum denies any theory of well-defined stages of history punctuated by sharp revolution. Emphasizing the persistence of long-term historical factors also implies a continuous historical evolution rather than sudden jumps from stage to stage. And if the evolution from stage to stage is supposed to be based almost exclusively upon changes in the economic base, then the attribution of a role to factors of superstructure affects the notion of a formation as it qualifies thoroughgoing economic determinism.

In fact, relatively few scholars have directly challenged the concept of a stage of history. Many, especially among the older generation and those teaching in the universities, deeply believe that the old categories (with qualifications) most accurately reflect reality.[103] Others may fear the party might react strongly if too many leading scholars followed an iconoclastic path. Still others—perhaps most of the serious research scholars—simply believe that the challenge is not worth the effort. No brief set of labels or categories can capture the complexities of historical development (the Western triad of traditional society, transitional society, and modern society is surely as oversimplified as the Marxist categories), and Soviet

102. Reisner and Simoniia, *Evoliutsiia vostochnykh obshchestv*, p. 194.

103. For a strong recent defense of a progressive succession of five stages (although with the possibility of jumping over stages—the slaveholding as well as the capitalist), see E. M. Zhukov, "Metodologicheskie problemy teorii obshchestvenno-ekonomicheskikh formatsii," in Kh. M. Momdzhian, ed., *Obshchestvenno-ekonomicheskie formatsii: problemy teorii* (Moscow: Mysl', 1978), pp. 35–39, 45.

historians of the third world, like most historians everywhere, have a suspicion of theorizing that gets away from the specifics of history. If "slaveholding" and "feudal" are defined loosely enough to give them freedom of operation, historians have little inclination to develop a new abstract scheme of their own.

Nevertheless, in a system in which ideological formulations are extremely sensitive, all sophisticated intellectuals are aware of possible implications of partial changes in formulations. In 1965 Evgenii Zhukov, the conservative academic secretary of the historical division of the Academy of Sciences, led off a discussion of the transition from feudalism to capitalism by noting that "it has recently become fashionable to subject to doubt the validity of Marxist historiography about the progressive changes in the course of a universal process of five socioeconomic formations." In this connection, he complained about "the heightened skepticism characteristic of a certain part of our scientific youth," and about the slogan "to subject all to doubt."[104] A decade later, Vladimir Nikiforov, the leading historiographer of Soviet oriental studies, made a similar complaint when he asserted that "if [the new hypotheses] were proven, then all the textbooks on history and historical materialism . . . would have to be written all over again."[105]

Nikiforov himself does not believe that the textbooks need to be rewritten, and essentially they have not been, but others think they should be. Some actually challenge the notion of a formation or stage of history fairly directly. "In recent years the concept of a 'socioeconomic formation' is all the more frequently combined with the word 'problem,'" one scholar wrote in 1978, and he defined "problem" as "a question, the answer to which is not contained in the knowledge accumulated by society."[106] Some are quite open in rejecting the whole idea of progress from stage to stage. "In general," Iurii Semenov has asserted, "all of world history up to late feudalism appears before us not in the form of a transition from stage to stage of a determined number of primordially existing social organisms, but as a process of the rise, development, and death of a multitude of social organisms. . . . Slaveholding social organisms of the ancient epoch

104. *Perekhod ot feodalizma k kapitalizmu v Rossii*, pp. 105–06.
105. Nikiforov, *Vostok i vsemirnaia istoriia*, p. 4.
106. M. A. Seleznev, "Poniatie obshchestvenno-ekonomicheskoi formatsii v strukture filosofskogo i istoricheskogo znaniia," in Momdzhian, ed., *Obshchestvenno-ekonomicheskie formatsii: problemy teorii*, p. 90.

were not transformed in their development into feudal ones—that is, 'passed' to a higher stage, but they disappeared or died."[107]

The implicit consequence of this view has been to define a formation as "only a type of society, [not] a stage of its development" and "inevitably to deny a necessary [zakonomernyi] connection between the level of development of productive forces and the type of productive relationships that lie at the base of this or that formation."[108] Vasil'ev was explicit in arguing against the concept of historical progress: "In not a small quantity of cases, history features cyclical and even regressive political development, the result of which was the return of more developed structures to their more primitive modifications."[109] Others, who did not raise this general issue, questioned whether development of the productive forces (rather than human development) was the major driving force in historical change.[110]

The notion of historical progress from stage to stage can also be challenged in indirect ways. Oleg Nepomnin, a historian of nineteenth and early twentieth century China, has attributed the revolutionary character of Chinese peasants not to feudal oppression but to peasant anger at the destruction of the traditional protections of the feudal system by the developing market relations.[111] Although Nepomnin did not say so explicitly, feudalism emerged as more "progressive" than capitalism from the point of view of the peasant. The basic idea of the unsettling character of capitalism and the peasants' attraction to traditional arrangements has been an increasingly popular theme among those emphasizing the importance of cultural factors.

Of course, if such statements were relevant only for ancient historians, few political problems would be raised. However, if the slaveholding and feudal stages do not exist in the way previously understood, then are not similar questions raised about capitalism and socialism? In studies of the

107. "Teoriia obshchestvenno-ekonomicheskikh formatsii i vsemirnyi istoricheskii protsess," *Narody Azii i Afriki*, no. 5 (1970), p. 90. The order of the sentences has been reversed.

108. Ibid., p. 85.

109. Vasil'ev, *Problemy genezisa kitaiskogo gosudarstva*, p. 50.

110. Iu. Aleksandrov and B. Slavnyi, "Chelovek v sisteme proizvoditel'nykh sil dokapitalisticheskikh vostochnykh obshchestv," *Aziia i Afrika segodnia*, no. 4 (1984), pp. 24, 26.

111. O. E. Nepomnin, "Nachalo 'agrarnogo' obnovleniia i zolotoe vremia' v Kitae," in L. P. Deliusin, ed., *Revoliutsiia 1925–1927 gg. v Kitae* (Moscow: Nauka, 1978), pp. 27–28.

contemporary third world, multistructural analysis tends to sidestep the problem, and other scholars also often solve the problem of defining the stage of history of third world countries in a simple manner: "In generalizing books on the problems of the contemporary East, the very concept of a 'socioeconomic formation' is used fairly rarely."[112]

The most serious implications of the debates on preindustrial third world evolution concern Western capitalism and socialism. If state ownership of a large proportion of the main means of production made the state the dominant socioeconomic force in ancient Asian society, should Western states be analyzed in similar terms when, as in the case of West Germany and France, they owned 30 to 40 percent of industry after World War II? In public this point was made primarily by critics of the Asiatic mode of production,[113] but for some at least, the criticism must have seemed less devastating to the Asiatic mode than to the conventional analysis of Western Europe.

Perhaps most explosive of all was the simple assertion, almost universally accepted even by the conservatives, that each of the early formations had many major variations. If this were true, then logically the socialist formation might have as much diversity. The question was to become especially acute in 1968 with the evolution in the Czechoslovakian Communist party and later with the development of Eurocommunism. After Czechoslovakia, discussion of such questions cooled, but as issues of economic reform came to the forefront in the 1980s, the problem of what is absolutely inherent to socialism and of how rigid are the laws of its inner workings became crucial once more.

112. Illarionov, "Problema formatsionnoi prinadlezhnosti afro-aziatskikh obshchestv," p. 159.

113. See Kachanovsky, *Rabovladenie, feodalizm, ili Aziatskii sposob proizvodstva?* pp. 126, 128.

# CHAPTER FOUR

# Economic Development and Western Investment

ULTIMATELY any predictions about the sociopolitical development of the third world have to be related to economic predictions. If third world communist countries significantly outperform noncommunist countries economically, nationalistic elements among the leaders will eventually be motivated to institute communist regimes. They would be able to charge that the old regimes' dependence on former colonial powers and multinational corporations caused economic stagnation, and they would have a good chance of successfully replacing them. If noncommunist countries outperform communist ones, the attractiveness of the communist model is likely to fade.

For many Soviet analysts in the Stalin era and in the decade after his death, the issue of the relative economic performance of communist and noncommunist systems was simple and reassuring. Lenin's major work on the subject, *Imperialism—The Highest Stage of Capitalism*, had treated colonialism as a thoroughly exploitive relationship. By exploiting cheap raw materials and selling expensive finished goods, he contended, Western capitalists had been able to extract sufficient surplus value from their colonies to keep the wages of Western workers high and stave off revolution.

"Neocolonialism" was treated little differently. Any country remaining within the capitalist framework was doomed to economic exploitation that was different from colonialism in form only. If a third world country remained capitalist and permitted foreign investment, the extraction of profit and the existence of unfair prices would destroy any chance for substantial, sustained economic growth.

From such a perspective, the answer to economic growth in the third world was simple. Because the West was taking more from these countries than it was putting in by way of investment and foreign aid, nationalizing foreign companies and preventing further foreign investment (and further extraction of foreign profits) would produce a net economic gain in and of itself. The way to create such growth was the Soviet model of industrialization. Although the Soviet Union had a mixed economy for seven or eight years (the New Economic Policy or NEP) and Mongolia experienced a period of transition that lasted nearly twenty years, Soviet scholars emphasized the model that the Soviet Union followed after 1929: a centrally planned and directed economy, virtually complete nationalization of industry and trade, concentration of investment in heavy industry, prohibition of foreign investment, thoroughgoing protectionism embodied in a government monopoly of foreign trade and nonconvertibility of the local currency into other currencies, and collectivization of agriculture. While the point was often made euphemistically ("the mobilization of internal reserves"), consumption was depressed in order to free resources for investment.

## The Persistence of Orthodoxy

The evolution of the public debates on third world economic development, although seemingly less sensitive in character, progressed much more slowly than those on revolutionary strategy until the second half of the 1960s. One reason may have been political caution. Yugoslavia began to proclaim the virtues of its own model of socialism in its 1958 program, and the pressure for change in Eastern Europe (especially Poland) remained strong. To have argued that alternative paths of economic development were viable in the third world so soon after the Hungarian revolt and the enunciation of the Yugoslavian program might have seemed real dissidence. Thus when a book spoke of "planning" in India in 1960, a reviewer objected on the same grounds from which Eugen Varga had been criticized in 1947—that planning was possible only under socialism and that India was not socialist.[1] This particular example of reluctance was

---

1. E. Ia. Bregel, review of V. I. Pavlov, *Ekonomicheskaia nezavisimost' Indii i Amerikanskie kredity* (Moscow: Izdatel'stvo vostochnoi literatury, 1960) in *Narody Azii i Afriki*, no. 1 (1961), p. 189.

extreme, but the prominence of the state sector in third world development intensified ideological problems for Soviet scholars.

Unorthodox thinking was also restrained by the pattern of developments in the third world. For instance, economic growth in Latin America from 1958 to the third quarter of 1963 was only 24 percent, compared with 31 percent for North America and 54 percent for Asia (excluding Japan).[2] Because Latin America was the most developed of the third world areas, such low growth was considered a harbinger of the future for capitalism there. At the same time, many of these countries seemed to be undergoing radical transformation. The evolution of the Cuban Revolution and the possibility of similar developments in Egypt, Indonesia, Burma, India, and a number of African countries provided yet another political reason for suppressing views that might provide propaganda against the radicals. The Cuban Revolution also affected the scholars more directly. As one remarked privately, they considered Fidel Castro's transformation a completely unexpected miracle, and it took a brave person to say or even believe that the pattern would not be repeated.

Another factor producing pessimism about third world capitalist development was doubts about economic prosperity in the West. Economists were confronted with the absence of a world economic crisis since 1938; previously the average interval between such crises had been seven years. The Korean War provided a convenient excuse for the failure of the 1948–49 American recession to deepen and spread, but the problem became especially severe for Soviet economists when the 1953–54 American recession at the end of the war proved similarly brief.

Debates about the nature of the business cycle developed over these issues. The scholar with the most authoritative post in this subject area—A. I. Bechin, deputy director for economics of the Institute of World Economics and International Relations (IMEMO)—presented the bleakest forecast of Western economic growth. He emphatically and continually contended that only military expenditures and the expansion of the credit system had prevented a major depression and that these palliatives ensured that the eventual crash would be even worse. In 1955 he argued that the 1953–54 recession would resume "in the immediate future" and deepen into a worldwide depression as in the 1930s, "but in a more serious form."

2. "Ekonomicheskoe polozhenie nekotorykh razvivaiushchikhsia stran Azii i Severnoi Afriki v 1963 g.," *Narody Azii i Afriki*, no. 4 (1964), p. 43.

He repeated this prediction in 1958.[3] In 1961 he asserted that the exact date was not important—only that there would definitely be a worldwide crisis and that the first postwar depression would be worse than 1929–33.[4]

Virtually all major Soviet economists thought Bechin went too far, and several prominent ones suggested that the pattern of shallow recessions would continue for some time.[5] From a political point of view, however, the crucial fact was that Eugen Varga, now approaching his eightieth birthday, gave partial support to Bechin's viewpoint. Varga retained many unconventional ideas; he was contemptuous of the opinion that the Western economies had not been developing in the postwar period, nor did he think there was sufficient basis for believing that the crisis must be worse than the Great Depression.[6] Nevertheless, his studies of the history of business cycles had convinced him that long periods of boom tended to be followed by more severe depressions than short booms were, and he thought that there would be a worldwide depression that would be deeper and longer than preceding postwar cycles.[7] Although he termed Bechin's scenario "not obligatory," he still thought that it was possible.[8] These views were not simply propagandistic or pro forma; they were criticized by a number of economists for being too pessimistic.[9]

The implications of Varga's analysis seemed to be that the West was in

3. A. Bechin, "K voprosu ob osobennostiakh poslevoennogo kapitalisticheskogo tsikla," *Voprosy ekonomiki*, no. 9 (September 1955), pp. 112, 115, 119; and "Ob ekonomicheskom polozhenii v stranakh kapitalizma," *Mirovaia ekonomika i mezhdunarodnye otnosheniia*, no. 5 (May 1958), p. 63, and no. 7 (July 1958), p. 151. (Hereafter *MEiMO*.)

4. "Problemy poslevoennogo tsiklicheskogo razvitiia kapitalizma," *MEiMO*, no. 4 (April 1961), p. 92. See also pp. 93, 96, 101–02, as well as E. Varga, "Marksistskaia teoriia krizisov i izuchenie kon'iunktury," *MEiMO*, no. 3 (March 1961), pp. 94, 102.

5. See, for example, the statements of Ia. A. Kronrod and S. M. Men'shikov, in "Problemy poslevoennogo tsiklicheskogo razvitiia kapitalizma," pp. 95–96, 98–99.

6. When Varga was given the chance in 1956, he cited examples of Western achievements that surely were deliberately chosen to shock the reader: 6 percent annual growth in industrial production in the capitalist world from 1948 to 1955; a growth in the American wheat reserve from 10.8 million tons in 1951 to 27.7 million tons in 1955; and an increase in electrical production between 1948 and 1955 that was greater than the entire annual production in the prewar period. See "Ob ekonomike poslevoennogo kapitalizma," *Kommunist*, no. 4 (March 1956), pp. 15, 19, 30; and "Obsuzhdenie doklada akademika E. S. Varga 'Problemy poslevoennego tsikla i novyi ekonomicheskii krizis pereproizvodstva,'" *MEiMO*, no. 7 (July 1958), p. 151.

7. "Problemy poslevoennogo promyshlennogo tsikla i novyi krizis pereproizvodstva," *Kommunist*, no. 8 (June 1958), pp. 152–53, 156.

8. A. Bechin in *MEiMO*, no. 7 (July 1958), p. 151.

9. For example, see footnote 5; the statements were specific answers to Varga.

the process of returning to the prewar pattern of economic cycles, which suggested long-term economic difficulties. This general view was expressed in an official statement by the conference of communist parties in November 1960 that said capitalism had reached a new and third stage of its "general crisis." The first stage began with the communist victory in Russia and the second with the world capitalist economy's loss of Eastern Europe after World War II. The new stage was associated with such factors as the accelerating collapse of the colonial empires and the movement of third world countries from a dependent economic position.[10]

That senior economists of the orthodox and nonorthodox schools were predicting Western economic troubles surely was a major factor in Khrushchev's optimistic claims about the ability of the Soviet Union to catch up with the West economically. If the Western economies were going to fall into a major depression, catching up would not be so difficult or utopian as it came to appear with the American boom of the 1960s. And if the West were going to have severe economic problems, then commodity prices would fall and Western business would likely contract investments as it had in the 1930s.[11] A third world country relying on commodity exports and on foreign investment for its capital formation would be in trouble, regardless of one's general theory of economic development.

A final factor retarding Soviet reconsiderations of Western economic performance was a shortage of qualified personnel. IMEMO had a group of capable scholars working on third world economies, but they were very young and inexperienced, with their first work usually on Western imperialism (economic policy) in the third world.[12] The Institute of Oriental Studies had a number of first-rate economic historians, especially those working on India, but few professional economists. Some studies were done on the history of the workers' movement but almost nothing on the

10. Surely IMEMO and its senior economists had a major role in working out this ideological innovation. For an article by the IMEMO director describing it, see A. Arzumanian, "Novyi etap obshchego krizisa kapitalizma," *MEiMO*, no. 2 (February 1961), pp. 3–19. For Arzumanian's extremely negative view of the American economy, see p. 15.

11. The impact of recessions on the third world was a frequent theme. See, for instance, A. Kodachenko, "Polozhenie ekonomicheski slaborazvitykh stran na mirovom rynke," *MEiMO*, no. 1 (January 1959), pp. 34–44.

12. See the complaint in "XX s"ezd Kommunisticheskoi partii Sovetskogo Soiuza i zadachi izucheniia sovremennogo Vostoka," *Sovetskoe vostokovedeniie*, no. 1 (1956), p. 5. Thumbing through the contents of the journals of the late 1950s allows one to see the phenomenon very clearly.

actual economic condition of workers.[13] The situation was particularly bad in the study of Africa, and the economic study of Latin America was so weak that the new Institute of Latin America appointed a specialist on Southeast Asia as its chief economist.[14]

All these factors kept many basic orthodoxies about the patterns of third world economic development from being challenged. Obviously no one asserted that economic growth was impossible under capitalism—after all, such growth was being achieved even in Latin America. Rather, it was assumed that the rate of growth would not be rapid enough to overcome the third world's underdevelopment and its rapid increase in population. Growth would begin to top out as Latin America's seemed to be doing.

The case against the possibility of sustained economic growth under capitalism was multifaceted, and no scholar accepted all of its parts. The case began with a recognition of the enormous amount of capital needed to bring the third world up to modern economic standards—three trillion dollars according to one estimate—and with the assumption that such sums could come only from radical land reform, which would open up "a colossal source of internal accumulation."[15] Thus there should be collectivization that, as in the Soviet Union, would permit the state to extract resources from agriculture to use as investment.

The orthodox case also assumed that the industrial countries were determined to prevent industrialization so that the third world would have to continue its old role as supplier of agricultural goods and raw materials and so that a politically dangerous industrial working class would not emerge.[16] "Some say," a critic observed in 1965, "that the term 'neocolonialism' should not be used because the same policy of colonialism is still being conducted and with the same means. Others assert that neocolonial-

13. L. A. Gordon, "Nekotorye osobennosti ekspluatatsii rabochego klassa v kolonial'noi Indii," *Sovetskoe vostokovedeniie,* no. 1 (1958), p. 18.

14. For Africa see "Ob izuchenii ekonomii stran Vostoka," *Sovetskoe vostokovedeniie,* no. 4 (1955), p. 7, and a similar official complaint a decade later in "O napravleniiakh raboty Instituta Afriki," *Vestnik Akademii Nauk,* no. 5 (1965), pp. 19–20. The specialist on Southeast Asia was Lev Klochkovsky; see Cole Blasier, "The Soviet Latin Americanists," *Latin American Research Review,* vol. 16 (1981), p. 110.

15. L. Stepanov, "Istoricheskaia dilemma ekonomicheski slaborazvitykh stran Vostoka," *Sovremennyi Vostok,* no. 2 (February 1960), p. 16.

16. See, for example, V. L. Tiagunenko, *Voiny i kolonii* (Moscow: Voenizdat, 1957), p. 57; and I. M. Lemin, "Ekonomicheskaia sushchnost' sovremennogo kolonializma," *Problemy vostokovedeniia,* no. 4 (1959), p. 19.

ism in general is the old colonial policy, but conducted with new methods that are adapted to new circumstances."[17] In this view, as another scholar charged, "when it was said that imperialism would not permit the industrial development of backward countries, this was based on an image of imperialism as some kind of center that plans and distributes resources, and so forth."[18] The logic of this position was that even if the third world wanted to rely on foreign investment, the West would not be willing to provide the funding for manufacturing that was needed for self-sustaining growth.

Even if the West were willing to invest, the argument continued, the results would be bad for economic growth. This logic was already implicit in the assertions about the determination of the West to focus on investment in agriculture and raw materials, but it went much further. Many continued to believe the profits and dividends that were sent from the third world to the West were greater than the funds invested from the West and that new investment would only continue the cycle. The most conservative scholars published estimates that the existing pattern of foreign investment caused 10 percent of the national income of the third world to be lost to foreign monopolies each year.[19]

The orthodox view also generally denied that the marketplace was a self-correcting mechanism and would direct resources into the proper areas. This skepticism concerned not only the possibility of building heavy industry in the presence of market forces but at times even denied the ability of price fluctuations to ensure that basic human needs were satisfied. For example, an article on African agriculture emphasized the inability of the existing communal form of agriculture and level of mechanization to achieve self-sufficiency in food production. But breaking up the communes into private farms would make the situation worse because it would inevitably lead to increased planting of more profitable export crops and to decreased production of food for the local population.[20] In these circumstances, it was not surprising that sometimes the "very simplified"

17. V. Rybakov in "Metropolii bez kolonii," *MEiMO*, no. 12 (December 1965), p. 113.

18. G. Mirsky in "Metropolii bez kolonii," *MEiMO*, no. 10 (October 1965), p. 106. For a scholar who did, indeed, say that it was a conscious decision of imperialism, see M. Iu. Bortnik, review of V. M. Kollontai, *Inostrannye investitsii v ekonomicheski slaborazvitykh stranakh*, in *Narody Azii i Afriki*, no. 4 (1961), p. 201.

19. V. Ia. Avarin, "O glavnykh chertakh zavershaiushchego etapa raspada kolonial'noi sistemy," *Narody Azii i Afriki*, no. 1 (1962), p. 24.

20. N. I. Gavrilov, "Tendentsii razvitiia sel'skogo khoziaistva v tropicheskoi Afrike," *Narody Azii i Afriki*, no. 6 (1962), p. 29.

assumption was made that "any measure that limits the private sector . . . is a progressive, anticapitalist step, and any encouragement or toleration of it is a departure from the noncapitalist path of development."[21]

## The Need for Western Investment

In the mid-1960s a number of the factors that had supported the old orthodoxy began to change drastically. The 1958–59 recession in the West was brief, and the 1961 stock market crash was followed by a period of unprecedented boom. Those who had been questioning older economists' predictions of a depression became increasingly bold. Their leader, the young economist Stanislav Men'shikov, argued that "a qualitative change" had occurred in "the way in which the law of crises manifested itself."[22]

Theory had assumed that Western countries were economically dependent on colonies, but the loss of colonies was actually being followed by unusually mild recessions. Obviously the old assumptions about the economic relationship between the industrial countries and the third world needed to be reconsidered. In the third world too, the actual course of events was also making "what recently seemed elementarily clear a subject for argument now."[23] Western governments were providing substantial amounts of direct and indirect aid, especially under President Kennedy and the Alliance for Progress, and manufacturing as well as extractive industries was beginning to grow. Instead of serving as a source of agricultural products for the industrial world, the third world was importing a substantial amount of food. And some of the radical economic measures were not working well: large new plants could not sell all their production and had unused capacity, and the nationalization of small industry and trade in countries such as Burma and Mali had led to severe economic difficulties.

At the same time, the quality of Soviet economists was improving rapidly. They now had a decade of experience, and the Soviet foreign aid

---

21. V. Kollontai, "Osvobodivshiesia strany: vybor puti razvitiia," *MEiMO*, no. 10 (October 1965), p. 32.

22. S. Men'shikov in "Deformatsiia kapitalisticheskogo tsikla i ee prichiny," *Problemy mira i sotsializma*, no. 3 (March 1962), p. 63.

23. L. Klochkovsky in "Metropolii bez kolonii," *MEiMO*, no. 11 (November 1965), p. 90.

program and participation in specialized United Nations organs was giving
them intimate exposure to Western theories of development and to the real
problems of the third world economies. Economists were providing concrete analyses and predictions to government agencies as well as publishing in scholarly journals. They sometimes worked in UN organizations or
served as consultants on Soviet aid programs. They had ample opportunity
to see their analysis and predictions tested by events.

The first questioning of the old orthodoxies was very cautious. A review of a book edited by two of the most conservative of the scholars
remarked upon its "unexpectedly extreme negative formulation" in asserting that existing socioeconomic conditions "do not permit the problem of
accumulation of capital to be successfully solved." The reviewer asked,
"would it not be better to say that the outcome will depend on struggle?"
He noted that capital investment was also difficult for socialist countries in
the first years.[24] A passing statement in an article on third world classes
that "the construction of industry is logically [zakonomerno] connected
with taxation and inflation" hardly seemed controversial until a conservative strongly criticized it and suggested that "nationalization was more
effective."[25]

Open attack on the old orthodoxies began with an article in 1963 by
Leonid Goncharov, deputy director of the Institute of Africa.[26] The essence of the old image of Western–third world economic relations was that
the West, either consciously or spontaneously through the workings of the
market, was using the third world as a source of maximum profit and
economic enrichment. Goncharov attributed another, more pressing goal
to Western governments. They "often have not had the goal of the direct
extraction of superprofits, but, first of all, the support of the general rule of
financial capital in the colonial and semicolonial periphery that has been
shaken and is disintegrating under the blows of the national liberation

24. A. S. Kaufman, review of V. Ia. Avarin and A. A. Poliak, eds., *Problemy industrializatsii sovremennykh slaborazvitykh stran Azii (Indiia, Indoneziia, Birma)* in *Narody
Azii i Afriki,* no. 1 (1962), p. 169.

25. The original statement was in L. A. Gordon and L. A. Fridman, "Polozhenie
rabochego klassa v ekonomicheski slaborazvitykh stranakh Azii i Afriki (na primere Indii i
OAR)," *Narody Azii i Afriki,* no. 1 (1962), p. 34. The criticism is in A. A. Iskenderov,
"Issledovaniia sovetskikh uchenykh o rabochem klasse Azii i Afriki," *Narody Azii i Afriki,*
no. 3 (1963), p. 111.

26. It is important to emphasize the timing of the debates and exchanges described here
and in the next few pages. There has been a tendency to think that debates and a Soviet
pessimism began only in the mid-1970s. Clearly this is inaccurate. See Elizabeth Kridl
Valkenier, *The Soviet Union and the Third World* (Praeger, 1983) pp. 43–46, 81.

movement." Western countries were trying to shore up third world regimes and prevent communist revolutions; they had to support these countries economically, not just exploit them. Goncharov indicated that one could not simply compare private capital investment with repatriated profits and dividends but instead had to take into account such things as foreign aid, technical assistance, state subsidies, state credits, and governmental guarantees of private loans. He noted that 15 percent of the English budget consisted of subsidies for the colonies.[27]

This argument came to be repeated by a large number of analysts. At a scholarly discussion held in 1963 a specialist on Southeast Asia noted that the annual level of American credits, loans, and subsidies was 40 percent higher than American private investment and that this was "a most important factor in balancing the state budget."[28] Another scholar spoke of "the tendency of imperialists to pay liberated countries a special compensation for preserving the existing system of the capitalist world economy."[29] Still another asserted that "neocolonialism is a new policy, carried out with new methods. . . . The basic content of the old colonial policy was to secure the economic exploitation of the colonies by noneconomic means. . . . Now the chief goal of the policy of the capitalist states is the . . . implantation and development in them of capitalist relations."[30]

A second line of attack on the old orthodoxies emphasized that the economic imperatives of the West had changed, as had the relative priority of their economic and political values. At a 1963 scholarly discussion, the main report by Gratsiia Kolykhalova focused on "serious structural changes in the world capitalist economy." In her opinion the development of synthetics had reduced the need for third world raw materials; advanced industrial countries had achieved self-sufficiency in agriculture and now were exporting food products; and Western machinery manufacturers needed to sell their goods and were thus interested in helping develop manufacturing in third world countries. As a consequence the West no

27. "Evropeiskii gosudarstvenno-monopolisticheskii kapital—orudie kolonial'noi ekspansii v Afrike," *Narody Azii i Afriki*, no. 3 (1963), p. 4.

28. L. L. Klochkovsky in "Nauchnaia diskussiia, posviashchennaia roli chastnykh inostrannykh investitsii v ekonomike stran Azii," *Narody Azii i Afriki*, no. 1 (1964), p. 224. The journal was signed to press on January 23, 1964. Another conference whose discussions were published in the same issue took place on July 11, 1963; see pp. 221, 248.

29. V. Kollontai in "Metropolii bez kolonii," *MEiMO*, no. 11 (November 1965), pp. 92–93.

30. V. Rybakov in "Metropolii bez kolonii," *MEiMO*, no. 12 (December 1965), pp. 113–14.

longer needed the underdeveloped countries as suppliers of agrarian or raw materials. Kolykhalova went so far as to assert that as a result, "imperialism now ceases to play a decisive role in defining the socioeconomic development of the liberated countries."[31]

Most scholars thought that Kolykhalova exaggerated some points about raw materials export and the decisive role of the West, but an increasing number began to worry not so much about a Western desire to develop and import third world raw materials as their desire not to do so. Concern was expressed about the "aggressive protectionism on raw materials" that was being instituted, especially in conjunction with the establishment of the Common Market.[32] While the importance of the third world's ability to sell goods for its economic growth was increasingly recognized,[33] one possible solution, Soviet Europe and Eastern Europe as major markets for these goods, was offered with decreasing frequency. The reasons were not often mentioned, but they must have been universally understood: the Soviet Union was exporting many of the same items as the third world countries and hence was not a natural importer.[34] It was also not producing machinery of high enough quality and was not setting up the necessary networks to provide spare parts and service; thus it could not sell enough of its finished goods.[35]

In addition to suggesting the need to sell to the West, scholars also began to think that the third world needed Western investment. At a 1963 conference a specialist on the United Arab Republic noted that "leading circles in a majority of underdeveloped countries willingly seek to attract foreign investment, plan the receipt of foreign loans for several years, including them in their five-year, ten-year, and other plans of economic development." She believed that limiting foreign capital would have significant adverse consequences for many countries.[36] In a short time this

31. In "Nauchnaia diskussiia, posviashchennaia roli chastnykh inostrannykh investitsii," pp. 223–24.

32. V. Pekshev and P. Khvoinik, review of B. M. Pinegin, *Nasushchnye problemy mezhdunarodnoi torgovli. K itogam Konferentsii OON po torgovle i razvitiiu* (Moscow: Mezhdunarodnye otnosheniia, 1966), in *MEiMO*, no. 5 (May 1967), p. 149.

33. The first to emphasize this point was Anatolii Ia. El'ianov. See his *Na puti XX vek. Razvivaiushchiesia strany: proizvodstvo i rynok* (Moscow: Mezhdunarodnye otnosheniia, 1969).

34. R. Andreasian, "Neft' i problema 'vzaimozavisimosti,'" *MEiMO*, no. 5 (May 1966), pp. 48–49.

35. Iu. F. Shamrai, "Nekotorye voprosy rynochnykh otnoshenii mezhdu sotsialisticheskimi i razvivaiushchimisia stranami," *Narody Azii i Afriki*, no. 2 (1969), pp. 21–24.

36. L. N. Vatolina in "Nauchnaia diskussiia, posviashchennaia roli chastnykh inostrannykh investitsii," p. 225.

attitude became widespread among serious economists. Increasingly they argued that "the extremely difficult [international] situation for Soviet Russia, which now is completely different for developing countries, did not permit another experiment of using the resources of imperialism in the interests of economic progress and socialism."[37] Leonid Goncharov was particularly insistent in warning that political instability and hasty nationalization would frighten foreign investors and have serious long-term economic consequences.[38]

A third line of attack focused on the appropriateness for the third world of the Soviet model of industrialization. By 1964 Georgii Mirsky, a leading third world specialist at IMEMO, questioned whether economic independence required an emphasis on heavy industry from the beginning.[39] Some thought the emphasis necessary in large countries, but the problem of excess capacity in many major third world enterprises quickly convinced virtually all economists that many small countries did not have the internal market to absorb the output of steel and significant machinery plants. Even those scholars with generally conservative positions on other third world development questions cited figures showing that to be economical a modern steel plant should produce 4 million to 5 million tons a year and that at third world rates of consumption only a country with 100 million to 120 million people could use that much.[40]

At the same conference at which he cast doubt on the need to concentrate on heavy industry, Mirsky asserted flatly that "the nationalization of small enterprises can only harm the economy in many countries."[41] After the difficulties that arose in Burma and Egypt with the nationalization of small trade, the belief became nearly universal that such policies were counterproductive because of the lack of trained personnel in the third world (and perhaps because of the unspoken feeling that Soviet experience with abolishing private trade had not worked out well for the consumer).

There seems to have been a movement toward consensus on these three major points in the mid-1960s. A. Kurshakov, a conservative economist at a 1967 conference noted, "it has been repeatedly emphasized in our litera-

37. V. A. Sandakov, review of E. A. Utkin, *Problemy planirovaniia v razvivaiushchikhsia stranakh*, in *Narody Azii i Afriki*, no. 4 (1966), p. 232.

38. *Narody Azii i Afriki*, no. 5 (1966), p. 229; and L. Goncharov, "Investitsii i pribyli inostrannykh kompanii," *MEiMO*, no. 11 (November 1968), pp. 105, 109.

39. G. Mirsky in "Sotsializm, kapitalizm, slaborazvitye strany," *MEiMO*, no. 4 (April 1964), p. 122.

40. N. P. Shmelev, review of A. El'ianov, *Na puti v XX vek*, in *Narody Azii i Afriki*, no. 5 (1970), p. 181.

41. G. Mirsky, in "Sotsializm, kapitalizm, slaborazvitye strany," p. 124.

ture that the former colonies that are oriented toward the capitalist model are not in a position to solve the fundamental problems standing before them." He then continued, "one would think that industrialization is among these problems. However, the majority of speakers [at this conference] not only admit of the possibility of industrialization in such countries, but give concrete technical-economic bases and calculations for it."[42]

This conservative asserted that "it is scarcely possible to agree with this point of view," but his complaint was certainly accurate. A substantial number of scholars continued to speak about the dependent and deformed nature of third world capitalist development. Some prominent ones repeated that the third world was still predominantly an agrarian-raw materials supplier for the West, that foreign investment had major adverse consequences, and that the state sector was good only if it focused on industry, preferably heavy industry.[43] Yet no seriously involved scholar could ignore that nearly all third world countries were accepting foreign investment, that they had a range of policies and practices, and that the Soviet Union had to make foreign aid decisions with respect to countries that were on capitalist as well as noncapitalist paths. Whatever their thoughts about long-term economic developments in the third world, they all gave thought to near-term economic strategy and expressed their opinions about it.

Beyond these general propositions, however, disagreements remained. Even statements about the attractiveness of the NEP contained a major ambiguity. After all, the NEP was conducted in a country under the leadership of a communist party, and it lasted for only eight years. Taken literally, an endorsement of the NEP could imply a very orthodox and rapid transition to Soviet socialism. Yet many who spoke of the NEP really seemed to be endorsing a very mixed economy that would persist for a very long time.

In addition, short-range economic policy invoked a variety of specific questions and responses. Some scholars continued to emphasize the need for third world countries to diversify their economies and rapidly reduce

---

42. A. Kurshakov in "Problemy industrializatsii razvivaiushchikhsia stran," *MEiMO,* no. 5 (May 1967), p. 94.

43. See for example, N. Shmelev, "Mirovaia torgovlia i osvobodivshiesia strany," *Voprosy ekonomiki,* no. 8 (August 1964), p. 79; V. Fetov, "Strategiia neokolonializma," *MEiMO,* no. 3 (March 1965), pp. 9–10; and R. A. Ul'ianovsky, "O nekotorykh chertakh sovremennogo etapa natsional'no-osvoboditel'nogo dvizheniia," *Narody Azii i Afriki,* no. 5 (1967), p. 29.

their dependence on the one or two crops or raw materials that they traditionally exported, while others argued that in the short run these countries should concentrate on their main export crop to obtain foreign currency.[44] Some wanted to reduce consumer imports in favor of machinery, but opponents warned that because feeding the population must be the primary goal, food imports or investment in agriculture or both were necessary.[45] Attitudes toward strategies of concentrating attention on infrastructure and agriculture were also divided. Some thought that third world countries had to increase productivity and economic growth; others saw the desirability of less productive but more labor-intensive technology to reduce unemployment.[46] The list could go on and on.

Overall economic development strategy had to include answers to each of these questions, and each had to be answered in terms of relative emphasis rather than strictly either/or. As a result, each scholar could have a slightly different combination of views. Debates moved toward the same level of sophistication as those in the West: the top scholars read the Western literature, and if a one saw an argument that convinced him or that bolstered his general position, he was inclined to adopt it. This, of course, was true for those on all sides of the debates.

One conclusion to which nearly all scholars came was that there was no single economic strategy that every country should follow. As Viktor Tiagunenko emphasized, there were many possible variants and paths of industrialization; the best one for a particular country depended on the

44. See N. Gavrilov, "Reshaiushchii faktor nezavisimosti," *Aziia i Afrika segodnia,* no. 8 (August 1963), pp. 4–6; R. Andreasian and A. El'ianov, "Razvivaiushchiesia strany: diversifikatsiia ekonomiki i strategiia promyshlennogo razvitiia," *MEiMO,* no. 1 (January 1968), p. 37; and Iu. G. Aleksandrov, review of P. G. Anan'ev, *Sel'skoe khoziaistvo sovremennogo Indonezii,* in *Narody Azii i Afriki,* no. 1 (1966), pp. 162–63.

45. Vl. Kondrat'ev, "Razvivaiushchiesia strany: bor'ba za preobrazovanie vneshnei torgovli," *MEiMO,* no. 10 (October 1966), p. 36; and I. S. Kazakevich and G. S. Matveeva, review of *Aktual'nye problemy stran Azii (sbornik statei)* in *Narody Azii i Afriki,* no. 1 (1967), p. 156.

46. For infrastructure and agriculture, see V. Tiagunenko in "Problemy industrializatsii razvivaiushchikhsia stran," *MEiMO,* no. 4 (April 1967), p. 107; Ul'ianovsky, "O nekotorykh chertakh sovremennogo etapa natsional'no-osvoboditel'nogo dvizheniia," p. 29; Andreasian and El'ianov, "Razvivaiushchiesia strany," p. 34; and N. Z. Volchek, S. D. Zak, and Iu. B. Il'in, "Itogi i perspektivy sotsial'no-ekonomicheskogo razvitiia molodykh soverennykh gosudarstv," *Narody Azii i Afriki,* no. 5 (1966), p. 226. L. V. Stepanov so emphasized increasing productivity that he made it the sole basis for his definition of economic independence. S. A. Kuz'min argued for reduced unemployment in *Razvivaiushchiesia strany: zaniatnost' i kapitalovlozheniia* (Moscow: Mysl', 1965). See also G. Skorov, "Poiski resheniia slozhnoi problemy," *MEiMO,* no. 11 (November 1969), p. 55.

country's level of economic development, its size, the character of its natural resources, and, of course, the relative strength of its various political forces. Such statements implied that the Soviet model should not be adopted universally, and Tiagunenko explicitly referred to the "special historical conditions" in which the Soviet Union had found itself in the late 1920s.[47]

By the 1970s all the sophisticated scholars had a sense of the excruciating dilemmas of the third world. The countries conducting radical transformations did not, on the average, turn out to have especially good records of economic growth. They did not have a "noticeable rise in productive forces" in the words of one article,[48] and in fact the average growth record of capitalist economies in Asia and Africa was better. In agriculture it became clear that egalitarian redistribution often left peasants with too little land to farm economically and that plantation agriculture was more efficient.[49] Nodari Simoniia of the Institute of Oriental Studies put the point starkly:

> If one compares in general the group of countries [of a socialist orientation] with the countries that are going on the path of capitalist development, then it will become obvious that the first group is unquestionably in the vanguard in the region of social and political transformations. However, the situation is much more complicated in the sphere of economics. . . . One can see a certain natural tendency [zakonomernost'] for countries of socialist orientation to lag in the economic sphere: a breaking and reconstruction of existing social and political relations . . . leads with objective inevitability to a retardation of tempos of economic growing at the beginning stage of their development. . . . [Moreover,] imperialism is not only immeasurably less generous in extending aid but takes all possible measures (right up to aggression) to slow their economic and social progress.[50]

Simoniia went on to discuss such other factors as unrealistic plans, bureaucratism, excessive nationalization, and corruption.

To the extent that poor growth records resulted from uneconomic projects undertaken to satisfy the ego of the dictator or from bureaucratic corruption, Soviet scholars could condemn and call for change. Yet the

47. "Problemy industrializatsii razvivaiushchikhsia stran," MEiMO, no. 4 (1967), pp. 107–08. Another participant of this 1967 conference noted that all participants "are agreed that a single universal scheme of industrialization does not exist"; V. Loginova, p. 103.

48. A. P. Kolontaev and V. I. Pavlov, "V. I. Lenin o preobrazovanii mnogoukladnykh struktur i chastnogo sektora (na primer razvivaiushchikhsia stran)," Narody Azii i Afriki, no. 2 (1970), p. 23.

49. Andreasian and El'ianov, "Razvivaiushchiesia strany," p. 32.

50. "Sotsialisticheskaia orientatsiia: problemy perspektivy," Aziia i Afrika segodnia, no. 1 (1976), p. 14.

thought could and did arise that such phenomena might be endemic to systems with dictators—even left-wing ones—or maybe even to large state sectors in general. What should one do if one concluded that competitive elections or the discipline of the marketplace or both were the solution?

In other cases no one could deny that a dilemma existed. If the radical regimes were too concerned with promoting full employment and hired excess workers in state enterprises, if they were too egalitarian in land reforms, they were not going to have the same increases in productivity as countries that neglected these concerns. As a result they might not prove competitive in the long run with the faster-growing capitalist countries, especially if achieving economic independence and equality with the West was the main driving force. Yet if radical regimes did not take social factors into account and emphasized only profitability, how were they any better than capitalist regimes?

Similarly, by 1969 no one challenged the proposition that "in no developing country [including radical ones] has any high degree of direction of socioeconomic development or control been achieved."[51] Indeed, one critic contemptuously denied that there was a crisis in third world planning on the grounds that one "could only call the present situation of planning in developing countries a crisis if there had been better days in the past. However, this is not so."[52] But, like some economists, did one thus conclude that "because it is difficult to plan a mixed economy, the private sector should be abolished," or did one lower one's expectation of what was possible in the third world?[53]

What choices should be made if one became convinced that small-scale enterprises were necessary, that pure nationalization was uneconomical, that the choice "to develop big or small industry means to strengthen the position either of the urban proletariat or the small businessmen,"[54] and that "it is impossible to have a strong class of private property owners in a country and isolate it from politics"?[55] One could try to square the circle

51. Kollontai, "Voprosy planirovaniia v 'tret'em mire,'" p. 99.
52. Bessonov, "Real'nye predposylki i vozmozhnosti planirovaniia," p. 90.
53. See B. Solov'ev in "Problemy industrializatsii razvivaiushchikhsia stran," p. 99; and G. Smirnov, "Vozmozhnosti i predely," MEiMO, no. 8 (August 1969), pp. 75–77.
54. Kollontai, "Voprosy planirovaniia v 'tret'em mire,'" p. 97.
55. G. Mirsky, " 'Novaia revoliutsiia' v OAR," MEiMO, no. 1 (January 1969), p. 46. Mirsky made the same point in 1964 when he first cautioned against excessive nationalization but said the private sector could lead to capitalism unless there was a strong political leadership such as existed in the USSR in the 1920s; see "Sotsializm, kapitalizm, slaborazvitye strany," p. 124.

by asserting that "the chief socioeconomic question is: should the small producers be subordinated to the large private producers or the state sector" and then by opting for the latter through cooperatives and the like.[56] Or one could conclude that the major third world countries were inexorably on a capitalist path, that the Soviet Union should not base its policy on wishful thinking, and that the socioeconomic transformation to be supported should center on perfecting the system of taxation, raising the effectiveness of the state sector, struggling against corruption, and reducing military expenditures.[57]

There were no straightforward answers to these questions; deeply held emotional values and psychological factors often seemed to determine responses. Analyses might change in response to changing circumstances and changing terms of the debate, but a scholar's basic posture toward the bourgeoisie and the market was much more stable. Thus Nikolai Shmelev, the most sophisticated of the economists with a clear-cut opposition to market-oriented regimes, forcefully argued in the mid-1960s that the market was not conducive to balanced economic growth, but when that argument was weakened by events, he became a forceful proponent of the theory that market forces must be overriden to promote social justice. By 1985 he took a much more cautious and balanced approach, but he was still pessimistic about the large Asian states and Africa, put great emphasis on social justice, and affirmed the decisive role of the state. Together with Simoniia—his protagonist of a quarter century earlier—he was chosen to give one of the conflicting reviews of a new book on third world economics.[58]

Those who were, above all, committed to a revolutionary strategy were inclined to say that their theory answered "the needs of the antiimperialist struggle," while their opponent's implied a reconciliation with capitalism. The latter in turn responded that their opponents were dogmatists ("ideologues" might be a better American translation) or accused them of naive revolutionary romanticism.[59] It is not our task to evaluate specific charges,

56. Tiagunenko in "Problemy industrializatsii razvivaiushchikhsia stran," p. 107.

57. "Finansirovanie ekonomiki razvivaiushchikhsia stran Azii," *Narody Azii i Afriki*, no. 1 (1968), p. 19.

58. "Mirovaia torgovlia i osvobodivshiesia strany," pp. 79–91, and "Stoimostnye kriterii i ikh rol' v ekonomike razvivaiushchikhsia stran," *MEiMO*, no. 6 (June 1968), pp. 40–51. See also "Nasushchnye problemy i strategii razvitiia osvobodivshikhsia stran," *MEiMO*, no. 3 (1985), pp. 118, 122, 124.

59. See V. L. Sheinis in "Kak otsenivat' osobennosti i uroven' razvitiia kapitalizma v Latinskoi Amerike?" *Latinskaia Amerika*, no. 2 (March–April 1979), p. 130; and E. A. Kosarev, "Ekonomika i mirnyi put' revoliutsii," *Latinskaia Amerika*, no. 5 (September–October 1974), pp. 92–100, esp. pp. 95, 96, 99–100.

but both groups were probably right in pointing to explanations that went beyond strictly rational analysis.

At an unconscious level, the divisions probably reflected instinctive attitudes toward good and evil or toward Soviet society. Does the world represent a Manichean struggle in which one has an obligation to bear continuing witness or does the real world always involve ambivalent choices and conflicts between relative goods and relative bads? Was one committed to the Soviet status quo and hence determined to emphasize the "objective laws" that produced it or was socialism an evolving process into which more market mechanisms should be introduced in order to improve economic performance and the quality of consumer services?

## Dependency, Level of Development, and the Uniformity of the Third World

The traditional Stalinist view of third world economic development was a very crude dependency theory. So long as a developing country remained within the capitalist world market, it would remain an economically dependent, exploited producer of raw materials and agricultural produce. In the mid-1960s, however, a more sophisticated version of dependency theory was developed in Latin America and introduced into the Soviet Union a few years later. This version, espoused by a number of the leading IMEMO scholars under the label "dependent capitalism," tended to focus on the historical origins of industrial development and the impact of these origins upon the internal economic and social development of third world countries. Because such a definition of dependency means a type of development, it is compatible with substantial economic growth and with a country's passing through different stages of development, but the IMEMO book was capable of real simplicity: "The greater the tie with state-monopoly capitalism, as a rule, the greater the dependence. The greater the dependence—in the final analysis—the greater the relative backwardness, which leads in turn to greater dependence, and so forth."[60]

The debate on dependent capitalism had many facets. No one denied that the third world countries were dependent in one sense or another and to some extent or another, although the oil crisis that occurred as the debate was heating up certainly provided an argument for those who wanted to talk about mutual dependence. The real issues were twofold:

60. R. M. Avakov and others, eds., *Razvivaiushchiesia strany: zakonomernosti, tendentsii, perspektivy* (Moscow: Mysl', 1974), p. 41.

what was the cause of the dependence and the best way to overcome it and how uniform was the third world?

The concept of dependent capitalism focused on capitalism as the cause of the trouble. It contained at least a whiff of the argument that, in the words of one critic, "entry onto the noncapitalist path of development is capable, like some talisman, of automatically solving the problem of economic dependence." The critics—especially those in the Institute of Oriental Studies, IMEMO's major competitor—believed that "such illusions facilitate the emergence of moods of pseudorevolutionary impatience and leftist deviations in economic policy." They spoke more of categories such as "economic progress" and defined "economic independence" more in terms of indicators such as productivity of labor that reflected level of development rather than the historical pattern of development.[61]

To attribute dependence to economic backwardness was to imply that capitalist economic growth was better than noncapitalist economic stagnation, and scholars who adopted this position could make it very explicit. In the words of Nodari Simoniia,

A real opportunity has opened up for the majority of liberated countries of Asia and Africa to conduct a nondependent economic policy, using it as a powerful lever to achieve economic independence. Such countries as Egypt [Anwar Sadat's Egypt by this time, it should be noted], Algeria or India and Pakistan can serve as an example of this. . . . [By contrast] the Republic of Indonesia from 1957 to 1963 conducted the "most nondependent" economic policy in its history. Its result was a significant erosion of existing productive forces and a general disorganization of the economy.[62]

This argument might have been relatively academic if in fact the countries on the noncapitalist path of development had been growing more rapidly than the countries on the capitalist path. The reality was very different. The degree of economic success did not correlate precisely with development strategy, but generally the radical regimes, especially those without petroleum reserves, were not doing well, while some of the more

61. B. G. Gafurov, ed., *Zarubezhnii Vostok i sovremennost'* (Moscow: Nauka, 1974), vol. 2, 477–83. This was a collective work of the Institute of Oriental Studies. The pages in question were written by N. A. Simoniia. Simoniia also presented these views under his own name. See his statement in "Konferentsiia po problemam bor'by za ekonomicheskuiu samostoiatel'nost' razvivaiushchikhsia stran," *Narody Azii i Afriki*, no. 2 (1970), pp. 227–28. For an early expression of the view, see S. I. Tiul'panov and V. L. Sheinis, review of V. V. Rymalov in *Narody Azii i Afriki*, no. 2 (1967), p. 173.

62. Gafurov, *Zarubezhnii Vostok i sovremennost'*, vol. 2, pp. 478–79.

spectacular successes (for example, South Korea and Taiwan) were favorably oriented toward foreign investment.

A second facet of the debate on dependent capitalism was disagreement on the degree of uniformity in the third world. Obviously the most traditional Soviet scholars had always distinguished between countries that were on the capitalist path and those that were labeled "socialist orientation," and the concept of dependent capitalism retained that distinction. While the book that introduced dependent capitalism discussed differences in level of development and singled out Latin America as being on a much higher level than Africa, it remained traditional in grouping Asia, Africa, and Latin America. The dependency thesis obviously implied that for most purposes the commonalities of third world historical experience and of membership in a capitalist world market outweighed the diversities.

In practice, the level of economic development in the major Latin American countries was much higher than that in most Asian countries and all African ones. Hence, as the most advanced area of the third world, Latin America was the obvious test of the thesis, and it became the subject of a heated debate.

A number of scholars led by Boris Koval', first of the Institute of Latin America and then deputy director of the Institute of the International Workers' Movement, insisted that Latin America was at so much higher a level of economic development that it was not really comparable with Asia and Africa and was approaching the state-monopoly capitalism found in the West.[63] A 1974 book Koval' coauthored with Sergei Semenov of the Central Committee's Institute of Social Sciences and Anatolii Shul'govsky, the chief sociopolitical specialist at the Institute of Latin America, did not mention any scholarly opponents in the Soviet Union, but it was blunt in its criticism of bourgeois literature that "still characterizes imperialism as having the chief and decisive role in the development of productive relations in Latin America." It was even more critical of the extreme views of "left radicals" abroad: "Here one can name the thesis about the colonial character of Latin American capitalism. . . . From this it is concluded that capitalism in Latin America is imported instead of being the result of the processes of internal development." The study concluded that "left radicals absolutize the tendency for foreign monopolistic capital

63. "Nauchno-tekhnicheskaia revoliutsiia i Latinskaia Amerika," *Latinskaia Amerika*, no. 5 (September–October 1972), pp. 14–22, esp. p. 21.

to be strengthened in Latin America, and they turn it into the dominating factor of the life of the Latin American countries."[64]

That Latin America should no longer really be discussed in conjunction with the underdeveloped countries of Asia and Africa was formalized by the most widely respected Soviet comparativist, Viktor Sheinis. When Sheinis explored the criteria for comparing third world countries, he argued that not only must the major countries of Latin America be differentiated from those in Asia and Africa but also that they should be considered countries of "medium-developed capitalism" rather than underdeveloped countries. He specifically grouped Argentina, Chile, Costa Rica, Jamaica, Mexico, Panama, and Uruguay (and probably Brazil and Venezuela) with Greece, Ireland, Malta, Portugal, Spain, and southern Italy.[65]

When Koval's book condemned bourgeois literature and left radicals abroad, there was little doubt about the real targets. One group was composed of Viktor Vol'sky, director of the Institute of Latin America, Lev Klochkovsky, the head of its economics department, and Igor Sheremet'ev, the institute's top specialist on Mexico, all of whom took an extreme position on the degree of Latin American dependence and its economic consequences. In 1970 Vol'sky asserted that Latin American dependence on international financial capital was growing and that the area was falling "all the more" behind in its economic development.[66] During the 1970s this group continued to cite statistics on trade and investment to argue that Latin America was becoming more dependent. This dependence made it very unlikely that the economies of countries such as Brazil and Mexico could continue to develop vigorously under capitalism, let alone that they could move on to more autonomous lines of development.[67]

The left-radical target was Kiva Maidanik, the leading Latin American-

64. B. I. Koval', S. I. Semenov, and A. E. Shul'govsky, eds., *Revoliutsionnye protsessy v Latinskoi Amerike* (Moscow: Nauka, 1974), pp. 29, 287, 298.

65. "Strany srednerazvitogo kapitalizma (nekotorye voprosy tipologii)," *MEiMO*, no. 9 (September 1977), p. 108.

66. "Leninizm i problemy revoliutsionnogo protsessa v Latinskoi Amerike," *Latinskaia Amerika*, no. 2 (March–April 1970), esp. pp. 8–11, 16–17, 23 (fn. 27).

67. L. Klochkovsky and I. Sheremet'ev, "Latinskaia Amerika: krizis zavisimogo kapitalizma," *MEiMO*, no. 4 (April 1978), pp. 53–66; and V. Vol'sky, "Otnositel'naia zrelost; bezuslovnaia zavisimost'," *Problemy mira i sotsializma*, no. 6 (June 1979), pp. 48–53. Also see the debate about Mexico, "O sovremennom etape razvitiia kapitalizma v Meksike," *Latinskaia Amerika*, no. 5 (September–October 1978), pp. 70–119, esp. 78–82, and that about dependence and level of development, "Kak otsenivat' osobennosti i uroven' razvitiia kapitalizma v Latinskoi Amerike," *Latinskaia Amerika*, no. 1 (January–February 1979), pp. 53–100, esp. pp. 56–62, 85–89, and no. 2 (March–April 1979), pp. 82–131, esp. 130–31.

ist at IMEMO. Maidanik was one of the driving forces behind the theory of dependent capitalism, but he agreed that Latin America had reached a higher level of development (middle-level capitalism) than Asia and Africa and that the area might be capable of substantially more growth. However, he argued that the occurrence of Latin American industrialization at a later stage than that of the United States and Western Europe had deformed it in very important ways. In his view the dependent and deformed development left Latin America trapped in a socioeconomic bog that gave the situation revolutionary potential.[68]

The surfacing of the argument about dependence coincided with the oil crisis of 1973 and the attendant dramatic increase in prices for petroleum and other commodities. Some scholars immediately asserted that the idea of dependence had been turned on its head: "In these conditions the capitalist world sharply felt its dependence on the developing world." They evinced considerable optimism: "The developing countries are taking into their own hands the control of resources and the extraction and export of raw materials. They are reestablishing national sovereignty over natural resources and are raising prices on raw materials."[69]

Such an opinion was, of course, not universal even at the height of the oil crisis. Leading economists on Latin America did not waver in their view of dependency. At IMEMO, Viktor Tiagunenko argued that the oil crisis actually increased the dependency of most of the third world because they were petroleum importers and had to come to the West for loans to purchase it.[70] Even an analyst who referred to "the demonstrated dependence of the economies of the leading capitalist countries on developing states for their supply of fuel and industrial raw materials" still cautioned, "we irrepressibly want to prove that dependence is absolute. If such dependence is not observed, we then go to the other extreme and hurry to deny it completely."[71]

---

68. K. L. Maidanik in "Kak otsenivat' osobennosti i uroven' razvitiia kapitalizma v Latinskoi Amerike?" *Latinskaia Amerika,* no. 2 (March–April 1979), pp. 89–91, 108–14; and V. M. Davydov in "O sovremennom etape razvitiia kapitalizma v Meksike," pp. 100–05, 112–14. Also see V. Davydov, "O stepeni zrelosti i osobennostiakh kapitalizma 'latino-amerikanskogo' tipa," *MEiMO,* no. 3 (March 1979), pp. 116–29.

69. R. Andreasian, "Strany OPEK protiv zasil'ia monopolii," *MEiMO,* no. 2 (February 1974), p. 77, and "Posledstviia dlia ekonomiki razvivaiushchikhsia stran," *MEiMO,* no. 6 (June 1975), p. 73.

70. "Vyvoz kapitala iz razvivaiushchikhsia stran," *MEiMO,* no. 3 (March 1975), p. 95.

71. V. Pavlov, "Vazhnyi aspekt mirokhoziastvennykh otnoshenii kapitalizma," *MEiMO,* no. 3 (March 1974), p. 79.

With the collapse of most commodity prices in the recession of 1974–75 and the inability of other producers' associations to duplicate OPEC's success, optimism about a transformation of the relationship between the developed and developing world tended to fade.[72] Economists continued to debate whether the prices of raw materials would tend to rise faster than those of finished goods, but even those who thought they would felt the likelihood of effective producers' action was very low.[73]

Basically, however, the oil crisis decided the issue about economic dependency in its old simplified global sense. No longer was it possible to say that capitalist development inevitably led to complete dependence and growth. Serious analysts began to single out the oil producers—at least those with relatively small populations—as a special group within the third world that, whatever their social system, had resources for very different patterns of economic development. This recognition in turn led to increasing efforts to differentiate among third world countries. Some of the Asian countries most dependent on foreign investment—South Korea, Taiwan, Hong Kong, and Singapore—could be treated as countries approaching European levels of economic development.[74]

In the early 1980s, a number of those insisting on the dependent character of third world economic development moved substantially away from their old position. Viktor Vol'sky, the director of the Institute of Latin America, made few changes in his analysis, but he was relatively unique. Even Lev Klochkovsky, head of the economics department of the institute, began to distance himself from his director.

The greatest change took place in IMEMO. In 1983 its top third world specialists published two collective books, *Developing Countries: Economic Growth and Social Progress* and *The Developing Countries in the*

72. Thus R. Andreasian, the leading specialist on Arab petroleum in IMEMO, and whose optimism in 1974 and 1975 was cited in footnote 69, said in 1977 that the situation was confused and that economic forecasting was as difficult as the forecasting of international relations. He predicted in 1978 that raw material prices in general would not outpace finished goods prices in the next quarter of a century; see "Vozmozhnye masshtaby i perspektivy progressivnykh izmenenii," *MEiMO*, no. 3 (March 1977), pp. 88–89; and no. 7 (July 1978), p. 99.

73. See the statements of A. Bel'chuk, a leading specialist on raw materials at IMEMO, in "Tovarnye soglasheniia i mirovye rynki syr'evykh tovarov," *MEiMO*, no. 4 (April 1977), p. 99; no. 5 (May 1977), p. 119; and no. 7 (July 1978), p. 101.

74. V. P. Lukin, in "Transnatsional'nye korporatsii i razvivaiushchiesia mir," *Latinskaia Amerika*, no. 8 (1983), p. 40.

*Contemporary World: Unity and Diversity.*[75] Both books still talked about
the dependent nature of the third world, but they did so in a far more
differentiated way. More important, the whole thrust of their argument
emphasized the diversity in the third world rather than its common features. As Nodari Simoniia noted in a review, "the impression is created
that the authors already have pushed off from one shore, but still haven't
decided to pull into the other.[76]

Clearly, however, the leaders of IMEMO have pushed a long way from
the old shore. They explicitly dissociated themselves from the emphasis of
the 1974 collective book on the crucial role of the external factor in third
world economic development (the essence of the dependency thesis) and
called for caution in the definition of dependence and the emphasis upon
its importance. They rejected out of hand the notion that the "vicious
circle of an increasing dependence could not be broken without social
revolution."[77] Moreover, the main line of analysis went in the opposite
direction. Their emphasis (discussed in the last chapter) upon a developing
society being "an integral and evolving social organism with its own logic
and social-genetic 'code' for this evolution" scarcely suggested that outside influences from the capitalist metropolis were the decisive factor.[78] In
their concrete economic analysis, they spoke not of connections with the
West leading to greater dependence, but about foreign economic relations
and export strategies being vital for growth and the development of domestic manufacturing.[79]

Perhaps most important, the use of the term "dependent" gradually
changed. It had always been implicitly used in both an economic and a
foreign policy sense. In the traditional analysis, a capitalist third world
country was a dependent part of the capitalist economy that could not have
sustained autonomous economic growth; it was also subordinated to the
West in its foreign policy. In the Khrushchev era it was impossible to say

75. V. L. Sheinis and A. Ia. El'ianov, *Razvivaiushchiesia strany: ekonomicheskii rost i
sotsial'nyi progress* (Moscow: Nauka, 1983); and I. V. Aleshina, I. D. Ivanov, and V. L.
Sheinis, eds., *Razvivaiushchiesia strany v sovremennom mire: edinstvo i mnogoobrazie*
(Moscow: Nauka, 1983).

76. N. Simoniia, "Dialektika vzaimosviazei," *MEiMO,* no. 3 (March 1985), p. 127.

77. Sheinis and El'ianov, *Razvivaiushchiesia strany,* pp. 54, 300; and Aleshina and
others, *Razvivaiushchiesia strany v sovremennom mire,* p. 6.

78. Aleshina and others, *Razvivaiushchiesia strany v sovremennom mire,* p. 8.

79. Sheinis and El'ianov, *Razvivaiushchiesia strany,* pp. 109, 126, 141–42.

that a capitalist third world country was inevitably dependent in its foreign relations (although one could hint at such tendencies), but few said openly that capitalist economic systems could have sustained growth. In the 1970s, especially after the oil crisis, fewer said that capitalist countries could not have strong growth. The arguments about dependence increasingly referred to the likelihood of an independent third world foreign policy. (For example, Tiagunenko's statement about dependence on loans to purchase petroleum may really have had this meaning.)

## An Internationalization of the World Economy?

The most interesting economic debates of the late 1970s and early 1980s dealt not with terminology but with the way the capitalist economy and implicitly the world economy functioned. Even innovative thinkers of the 1960s tended to see imperialists' granting economic concessions to the third world for political reasons in a way that implied Western initiative. Trade between industrial goods producers and raw materials producers was inherently exploitive ("nonequivalent"), with only a political decision by Western governments or concerted action by producers being able to correct the situation in part.[80]

In the West the theory of comparative advantage had insisted that foreign trade was always advantageous if based on market prices and free trade. The 200th anniversary of David Ricardo's birth in 1972 provided the occasion for reminding scholars that Marx's analysis rested on classic economics and that classic economics had featured the theory of comparative advantage in foreign trade.[81] Soviet scholars shied away from Western phraseology, but increasingly they used language that was roughly equivalent. In 1983 Ivan Ivanov, the deputy director of IMEMO who supervised studies of foreign economies, was particularly blunt:

It has already been repeatedly disproved, but now the thesis about "the price scissors" [industrial prices rising faster on the graph than commodity prices] as a quantitative expression of "nonequivalent trade" has again arisen in the pages of

80. For a relatively recent book containing a strong repetition of the thesis of non-equivalent trade, see A. S. Kodachenko, *Vneshne-ekonomicheskaia politika imperializma i razvivaiushchiesia strany* (Moscow: Nauka, 1977), pp. 74–80.

81. "D. Rikardo i sovremennost'," *MEiMO*, no. 5 (May 1972), pp. 116–24; and "Ob-suzhdenie teorii ekonomicheskogo rosta razvivaiushchikhsia stran," *Narody Azii i Afriki*, no. 3 (1972), pp. 243–44.

our scientific journals. They say, for example, that if Colombia paid 20 bags of coffee for a tractor in the 1930s and now 50, then this is an increase in the degree of exploitation. I think that it is necessary to abandon this simplified approach. Such a conclusion contradicts the law of labor value, according to which the exchange of goods should be carried out not by individual values, but by socially necessary ones. On the level of the world market, the latter are expressed in world prices. However inconvenient these prices are for this or that country, they are objective. The Soviet Union trades on these bases, and they serve, although in average [*usrednennom*] form, as the basis of prices and trade inside SEV. There-fore, to interpret them as monopoly prices (this also occurs) means to contradict not only political economy but also world economic practice.[82]

A second change in the image of the capitalist economy concerned the role of the international corporation, and to a considerable extent it re-flected changes occurring in the real world. Originally, foreign factories of an international corporation were either plants for extracting raw materials or duplications of the domestic factory that produced for the local foreign market. Increasingly, however, production has become more internation-alized; parts of a complex product may be manufactured in a variety of countries to take advantage of different levels of skills and wages. The division of labor can take place not only between corporations but within a corporation, and it can involve subcontracting, establishing joint compa-nies, and so forth. One Soviet scholar cited the statistic that the Boeing 747 uses parts from 16,000 companies of the United States and other countries.[83]

For some, this phenomenon had little fundamental significance. The joint companies could be called no more than a cover and the division of labor seen as of importance only to the corporation, not the national development of the foreign country.[84] Yet for others a fundamental change was occurring, "a new state of development . . . a transition of the internationalization of production to a new, higher level," in the words of Pavel Khvoinik, a foreign economics relations specialist at IMEMO. Khvoinik and others of like views ascribed the change not to the exploitive tendency of the corporations but to "the objective need of productive

82. I. D. Ivanov in *Latinskaia Amerika,* no. 8 (1983), p. 50.

83. P. Khvoinik, "Vneshneekonomicheskaia sfera kapitalizma: novyi etap razvitiia," *MEiMO,* no. 5 (May 1976), p. 77.

84. S. Kuz'min, "Mnogonatsional'nye korporatsii i integratsiia v 'tret'em mire,'" *MEiMO,* no. 6 (June 1975), pp. 117, 122, 124.

forces for a further deepening of the specialization or cooperation of production in conditions of the scientific-technical revolution.[85]

In this view the transnational corporation had a very different role than had been attributed to it in the past. Viktor Sheinis, the leading comparativist at IMEMO, called the transnational corporation "one of the 'motor' forces of development."[86] Ivan Ivanov, who was just cited on nonequivalent prices, spelled out the reasons for Sheinis's point:

The young states . . . all the more often receive access to the technical-financial potential of the transnational corporation while perserving national sovereignty over natural resources and their economies. . . . So far as the transnational corporation is concerned, the profits they receive in the framework of the new forms now are dependent in much greater degree on the work of their subsidiaries.[87]

This debate about the internationalization of the world economy had implications for the Soviet Union itself, which was moving toward greater economic collaboration with the West—basically on the "colonial" pattern of exporting raw materials and importing technology.[88] As Ivanov's statement about world prices indicated, an assertion about nonequivalent trade really implied that expanded economic collaboration with the West was probably not very advantageous to the Soviet Union. The conservatives argued that economic relations with the West should be strengthened by a removal of Western discriminatory measures, but they rarely went beyond this.[89]

To say that internationalization of the capitalist economy was required by "the objective needs of the productive forces . . . in conditions of the scientific-technical revolution" was another matter altogether. As the late director of IMEMO, Nikolai Inozemtsev, once reported,

Marxist investigators naturally ask themselves the question: What has produced these changes [in capitalism] and what do they reflect—the objective needs

85. "Vneshneekonomicheskaia sfera kapitalizma," pp. 78–79; and "Mezhdunarodnye monopolii i mezhdunarodnaia torgovlia," MEiMO, no. 4 (April 1975), p. 109.

86. "Transnatsional'nye korporatsii i razvivaiushchii mir," p. 65.

87. "Gosudarstvo i inostrannyi kapital: modifikatsiia otnoshenii," Azii i Afriki segodnia, no. 2 (1984), p. 31.

88. See the discussion in Erik P. Hoffmann and Robbin F. Laird, The Politics of Economic Modernization in the Soviet Union (Cornell University Press, 1982), pp. 99–187.

89. Khvoinik explicitly criticized a conservative author for limiting his appeal for greater collaboration to this level. "It is scarcely possible to agree completely with the author's formulation of the tasks of the normalization of international trade only as a struggle against discrimination." Review of Iu. N. Kapelinsky, Na vzaimovygodnoi osnove (torgovlia SSSR s razvytymi kapitalisticheskimi stranami) (Moscow, 1975) in Khvoinik, "Shirokie perspektivy sotrudnichestva," MEiMO, no. 10 (October 1975), p. 134.

of the development of productive forces, or the nature of imperialism and the features that are inherent in it? We, of course, have a fundamentally different attitude to these two groups of factors. The socialist states cannot ignore the objective laws of the development of productive forces.[90]

Ivanov advocated that Soviet enterprises also farm out production of components in the third world.[91] While it might be politically difficult to say, Soviet production of component parts for Western firms would be an ideal way to force Soviet managers to achieve higher quality standards.

As Soviet economic performance worsened in the 1970s, the number of statements about third world economic strategy that clearly also referred to economic reform in the Soviet Union multiplied. The following is a typical example: "A course toward a closed economy or, in other words, toward economic autarchy is, as history shows, a course without a future. It is a path leading to a dead end. . . . The higher the level of participation in the system of the international division of labor, the higher the tempos of economic growth." The author later notes that extreme protectionism, carried out over an unjustifiably long time, is fraught with negative consequences (the preservation and extension of backward, noncompetitive, inefficient production with high costs of production, low productivity of labor, and low quality of production).[92]

Of course, a variety of positions on this issue continue to be expressed. In the spring of 1985, for example, Viktor Vol'sky published an extremely strong attack in *Pravda* on the consequences of foreign investment in Latin America. While the main policy point of his article may have been to warn against Soviet optimism about prospects in Central America and against excessive investment of resources there, some of his language scarcely suggested an enthusiasm for Soviet integration into the world economy:

Recently the U.S.A. was able to impose monetarist recipes of economic development on not a few Latin American countries. These recipes foresaw the "strengthening" of the economy by opening the national markets to the free competition of foreign capital and uncontrolled exchange of currency by foreign banks. . . . "Freedom of competition" in Argentina led in the last 10 years to a reduction of the industrial proletariat by almost 30 percent. Argentine economists called this process "deindustrialization." The U.S.A. itself by no means follows

90. N. N. Inozemtsev, A. G. Mileikovsky, and V. A. Martynov, eds., *Politicheskaia ekonomiia sovremennogo monopolisticheskogo kapitalizma* (Moscow: Mysl', 1971), vol. 2, p. 391.

91. "Transnatsionalynye korporatsii i razvivaiushchiesia mir," pp. 49–50.

92. A. I. Dinkevich, "O strategii ekonomicheskogo razvitiia osvobodivshikhsia stran," in A. I. Dinkevich, ed., *Razvivaiushchiesia strany: nakoplenie i ekonomicheskii rost* (Moscow: Nauka, 1977), pp. 8, 12.

the recommendation of tolerating freedom of competition on its domestic markets. On the contrary, it carries out a policy of rigid protectionism in relation to Latin American goods."[93]

Glerii Shirokov, deputy director of economics at the Institute of Oriental Studies, took a somewhat intermediate position. He was very critical of the import-substitution strategy in the third world, but suggested that this strategy could be much more important if the spontaneous market mechanism were limited, income inequality were reduced, and strict control over foreign monopolies were exercised. He cautioned that the 1970s had seen slower growth for countries strongly integrated in the world market and that exports had far less impact on larger countries than small ones. Yet he insisted that "entering the world market forces the technological structure and productivity of labor to be dragged up to world levels," and he saw the export of machinery, metal fabricated goods, and chemical items as extremely beneficial to a country, if also very difficult. He called for a mixture of the strategies of export orientation and import substitution, and for a country such as the Soviet Union that had been almost totally import substitution, his advice about the direction of movement was clear.[94]

## Economic Growth vs. Social Justice

Soviet officials and scholars do not, of course, praise capitalism as the optimal form of economic development. In the United Nations they generally support the third world complaints about multinational corporations, although they have acted with outrage at the assertion that they themselves are part of the "rich North" that has a special responsibility to help the "poor South."[95] All Western economists not wholeheartedly in the Chicago school warn third world countries that adopting an absolutely free market can lead to devastating consequences in times of economic downturn in the West and can fail to provide citizens with the protections against the market that are taken for granted in the United States. Soviet economists all join this attack on the postulates of the Chicago school, and

93. "Latinskaia Amerika: Est' li vykhod?" Pravda, April 20, 1985.

94. G. K. Shirokov, Promyshlennaia revoliutsiia v stranakh Vostoka (Moscow: Nauka, 1981), pp. 128, 130, 132–33.

95. For a good discussion of the growing wariness in Soviet support of third world positions in the United Nations Conference on Trade and Development (UNCTAD), see Valkenier, The Soviet Union and the Third World, pp. 109–27.

at a minimum they call for regulation of the activity of international corporations by the host countries.

Yet this continually negative tone about capitalism and the multinational corporation should not mislead us. An economist who wrote about third world political positions in the United Nations Conference on Trade and Development (and who apparently participated in the discussions) cautioned against pessimism about the effort to promote a new economic order while tacitly painting a most pessimistic picture himself. He simply said, for example, that all that is required for a new economic order is third world unity and then included scathing comments about "a narrow understanding of the interests of the developing countries," the selfish interests of energy producers, the divisions between reactionary and progressive third world countries, and the economic weapons in the hands of the West.[96]

If read carefully, criticisms of "capitalism" in the Soviet literature are often criticisms of the capitalism of Milton Friedman in which many Western non-Marxist economists would also join. Even so, economists specializing on third world issues are less and less often debating the major economic issues of the past, because the issues have been at least temporarily resolved. The economic performance of the socialist-oriented countries has on the whole been poor, while the economic stars have followed an aggressive strategy of attracting foreign investment and promoting the private sector.

Soviet economists still have sharp disagreements on detailed questions of the best economic strategy—and implicitly, therefore, on the proper Soviet foreign aid program—but it is impossible to find a serious economist who accepts the traditional economic analysis of the third world as a whole. It is difficult to find those who treat the socialist path as the preferable path of development from an economic point of view. The international debt crisis has breathed new life into the pessimists, and if it has disastrous consequences, that will affect everyone. Nevertheless, even

96. E. E. Obminsky, *Gruppa 77: mnogostoronniaia ekonomicheskaia diplomatiia razvivaiushchikhsia stran* (Moscow: Mezhdunarodnye otnosheniia, 1981), pp. 4, 19–20, 48, 49, 161, and 235–36. Valkenier describes the issues on the world economy very well in *The Soviet Union and the Third World*, pp. 37–69, 109–43, but Obminsky's views are misunderstood by a reviewer of the Valkenier book who did not see the way that Obminsky had to argue his case in the *Gruppa 77* book—one on diplomacy rather than economics, published by a fairly propagandistic publishing house. See Robert M. Cutler, "Economic Issues in East-South Relations," *Problems of Communism*, vol. 33 (July–August 1984), pp. 76–77.

the debt crisis has not shown that socialist orientation is more effective for economic growth but has suggested that third world countries now have a special need for Western patronage.

A move toward consensus is difficult to document because of the increasing disappearance of scholarly exchanges on the topic, but the best indication is the change in the terms of the debate. Except in the case of Latin America, the statements of those who take for granted that third world integration into the capitalist economy and use of market mechanisms are conducive to economic growth have become quite bald. One scholar will simply state in a matter-of-fact way that "the prospects for the development of the third World countries in the coming years will, as in the past, depend on the economic conditions in the industrial capitalist countries." Another will be emphatic in warning against excessive nationalization and will point to the need to nurture the private sector in a "mixed economy."[97] The deputy director of the Institute of Oriental Studies could write a book on the "industrial revolution in the countries of the East" without even discussing the socialist or social-orientation model, let alone advocating it.[98]

What is interesting is not only the self-confidence in such statements but also the reaction to them. The statements are almost never criticized on their own terms. A critical review of the book that damned nationalization conceded that "from a narrow economic point of view, such an approach is justified." It then continued, "However . . . many of the reasons [for nationalization] lie in the social or even purely political sphere."[99] A reviewer of another book noted that the author is "one of the economists who consider growth of national income or efficiency the only criterion" in evaluating economic relations. Again, the criticism was made: "in many cases, precisely the political and social criteria determine the priority of the direction and form of economic collaboration."[100] Still another

97. See, respectively, I. Korolev in "Sovremennoe polozhenie kapitalisticheskoi ekonomiki i blizhaishie perspektivy ee razvitiia," *MEiMO*, no. 5 (May 1977), p. 111; and E. A. Bragina, *Razvivaiushchiesia strany: gosudarstvennnaia politika i promyshlennost'* (Moscow: Mysl', 1977), pp. 245–46.

98. Shirokov, *Promyshlennaia revoliutsiia v stranakh Vostoka*.

99. The reviewers are L. Aleksandrovskaia and S. Bessonov, two major scholars of the Institute of Africa who are strongly supportive of socialist orientation; see "Vazhnyi rychag sotsial' no-ekonomicheskogo progressa," *MEiMO*, no. 2 (February 1978), p. 149.

100. V. Karavaev, review of S. N. Zakharov, *Raschety effektivnosti vneshneekonomicheskikh sviazei (voprosy metodologii i metodiki raschetov)*, in "Izmerenie effekta ekonomicheskogo sotrudnichestva," *MEiMO*, no. 5 (May 1976), p. 144.

reviewer remarked, "a book by an economist does not speak about morality," and then went to speak of the moral outrage of the increase in the difference in per capita income between the developed and developing countries—from two to one in 1800 to thirteen to one in 1970 and fifteen to one in 1975.[101] The leading conservative specialist on the economy of Mexico conceded that "the scale of private foreign capital . . . was undoubtedly one of the mainsprings of 'the economic sprint' of Mexico—a fairly quick development of its economy, chiefly industrial potential," but he argued that the consequences of this growth were negative.[102]

Even those who are most prorevolution have usually been writing about the "new approach . . . to foreign capital" in radical countries, about "the necessity of partial attraction of foreign resources, including from the capitalist states of the West."[103] They defend socialist-oriented systems on grounds of political and social justice. In particular, they argue that in conditions in which private farming drives increasing numbers of peasants from the land, the small modern capitalist sector will be an island in "a sea of pauperism, unemployment, and poverty."[104] A country divided into a modern and a traditional sector will be politically and socially intolerable.

A second defense of socialist-oriented systems focuses on foreign policy. In the words of one conservative, "the concept of 'mutual dependence' of nations, which contravenes the principle of national sovereignty, ignores the main thing that defines the character of international economic relations in the world capitalist economy—namely their antagonistic and exploitive content." This author was blunt in damning "the proponents of the concept of 'mutual dependence' [who] call upon the developing countries to sacrifice their sovereignty for the sake of an acceleration of technical and economic progress."[105]

101. E. Pletnev, review of A. S. Kodachenko, *Vneshneekonomicheskaia politika imperializma i razvivaiushchiesia strany* (Moscow: Nauka, 1977), in "Moral'nyi iznos neokolonializma," *MEiMO,* no. 8 (August 1978), pp. 135–36.

102. I. Sheremet'ev, "Meksika: sovremennye problemy razvitiia," *MEiMO,* no. 2 (February 1983), pp. 67–68.

103. Vl. Li, "V. I. Lenin o preobrazovaniiakh perekhodnogo tipa i razvivaiushchiesia strany," *Azii i Afrika segodnia,* no. 4 (April 1983), p. 5.

104. V. V. Krylov, "Kapitalisticheski orientirovannaia forma obshchestvennogo razvitiia osvobodivshikhsia stran," *Rabochii klass i sovremennyi mir,* no. 2 (March–April 1983), p. 34. It is striking how similar such arguments are to those of the nineteenth century Russian populists. See Arthur P. Mendel, *Dilemmas of Progress in Tsarist Russia* (Harvard University Press, 1961), pp. 38–50, 63–64.

105. M. Volkov, "Kontseptsiia 'vzaimozavisimosti natsii' i ideologiia neokolonializma," *MEiMO,* no. 9 (September 1980), pp. 71, 72.

The most subtle and fundamental way of insisting on the importance of the political factor is to use it to differentiate among developing countries. Those who play down the absolute importance of the difference between socialist-oriented and capitalist-oriented countries choose other criteria for distinguishing among third world countries—the level of GNP per capita, the size of the countries, or petroleum resources.[106] Conservatives still insist that "the basic indicators of the dynamics of the liberation struggle in the economic sphere are the development of the productive forces in the state and cooperative sector . . . [and] the regulation and limitation of foreign and national capital."[107]

While the conservatives act as if they have conceded that socialism is not necessarily most conducive to economic growth, their opponents have not conceded that economic growth is incompatible with social justice or national honor. Viktor Sheinis has argued that one can examine social indicators closely and conclude that "in the majority [of cases] they correlate with economic growth" and that "the higher the level of economic development, other conditions held equal, the more favorable the social indicators."[108] The implication is absolutely clear that sacrificing economic growth for social justice can be a self-defeating process in the long run. Nodari Simoniia actually criticized Sheinis for not going far enough. He believes that indicators such as "growth of productive forces" should be as indicators of social progress.[109] As will be discussed in the next two chapters, the question of social justice can also be raised by questioning the progressiveness of left-wing dictatorships or by suggesting the virtues of representative democracy.

Of course, to say that Moscow economists who lead the debates on economic development have moved in a certain direction is not to say that Soviet thinking as a whole has been transformed. There are many non-

106. See V. Sheinis, "Sotsial'no-ekonomicheskaia differentsiatsiia i problemy tipologii razvivaiushchikhsia stran," *MEiMO*, no. 8 (August 1978), pp. 93–110, and "Differentsiatsiia razvivaiushchikhsia stran: ochertaniia i masshtaby," *Azii i Afrika segodnia*, no. 1 (January 1980), pp. 31–36.

107. E. Tarabrin, "Afrika na novom vitke osvoboditel'noi bor'by," *MEiMO*, no. 2 (February 1979), p. 43.

108. "Sotsial'nye izmeneniia v razvivaiushchikhsia stranakh," *Azii i Afrika segodnia*, no. 3 (March 1983), pp. 26, 27. In his major book Sheinis outlined the criteria of social progress without distinguishing between "capitalist orientation" and "socialist orientation," even cautioning that "anti-imperialism is not in all cases connected with really progressive economic and social relations"; see Sheinis and El'ianov, *Razvivaiushchiesia strany*, pp. 543–68. The quotation is from p. 550.

109. Simoniia, "Dialektika vzaimosviazei," p. 131.

economists among third world specialists in Moscow, there are many scholars in universities in the provinces, and there are many relevant participants in the foreign policy process who are not specialists on the third world. In private, for instance, some of the most sophisticated and iconoclastic specialists on the third world retain primitive ideas about the American political system that they learned in their youth, while some of the most sophisticated specialists on the United States sometimes retain assorted traditional ideas about the third world.

Nevertheless, a real shift in general Soviet thinking has surely occurred; the debates on autarchy and protectionism, on the priority of economic growth and social justice, and on the relationship of foreign economic ties and national sovereignty have heavy domestic implications. The central issues with respect to Soviet economic reform are how much the principles of egalitarianism and full employment should be sacrificed in an attempt to achieve economic growth and technological progress and how much integration of the Soviet economy into the world economy is desirable. Strong movement toward the greater use of market mechanisms and decentralization of authority to managers would require an end to food subsidies (that is, a major increase in consumer prices for them), more freedom for managers to fire workers, and ultimately foreign competition for sheltered Soviet industrialists.[110] It is not hard to guess the position of many specialists on the third world with respect to these questions, nor is it accidental that greater pessimism about economic growth in socialist-orientation countries and greater sensitivity to the possible benefits of internationalization of the world economy have followed the slowdown in Soviet economic growth.

110. See the discussion of the issues on the Soviet domestic scene in Jerry F. Hough, "Soviet Succession: Issues and Personalities," *Problems of Communism*, vol. 31 (September–October 1982), pp. 21–28.

# CHAPTER FIVE

# Nature of the Political System

FOR ANYONE in the Soviet Union interested in revolution, the crucial question has been the nature of the foreign state (or political system, as it would be more typically called in the United States).[1] Can the Soviet Union promote political change through existing political systems or does it have to work to overthrow them? Similarly, in the conduct of its foreign policy, is the Soviet Union facing governments that are inexorably the tool of some one group with a defined attitude toward the Soviet Union or is it facing governments subject to a variety of social forces with a variety of political attitudes?

The nature of the state has long been an issue at the heart of Marxism-Leninism, although both Marx and Lenin were somewhat ambiguous about it. In his basic works Marx described the state as part of a super-structure whose character and activities were determined by the economic base in society. The state had been created by the propertied class to maintain its dominance over those who were not owners; Western governments—even those with competitive elections—were "but a committee for managing the common affairs of the whole bourgeoisie."[2] Marx insisted on the necessity of a revolutionary overthrow of Western states—even of "bourgeois democracy," as he called constitutional democracy—if social-ism were to be introduced. Yet for all his stark generalizing language, his own journalistic and historical analyses of political events (for example, in *The Eighteenth Brunmaire of Louis Bonaparte* and *The Civil War in*

---

1. As a Soviet political theorist noted, the word "state" (*gosudarstvo*) has two mean-ings: "In the narrow meaning, it is one of the institutions of the political system that disposes of the apparatus of repression, but in the broad meaning, it is the entire political structure of society. In the latter case, 'state,' in practice, is used as a synonym for 'political system.'" See F. M. Burlatsky, *Lenin, gosudarstvo, politika* (Moscow: Nauka, 1970), pp. 121–22.

2. Karl Marx and Friedrich Engels, *The Communist Manifesto* (New York Labor News, 1948), p. 11.

*France*) did not feature a simpleminded economic determinism. Rather, in such works he treated policy as the result of the interplay of a variety of factors and political forces.

By the 1890s, Marxists faced a serious problem. Nearly half a century had passed since Marx had predicted imminent revolution in *The Communist Manifesto*. Not only had revolution not occurred, but the living conditions of Western European workers seemed to be improving, and the workers themselves appeared to be in a less revolutionary mood. A number of Marxists, led by Eduard Bernstein of the German Social Democratic party, concluded that Marx's image of the state was flawed. In their view, universal suffrage, essentially a phenomenon of the post-1850 period, had given workers the ability to effect change through the political process and ultimately even to nationalize industry if they achieved a parliamentary majority.

But when Lenin entered the political scene in the 1890s, he was determined to establish a party that would uphold the original Marxist insistence on revolution. While he did argue that Western governments had become more important participants in economic management (he sometimes described this development with the phrase "state-monopoly capitalism"), he remained passionately opposed to the idea that the state could be used by the workers for their purposes. Lenin's major theoretical work, *State and Revolution* (1917), argued in strong terms that "the state . . . is the organization of violence for the suppression of some class." Those who think that the state tries to reconcile class conflicts are espousing a "petty-bourgeois and philistine theory" and are not socialists. Those who think that a government, even one based on universal suffrage, can further socialism and democracy are presenting a petty-bourgeois utopia and are the victims of "common opportunist prejudices and philistine illusions." He concluded that for voters to decide periodically "which member of the ruling class is to repress and oppress the people through parliament—that is the real essence of bourgeois parliamentarism, not only in parliamentary constitutional monarchy, but also in the most democratic republics."[3]

Nevertheless, Lenin implicitly introduced major changes in his analysis of the bourgeois state after the Bolshevik Revolution. Originally he had assumed that the Bolshevik regime could not survive without the spread of

3. V. I. Lenin, *State and Revolution* (Westport, Conn.: Greenwood Press, 1978), pp. 9, 22, 23, 46.

the revolution to the West. Yet a European revolution did not occur, and Western intervention in the Russian civil war failed. In explaining these events, Lenin argued that they resulted from the influence of the workers on Western governments: "the workers and peasants in capitalist states could not be compelled to fight against us. . . . Our allies actually turned out to be the exploited masses in every capitalist state, for these masses wrecked the war."[4]

If workers had been able to affect the policy of Western governments on the question of intervention, then it would seem logical that they might also affect policy on other issues. Indeed, when the Communist International (the Comintern) was established in 1919, the conditions of admission included the obligation of foreign communist parties to support Soviet foreign policy. The assumption seemed to be that while the capitalist state was basically a representative of the business class, it might sometimes respond to mass pressures. Otherwise, how could communist support of Soviet foreign policy matter? Just as the doctrine of the impossibility of Bolshevik survival in a capitalist sea had been modified, so the same might be necessary for the more extreme and polemical images of the bourgeois state. However, Lenin died before any such modification was made.


### The Varga Controversy

In the late 1920s and early 1930s, Joseph Stalin must have strongly believed that Western governments merely carried out the desires of their respective bourgeoisie. Despite the advice of his foreign minister, his ambassador to Germany, and the leading Soviet representative to the Comintern, he refused to permit German communists to cooperate with the Social Democrats to prevent the rise of Hitler.[5] Because Hitler had explicitly described his territorial designs on Russia, the only reasonable explanation for Stalin's behavior was that he must have thought that no matter who the formal head of the German government might be, German capitalists would inevitably determine the country's foreign policy.

---

4. V. I. Lenin, "Nashe vneshnee i vnutrennoe polozhenie i zadachi partii," in V. I. Lenin, ed., *Polnoe sobranie sochineniia* (Moscow: Politizdat, 1970), vol. 42, pp. 21–22.

5. *Dokumenty vneshnei politiki SSSR* (Moscow: Nauka, 1969), vol. 15, pp. 287–88, 387–89, 485, 621; and E. H. Carr, *Twilight of the Comintern, 1930–1935* (Pantheon, 1982), p. 5.

The experience with Hitler should have altered these preconceptions, and, in fact, after Germany attacked the Soviet Union in June 1941, Soviet official language did change radically. No longer an unjust imperialist conflict, the war was now described as a struggle between aggressive fascist nations and peace-loving countries, including the United States and Great Britain. Criticism of the internal systems of the latter became gentler, although it scarcely disappeared.[6]

In the mid-1940s a number of prominent policy intellectuals implicitly argued for some theoretical modification of the most extreme views of the Western state. As late as March 1946, Il'ia Trainin, director of the Institute of Law and the academic secretary of the economics and law division of the Academy of Sciences (he had worked with Stalin in the early 1920s), wrote of Soviet democracy as the highest form of democracy rather than the only form and suggested that bourgeois democracy could be widened under the pressure of the working class. He described President Franklin D. Roosevelt as a sober politician who had made many concessions to workers and farmers in an effort to save capitalism and who had made an advance in the definition of freedom—including freedom from fear.[7] And Mikhail Strogovich, head of the department of the theory of state and law of the Central Committee's Academy of Social Sciences, wrote a textbook on criminal procedure asserting that Russia had adopted (and no doubt should continue to adopt) the most progressive experience of the West.[8]

By far the most important advocate of a partial redefinition of the capitalist state was Eugen Varga, director of the Institute of World Economics and World Politics and a regular consultant to Stalin for two decades.[9] Varga had been presenting his views for some time, but he summarized his position in striking form in a book signed to press in September 1946. Although titled *Changes in the Economics of Capitalism*

6. Frederick C. Barghoorn, *The Soviet Image of the United States: A Study in Distortion* (Harcourt, Brace, 1950), pp. 39–102.

7. "O demokratii," *Sovetskoe gosudarstvo i pravo*, no. 1 (1946), pp. 13, 19.

8. *Ugolovnyi protsess* (Moscow: Luridicheskoe izdatel'stvo, 1946). For a selection of the statements the dogmatists found most offensive, see S. I. Bouden, "O knige professora Strogovicha 'Ugolovnyi protsess,'" *Sovetskoe gosudarstvo i pravo*, no. 6 (June 1948), pp. 73–86; and M. Iakovlev, "B Institute prava Akademii nauk SSSR," ibid., no. 4 (April 1949), pp. 43–44.

9. Varga reportedly delivered a packet of analysis from his institute to Stalin once a week with his own comments attached.

*as a Result of World War II*, the book's most crucial arguments focused on Western political systems.[10] Adopting Lenin's phrase, "state-monopoly capitalism," Varga argued that the state had become an increasingly important force in Western economic life. It had a decisive role in the wartime economy and even afterward remained more powerful than before the war. Moreover, Varga asserted that although Western governments were withdrawing somewhat from economic decisionmaking after the war, "the question of 'planning' . . . will again become urgent in two or three years when the regular crisis of overproduction occurs."[11]

The most controversial aspect of Varga's analysis was his treatment of the determinants of governmental action. In the orthodox view the state was not simply the tool of the bourgeoisie but also of the "monopolies" (big business). The most extreme version of this argument considered the state completely subordinated to the monopolies and to them alone; a slightly more moderate view posited a coalescence (*srashchivanie*) of the state and monopolies. Varga contended, however, that Western government, while ultimately controlled by "the financial oligarchy," sometimes defended the interests of the bourgeois class as a whole, instead of the immediate, narrow interests of the monopolistic bosses.[12] Because the basic interest of the bourgeoisie was preservation of the capitalist system and because this goal sometimes required policies (price controls in wartime, for example) contrary to the interests of immediate private profit, government policy could not always reflect the interests of the monopolies.

10. Many Westerners have argued that the essence of Varga's argument (and the reason that he was punished) was his prediction of a long-term postponement of a Western depression, but this is not accurate. Although he suggested that capitalism would not experience a full-scale depression for ten years, this prediction assumed that Europe was so devastated that it would require a decade to reach prewar production levels (in actuality, it was to take only three to five years). He also predicted an interim moderate depression in the United States in two or three years. This scenario was sometimes criticized, but it was never treated as unforgivable heresy. When Varga was forced to write an abject ten-page recantation in 1949, he did not even mention this question. A year earlier he had had to acknowledge that the interim American depression had not occurred as soon as he had predicted. See *Izmeneniia v ekonomike kapitalizma v itoge vtoroi mirovoi voiny* (Moscow: Gospolitizdat, 1946); "Protiv reformistskogo napravleniia v rabotakh po imperializmu," *Voprosy ekonomiki*, no. 3 (March 1949), pp. 79–88; and "O nedostatkakh i zadachakh nauchno-issledovatel'skoi raboty v oblasti ekonomiki," ibid., no. 9 (September 1948), p. 56.

11. *Izmeneniia v ekonomike kapitalizma*, pp. 32–313, 318.

12. "Diskussiia po knige E. Varga, 'Izmeneniia v ekonomike kapitalizma v itoge vtoroi mirovoi voiny,' 2, 14, 21 maia 1947 g., Stenograficheskii otchet," *Mirovoe khoziaistvo i mirovaia politika*, no. 11 (November 1947), supplement, p. 50.

In practice, Varga treated government and the political forces in society as having a considerable independence in immediate terms. For example, he explained the end of price controls in the United States by strictly political factors—the death of President Roosevelt and the election of a Republican Congress in 1946.[13] In response to criticism, he expressed scorn at the idea that "now in 1947 the working class and the Labour party have no influence on the policy of England, that the financial oligarchy makes all the policy."[14] Most remarkably, he suggested in his book that the democratic forces in all countries were so strong and had such a strong potential impact on government policy that "the relationship of the capitalist countries to the Soviet Union will not be the same as it was in the prewar period."[15]

Varga went even further. He suggested the influence of the masses on the bourgeois state could become so great that the state could serve as the vehicle for the transformation of capitalism and the peaceful transition to socialism. He treated the Eastern European countries as being part of the capitalist world, but as having "economies of a new type," as being "democracies of a new type."[16] In itself such a statement might not have been so controversial, but Varga also asserted that "bourgeois nationalization . . . means progress in the direction of democracy of a new type."[17] This view of the bourgeois state was perilously close to that of the so-called revisionists Lenin had so vehemently damned at the turn of the century—identical to that view, many of Varga's critics contended. Despite the criticism, including that at a conference specifically called in May 1947 to discuss his book, Varga expressed his opinion with greater sharpness in October 1947:

Bourgeois Europe . . . itself now recognizes that the capitalist social order needs basic reform, that it is impossible to get by without such measures as nationalization of the important branches of production, state control over the economy, 'planning of the economy.' . . . Many bourgeois theorists proclaim the possibility of a slow, gradual, and peaceful transition to 'democratic socialism.' . . . This is not only a play on words, not only a maneuver. . . .

Today, thirty years after the victory of the Great October Revolution, *the struggle in Europe is becoming in its historical development more and more a*

13. Ibid., p. 2.
14. Ibid., p. 61.
15. *Izmeneniia v ekonomike kapitalizma*, p. 319.
16. Ibid., pp. 291–92.
17. "Demokratiia novogo tipa," *Mirovoe khoziaistvo i mirovaia politika*, no. 3 (March 1947), p. 5.

*struggle for the tempos and forms of the transition from capitalism to socialism.* Although the Russian path, the Soviet system, is undoubtedly the best and the fastest path of transition from capitalism to socialism, historical development, as Lenin had theoretically predicted, shows that other paths are also available for the achievement of this goal.[18]

This persistence—this "nonparty relationship to criticism" and repetition of "a clearly revisionist thesis," as Konstantin Ostrovitianov, the academic secretary of the economics division of the Academy of Sciences and a relative moderate, expressed it—was the last straw.[19] Varga's institute was abolished, and he seldom appeared in print for the rest of the Stalin period.

During and immediately after World War II, conservative critics of Varga's position had to be cautious so that they would not be too offensive to the United States. Yet even at the time of the Yalta conference, Mark Mitin, one of the two leading ideologists on the Central Committee, was able to describe Western democracy in the most negative terms and to emphasize that European workers had to have "a complete reconstruction of all contemporary social life" in order to enjoy any democratic rights.[20] As relations with the West deteriorated, conservatives were able to speak more openly.

The conservative attack on Varga became the basis for the orthodoxy of the late Stalin era.[21] Some of the more extreme argued that the role of Western government in economic life had increased only marginally. Most, however, focused on the notion—which they attributed to Varga— that the state could stand above classes and partly mediate among them. In their view the kind of nationalization being conducted by the British Labour party had nothing to do with socialism. The European social

18. "Sotsializm i kapitalizm za tridtsat' let," *Mirovoe khoziastvo i mirovaia politika,* no. 10 (October 1947), pp. 4–5. The italics are Varga's.

19. K. Ostrovitianov, "Ob itogakh i napravlenii raboty instituta ekonomiki akademii nauk SSSR," *Voprosy ekonomiki,* no. 1 (January 1948), p. 88; and no. 8 (August 1948), pp. 71, 98–99.

20. "Istoricheskoe znachenie A. I. Gertsena," *Bol'shevik,* no. 2 (January 1945), p. 23.

21. See Richard Nordahl, "Stalinist Ideology: the Case of the Stalinist Interpretation of Monopoly Capitalist Politics," *Soviet Studies,* vol. 26 (April 1974), pp. 243–47.

22. Thus in 1948 the Ostrovitianov who was quoted damning Varga for "a clearly revisionist thesis" used "coalescence" in the midst of this criticism, and he combined it with an intermediate position on the role of the state: "The state, which acts in the interests of monopolistic capital, is sometimes required by the threat of strikes and a revolutionary uprising to make concessions to the working class in order to clutch it more strongly in the grip of its dictatorship." *Voprosy ekonomiki,* no. 9 (September 1948), p. 98.

democrats were not only tools of the bourgeoisie but the most despicable of tools because they were so dishonest in their claims to represent the workers.

Moderate critics tried to preserve the notion of some limited independence of the government by talking of a coalescence of government and monopolies instead of direct subordination.[22] Others tried to make the same point by speaking of the partial independence of the superstructure from the economic base (they usually cited relatively uncontroversial examples, such as the continuing value of nineteenth century Russian literature in a socialist Russia with a very different base).[23] Stalin would have none of it. In the last year of his life, he declared that "the expression 'coalescence' is not appropriate. . . . What is occurring is not simply coalescence, but the subordination of the state apparatus to the monopolies. Consequently, we ought to get rid of the word 'coalescence,' but speak of the 'subordination of the state apparatus to the monopolies.'"[24]

This debate was not an abstract one; it was intimately related to the most fundamental foreign policy questions. When Varga declared in September 1946 that the strength of the democratic forces in all countries was great enough to ensure that the relationship of the capitalist countries to the Soviet Union would change, he was scarcely making a dispassionate prediction. Instead, in the face of the rapidly developing cold war, he was appealing to the Soviet leadership to base its policy on the assumption that good relations were possible. His discussion of different possible roads to socialism was surely a subtle suggestion that the communization of Eastern Europe not be carried through to its conclusion, perhaps to strengthen the "democratic forces" in Western foreign policy, perhaps to make a gradual transformation of Western Europe more likely because less threatening (communists were still members of coalition governments in France and Italy) or even to save his native Hungary from the worst features of Stalinism. Those who asserted the complete subordination of Western governments to the monopolies were really talking about the complete and implacable hostility of those governments to the Soviet Union and the impossibility of any socialist model other than the Soviet.[25]

23. For references to the discussion, see "O meste i roli iskusstva v obshchestvennoi zhizni (k itogam diskussii)," *Voprosy filosofii,* no. 6 (1952), pp. 155–70.

24. "Ekonomicheskie problemy sotsializma v SSSR," *Bol'shevik,* no. 18 (September 1952), p. 23.

25. See the discussion in Franklyn Griffiths, "Images, Politics, and Learning in Soviet Behavior toward the United States" (Ph.D. dissertation, Columbia University, 1972). pp. 236–40.

Because the nature of the state was so central a concept in the Varga controversy and in the discussion of Soviet-American relations, scholars interested in discussing the new third world governments had to deal with the subject in a gingerly manner if they wanted to be at all unorthodox. The position that became the official one, first enunciated by Evgenii Zhukov, director of the Pacific Institute, treated the governments of countries such as India as the representatives of the monopolistic or big (*krupnyi*) bourgeoisie and the big landlords. Governments of more underdeveloped countries such as Saudi Arabia were described as feudal. From 1947 to 1949 the leading specialists on India—Vladimir Balabushevich of Varga's institute and Aleksei D'iakov of the Pacific Institute—presented the opposing point of view that the Nehru government and the Congress party represented the interests of the Indian and, first of all, the Hindu bourgeoisie.[26] This formulation meant the bourgeoisie as a whole, including the petty bourgeoisie. The reference to the Hindu bourgeoisie was a subtle reminder of a point often blurred in orthodox analysis—the internal ethnic divisions in nearly all of the new countries.

This seemingly abstract exchange about the Indian bourgeoisie reflected serious differences of opinion on foreign policy. Like Varga, Balabushevich was using an argument about the broad support for the Indian government as a way of suggesting the possibility of Soviet cooperation with new governments. "Without doubt," he wrote, "the Indian bourgeoisie now has received more freedom of action and wider opportunities for strengthening its position. . . . The Indian representatives can now take a more independent position in the organizations of the United Nations."[27]

In the context of the third world this position also had implications for revolutionary strategy. By asserting that the Nehru government rested only on the big bourgeoisie, Zhukov argued the "complete isolation [of the latter and by implication the government] in the population."[28] This meant that the Communist party could gain the support of substantial numbers of other groups, including some from within the bourgeoisie, for its programs. By contending that the Indian government was supported by the

26. V. V. Balabushevich, "Indiia posle razdela," *Mirovoe khoziaistvo i mirovaia politika*, no. 12 (December 1947), p. 55. This distinction was first discussed in John H. Kautsky, *Moscow and the Communist Party of India: A Study in the Postwar Evolution of International Communist Strategy* (John Wiley, 1956), pp. 24–26, 29–30, 33.

27. "Indiia posle razdela," p. 49. Varga himself also took this position.

28. "Obostrenie krizisa kolonial'noi sistemy," *Bol'shevik*, no. 23 (December 1947), p. 54.

entire bourgeoisie, D'iakov and Balabushevich were saying that the petty bourgeoisie, including the peasantry, were nonrevolutionary in the short run and that a Mao-like strategy of communist revolutionary cooperation with such social forces could not be successful. American scholar John Kautsky believed that by this formulation D'iakov and Balabushevich were supporting a left-wing revolutionary strategy of struggle against all the bourgeoisie.[29] It is virtually certain, however, that they were expressing general pessimism about the possibility of overthrowing the Congress party and were really favoring a more accommodating posture toward the government in the near term.

Despite appeals for change from the leading specialists and almost surely from leading figures in the Politburo, Stalin would not modify his policy. In 1947 Andrei Zhdanov, a leading Central Committee secretary, enunciated a two-camp theory that depicted the third world (and Western Europe) in simple East-West terms: if a third world country were not communist, then it was in the imperialist camp, even if its leaders proclaimed a policy of neutrality. Scholars later reported that Turkey was the model that dominated thinking.[30] Kemal Ataturk had been the "bourgeois" leader of a "national liberation movement" supported by the Soviet Union with military assistance in the early 1920s, but he had suppressed local communists and did not support the Soviet Union on the issue of the Dardenelles and Bosporous at the Lausanne conference. In 1952 Turkey became a member of NATO. Stalin must also have been deeply affected by the experience in China, where Chiang Kai-shek, after a close association with the Soviet Union and the Chinese communists in the civil war, had turned against the communists with a crushing blow in 1927 and had broken relations with the Soviet Union.[31] The outcomes in Turkey and China may have only reinforced views that Stalin had already held, because in 1922 he had opposed significant military aid to Turkey.[32]

In his last speech, at the Nineteenth Party Congress in 1952, Stalin was scathing in his denunciation of the bourgeoisie:

29. See Kautsky, *Moscow and the Communist Party of India*, pp. 23–34, for a discussion of the "neo-Maoist" strategy implied in the official definition.

30. G. Akopian, "O roli i kharaktere natsional'noi burzhuazii stran Vostoka," *Mirovaia ekonomika i mezhdunarodnye otnosheniia*, no. 6 (June 1962), p. 101. (Hereafter *MEiMO*.)

31. Eugen Varga later emphasized the importance of this factor for Stalin. See his *Ocherki po problemam politekonomii kapitalizma* (Moscow: Politzdat, 1964), p. 91.

32. Louis Fischer, *The Soviets in World Affairs: A History of the Relations Between the Soviet Union and the Rest of the World*, 2d ed. (Princeton University Press, 1951), vol. 1, p. xv.

The bourgeoisie itself—the chief enemy of the liberation movement—has become different than it was. . . . Earlier the bourgeoisie allowed itself to take liberal actions. It defended bourgeois-democratic freedom and thus created popularity for itself in the people. Now not a trace of the liberalism remains. . . . Earlier the bourgeoisie was considered the head of the nation. It defended the rights and independence of the nation, placing it "highest of all." Now not a trace of the "national principle" remains. Now the bourgeoisie sells the rights and dependence of the nation for dollars.[33]

As will be discussed in chapter 6, cooperation with some elements of the bourgeoisie was still deemed possible at the end of Stalin's life, but only under the leadership of "the working class"—that is, the Communist party.

## The Breakup of the Old Rigidities

Just as the nature of the bourgeois state had been a vehicle for debates about détente in the mid-1940s, so it fulfilled the same function when the debates reemerged in the first years after Stalin's death. In 1954 one article in favor of détente by Valentin Zorin described divisions within American ruling circles in great detail—the competition between the Morgans, the Rockefellers, and the Du Ponts within Wall Street, as well as that between Wall Street and the new financial groups of Chicago, Texas, and California. Zorin discussed divisions in foreign policy among these groups (essentially the divisions between the Eisenhower and Taft wings of the Republican party) and contended that the liberal wing of the Democratic party was "under a certain influence of the trade union and farmer organizations" and "to a greater degree than the others reacts to the pressure of the masses."[34]

A year later Georgii (or Iurii, as he then signed himself) Arbatov, future director of the Institute of the USA and Canada, emphasized "the growing dependence of foreign policy on the masses." Arbatov contended that "the masses in our day display a vital interest in foreign policy, and the imperialist governments cannot fail to take their opinion into account to this or

33. *Pravda*, October 15, 1952.

34. "Predstoiashchie vybory i vnutripoliticheskaia obstanovka v SShA," *Kommunist*, no. 8 (May 1954), pp. 86–89, 91.

NATURE OF THE POLITICAL SYSTEM 115

that extent."[35] Gradually, the old word "coalescence" reappeared and was advanced with increasing boldness.[36]

Opponents of détente defended the old images of the state, although it was difficult to attack the "role of the masses" theme directly because the new regime was endorsing it at home.[37] The legitimate way of saying that Western governments were not subject to significant influence by the masses—or by the Soviet Union—was to reaffirm that they were strictly subordinated to the "monopolies," and a fairly united monopolistic group at that. In what was surely a direct answer to Zorin, Ivan Kuz'minov, the most vocal conservative theorist, insisted that

the subordination of the apparatus of the bourgeois state to the monopolies and their use of it to secure maximum profits flows inevitably from the action of the basic economic law of contemporary capitalism and is the essence of state-monopoly capitalism. . . .

The development of state-monopoly capitalism is always connected with the growth of reaction, with the oppression of the toilers, with the suppression of democratic freedoms, with an aggressive foreign policy. On the eve of World War II, the country with the highest level of development of state-monopoly capitalism—Germany—became the seat [ochag] of the blackest reaction, fascism. Similarly, after World War II, America, which stands ahead of other capitalist countries in the level of development of state-monopoly capitalism, became the country with the most reactionary and aggressive domestic and foreign policy.[38]

As chapter 7 will note, a closely related technique for discussing détente was to debate the priority of economics and politics and the relationship between them. Here too the traditional position was hard to express directly because it was aimed so directly at Nikita Khrushchev's own policy and ideological modifications, but the case could be made in its strongest form in attacks on "revisionism" in Eastern Europe. The Yugoslavian party program, for example, contained statements that almost any member of the Soviet establishment would reject, and in criticizing

35. "K voprosu o roli narodnykh mass v mezhdunarodnykh otnosheniiakh," *Mezhdunarodnaia zhizn'*, no. 9 (September 1955), pp. 64, 67.
36. See Griffiths, "Images, Politics, and Learning," p. 49.
37. Vladimir Kruzhkov, the outspoken conservative head of the Central Committee's propaganda-agitation department, came close to a direct attack. He strongly criticized the "reactionary theory" of the "amorphous crowd," and in his description of this theory the word "crowd" seemed indistinguishable from "masses." See "V. I. Lenin—korifei revoliutsionnoi nauki," *Kommunist*, no. 1 (January 1954), p. 23.
38. "Burzhuaznoe gosudarstvo—orudie obogashcheniia monopolii," *Kommunist*, no. 9 (June 1954), p. 61, 73.

them a conservative could include statements that clearly had broader applicability:

Marxists always have begun and still begin with the existence of an inseparable link between politics and economics ("politics is concentrated economics"), between domestic and foreign policy. . . . Consequently, the two camps must be and actually are the bearers of different orientations in international politics. . . . A description of contemporary world politics as a competition of two "superpowers" . . . is intended . . . to hide the true class essence of the struggle. . . . An underestimation of the military danger is connected with direct or indirect apologetics of American imperialism.[39]

The opposing position, and almost surely the real target of the attack on Yugoslavian revisionism, had been published two months earlier. In one of the first issues of the new journal of the Institute of World Economics and International Relations (IMEMO), Iosif Lemin, a long-time associate of Eugen Varga, emphasized the importance of politics in strong terms:

Economics provides the key to an understanding and a correct definition of politics. . . . But it is not so simple to use this key. Politics is not simply a reflection of economics and social relations based on economics. . . . To infer policy directly from economics alone, ignoring the intermediate links, forgetting the reverse influence of politics on economics, losing sight of the tendency for political processes to move in a relatively independent manner, would be a vulgarization of Marxism. . . . In the works of Marx, foreign policy is always examined in inseparable connection with the internal politics of the state and the different classes inside these states.[40]

Seven years later, Lemin edited the first major Soviet book on the domestic sources of American foreign policy, and he reiterated his thesis: "The classics of Marxism decisively warned against seeing superstructure phenomena as a passive element and ignoring the extremely active role of the superstructure and its influence on the base. Besides economic class interests, such factors as ideology, historical traditions, national character, and individual personality play a certain role—sometimes even a very important one—among the chief moving forces of policy."[41]

In the case of the third world, a certain inconsistency in the Stalinist analysis of government provided the basis for a further line of argument.

---

39. N. Nazarov, "Ideinye korni revizionizma v voprosakh mezhdunarodnykh otnoshenii," *MEiMO*, no. 7 (July 1958), pp. 20, 27, 28.

40. "Marks i voprosy vneshnei politiki," *MEiMO*, no. 5 (May 1958), pp. 21–22. For a discussion of the analysis of 1956–61 articles that assumes that they reflect ambivalence rather than debate, see William Zimmerman, *Soviet Perspectives on International Relations, 1956–1967* (Princeton University Press, 1969), pp. 85–90.

41. *Dvizhushchie sily vneshnei politiki* (Moscow: Nauka, 1965), p. 7.

On one hand the third world state had been said to be strictly subordinated to the local monopolies or large landlords or both; on the other it had been said to be slavishly subordinated to a United States that was following a policy of maximum economic exploitation of third world countries. The early post-Stalin hints of innovation focused on this inconsistency. In an otherwise orthodox analysis of the bourgeois state, a young scholar wondered whether it was not a contradiction that while the English and French governments were subordinated to the local monopolies and had the goal of "helping 'national' monopolies to exploit their own and other peoples, they still help the U.S. in extracting profits from the country." His answer was, "unquestionably," and he suggested that there was a struggle between capitalist states.[42] A *Pravda* correspondent implied the same thing when he asserted that the local Latin American bourgeoisie "themselves want to receive the profits from the exploitation and ravaging of the working people."[43]

Consequently, the change in third world foreign policy in these years—first the arms sales to Guatemala and then the reevaluation ("at the initiative of the Central Committee of the Communist party"[44]) of such "bourgeois nationalist" leaders as Nehru, Sukarno, and Nasser—required little modification in the theory of the state. One had only to assert that local monopolistic bourgeoisie themselves wanted to receive the profits from exploiting workers and hence opposed Western exploitation. Analysis gradually went further. A critical review of a major book on Latin America emphasized the divisions among the bourgeoisie, and among the petty bourgeoisie and the intelligentsia, and thus implicitly opened up the question of the social support for and degree of independence of Latin American governments. As in the mid-1940s, such an analysis suggested that policy could reflect these broader forces.

Then in 1956 Khrushchev asserted that there were different possible paths to socialism, including peaceful ones: "The forms of the transition to socialism will become all the more varied. . . . It is not obligatory that these forms will always be connected with civil war." He went on to

---

42. G. Kh. Shakhnazarov, "Osnovnoi ekonomicheskii zakon sovremennogo kapitalizma i burzhuaznoe gosudarstvo," *Sovetskoe gosudarstvo i pravo*, no. 4 (April 1953), p. 46.

43. V. Chichkov, "Obostrenie sopernichestva imperialisticheskikh derzhav v stranakh Latinskoi Ameriki," *Kommunist*, no. 13 (September 1953), p. 107.

44. R. Avakov and G. Mirsky, "O klassovoi strukture v slaborazvitykh stranakh," *MEiMO*, no. 4 (April 1962), p. 81.

suggest that parliamentary means might be used for the transition to socialism if the communists were able to secure a solid majority in a parliament.[45] This possibility raised various questions. In particular, if communists could use parliaments to introduce socialism when they achieved a
solid majority, why could they not affect policy partially when their
strength was somewhat weaker? Khrushchev's analysis was vague, and
reactions after the Twentieth Party Congress did nothing to encourage his
clarification or elaboration. East European communists argued that the
possibility of different roads to socialism should legitimize deviations
from the Soviet model, an interpretation Soviet leaders did not want. Some
West European communists, disillusioned by the attack on Stalin at the
party congress, wanted their parties to become almost exclusively parliamentary—another development Soviet leaders did not favor. The Chinese
became angry at the new formulation, and the Soviet leaders were still
trying to appease them. Finally, the regime was seeking good relations
with neutral, noncommunist governments of the third world, and it was
scarcely diplomatic to talk too loudly about plans to overthrow them. In
these circumstances, Soviet theorists tended to emphasize obstacles to the
parliamentary route in the West and insisted on "the dictatorship of the
proletariat" (Communist party rule) as an indispensable part of socialism.
Third world governments continued to be analyzed as instruments of the
bourgeoisie alone or of the bourgeoisie in alliance with the landlords.

Variations in the early debates about the state in the third world were
expressed in differences in the definition of the "bourgeoisie" upon which
the governments rested. Thus, Vladimir Balabushevich asserted that the
Congress party in India was "the party of the national bourgeoisie and that
part of the landlords who are interested in capitalist development," but he
defined the national bourgeoisie as including small businessmen and the
agricultural bourgeoisie (reasonably well-to-do peasants) as well as big
business. Others still insisted that these governments (including the Congress party) were subordinated only to the monopolies and landlords.[46]

Any other position had to be expressed with the greatest of care. A 1958
assertion that "state capitalism [in India] in the form in which it exists at

45. *XX s'ezd Kommunisticheskoi partii Sovetskogo Soiuza [14–25 fevralia 1956 goda],
Stenograficheskii otchet* (Moscow: Gospolitizdat, 1956), vol. 1, pp. 39–40.

46. It was reported that G. Ia. Schmidt and P. M. Shastitko "stubbornly" stuck to this
position. See "Diskussiia ob ekonomicheskikh i politicheskikh pozitsiiakh natsional'noi
burzhuazii v stranakh Vostoka," *Sovetskoe vostokovedenie,* no. 1 (1957), p. 183.

the present time . . . is produced by the contradiction between its economic backwardness and the need for its rapid independent economic and political development" was a way of saying that the Indian government was serving the interests of a broader group than just the bourgeoisie, for everyone benefited from rapid independent economic growth.[47] The strength of the attack upon this position revealed its controversial nature, but the meaning was scarcely apparent to the casual reader.

Some scholars even took Khrushchev's statement about different paths to socialism to legitimize the concept that "the state sector in India and a series of other countries is the beginning point for socialist transformation of the economy. This concept essentially admitted the possibility of building socialism under the leadership of the bourgeoisie."[48] Scholars could hint at this position,[49] but basically it was denounced as revisionism. At the other extreme, an unknown number of persons were said not to "see anything new in the economic and political development of India, Indonesia, Burma, and other countries of the East,"[50] but they too had difficulty in expressing their views.

## Toward a More Complex View of the State

In the early 1960s a number of factors converged to open the question of the state to serious discussion. First, the debates about economic growth in the West had important implications for understanding Western political systems. If Western economies were growing without the anticipated major depression and if standards of living were increasing at a time when colonies were being lost, then obviously Western governments were having some success in managing their economies. The social welfare legislation of the previous thirty years also cried for explanation. A number of scholars began to argue that the bourgeois parliament could, in fact, pass

47. A. Levkovsky, "Gosudarstvennyi kapitalizm v Indii," *Sovremennyi vostok*, no. 5 (May 1958), p. 10.
48. B. G. Gafurov, "Aktual'nye zadachi sovetskogo vostokovedeniia," *Vestnik Akademii Nauk SSSR*, no. 9 (1957), p. 23.
49. Ts. A. Stepanian, "Obshchie zakonomernosti i osobennosti vozniknoveniia kommunisticheskoi formatsii," in F. T. Konstantinov and A. I. Arnol'dov, eds., *Sodruzhestvo stran sotsializma* (Moscow: Izdatel'stvo Akademii Nauk SSSR, 1958), pp. 79–92.
50. I. V. Dudinsky, "Kniga no aktual'nym problemam razvitiia mirovogo sotsializma," *Voprosy filosofii*, no. 12 (1958), p. 135.

laws of benefit to other classes (they did this largely by insisting that Western governments served economic and social functions as well as repressive ones). In the course of such an argument, a scholar could explicitly deny the proposition that "the bourgeois legislature cannot by its essence contain norms that answer the interests of the toilers."[51]

The most innovative theorist on the state was Fedor Burlatsky.[52] In 1963 while he was a Central Committee official, Burlatsky cited a statement of Friedrich Engels that there are certain functions without which society cannot get along and that the state arose as part of a division of labor to fulfill these needs. Burlatsky warned against a vulgarized image of the state as a mechanism imposed upon society solely from the outside (that is, by a separate ruling class). He contended that even in advanced industrial countries the bourgeois state performed not only a repressive role but also "an economic function . . . as an answer to societal needs connected with the high level of production."[53]

Developments in the third world posed a significant challenge for the theory of the state. In 1957 communists won elections in Kerala, and the Sukarno government in Indonesia nationalized Dutch property. In 1960 and 1962 the Nasser government became much more radical in its attack on private property; in 1962, also, Ne Win led a military coup in Burma and undertook radical transformation of the economy, including the nationalization of private trade. Finally, of course, during these years the "bourgeois national" leader of the Cuban Revolution, Fidel Castro, quickly led Cuba to a socialist revolution—an event unexpected in the Soviet Union and impossible according to the traditional ideology. Thus in 1964, Georgii Mirsky could summarize,

51. V. I. Usenin, "Ob otsenke sotsial'nykh zavoevanii proletariata kapitalisticheskikh stran," *Sovetskoe gosudarstvo i pravo*, no. 12 (December 1965), p. 50. Also see M. V. Baglai, "O funktsii sotsial'noi deiatel'nosti imperialisticheskogo gosudarstva," ibid., no. 6 (June 1966), pp. 77–85. An earlier cautious version of this point can be found in M. Baglai, "Ideia 'klassovogo mira' i kapitalisticheskaia deistvitel'nost,'" *Kommunist*, no. 6 (April 1961), p. 86.

52. From 1959 to 1964 Burlatsky worked in the Central Committee apparatus under Otto Kuusinen and Yuri Andropov, for a time serving as head of a subdepartment (later termed "group of consultants") of the Socialist Countries Department. He was the key staff member in developing the concept of the all-people's state in the party program of 1961.

53. *Gosudarstvo i kommunizm* (Moscow: Izdatel'stvo sotsial'no-ekomicheskoi literatury, 1963), p. 340. For a later article that, with many citations, insisted Marx and Engels had a subtle view of the state, see L. S. Mamut, "K. Marks o gosudarstve kak politicheskoi organizatsii obshchestva," *Voprosy filosofii*, no. 7 (1968), pp. 29–39.

[According to] the traditional scheme, the national bourgeoisie have come to power in the young states and all reforms—even extremely radical ones—that go beyond the framework of capitalist productive relationships have the goal of hiding the rule of the bourgeoisie and of fooling the masses. This is said even about countries where, in essence, there is no national bourgeoisie or, if it exists, where the reforms are directed against it. ... How is it possible to assert that the national bourgeoisie is in power in the UAR [Egypt]? Why, it is well known that the big bourgeoisie have been liquidated there, and the activity of the middle bourgeoisie restricted to the utmost.[54]

One way in which theorists dealt with this dilemma was to say that more conservative and pro-Western regimes essentially rested on the class base of the bourgeoisie or the feudal class (or some combination of elements of the two), while more radical and pro-Soviet regimes had the class support of the medium strata, the petty bourgeoisie, and the intellectuals.[55] The problem with this solution, as critics were to charge, was that the class structure of radical and conservative states often looked very similar, especially if "feudal" states like Saudi Arabia or industrializing ones like India were excluded. It was possible to say that the leaders "objectively" represented the interests of this or that class, depending on the Soviet definition of class interests, but this only begged the question. In countries with nearly identical socioeconomic structures, how could leaders come to take such different positions?

The obvious implication of the third world experience was that the state and its leaders (at least in that part of the world) were far more independent of the ruling classes than the old discussion of subordination or even coalescence suggested. In 1963 Burlatsky made the point directly: "Marx and Lenin wrote that in some historical situations the state can function as a more or less independent force, maneuvering between the struggling classes. . . . In our days one can still speak about a certain independence of the state in relations to different classes in some young national states of Africa and Asia, where class relations have still not developed with as much force as in the developed countries and where the state tries to strike a balance between different strata of the population."[56] At the same time, theorists of historical development began to treat "feudalism" as some-

54. "Sotsializm, kapitalizm, slaborazvitye strany," *MEiMO,* no. 6 (June 1964), p. 62.
55. Iu. Ostrovitianov, "Sotsialisticheskie doktriny razvivaiushchikhsia stran: formy, sotsial'noe soderzhanie," *MEiMO,* no. 6 (June 1964), pp. 84–87.
56. *Gosudarstvo i kommunizm,* pp. 34–35.

thing that did not require landlords and to speak about an Asiatic mode of production in which the state had a dominant and independent role, a position that also undermined the Stalinist image of a state that was simply a tool of the owning class. Any talk about the contemporary third world as multistructural, especially if there was not a dominant substructure (*uklad*) and class, had similar implications.

No doubt because the concept of state had so many overtones from the past and tended to focus attention on formal governmental institutions, a number of scholars introduced newer and broader concepts that incorporated nongovernmental institutions and political phenomena, often ones that did not support the existing economic base. The 1961 party program had referred to "the political organization of society" and, as a Soviet scholar later noted, this concept played "an important role in permitting a comprehensive characterization of the whole political mechanism of society."[57] Those who wanted to break with old sterotypes about the state included parties, interest groups, and political relationships within the concept of the "political organization of society" and included antibourgeois parties and groups as well as those representing the owning class of the "economic base."[58]

The effort to develop a new image of the state also found expression in a movement to develop a separate discipline of political science, that would focus analysis on "the political system." The appeals for a political science research institute and political science departments in colleges were unsuccessful, but an Association of Political Science was formed and the number of scholars who privately called themselves political scientists (*politology*) sharply increased.[59] Calls for the formal acceptance of politi-

57. Iu. Tikhomirov, "Sotsial'nye upravlaiushchie sistemy," *Sovetskoe gosudarstvo i pravo*, no. 5 (May 1970), p. 63.

58. G. N. Manov, "Poniatie politicheskoi organizatsii obshchestva," *Sovetskoe gosudarstvo i pravo*, no. 10 (October 1972), pp. 32, 33.

59. For a description of the struggle to establish a political science, see Gordon Skilling, "In Search of Political Science in the USSR," *The Canadian Journal of Economics and Political Science*, vol. 29 (November 1963), pp. 519–29; David E. Powell and Paul Shoup, "The Emergence of Political Science in Communist Countries," *American Political Science Review*, vol. 64 (June 1970), pp. 572–80; Ronald J. Hill, *Soviet Politics: Political Science and Reform* (White Plains, N. Y.: Sharpe, 1980), pp. 1–22; and Archie Brown, "Political Science in the Soviet Union: A New Stage of Development," *Soviet Studies*, vol. 36 (July 1984), pp. 317–44. The economic debates also spilled into a critique of the old conceptions of the state; see Moshe Lewin, *Political Undercurrents in Soviet Economic Debates: From Bukharin to the Modern Reformers* (Princeton University Press, 1974), pp. 189–246. (However Hill is right in *Soviet Politics*, p. 7, in criticizing Lewin for suggesting that certain critiques emerged for the first time in this context.)

cal science continued to be made, and an invitation was issued to the International Political Science Association to hold a world congress in Moscow in 1978 as part of the effort to legitimize the discipline.[60]

The phrase "political system" fared much better than "political science." Both the content of the former and its relationship to the concept of the political organization of society remained controversial, but it certainly was possible to define "political system" broadly. The major innovative book of the 1970s on the subject was again written by Burlatsky, and it presented a sweeping "systems analysis of political structures":

The political system includes, first of all, political institutions—the state, law, political parties, and organizations, and so forth—and also the system of communications, which connects the members of society and the social groups with its center—the political authority. The political system is one of the subsystems of society (together with such subsystems as the socioeconomic, the social-cultural, the personality [*lichnostnaia*], and others) and plays the basic role in the mobilization of the resources of society. . . .

The mobilization of the social forces and resources for the achievement of general social goals formulated and thrust forward by the ruling classes is the specific social function of the political system. At the same time, the latter, together with other social systems, takes part in the solution of such tasks as the integration of society, the distribution of different values and costs, the definition of goals and tasks in the solution of concrete economic, cultural, and other problems.

Burlatsky's 1985 book on the "contemporary leviathan" was organized under such chapter headings as "Social Components of Political Authority," "Political Culture," and "Political Behavior." [61] It was a long way from such language to the old insistence on complete subordination to the monopolies.

Of course, all such views remained controversial. The assertions that the bourgeois state had a social function were criticized on the ground that it did not have the interests of the toilers as a goal.[62] As late as 1977 Kuz'minov still believed that "the imperialist state . . . independent of its form is a tool of a handful of the most important monopolies, which exert

60. G. Kh. Shakhnazarov and F. M. Burlatsky, "O razvitii marksistsko-leninskoi politicheskoi nauki," *Voprosy filosofii*, no. 12 (1980), pp. 10–23.

61. *Lenin, gosudarstvo, politika*, pp. 118–19; and F. M. Burlatsky and A. A. Galkin, *Sovremennyi leviafan* (Moscow: Mysl', 1965), p. 383.

62. V. E. Guliev, *Imperialisticheskoe gosudarstvo (ocherk kritiki burzhuaznykh teorii)* (Moscow: Izdatel'stvo Moskovskogo universiteta, 1965), p. 124. Also see V. E. Guliev in G. P. Kaliamin, "Obsuzhdenie monografii ob imperialisticheskom gosudarstve," *Sovetskoe gosudarstvo i pravo*, no. 7 (July 1966), p. 152.

decisive influence on its policy." Others went so far as to talk about the totalitarian rule of the monopolies that reduced the automony of the individual "in a catastrophic way."[63]

A Soviet author making a survey of the literature in 1981 reported "unceasing arguments" about whether it is possible to include in the political system of society all those units that take some part in the political life of the country:

> Many authors call the political organization of bourgeois society, like that of any other class society, nothing but the "mechanism of the realization of political power," the system of organizations of the ruling class that achieves "the leadership and control of the development of social life in the interests of this class," the system of state and social organizations, by means of which the ruling class "realizes its policy, the administration of all the affairs of society," and so forth.[64]

Among the establishment research scholars, however, there seemed to be movement toward a less harsh image of the Western state. The author of the statement about unceasing arguments reported that the defenders of the old views were "comparatively few in number, but no less active in defending their views."[65] The change was also suggested in a textbook written by the Institute of World Economics and International Relations that incorporated much new and sophisticated analysis. For the 1971 first edition, the editors chose S. S. Salychev as the author of a key section on the Western political system, and he wrote about the subject in a very traditional way. In the 1975 second edition, which often copied the first edition word for word, this section was entrusted to another author.[66] A comparison of passages in the two editions shows striking contrasts:

| *First edition* | *Second edition* |
|---|---|
| Under the influence of the objective laws of state-monopolistic development and of the political conditions en- | The internal political development in the capitalist countries takes place under the continuous influence of the |

63. I. Kuz'minov, "Leninskaia teoriia imperializma i sovremennyi mir," *Mezhdunarodnaia zhizn'*, no. 5 (May 1977), pp. 113–14; and D. A. Kerimov and N. M. Keizerov, "Nesostoiatel'nost' burzhuaznykh kontseptsii demokratii," *Sovetskoe gosudarstvo i pravo*, no. 1 (January 1972), p. 27.

64. M. N. Marchenko, *Politicheskaia sistema sovremennogo burzhuaznogo obshchestva (politiko-pravovoe issledovanie)* (Moscow: Izdatel'stvo Moskovskogo universiteta, 1981), p. 11. See pp. 7–30 for a discussion of the literature.

65. Ibid., p. 12.

66. N. N. Inozemtsev, A. G. Mileikovsky, and V. A. Martynov, eds., *Politicheskaia ekonomiia sovremennogo monopolisticheskogo kapitalizma* (Moscow: Mysl', 1971, 1975). The differences and similarities of the two editions are analyzed in Jerry F. Hough, "The Evolution in the Soviet World View," *World Politics*, vol. 32 (July 1980), pp. 509–30.

gendered by the general crisis of capitalism, the tendencies toward reaction that are inherent in imperialism acquire particularly threatening dimensions.

The more deeply the bourgeois state penetrates into all spheres of public life, the less capable society is of controlling its activity. . . . The antidemocratic tendencies in bourgeois politics rise sharply, fed by the concentration of economic power and by the aspiration common to all the bourgeoisie to rely upon authoritarian methods in the face of an intensifying revolutionary movement. The establishment of fascist regimes expresses in the most concentrated form a political tendency that is common in all countries that have entered the stage of state-monopoly capitalism.

Political freedom in the bourgeois-liberal interpretation comes into irreconcilable conflict with the interests of economic development. . . . It is not surprising that now even bourgeois proponents of democracy doubt the effectiveness of liberal-bourgeois politics and traditional bourgeois-democratic institutions.

competition and struggle between the two social systems on the world scale and of the historical achievements of socialism in different spheres of life. This compels the monopolistic bourgeoisie to make maneuvers that adjust to the changing conditions of the class struggle.

The times of the undivided rule of the monopolistic bourgeoisie have passed. . . . As before, imperialism gives birth to tendencies toward extreme reaction that are fed by an ever greater concentration of economic power, a sharp increase in the role of the state, and an aspiration of the bourgeoisie to "introduce order in its own house." . . . But this is only one side of the question. . . .

Direct attacks on democratic rights and freedoms run up against the opposition of the broad masses. . . . This makes it difficult for the ruling class to turn to openly terroristic methods of exercising its authority. . . . The ruling class in the capitalist countries is not as free as it used to be in selecting its methods of rule.

The preservation of the attributes of bourgeois democracy better guarantees that flexibility that is so indispensable to the capitalist system under present conditions. . . . It facilitates the possibility of conducting the improvements and reforms without which the further functioning of the capitalist system is impossible under contemporary conditions.

In the late 1970s and early 1980s, general evolution in the analysis of political systems continued. As Archie Brown reported, "the period since 1970 has seen the publication of a number of important books in terms of ideas which are innovative in the contexts both of Soviet political science and of Soviet politics. A number of them are concerned with theory of the state and the political system, some by way of extended critiques of

Western writing on the subject, others with the relationship between public administration. Others venture into the field of comparative politics or take further the application of systems analysis to administrative problems."[67]

At the same time, the evolution toward recognition of popular influence on Western governments has been retarded because insistence that the "masses" have a significant role and that there are broader influences on Western policy had traditionally been a technique for taking such a position favoring détente. Clearly, however, American policy toward the Soviet Union has not been very warm under Presidents Carter and Reagan. If the U.S. government has been responsive to the masses and if the policy toward the Soviet Union has reflected American public opinion, then this is disconcerting in the extreme in terms of the prodétente argument about the "good" American people.

Some authors, such as Iurii Zamoshkin of the Institute of the USA and Canada, have moved beyond the traditional prodétente position and have suggested that public opinion has been both powerful and a force at least temporarily against détente. Zamoshkin wrote in 1982 that the "proponents of détente represent, so to speak, the political establishment of the USA," and he described the antidétente forces in ways that showed they were often outside the central establishment.[68] In 1985 he was even more explicit. He described "mass consciousness" as an important factor shaping American foreign policy and then cited public opinion poll after poll showing genuine, if irrational, fear of Soviet military superiority pushing the majority of Americans in an anti-Soviet direction in the late 1970s. He showed the decline of such opinions under Reagan and the large percentage of Americans now seeking cooperation with the Soviet Union in a way that must have led some Soviet readers to see the consequences of the American buildup in a more nuanced way than is usually presented in the Soviet press.[69]

Nevertheless, the argument that public opinion had been a major factor in the worsening of Soviet-American relations remained a difficult one. It involved two breaks with the old orthodoxy—that the monopolies (or "establishment") ruled and that the masses were always in favor of good

67. "Political Science in the Soviet Union," p. 326. In the original, this paragraph includes footnotes that provide a substantial number of citations to the Soviet literature.

68. Iu. A. Zamoshkin, "Ideologiia v SShA: za razriadku i protiv nee," SShA, no. 4 (1982), p. 8.

69. Iu. A. Zamoshkin, "Iadernaia opasnost' i faktor strakha," SShA, no. 3 (1985), pp. 3–9.

relations with the Soviet Union. Such a complex argument is not an easy one politically in any country. Moreover, it led to serious thought about Soviet responsibility for the breakdown in détente, at least because of secrecy if not actual military policy. Both in 1982 and 1985 Zamoshkin made clear his belief that "the vicious circle" in Soviet-American relations would not be broken unless Americans believed that the correlation of forces was not moving against the United States and unless "the idea of military lag from the USSR that frightens them so much is destroyed."[70]

In practice, most Soviet scholars writing about the United States have not wanted to take on this argument. As a consequence, they have avoided the questions produced by the collapse of détente by limiting their summary statements about the American political system and casting them in a semitraditional direction.[71] One should not, however, be misled by this essentially political decision. The actual analysis of Western political systems has progressively moved in a more nontraditional direction. Books now include long sections titled "Social-psychological Mechanisms of the Evolution and Inversion of Traditional Types of Political Consciousness in the USA."[72] Scholars may now simply state in a matter-of-fact way that "the White House and Congress are leading institutions in the American governmental system. The governmental policy of the USA—the basic direction of its foreign and domestic policy—depends on how the relations between them take shape," and then go on to a detailed analysis of their relation.[73] It is in this detailed analysis—and, as Archie Brown emphasized, in the use of nontraditional categories and methodologies of analysis—that the real evolution in Soviet thinking about political systems is seen.

## Four Images of the State in the Third World

It is, of course, one thing to say that the state has some independence from the capitalist class, at least to the extent of being forced to make

70. Zamoshkin, "Ideologiia v SShA: za razriadku i protiv nee," p. 16; and Zamoshkin "Iadernaia opasnost' i faktor strakha," p. 6.

71. For a discussion of this evolution in a more cautious direction, see Franklyn Griffiths, "The Sources of American Conduct: Soviet Perspectives and Their Policy Implications," *International Security*, vol. 9 (Fall 1984), pp. 3–50.

72. Iu. A. Zamoshkin and E. Ia. Batalov, eds., *Sovremennoe politicheskoe soznanie v SShA* (Moscow: Nauka, 1980), p. 367.

73. V. A. Savel'ev, "President i kongress v god vyborov," *SShA*, no. 8 (1984), p. 5.

some concessions to other groups, but it is something else to say what the state is. One of the manifestations of the Stalinist orthodoxy had been its almost total disinterest in the institutional forms of government. Stage of history had been the traditional basis for comparing types of government, and a scholar complained in 1966 that even in the writing of ancient history "as a rule, only the class nature of the state has been investigated. . . . Everything that concerns the form, structure, and functions of state power and its individual organs fell outside the field of view of historians."[74]

Although the 1960s and 1970s saw an increase in work done on third world political institutions, they remained a secondary interest in Soviet scholarship. Scholars continued to focus on the class character of third world political systems: "Which classes struggle for the creation [of the political system] and support it? In whose interests does the state act?"[75] Nearly all rejected an institutional or structural-functional analysis (the "formal-dogmatic analysis") in which American political scientists have compared regimes by discussing the number of parties, the role of the military, the mass or elite character of parties, and the like.[76] With such a methodology, the Soviets asserted, American political scientists may group Chad with Tanzania and Burma with pre-1975 South Vietnam, even though they have "diametrically opposed systems in character."[77] Participants in a 1979 discussion of a book on the Kuomintang in China from 1927 to 1949 could justly note that there had been many general statements in the Soviet literature about the importance of the state and the state sector, but that this book was one of the first to examine the state in detail in a particular country.[78]

74. V. A. Rubin, "Problemy vostochnoi despotii v rabotakh sovetskikh issledovatelei," *Narody Azii i Afriki*, no. 4 (1966), p. 95.

75. G. B. Starushenko, "Sotsial'noe soderzhanie i politicheskaia forma nekapitalisticheskogo razvitiia molodykh gosudarstv," *Sovetskoe gosudarstvo i pravo*, no. 4 (April 1966), p. 108.

76. N. Savel'ev, "Puti razvitiia novoi Afriki," *MEiMO*, no. 2 (February 1966), p. 153; V. G. Solodovnikov, ed., *Politicheskie partii Afriki* (Moscow: Nauka, 1970), p. 51; and L. M. Entin, "Sotsial'naia priroda vlasti v strankakh tropicheskoi Afriki," *Sovetskoe gosudarstvo i pravo*, no. 8 (August 1965), p. 56.

77. F. M. Burlatsky and V. E. Chirkin, eds., *Politicheskie sistemy sovremennosti* (Moscow: Nauka, 1978), p. 186.

78. M. S. Meier and M. A. Cheskov in "Biurokraticheskaia burzhuaziia—biurokraticheskii kapital—gossektor—goskapitalizm," *Narody Azii i Afriki*, no. 5 (1979), pp. 186, 191. The book is A. V. Meliksetov, *Sotsial'no-ekonomicheskaia politika Gomin'dana v Kitae (1927–1949)* (Moscow: Nauka, 1977).

While the analysis of a third world state has frequently been more implicit than explicit, scholars have tended to define it in four ways in the past two decades. The first definition has been the traditional one, now usually with qualifications attached, focusing on the state's presumed class base and implying that this is the sole key to understanding. A second has focused on the bureaucracy as an institution or the bureaucrats as a class. A third has analyzed the leader and his values—or later the leader, his party, and their values. A fourth, although it has been much more vague in specifying its institutional meaning, has treated the state as an ongoing political process in which the different groups and classes (including bureaucratic ones) struggle to have their interests represented in policy and in which the government sometimes acts as mediator. Each definition has tended to be associated with a different view about the future course of developments in a country.

The most traditional scholars continue to look for the dominant class in third world countries and to see the state as its instrument. To some extent this view reflects the influence of Marxism-Leninism as it has been understood in the Soviet Union in the past, and to some extent it is also a product of the strong continuing impact of traditional jurisprudence and its conceptions about sovereignty. Thus Veniamin Chirkin, the most sophisticated of the scholars presenting a neotraditional view, spoke of the state as "an indivisible institution" and "an indivisible power," treating this assumption as a self-evident fact because "there cannot be two sovereign powers in the state."[79]

The traditional view of the state has continued to dominate textbooks and propagandistic articles, but it also emerges in specific analyses. For example, a 1980 book edited by Anatolii Gromyko, director of the Institute of Africa, sharply criticized military rule in countries with a capitalist orientation, but insisted that in countries of socialist orientation under military rule, "the political regime by its social essence is democratic, although it is realized by military methods that limit the sphere of political democracy. It cannot (as is sometimes done) be classified as a military dictatorship."[80]

The same point of view emerges in a rather nasty critique of an article

---

79. "Gosudarstvo sovremennogo perekhodnogo obshchestva," *Azii i Afrika segodnia,* no. 9 (1978), p. 29.

80. *Velikii Oktiabr' i Afrika* (Moscow: Nauka, 1980), p. 144. The chapter in which these lines appeared was written by V. E. Chirkin.

written by a foreigner (but really a critique of Soviet scholars who shared the foreigner's views—views that fit the fourth definition of the state): "[From the author's argument] it follows that the progressive forces need to struggle not so much against imperialism, the transnational corporations, their Latin American allies and agents as . . . against the strengthening of the state. It is by no means accidental that the struggle against the strengthening of the role of the state, particularly in the economy, is led by the transnational corporations in alliance with their proimperialist agents in the countries of the continent."[81]

A slightly more nuanced traditional image was presented by Chirkin. Except in a rare case such as India, Chirkin saw the third world state as more than the tool of a single ruling class as it was in the West. He saw a coalition of more progressive class forces in charge in radical countries such as Angola. To the extent that these various states were transitional, Chirkin insisted that this coalition did not result from the multistructural nature of society but from unresolved political struggle among classes that were still being formed. In "the exploiting state of the liberated countries . . . the state apparatus tries to base itself on [a combination of] different exploiting classes and strata of the population." However, it was a coalition *only* of exploiting classes.

Chirkin did see the third world state as having a broad role and relative independence from the ruling classes, but he attributed this to a factor that had been used to justify Stalin—the scale of the tasks and the need to solve them quickly. Conceding that "in fulfillment of broad national tasks, even an exploiting state power can infringe upon the interests of some categories of exploiters," he insisted that "it must not be forgotten that in the final analysis this is done in the interests of the exploiting class as a whole."[82]

The type of analysis advanced by Chirkin can be either optimistic or pessimistic about revolutionary prospects, depending upon what the scholar thinks about the workings of the economic laws of development in the third world. In practice, authors such as Chirkin normally retain not only the traditional view about the state but also the traditional skepticism about the prospects of capitalism. At a minimum, the analyses lead to qualitatively different evaluations of "exploiting" states and those of so-

81. V. P. Totsky, in "Latinskaia Amerika: vneshniaia politika i ekonomicheskaia zavisimost'," *Latinskaia Amerika*, no. 8 (1981), p. 60. The ellipsis was inserted by Totsky and was meant to imply incredulity.

82. "Gosudarstvo sovremennogo perekhodnogo obshchestva," pp. 28–31.

cialist orientation. As the next chapter shows, Chirkin was very optimistic about the radical states and by implication strongly advocated Soviet support for them.

A second optimistic point of view treats the state as much more independent, with a political leadership that represents its own ideology rather than that of preexisting classes. Obviously the traditional Soviet focus on a seizure of power by the Communist party implied the importance of political leadership, but doctrine had always insisted on some kind of mass base for a communist coup—not necessarily a communist majority but at least substantial revolutionary activity among workers or peasants or both. Some theorists, however—most notably among them, Georgii Mirsky— insisted from the early 1960s that the third world superstructure or state could be virtually independent of the economic base and that, indeed, "the superstructure tries to change the old base in its own image":[83]

> The societies of the underdeveloped countries [have] social elements that are not included in the concept of "bourgeoisie," but that in many cases play a huge and even leading role. I have in mind the intelligentsia and the army. It is precisely from these elements that the revolutionary or national democrats come. This is not a force that is independent of classes or above classes; it expresses the interests of definite classes. But the society in which it acts bears a transitional character, the world view of these people can evolve, and if they possess real power, they are in a position to turn the rudder sharply. The direction in which the rudder will be turned depends on the political views of the leaders and on the degree they are connected with the masses and express their interests.[84]

The third line of analysis, that which focuses on the bureaucracy as the essential element of the state, tends to be the most pessimistic about the possibility of revolutionary progress, even in radical states. After 1955 it was virtually unquestionable dogma that the sector of the economy run by the state was more progressive than the private sector. The state sector promoted nationalization and concentrated on heavy industry; hence almost by definition it was building the base for socialism and had to be better than the private sector.

Yet while a few scholars called the state sector "the people's sector" (or even "semisocialist" in radical regimes),[85] most of those who were really

83. G. Mirsky and T. Pokataeva, "Klassy i klassovaia bor'ba v razvivaiushchikhsia stranakh," *MEiMO,* no. 3 (March 1966), p. 60.

84. G. Mirsky, "Tvorcheskii marksizm i problemy natsional'no-osvoboditel'nykh revoliutsii," *MEiMO,* no. 2 (February 1963), pp. 65–66.

85. See *Razvivaiushchie strany v bor'be za nezavisimuiu natsional'nuiu ekonomiiu* (1967), pp. 20, 176; and V. Tiagunenko, "Oktiabr' i sovremennaia natsional'no-osvoboditel'naia revoliutsiia," *MEiMO,* no. 1 (January 1967), pp. 14–15.

optimistic about the prospects of revolutionary transformation did not speak about the state bureaucracy as an institution, especially in a positive manner. If they had a favorable view of the employees of the economic ministries and state-run factories, they usually lumped them together with other intelligentsia and urban white collar workers who were driven to the left by the forces of nationalism. The standard optimistic analysis treated the bureaucracies of the state sector as politically neutral entities that would follow the directives of the political leaders: "it is impossible to expect that the state and cooperative sectors . . . will by themselves . . . fulfill their role of enzyme and catalyst in the process of the transition of the country to noncapitalist development. . . . That is determined by the socialist evolution of the state power itself."[86]

Those who took the employees of the state bureaucracy seriously as a social group and who focused on them seldom had any faith in their neutrality. They often used phrases such as "a special bureaucratic elite," "a bourgeoisie of officials," and especially "the bureaucratic bourgeoisie."[87] As a scholar noted in 1977, these phrases were attractive because of their breadth and undefined nature,[88] but they usually had negative connotations. One scholar, for example, asserted that "the bureaucratic bourgeoisie, in essence, prepares the soil for subverting the state sector," while another said that "the bureaucrats . . . see the imperialistic monopolies not as an enemy, but as an ally that facilitates their enrichment."[89] Although these authors believed that political forces could overcome this new type of bourgeoisie, others thought that the bureaucracy was the dominant social force in the third world and would generally ensure a bourgeois development in the foreseeable future. (This analysis usually was not extended to the most economically backward countries, which did not have significant state or private industrial sectors.)

86. R. A. Ul'ianovsky, "Birma na novom puti razvitiia," *Narody Azii i Afriki*, no. 6 (1963), p. 44.

87. G. Mirsky, "Tvorcheskii marksizm i problemy natsional'no-osvoboditel'nykh revoliutsii," *MEiMO*, no. 2 (February 1963), p. 65; and M. A. Andreev, "Trudnosti razvitiia gosudarstvennogo sektora Indonezii," *Narody Azii i Afriki*, no. 5 (1963), p. 35.

88. Meliksetov, *Sotsial'no-ekonomicheskaia politika Gomin'dana v Kitae*, p. 258. Nodari Simoniia agreed, but responded that the lack of definition was their least attractive feature. See "Biurokraticheskaia burzhuaziia—burokraticheskii kapital—gossektor—goskapitalizm," p. 199.

89. Andreev, "Trudnosti razvitiia gosudarstvennogo sektora Indonezii," p. 40; and Mirsky, "Tvorcheskii marksizm i problemy natsional'no-osvoboditel'nykh revoliutsii," p. 65.

At first this viewpoint was expressed cautiously. Perhaps the old view of the state as the instrument of the owning class made it difficult to conceive of bureaucrats as a crucial class in their own right, or perhaps there were political restraints because of Khrushchev's optimism. When the chief specialist on Turkey at the Institute of Oriental Studies wrote of state-monopoly capitalism in Turkey and was pessimistic about any changes for the better, a critical reviewer noted, "in such a case we would be required to consider that all enterprises created in the state sector of underdeveloped countries like, for instance, India, OAR, or other countries that recently have become politically independent are monopolistic organizations."[90]

After the overthrow of Kwame Nkrumah in Ghana and especially the post-Nasser evolution of Egypt, a number of scholars created broader generalizations about the dominance of the bureaucracy as a social force in the third world. "The 'elite,' who occupy high posts of the state hierarchy," one scholar wrote, "act not simply as a political representative of 'other' class interests, but as some special social community, which personifies a state-owner."[91] This author, like many others, linked the analysis with that of the Asiatic mode of production and spoke of the continuation of "the tradition of a strong centralized state."[92] In fact, the Soviet discussion of the Asiatic mode, analyzed in the last chapter, was to a considerable extent an analysis of the contemporary state.

A fourth implicit definition of the state had more neutral long-term implications on the surface, but in some respects it moved toward the most decisive break with old orthodoxies. It saw the state not as a reified entity, but as an arena in which political and social forces could compete or even as a process in which state officials could serve mediating functions.

This view was at least partly implicit in Khrushchev's general declaration at the Twentieth Party Congress in 1956 that there were different

90. B. M. Dantsig, "K voprosu o razvitii kapitalizma v Turtsii (po povodu knigi Iu. N. Rozalieva)," *Narody Azii i Afriki*, no. 6 (1963), p. 160. The book reviewed was Iu. N. Rozaliev, *Osobennosti razvitiia kapitalizma v Turtsii (1923-1960 gg.)* (Moscow: Izdatel'stvo vostochnoi literatury, 1962). Rozaliev was consistent. For a similar review of his previous book, see *Sovetskoe vostokovedenie*, no. 1 (1958), pp. 126-27, and for his response to Dantsig, see "Eshche raz ob osobennostiakh razvitiia kapitalizma v Turtsii," *Narody Azii i Afriki*, no. 3 (1964), pp. 129-37.

91. M. Cheshkov, "'Elita' i klass v razvivaiushchikhsia stranakh," *MEiMO*, no. 1 (January 1970), p. 88.

92. Also see A. B. Meliksetov's review of O. E. Nepomnin, *Sotsial'no-ekonomicheskaia istoriia Kitaia, 1894-1914* in *Narody Azii i Afriki*, no. 2 (1981), p. 222-24.

roads to socialism, including parliamentary ones. In 1958, however, Sergei Mikoian, the son of one of Khrushchev's closest associates in the party leadership, wrote a critical book review presenting an analysis that seemed to follow from Khrushchev's speech:

[The author] dwells little on the role of the masses in [India]. Of course, state power in the country belongs to the bourgeoisie. Nevertheless, as V. I. Lenin indicated—politics is the relationship between classes. Policy is determined by the interests of different classes, their struggles for their own interests, and their respective power in this struggle. The role of the working classes in India grows with every year, and it is wrong to underestimate their influence on the foreign policy of the ruling classes.[93]

In the 1950s and 1960s this image was usually expressed in more cautious terms, especially in theoretical discussions, but by the end of the decade it was possible to be more open. As was discussed in chapter 3, Aleksei Levkovsky developed a multistructural analysis of third world society that insisted no mode of production, and therefore no class, occupied a dominant position in the economies of these societies. For a Marxist the question obviously arose that if government is an instrument of the dominant owning class and there is no such class, who does the government represent?

Unlike more cautious scholars, Levkovsky answered that a ruling elite "usually exercises political power not in the name of one class but of a broad coalition of classes" and that it "usually tries to play the role of an arbiter that stands above classes."[94] It was, of course, a position that was sharply attacked for its unorthodoxy,[95] but it was also a position Levkovsky was to maintain resolutely, although with language that was a bit more cautious. Thus, in 1978 he pulled back from any suggestion that the third world state represented all classes equally, but he did not pull back very far:

Each economic base has its corresponding political structure, or to be more accurate, the former begets the latter. . . . Multistructureness [*mnogoukladnost'*] is

93. S. A. Mikoian, *Sovetskoe vostokovedenie*, no. 6 (1958), pp. 107–08.

94. B. G. Gafurov, ed., *Zarubezhnyi Vostok i sovremennost': osnovnye zakonomernosti i spetsifika razvitiia osvobodivshikhsia stran* (Moscow: Nauka, 1974), vol. 2, p. 669. The section in which these words appeared was officially said to be written by G. F. Kim, but the analysis was Levkovsky's.

95. A. U. Roslavlev, "O klassovom podkhode k problemam osvobodivshikhsia stran," *Rabochii klass i sovremennyi mir*, no. 6 (November–December 1974), pp. 103–14. "Roslavlev" is the pseudonym of the deputy head of the international department, R. A. Ul'ianovsky.

always a relative and temporary, more or less stable, equilibrium between several substructures in the socioeconomic base. . . . In the transition period from one means of production to another, the heterogeneity of the superstructure, including the state, corresponds to the heterogeneity of the economic base.

The dominant superstructure answers the interest not of all but only some of the economic substructures and some of the classes associated with them. . . . However . . . the necessity to regulate the harmonizing of all the substructures for the use of some selected ones (and the classes they represent) strengthened the eclectic nature of the state superstructure. . . . Consequently in the transitional society, the state serves the basic needs of *several* social forces that enter the ruling coalition. Consequently such a state cannot be characterized as *one-class* in nature.[96]

The slightly qualified formulation did not end controversy. The Chirkin article cited at length above was a direct response to and criticism of the Levkovsky article from which this quotation was drawn.

The same general position could also arise from a theory similar to the Asiatic mode of production. While the latter traditionally had tended to see the state as the owner and thus a force that suppressed society, it was possible simply to focus on the lack of a class base: "In contrast to the bourgeois state of the West, which was formed as a superstructure over civilian society, the national state in Asia and Africa preceded civilian society. . . . In the conditions of postcolonial social development, the rule of a single class cannot be imposed. The political authority in developing countries has a persistently coalitional, compromising character."[97]

Nodari Simoniia, however, took the position that the differences between the West and the East should not be exaggerated. "The counterpoising . . . of some universal and timeless Western democratic type of state to an authoritarian Eastern one is unproductive from a scientific point of view." For Simoniia, "bourgeois democracy" was not really bourgeois at all, for "parliaments arose as an expression of the interests of traditional— that is, feudal—forces," and he argued that "a bonapartist state is characteristic for the phase of early capitalist development." He asserted that "authoritarianism means a certain independence from classes. . . . The essence of the class relations expressed by the autocracy is an equilibrium and compromise of classes. . . . The concrete class contents of each type of authoritarian state objectively depend on the character of classes whose

96. "O spetsifike gosudarstva v mnogoukladnykh stranakh," *Aziia i Afrika segodnia,* no. 2 (February 1978), pp. 25, 27, 28. The order of the sentences has been rearranged.

97. V. I. Maksimenko, "Evoliutsiia politicheskikh struktur v razvivaiushchikhsia stranakh Azii," *Narody Azii i Afriki,* no. 4 (1984), p. 118.

compromise it expresses." He labeled the governments of India and Maylasia "parliamentary authoritarianism," Iran of the shah "an absolutist-bonapartist regime," and Indonesia, Thailand, and the Philippines "neobonapartist regimes, or controlled democracy."[98]

The Soviet literature on the third world was slow to put a value on competitive elections as such. If such institutions provided the mechanism for communist victories, as in the state of Kerala, they were, of course, a good thing. Yet, when "the national democratic state" was proclaimed as a model, when it was defined in part as "a state that repudiates dictatorial despotic methods of rule [and] in which the people are guaranteed broad democratic rights and freedoms," the word "democratic" almost always carried its old connotations. The radical regimes that were called national democratic states were basically dictatorial regimes by Western definitions, and the Soviet Union was scarcely advising them to establish elections in which villagers under the influence of tribal and religious leaders were likely to vote conservatively or for separatism. Indeed, in 1984 Chirkin still included "bourgeois democratic conceptions of constitutional law" as one of the old norms of society that had to be overcome.[99] The stipulation that such states be democratic meant that the Communist party or other radical forces be free to organize and push the revolution in a more left-wing direction. While some Soviet specialists implicitly objected, the Soviet Union still applied the national democratic label to regimes that outlawed the Communist party so long as they remained radical and pro-Soviet.

In the late 1960s, however, an increasing number of scholars began to treat the achievement and maintenance of democratic institutions as a goal worth fighting for until the socialist revolution occurred. This theme was particularly pronounced in work on Europe, and in the second half of the 1970s scholars increasingly began to suggest that various types of democratic transformation (for example, workers' participation in management) in Western Europe could be the mechanism by which a gradual transition to socialism might take place.[100]

In terms of the third world the issue first arose seriously in the context

98. L. I. Reisner and N. A. Simoniia, eds., *Evoliutsiia vostochnykh obshchestv: sintez traditsionnogo i sovremennogo* (Moscow: Nauka, 1984), pp. 195–200, 210, 296, 382, 391.

99. "Novoe i staroe v konstitutsionnom prave stran sotsialisticheskoi orientatsii," *Sovetskoe gosudarstvo i pravo*, no. 1 (1984), pp. 86–87.

100. This theme is beyond the scope of this book, but a representative sample of citations on it is found in V. N. Shevchenko, "K kharakteristike dialektiki perekhoda ot kapitalizma k sotsializmu," *Filosofskie nauki*, no. 1 (1981), pp. 13–25.

of the Salvador Allende experiment in Chile. Irina Zorina, a specialist on Chile, was one of those severely critical of what they saw as the excessive radicalism of Allende's regime. It should have sought, she insisted, "political compromise, collaboration, and alliances" with the parties representing the peasants and the middle strata, especially the Christian Democrats.[101] When she asserted that "the participation of the Christian Democrats would not have hindered the enactment of the planned program of democratic transformation but could have achieved its full realization and made it really irreversible,"[102] she seemed to have in mind a concept of democratic transformation whose substance and gradualness would have made it acceptable to the center as well as the radicals.

In the second half of the 1970s this position was expressed by those Latin Americanists who, as discussed in chapter 4, insisted that the economies of Latin America were becoming more like those of southern Europe than like those in the bulk of Asia and Africa. With such a perspective it was natural to ask whether Latin American politics might be on the verge of Europeanization as well—in particular, whether the movement from military dictatorship to representative democracy in Portugal, Spain, and Greece (and the evolution of the Italian Communist party in a social-democratic direction) did not foreshadow a similar development in Latin America in the relatively near future.

The thesis about a Europeanization of Latin American politics was already implicit in the writings of Boris Koval' in the early 1970s, and it subsequently appeared in partial form in various statements by participants in roundtable discussions in the journal, *Latin America*. However, in 1978 I. V. Danilevich, the daughter of the leading Latin Americanist of two decades before, published an article on the relationship of the Socialist International and Latin America asserting that "essential socioeconomic changes had occurred . . . that had transformed the face of the continent and that on a series of parameters have brought it closer to the countries of developed capitalism."[103] Acknowledging that in the 1960s she had seen little future for social democracy in Latin America, she argued that social

101. I. N. Zorina and Iu. F. Kariakin, "Politicheskaia khronika chiliiskoi revoliutsii," pt. 2, *Rabochii klass i sovremennyi mir*, no. 5 (September–October 1974), p. 148. Also see Zorina's statement in the discussion published in M. O. Karamanov, "Opyt Chili i revoliutsionnyi protsess," ibid., no. 6 (November–December 1974), p. 136.

102. I. N. Zorina, "Revoliutsiia i khristiansko-demokraticheskaia partiia," in M. F. Kudachkin and A .A. Kutsenkov, eds., *Uroki Chili* (Moscow: Nauka, 1977), p. 197.

103. "Mezhdunarodnaia sotsial-demokratiia i Latinskaia Amerika," *Latinskaia Amerika*, no. 2 (March–April 1978), p. 81.

democracy's tendency to become more nationalistic had changed the situation in a substantial way.[104] The same issue of *Latin America* included a long roundtable discussion on the subject, with a full spectrum of views expressed.

A similar discussion was held in 1981 on Christian democracy, with Sergei Semenov the reporter. At the end of the discussion Semenov suggested that two basic positions had been presented. "The first [essentially his own] sees Latin America passing through the same stages of development as Western Europe, but with a delay. Having cleaned away 'the dirty aquarium,' the military dictatorships create the optimal conditions for the activity of Christian democracy and social democracy." In answering the opposing position that the transnational corporations and the local bourgeoisie wanted an authoritarian state instead of bourgeois democracy, Semenov was blunt: "[For the bourgeoisie] bourgeois democracy is not a luxury, not a gift of nature, and not only a passion of the masses. It is a definite economic need, a need of the functioning of production. It is a demand of social progress as a whole. Therefore, fascism is an anomaly, an extreme situation that interferes with the normal functioning of production."[105]

In terms of Soviet images of the state, what was important was not the prediction but the evaluation of it. The movement toward bourgeois democracy in Latin America was described by these scholars not as a typical trick perpetrated by the bourgeoisie but as a positive development. Thus in 1982 and 1983 Anatolii Shul'govsky, who at least in private expressed this position most vigorously, wrote three articles on Latin American theoretical conceptions of the state in which he sharply distinguished between countries that were authoritarian repressive regimes and those that were representative democracies. While putting the latter words in quotation marks and being highly critical of such governments, he was even more critical of those theorists who treated the Latin American state—whatever its form—as inevitably an extraordinary or satellitized one that always resorted to open violence and terror for the benefit of American corporations.[106]

104. "Mezhdunarodnaia sotsial-demokratiia i Latinskaia Amerika," *Latinskaia Amerika*, no. 4 (July–August 1978), pp. 89–90.

105. "Vmesto zakliucheniia," in "Khristianskaia demokratiia v politicheskoi sisteme stran Latinskoi Ameriki," *Latinskaia Amerika*, no. 3 (1982), p. 76.

106. "Gosudarstvo i bor'ba za demokratiiu," *Latinskaia Amerika*, no. 4 (July–August 1983), pp. 5–10. Also see his "Gosudarstvo 'vseobshchego blagodenstviia': teoriia i

Similarly, Boris Koval' suggested that the struggle for democracy (in a presocialist system) would be the determining feature of Latin American politics for many years and perhaps decades ("in a whole group of countries the toilers, in practice, have to select not between capitalism and socialism, but between bourgeois democracy and fascism"). He left no doubt on his opinion about the position of the communists in this struggle. While maintaining their independence, they should be willing to cooperate with the moderates when there was a coincidence of interests—and the preservation of representative democracy was certainly one such case. "A widening of democracy is a necessary precondition for a successful struggle against imperialism and for socialism."[107] In 1982 Koval specifically cautioned against an underestimation of the revolutions in Peru in 1968–75 and in Zimbabwe in 1980. At a 1984 seminar Semenov cautioned that while the Peruvian regime had instituted deep transformations, they "scarcely should be evaluated as a 'revolution' or a 'revolutionary process,'" but Koval' objected that "revolutionary process" is fully justified. Although the transformations did not produce socialism, they did lead to a change in political system, and in his opinion that was not insignificant.[108]

In discussions of Africa, too, expressions of disillusionment with the left-wing dictatorships were expressed more openly. By the mid-1970s some scholars were emphasizing the common features of Asian and African countries of both capitalist and socialist orientation, and their observations were not flattering. One general study suggested that almost all political systems in Asia and Africa have the following characteristics in common: "an exceptionally large role for the executive; the hegemony of one political organization, which at the same time does not represent the interests of any one class; a growing influence of the bureaucracy, and in a

---

real'nost'," *Latinskaia Amerika,* no. 10 (1982), pp. 5–19, and "Gosudarstvo i 'grazhdanskoe obshchestvo': novye konseptsii," *Latinskaia Amerika,* no. 11 (1982), pp. 24–40. Shul'govsky's articles seem, if anything, more cautious than Boris Koval's, but conservative Soviet Latin Americanists clearly perceive Koval' to be the more moderate of the two.

107. *Latinskaia Amerika,* no. 6 (November–December 1975), p. 111; no. 4 (July–August) 1978, p. 103. Also see B. I. Koval' and S. I. Semenov, "Latinskaia Amerika i mezhdunarodnaia sotsial-demokratiia," *Rabochii klass i sovremennyi mir,* no. 4 (July–August 1978), p. 101.

108. See "Revoluitsionnoe dvizhenie v Peru: uroki, problemy, perspektivy," *Latinskaia Amerika,* no. 1 (1984), pp. 162–63; and "Rabochii klass i revoliutsionnost' narodnykh mass: opyt 70kh godov," *Rabochii klass i sovremenny mir,* no. 2 (1983), p. 13.

series of cases, the military; weakness of the opposition; the 'political stratum' being out of touch with the masses; a subordination of parties and trade unions to the state."[109]

Others with this fourth image of the state were even more critical. Nodari Simoniia explicitly warned against the "illusions" that "alliances with 'left-wing' dictators can bring success to proletarian forces."[110] Viktor Sheinis, the leading comparativist at IMEMO in the 1980s, referred to "the corruption, nepotism, economic and administrative inefficiency, stagnation or slow increase in living standards, the passivity of the masses, undemocratic methods of administration, and so forth" that often had been a cause of counterrevolution in countries of socialist orientation. He then launched into a virulent attack on Idi Amin that must have been directed at those in the Soviet Union who had taken the Ugandan leader's socialist and pro-Soviet language seriously in the the past.[111]

As already noted, however, Simoniia cautioned against the widespread practice of "comparing noncomparable types of states. Often the political system of the transition period in the development of societies in the East is contrasted with systems that correspond to the phase of organically integrated societies in the West." He forcefully reminded his readers that "even the liberal idea of the 'absolute value'" of bourgeois democracy took root comparatively recently on the European continent and that the process by which the ideas of democratism really took root required decades of the most persistent struggle.[112] In the context of his discussion of the variety of authoritarian regimes and their social supports, Simoniia was warning against the notion of perpetual oriental despotism and against the notion that the fight for democratism be limited to the struggle for twentieth century parliamentary institutions.

These views occupy just one portion of the spectrum of opinions on the third world state or political system. Treating Latin American governments, regardless of their form, as little more than tools of the bourgeoisie while treating radical left-wing dictatorships in Africa as progressive has remained the most common approach in print. Even those who see the state—especially one with representative institutions—as a political arena

109. V. L. Tiagunenko, ed. *Razvivaiushchiesia strany: zakonomernosti, tendentsii, perspektivy* (Moscow: Mysl', 1974), p. 342.

110. *Strany Vostoka: puti razvitiia* (Moscow: Nauka, 1975), p. 320.

111. "O kriteriiakh sotsial'nogo progressa v razvivaiushchikhsia stranakh (diskussiia)," *Narody Azii i Afriki*, no. 5 (1981), pp. 66, 67.

112. Reisner and Simoniia, *Evoliutsiia vostochnykh obshchestv*, p. 19.

in which the owning class has an undue advantage have not developed this view with any great thoroughness or theoretical sophistication. Yet these four views of the state are not abstract arguments in political science. In the Soviet Union they are a way of implying different revolutionary strategies and different foreign policy postures, matters discussed in the following three chapters.

These various views are also, of course, ways of discussing the Soviet future. A Chirkin who speaks with contempt about "bourgeois democratic conceptions of constitutional law" is hardly suggesting that they be introduced in the Soviet Union. Those who attack "bureaucratic bourgeoisies" usually also have the Soviet ministries in mind. And a Simoniia who writes about the variations in authoritarian regimes and their coalitional bases surely is trying to stimulate thought about the possibility of evolution within the Soviet one-party system.

# CHAPTER SIX

# Political Development and Revolutionary Strategy

OVER THE YEARS the Soviet debates on revolutionary strategy have focused on two related sets of questions. What is the nature of the state in foreign countries and does it have to be overthrown by violent revolution if there is to be hope for social progress? What is the natural tendency of historical development as feudalism—or preindustrial society, however defined—begins to disintegrate with the growth of capitalism or industrialization or both? Are major historical forces leading to socialist revolution in the near term?

Marxism-Leninism is far more ambiguous on the probability and the course of development of third world revolution than it is on the nature of the state. Marx's basic analysis of historical development presented the concept of progress from one fairly well defined stage to another. Each stage is economically more productive than its predecessor, but the inner workings of each create forces that will eventually destroy it. From this perspective, capitalism is a highly progressive development in comparison with feudalism, and it should be the first (and judging by the Western European experience, a long-term) natural consequence of industrialization.[1] If capitalist economic relations have already begun to develop, then

1. One of the passages in *The Communist Manifesto,* for example, could have been written by the U.S. Chamber of Commerce. "The bourgeoisie, during rule of scarcely one hundred years, has created more massive and more colossal productive forces than have all preceding generations together. Subjection of nature's forces to man, machinery, application of chemistry to industry and agriculture, steam navigation, railways, electric telegraphs, clearing of whole continents for cultivation, canalization of rivers." Karl Marx and Friedrich Engels, *The Communist Manifesto* (Labor News, 1948), p. 14.

a change in the political structure is to be expected, and the bourgeoisie is the group that is supposed to lead this revolution. It would seem logical for the communists to cooperate with them in order to push history forward. Yet Marx wrote optimistically about imminent communist revolution in 1848, when Western Europe was undeveloped by today's standards. Lenin then led a socialist revolution in a Russia less industrialized than the Western Europe of 1848. He argued that it was possible for the bourgeois revolution to grow over (*pererastat'*) into the socialist one, and in fact this "growing over" required only eight months in Russia. For postrevolutionary Soviet leaders, the question obviously arose: was Russia to be the rule or the exception so far as subsequent historical development was concerned?

When, contrary to predictions, the revolution did not spread to Western Europe, it would have been easy to see the Russian Revolution simply as the product of very peculiar historical circumstances, especially the impact of World War I on a political order already near collapse. It could have been argued that Marx was right—that "feudalism" normally gives rise to capitalism, which normally lasts for a long time, as in Western Europe. Or it could have been argued that Russia was the first developing country and that the socialist revolution there was the natural product of capitalism, which developed subsequent to that in Western Europe. If the capitalism introduced later was inherently different because of the influence of advanced Western countries, it would logically follow that the political development during the transition away from "feudalism" would also have an inherently different character. Such a judgment would obviously affect communist revolutionary tactics in these areas.

For Soviet policymakers the issue of the uniqueness of Russian history was not an abstract one, and it did not arise in a vacuum. Except in a rare country such as Vietnam, communist parties proved not to be the dominant force in the revolutionary movements that arose to fight Western domination. The major figures in the countries of most direct relevance to the Soviet Union—Kemal Ataturk in Turkey, Chiang Kai-shek in China, and Mahatma Gandhi in India—were anti-Western and with the partial exception of Gandhi (but not many of his supporters) were strong proponents of industrialization. Yet they were scarcely communists. Ataturk killed a number of leading Turkish communists, and Chiang Kai-shek, while cooperating closely with the communists in the early stages of his revolution, turned brutally against them in 1927 as he began to win. In

Soviet terminology, such a person—anticommunist, anti-Western, and proindustrialization—was a "bourgeois nationalist," and the crucial question was what the correct Soviet posture toward him should be. If capitalism was the normal, long-term future of the third world, the answer might be different than if Russia was to be the model.

### The National Liberation Movement and Communist Revolutionary Strategy

Lenin was first of all a theorist who was unusually sensitive to the importance of nationality in social revolution, but before the Bolshevik Revolution his attention was riveted on Russia and Western Europe. While he recognized the possibility of anticolonial revolutions, he did not attach great significance to them. "A blow delivered against the English imperialist bourgeoisie by a rebellion in Ireland is a hundred times more significant politically than a blow of equal weight delivered in Asia or in Africa," he wrote in 1916. In March 1919 the manifesto of the newly created Communist International gave little more attention to the subject: "The liberation of the colonies is only possible accompanied by that of the metropoles. The workers and peasants not only of Annam, Algeria, Bengal, but also of Persia and Armenia will only obtain the possibility for independent existence on the day when the workers of England and France will have overthrown Lloyd George and [Georges] Clemenceau and taken the state power into their own hands."[2]

As the prospects for revolution in the West faded, however, Soviet eyes turned to the East. During the summer of 1919 the Hungarian and Bavarian revolutions began to fail, and Defense Minister Leon Trotsky wrote an impassioned memorandum to other members of the Central Committee advocating the use of the Red Army as an instrument to support the revolution in Asia:

There is no doubt that our Red Army is an incomparably more significant force on the Asian fields of world politics than on the European fields. . . . The road to India can be more passable and shorter for us at the present time than the road to Soviet Hungary. An army that now cannot have important significance in the European scales can destroy the unstable equilibrium of Asiatic relations of colo-

2. This paragraph is based on Demetrio Boersner, *The Bolsheviks and the National and Colonial Question (1917-1928)* (Geneva: Librairie E. Droz, 1957), pp. 49-56, 64-66. The quotations are from pp. 55, 66.

nial dependence, give a direct push to the rebellious and oppressed masses, and secure a victory for an uprising in Asia. . . . The path to Paris and London lies through the cities of Afghanistan, Pendzhab, and Bengalia.[3]

The Red Army was in fact used in successful support of the pro-Bolshevik forces in the old Soviet Asian borderlands of central Asia and the Transcaucasus, and the old Russian empire was reestablished in these areas. There were also some efforts to extend military activity into northern Persia, but employing Soviet military power to promote revolution outside the boundaries of the old Russian empire quickly came to an end.

Inevitably the question arose as to what the Soviet Union should do to support revolution and what its relationship should be to the bourgeois nationalists. In 1916 Lenin stated that "socialists should in the most decisive manner support the most revolutionary elements of the bourgeois democratic nationalist movements in [colonies and semicolonial countries] and help in their uprising."[4] In 1920 as the Ottoman Empire dissolved, the British occupied Constantinople and the Soviet Union moved to support Kemal Ataturk, a noncommunist but anti-British modernizer. Lenin's theses for the Second Congress of the Comintern in August 1920 reiterated that all communist parties must help "the peasant movement against landlords" in backward countries, but he cautioned that this was "a temporary alliance" and that the communists should "unconditionally preserve their independence."[5] These theses provoked disagreements, and as a result Lenin agreed to change the term "bourgeois democratic movement" to "national revolutionary movement" to emphasize that "the Soviet Union would support bourgeois liberation movements in colonial countries only in those cases when those movements are actually revolutionary."[6] It is unclear whether the linguistic change was of any significance for Lenin himself.

Although the basic principle of support for the movements and national liberation revolutions has remained unchanged since Lenin's time, ambi-

3. Letter to the Central Committee, August 5, 1919, Trotsky Archives, Harvard University, document T-2956. He repeated the appeal on September 20, 1919, Trotsky Archives, document T-2957.

4. "Sotsialisticheskaia revoliutsiia i pravo natsii na samoopredelenie" in V. I. Lenin, *Polnoe sobranie sochinenii,* 5th ed. (Moscow: Gospolitizdat, 1962), vol. 27, p. 261.

5. "Pervonachal'nyi nabrosok tezisov po natsional'nomu i kolonial'nomu voprosam (dlia vtorogo s'ezda Kommunisticheskogo Internatsionala" in Lenin, *Polnoe sobranie sochinenii,* vol. 41, pp. 166–67.

6. "Doklad komissii po natsional'nomu i kolonial'nomu voprosam 26 iulia" in Lenin, *Polnoe sobranie sochinenii,* vol. 41, pp. 243, 247.

guities or problems have arisen in applying the principle. One problem has been in defining the nation whose liberation movement deserves support. In the third world in particular, the meaningful nations in terms of common historical background, culture, language, and self-identification (the usual Soviet definition of a nation) do not live in geographical areas that correspond with state boundaries. Does the Soviet Union support the liberation of the Nigerian people or the Ibos when a secession movement arises in Biafra? Does it support national liberation for the Kurds who straddle Turkey, Syria, Iraq, and Iran, or for the Baluchis in Pakistan and Afghanistan? These are not trivial theoretical questions, for most people in most third world countries identify more strongly with their ethnic group than with the nation as defined by membership in the United Nations. Moreover these ethnic groups frequently are not small, economically unviable units like the Hopi Indians in the United States. There are perhaps 10 million Kurds and 3 million Baluchis in their respective areas.

In practice the Soviet Union has generally supported national liberation for nations that correspond to state boundaries, however irrational. It has occasionally toyed with supporting the Kurds and no doubt provides a little covert aid to separatist movements in pro-Western countries in order to harass their governments. Moreover, when a separatist movement in the Soviet interest looks like it will win (for example, in Bangladesh), the Soviet Union can shift policy very quickly. Yet in the case of the Biafran secession, in which the rebels were more left-wing than the Nigerian government, the Nigerian government was essentially pro-Western, and Biafra had the petroleum to be economically viable, the Soviet Union still supported the Nigerian government. This typical pattern seems explained both by a desire not to offend third world governments (who are strongly opposed to separatism in general for reasons of self-interest) and by sensitivity to potential separatist movements within the Soviet Union itself.

The second potential ambiguity in the concept of national liberation is in the word "liberation": from what is the nation being liberated? To an American, national liberation implies anticolonial movements and perhaps also efforts to prevent third world military alliances with the West. Such assumptions are certainly correct, but traditionally Soviet theorists assigned a far broader meaning to national liberation. Since capitalist development was said inevitably to lead to dependence on the Western powers, it logically followed that real national liberation required the overthrow of capitalism.

Although Soviet doctrine has changed from time to time, the national liberation revolution was generally described as having two stages. In the first a colony achieves political independence, often under the leadership of the bourgeoisie. In the second it achieves economic independence under the leadership of the workers, that is, the Communist party. In this stage the national liberation movement and the national liberation revolution become euphemisms for the socialist revolution.

During the Stalinist period this two-stage concept was expressed in jargonized language about the "national bourgeoisie":

Stalin considered that only in the first stage of the Chinese revolution . . . [did] the Chinese national bourgeoisie [possess] revolutionary potential . . . and there-fore supported the revolution and entered into alliance with the Chinese proletariat on the platform of a general struggle for the expulsion of the imperialists from China. In the second stage of the Chinese revolution, which began after the counterrevolutionary coup by Chiang Kai-shek in April 1927, Stalin considered that the Chinese national bourgeoisie had already exhausted its revolutionary possibilities, and had left the national revolutionary front for the camp of the counterrevolutionaries. . . . This evaluation of the Chinese national bourgeoisie . . . was mechanically transferred to the national bourgeoisie of the colonial and semicolonial East.[7]

This post-Stalin statement is somewhat too sweeping, however. During the Popular Front period and World War II, Stalin had not cared at all about the revolutionary potential of the bourgeoisie but had been eager to cooperate with anyone who was opposed to Hitler. Immediately after the war the local communists generally continued to cooperate with the non-communist anticolonial movements in what one scholar has called "a united front from inertia."[8]

In addition, Stalin distinguished between the "collaborationist" and the "revolutionary" bourgeoisie during the colonial period. In the first stage of the national liberation struggle, it was quite proper for the communist parties to cooperate with the latter, but those bourgeoisie who collaborated with the colonial powers were lost causes. In and of itself, this distinction was reasonable, but the crucial question was which political parties and movements were in which category?

---

7. E. F. Kovalev, "Sun' Iat-sen o 'preduprezhdenii' kapitalizma v Kitae," *Narody Azii i Afriki*, no. 2 (1963), p. 71. See also A. M. D'iakov and I. M. Reisner, "Rol' Gandi v natsional'no-osvoboditel'noi bor'be narodov Indii," *Sovetskoe vostokovedenie*, no. 5 (1956), pp. 22–23.

8. Donald Steven Carlisle, "Soviet Policy in the United Nations and the Problem of Economic Development, 1946–1956" (Ph.D. dissertation, Harvard University, 1962), p. 48.

For instance, although many of the leading specialists on India used esoteric language to argue that the Congress party had broad support after 1947 and that the common front with these bourgeoisie should be continued,[9] after 1947–48 third world governments were officially treated as tools of the big bourgeoisie, and all the politically significant bourgeoisie were essentially treated as collaborationist. The Chinese strategy of revolutionary war was essentially endorsed and implicitly justified by the analysis that the new governments lacked any broad class support.

In 1949 communist tactics in Europe were changed to encourage cooperation with those who opposed the United States and European unity,[10] and in the early 1950s a similar change was introduced in Asia. Although some scholars continued to espouse the doctrine of revolutionary war, the most important argued that the time was not ripe for it in most of Asia.[11] Soviet doctrine recognized the possibility and desirability of cooperation with the bourgeoisie in the second stage of the national liberation revolution as well as the first stage.

This change in the late Stalinist period should not, however, be misunderstood. If members of any class, including the bourgeoisie, wanted to participate in front organizations and movements that stood for "peace," "antifeudalism," or "antiimperialism," they were more than welcome, but those elements in power in countries such as India were still collaborationist bourgeoisie, and cooperation with them was impossible. Indeed, even major noncommunist anticolonial movements such as that of the Mau Mau in Kenya were treated suspiciously at best. As a Soviet scholar was later to write: "[in the early 1950s] it was thought that the united front should be under the leadership of the proletariat from the moment of its creation, that the hegemony of the proletariat and its Communist vanguard was a preliminary condition of its creation." Earlier he had noted, "it was thought that in the economically underdeveloped countries (in particular, the Latin American ones) the basic blow should be directed at the reformist national bourgeoisie."[12]

9. See chapter 5, pp. 112, 118–19.

10. Marshall D. Shulman, *Stalin's Foreign Policy Reappraised* (Harvard University Press, 1963). For a summary of the position, see pp. 80–103, 257–59.

11. E. M. Zhukov and V. V. Balabushevich in "O kharaktere i osobennostiiakh narodnoi demokratii v stranakh Vostoka," *Izvestiia Akademii Nauk SSSR, Seriia istorii i filosofii*, no. 1 (January–February 1952), pp. 81, 84–85. The opposing position is also argued on pp. 84–85.

12. G. B. Starushenko, *Natsiia i gosudarstvo v osvobozhdaiushchikhsia stranakh* (Moscow: Mezhdunarodnye otnosheniia, 1967), pp. 200–02.

Similar caution must be exercised in interpreting an early 1950s change of doctrine asserting that the transition to socialism in Asia would have a different character than in Europe. The most official of the Soviet scholars of the time, Evgenii Zhukov, emphasized that "people's democracy" in the Orient would be unlike that in Eastern Europe: it "does not have as a near-term task the building of socialism and, consequently, does not perform the functions of the dictatorship of the proletariat. . . . Overcoming the general economic and cultural backwardness that is the inevitable consequence of the past colonial yoke requires a long time." Zhukov acknowledged that "elements of capitalism . . . exist and perhaps will grow for a certain period (in China, for example)."[13] Yet, these statements referred to the speed of social transformation and especially to a Soviet decision not to read China out of the socialist movement because of its deviation from the Eastern European path in its treatment of the bourgeoisie. It involved no retreat from the principle that a communist party loyal to Moscow must be in charge in a people's democracy.

## The Many Roads to Socialism and the National Bourgeoisie

The first fundamental change in Soviet third world policy after Stalin's death concerned foreign policy rather than revolutionary strategy. In August 1953 Premier Georgii Malenkov spoke warmly of Jawaharlal Nehru's foreign policy, and by mid-1955 party leader Nikita Khrushchev was courting the neutral governments of Asia vigorously. The local communists must have found it embarrassing that Soviet leaders embraced men whom they too had previously denounced as lackeys of imperialism. What was to be their posture toward governments whose virtues were now being extolled by the Soviet leadership?

The Soviet response to this question was to abandon the position that the basic blow should be directed at the reformist bourgeoisie. Now there was a new strategic line: "the chief blow will be directed against the landlords, foreign imperialists, and the big bourgeoisie connected with them. . . . If the medium bourgeoisie supports the big bourgeoisie, then the people's movement will be directed against the medium bourgeoisie as well. Conditions may develop when part of the medium bourgeoisie go for

---

13. I. S. Braginsky in "O kharaktere i osobennostiiakh narodnoi demokratii v stranakh Vostoka," p. 86.

a certain period with the people, and, naturally, the relationship to it will then be different."[14]

In itself, this language was not radically different from that used in the late Stalinist period. However, the "bourgeoisie" of the type who were heading the Indian and Indonesian governments now were considered sufficiently antiimperialist to be going "for a certain period with the people," despite their continuing acceptance of foreign investment. Moreover, foreign communists were encouraged to cooperate with those forces that were antiimperialist—those who were against multinational corporations and additional foreign investment—even if the cooperation was not always in the form of front organizations under communist control. But the purpose of this activity was still "the establishment of the authority of the toilers under the leadership of the working class [that is, the Communist party]."[15] It was to be years before anyone publicly challenged the two-stage definition of a national liberation revolution.

Thus officially at least, the new revolutionary strategy entailed no change in goals. It rested on the assumption that anti-Western nationalism was still the strongest force in the third world and that it could provide the vehicle for a victory if only the communists demonstrated their dedication by cooperating with anyone who advocated anti-Western measures. While one may suspect that the new revolutionary strategy was simply a rationale for the new foreign policy, the reverse may be true. In areas such as the Middle East, continuing Soviet support for local communists and radical reforms seriously interfered with the promotion of governmental interests.

A second major change in Soviet revolutionary theory in 1956 was the declaration by Khrushchev at the Twentieth Party Congress that the forms of the transition to socialism will become all the more varied [and that] "it is not obligatory that these forms will always be connected with civil war."[16] As his associate, Anastas Mikoian, expressed it, "The means of seizing power cannot be identical in different countries, in different times, and in different internal settings. All depends on the concrete alignment of class forces, on the degree to which the working class is organized, and on the ability of the working class to attract allies, first of all, among the

14. A. Sobolev, "O parlamentskoi forme perekhoda k sotsializmu," *Kommunist*, no. 14 (September 1956), p. 27.

15. Ibid., pp. 26–27.

16. *XX s"ezd Kommunisticheskoi partii Sovetskogo Soiuza [14-25 fevralia 1956 goda]: Stenograficheskii otchet* (Moscow: Gospolizdat, 1956), vol. 1, pp. 39–40.

peasantry."[17] A full debate of the implications of this position was complicated by the unrest in Eastern Europe and in the Western European communist movement. In these circumstances Soviet theorists tended to emphasize the obstacles to the parliamentary route in the West, and the diversity of the roads to socialism was primarily discussed in the context of the third world. There it served to legitimize almost anything that third world communists wanted to do. The decreasing Soviet control over the communist movement that resulted from the Twentieth Party Congress and the growing Soviet-Chinese conflict made acknowledgment of such diversity politically wise in the third world in any case, and deviations in those countries had few dangerous ramifications for the more developed Eastern Europe.

Soviet scholars who wanted to discuss revolutionary strategy in the 1950s essentially had to do so in code, especially if they were opposing Khrushchev's line and implicitly were endorsing the Chinese pattern of revolution (and the Chinese criticism of Khrushchev). Doubts could be implied in reaffirmations of Lenin's attacks on the utopianism of the Russian populists or of the Chinese revolutionary leader, Sun Yat-sen.[18] Others made the same point somewhat more subtly by emphasizing the experience of Mongolia and the central Asian republics of the Soviet Union as models of development for the third world.[19] Those who supported Khrushchev often quietly failed to mention the role of the Communist party in the revolutionary process, while their opponents mentioned the communists and "the working class" as key elements.[20] (All the participants knew very well that radical regimes in, for example, Egypt and Iraq were abolishing communist parties.)

Probably the major way of discussing revolutionary strategy was to

17. Ibid., p. 314.

18. V. Martynovskaia, "K voprosu o russkom utopicheskom sotsializme 40-kh godov," *Voprosy ekonomiki,* no. 8 (August 1958), pp. 81–89.

19. For example, see V. Zhamin, "O perekhode k sotsializmu slaborazvitykh v ekonomicheskom otnoshenii stran," *Voprosy ekonomiki,* no. 6 (June 1959), pp. 59–66.

20. See the discussion in Oded Eran, *Mezhdunarodniki: An Assessment of Professional Expertise in the Making of Soviet Foreign Policy* (Ramat Gan, Israel: Turtledove, 1979), pp. 175–203. For an article that emphasizes the "working class" and its vanguard, see A. Iskenderov, "Rabochii klass i natsional'no-osvoboditel'nye revoliutsii," *Aziia i Afrika segodnia,* no. 5 (1962), pp. 6–8. See also V. Ia. Avarin, *Raspad kolonial'noi sistemy* (Moscow: Gospolitizdat, 1957), pp. 178, 182. For a discussion of the difficulty that the latter author had in getting his book published, see F. Burlatsky and S. Mezentsev, "Avtor i izdatel'stvo," *Kommunist,* no. 17 (November 1956), p. 89.

recast the description of the class support for third world governments and redefine classes. Thus although it was difficult to deny the possibility of cooperation with the national bourgeoisie, those bourgeoisie who were not national were a different matter.[21] Khrushchev's supporters spoke of the national bourgeoisie with enthusiasm and excluded from their definition only those persons whose economic interests were directly associated with foreign companies and imperialism.[22] In 1956 Aleksei Levkovsky defined the national bourgeoisie purely in terms of economic interests and included not only the petty bourgeoisie, the medium bourgeoisie, and the big bourgeoisie, but also "the monopoly bourgeoisie." Balabushevich agreed but argued that the definition should be widened to include the agricultural bourgeoisie as well—the comparatively well-off peasants.[23]

Those who were pessimistic about the progress of countries headed by the national bourgeoisie narrowed their definition of the group, retaining all the negative words to describe those whom they did not include in it. They contended that the number of bourgeoisie associated with the West was fairly large, especially when indirect associations were counted.[24] They also raised doubts about the revolutionary potential of the national bourgeoisie and emphasized its inclination to collaborate with the imperialists.[25]

The more traditional scholars also insisted that political role as well as economic interests be a factor in defining the national bourgeoisie.[26] In one extreme case this class was characterized as "only that part of the local bourgeoisie of colonial and dependent countries that stands for political and economic development of its country that is independent from

21. For an analysis of these differences, see Richard B. Remnek, *Soviet Scholars and Soviet Foreign Policy: A Case in Soviet Policy Toward India* (Durham: Carolina Academic Press, 1975), pp. 139–43.

22. See A. M. Rumiantsev, ed., *Sovremennoe osvoboditel'noe dvizhenie i natsional'naia burzhuaziia* (Prague: Mir i sotsialism, 1961), p. 335.

23. "Diskussiia ob ekonomicheskikh i politicheskikh pozitsiiakh natsional'noi burzhuazii v stranakh Vostoka," *Sovetskoe vostokovedenie*, no. 1 (1957), pp. 75, 183.

24. See the statements of G. I. Levinson and E. M. Komarov, ibid., pp. 176, 181; and E. M. Zhukov, "O nekotorykh voprosakh natsional'no-osvoboditel'nogo dvizheniia v stranakh Vostoka," in Iu. P. Frantsev, ed., *Stroitel'stvo kommunizma—delo millionov liudei truda* (Moscow: Izdatel'stvo VPSh i AON pri TsK KPSS, 1959), p. 353.

25. V. Li, "O nekapitalisticheskom puti razvitii," *Sovetskoe vostokovedenie*, no. 11 (1961), pp. 12–13.

26. A. Guber in "Diskussiia ob ekonomicheskikh i politicheskikh pozitsiiakh natsional'noi burzhuazii v stranakh Vostoka," p. 181.

imperialism."[27] Because toleration of foreign investment could denote a lack of such support, this definition comes very close to the old Stalinist formulation. Scholars could also make the point more directly, although often in more obscure places, by cautioning against any idealization of the national bourgeoisie and by reminding the reader that the interests of the workers and bourgeoisie were often in direct opposition.[28]

Critics of the Khrushchev position who referred to the Indian government and others like it as representatives only of the important bourgeoisie and the landlords or asserted that "as long as the bourgeoisie is in power, the agrarian question can be decided only in the interests of the landlord" scarcely considered the bourgeoisie as a likely ally for the communists for any significant time.[29] Indeed, one scholar who insisted that the Indian government was subordinated to the big bourgeoisie and the landlords later made the meaning of this analysis explicit: "Economic independence [should not be] the basic political slogan for the struggle of progressive elements in many underdeveloped countries. The basic slogan . . . should be a democratic solution of the agrarian question."[30] Obviously any such slogan required a far sharper attack on the existing government than the call for economic independence—that is, first of all, an attack on the multinational corporation.

The words used to describe and define other social strata could be just as revealing. In the early years almost everyone used the terms "workers" and "proletariat" to describe the urban employed, but in the 1970s, words such as "lumpen-proletariat," "marginal strata," and "declassed elements" were employed to denote skepticism about the revolutionary po-

27. A. A. Iskenderov in Rumiantsev, ed., *Sovremennoe osvoboditel'noe dvizhenie i natsional'naia burzhuaziia*, pp. 7–8. For a book review that points up the meaning of this definition in comparison with Rumiantsev, see V. I. Pavlov in *Narody Azii i Afriki*, no. 5 (1961), p. 221.

28. Zhukov, "O nekotorykh voprosakh natsional'no-osvoboditel'nogo dvizheniia v stranakh Vostoka," in Frantsev, ed., *Stroitel'stvo kommunizma*, pp. 352, 357.

29. A. A. Poliak in "Agrarnye reformy v stranakh zarubezhnogo Vostoka," *Problemy vostokovedeniia*, no. 4 (1959), p. 216.

30. G. Shmidt in "Kratkii obzor vystuplenii," *Mirovaia ekonomika i mezhdunarodnye otnosheniia*, no. 6 (June 1962), p. 105. (Hereafter *MEiMO*.) For his earlier statement about the class character of the Indian government, see "Diskussiia ob ekonomicheskikh i politicheskikh pozitsiiakh natsional'noi burzhuazii v stranakh Vostoka," *Sovetskoe vostokovedenie*, no. 1 (1957), p. 183.

tential of this class.[31] In the late 1950s and early 1960s those who wanted a large working class, and by implication excellent prospects for revolution, talked about "hired labor," and included everyone who worked for someone else. As the Soviet scholars pointed out, this could include people whom Western scholars talked about as rural overpopulation.[32] By adding all the different kinds of hired labor together, the optimists could come up with substantial figures: one estimated 25 percent of the population in Africa in the 1950s was proletarian and concluded that "this provides some idea of the quantity of the working class of the colonies."[33] Some spoke of the "rapid proletarization of the population," emphasizing the formation of the proletariat as a class.[34]

The more pessimistic scholars were highly skeptical about counting white collar employees, peasants engaged in part-time city work, and agricultural hired hands as part of the working class. In 1960 the director of the Institute of Africa put the figure of full-time African industrial workers who had broken ties with the village at only 2 or 3 percent of the population, and he cautioned that even they were only first or second generation workers.[35] Two scholars doing seminal work on third world class structure were even more restrictive: "as V. I. Lenin noted, only important machine industry creates a contemporary proletariat as a 'special class of the population.'" They added that the various ideas on class structure "do not, in our opinion, have only academic interest."[36] Scholars who wanted to emphasize the possibility of revolution usually spoke of the working class in united terms. Their opponents broke away from such analyses and began to write about ethnic divisions among the workers: most Burmese workers came from India, over one-third of Malay workers

31. For a survey of different Soviet analyses of the working class, see A. M. Razinkina, "Problemy formirovaniia rabochego klassa afro-aziatskikh stran v sovetskoi literatury 20–70 kh godov," Narody Azii i Afriki, no. 1 (1983), pp. 162–69.

32. M. A. Maksimov and V. G. Rastiannikov, "Nekotorye osobennosti formirovaniia i ekspluatatsii sel'skokhoziaistvennogo proletariata v kolonial'noi Indii," Sovetskoe vostokovedenie, no. 6 (1956), p. 42.

33. M. I. Braginsky, "O polozhenii rabochego klassa i profsoiuznom dvizhenii v kolonial'nykh stranakh Afriki (obzor)," Problemy vostokovedeniia, no. 5 (1959), pp. 104–05.

34. V. Kiselev, "Rabochii klass i natsional'no-osvoboditel'nye revoliutsii," MEiMO, no. 10 (October 1963), pp. 94–95.

35. I. I. Potekhin, "Kharakternye cherty raspada kolonial'noi sistemy imperializma v Afrike," MEiMO, no. 1 (January 1960), p. 117.

36. L. A. Gordon and L. A. Fridman, "Osobennosti sostava i struktury rabochego klassa v ekonomicheski slaborazvitykh stranakh Azii i Afriki (na primere Indii i OAR)," Narody Azii i Afriki, no. 2 (1963), pp. 6, 18.

were from China and another third were from India, and so forth. Such analyses always implied difficulties in organizing united class action, but sometimes the point was made explicitly.[37] A scholar who wanted to imply the good prospects for revolution in Malaya, by contrast, wrote that the workers came from inside the country.[38]

When Soviet scholars talked about the peasants, no one had any need to exaggerate the numbers; obviously a great many people lived on the land. The question was, what kind of people were they? Those who saw the countryside as revolutionary emphasized the continued existence of land-lords, the meaningless character of land reform, and a united, dissatisfied peasantry. Rostislav Ul'ianovsky, then deputy director of the Institute of Oriental Studies, spoke of "the toiling peasants," of "the basic mass of the rural population" who have no possibility of acquiring property.[39] Scholars who insisted that African peasants were still at the communal-tribal stage of development and were therefore "not infected with private property moods" were advancing a similar position.[40]

Those who doubted the revolutionary potential in the countryside wrote about the development of capitalist relations there. Georgii Kim, a leading scholar of the Institute of Oriental Studies, was typical in arguing that agrarian reforms "are leading to a certain limitation of feudal-landlord agriculture and to a gradual transformation of it into capitalist agriculture and to a strengthening of the kulaks [rich peasants] and an increased differentiation of the peasants." He also noted that "the withdrawal from the democratic movement of the well-to-do and, in part, the medium peasantry who received land as a result of the reforms led to a split and, consequently, to a significant weakening of the front of the all-peasant struggle."[41]

37. A. S. Kaufman, *Rabochii klass i natsional'no-osvoboditel'noe dvizhenie v Birme* (Moscow: Izdatel'stvo vostochnoi literatury, 1961); and I. Latysheva's review of V. A. Zherebilov, *Rabochii klass Malaii* (Moscow: Izdatel'stvo vostochnoi literatury, 1962) in *Narody Azii i Afriki*, no. 4 (1964), pp. 230–31. The review of Kaufman's book also argued that the negative consequences of ethnic division should be emphasized more; see *Narody Azii i Afriki*, no. 6 (1961), p. 171.

38. A. A. Iskenderov, "Issledovaniia sovetskikh uchenykh o rabochem klasse Azii i Afriki," *Narody Azii i Afriki*, no. 3 (1963), p. 111.

39. "Agrarnye reformy v stranakh Blizhnego i Srednego Vostoka, Indii i iugo-vostochnoi Azii," *Narody Azii i Afriki*, no. 2 (1961), pp. 16, 18.

40. R. Avakov and L. Stepanov, "Sotsial'nye problemy natsional'no-osvoboditel'noi revoliutsii," *MEiMO*, no. 5 (May 1963), p. 50.

41. "Soiuz rabochego klassa i krest'ianstva v natsional'no-osvoboditel'nykh revoliut-siiakh," *Narody Azii i Afriki*, no. 5 (1962), pp. 7–8.

This difference in characterization of the peasantry broke into open debate with the publication in 1967 of an important collective book by IMEMO on classes and class struggle in developing countries. It described the peasants as "nonproletarian and semiproletarian working poor," who have "only one prospect under capitalism—the prospect of pauperization." The authors asserted that the peasants were not petty bourgeois, even in societies with a medium level of development of industrial capitalism (for instance, in Latin America). This conclusion reflected not only a judgment about landholding but also about the impossibility of the development of "a soul of a small owner." In an independent article, Viktor Tiagunenko, the leading IMEMO specialist on the third world, also spoke of the "working [*trudovoe*] peasantry" and contended that their ideology was different from that of the petty bourgeoisie.[42]

This analysis was explicitly challenged in a long article-review by Iurii Aleksandrov and Nodari Simoniia of the Institute of Oriental Studies. They insisted that the peasants were petty bourgeoisie, and emphasized that they constituted "a new class, organically connected with the rise and development of capitalist society." They thought that a bourgeois evolution of the rural system was taking place but said that the concept had a broader meaning than ownership alone. "The concept embraces a complex of socioeconomic, political, and social-psychological factors that . . . turn [the peasant] into an unconscious supporter of arrangements that give rise to capitalism." An understanding of this, they contended, was crucial for "a correct evaluation of prospects for the development of the political situation."[43]

## The Noncapitalist Path of Development and Socialist Orientation

During the 1950s the arguments over revolutionary strategy had one thing in common: an acceptance of the proposition that the eventual transition to socialism would have to be under the leadership of the Communist party. After all, at the Twentieth Party Congress, Khrushchev had insisted

42. See IMEMO, *Klassy i klassovaia bor'ba v razvivaiushchikhsia stranakh* (Moscow: 1967), vol. 1, pp. 42, 43; and vol. 2, pp. 192, 193; and V. Tiagunenko, "Oktiabr' i sovremennaia natsional'no-osvoboditel'naia revoliutsiia," *MEiMO*, no. 1 (January 1967), p. 10.

43. "Po povodu monografii 'Klassy i klassovaia bor'ba v razvivaiushchikhsia stranakh'," *Narody Azii i Afriki*, no. 1 (1969), pp. 46, 49.

that "in all forms of transition to socialism, the absolute and decisive condition is the political leadership of the working class, headed by its vanguard. The transition to socialism is impossible without it."[44]

Then to the Soviets' surprise, bourgeois nationalist Fidel Castro adopted increasingly radical measures and soon called himself a Marxist-Leninist.[45] Algeria, Ghana, Guinea, and Mali adopted more radical programs than older independent countries; and Burma, Egypt, and Indonesia moved to the left. These cases demonstrated that there were more paths to socialism than had been imagined in 1956, and the Soviet Union had to decide whether such diversity was the wave of the future. It also had to decide how to explain what theory had said would be impossible.

In November 1960 the first official discussion of these radical developments declared the possibility of "the state of national democracy" and "the noncapitalist path of development." The state of national democracy was a nonsocialist state that conducted a policy of social transformation at home and a basically pro-Soviet foreign policy. This concept did not cause major theoretical problems, for even a conservative Marxist might find it reasonable to say that in countries without a strong feudal, capitalist, or working class a coalition of progressive or perhaps "intermediate" forces might be able to seize power and—at least for a short time—take left-wing measures while the fate of the country was being decided.

The noncapitalist path of development caused more difficulties. The basic problem, of course, was that Marx had already described a noncapitalist path—the socialist one. At the end of the Stalinist period the phrase had been used to describe the slower path to socialism taken by the Asian people's democracies. The noncapitalist path of development was defined as this slower path—"the path of development to socialism by a special route, the route of permitting capitalism as a subsector."[46] Nevertheless, it was an unequivocal path to socialism; for instance, it was asserted that capitalistic elements would never turn China back onto the path of capitalism.[47]

---

44. *XX s "ezd Kommunisticheskoi partii Sovetskogo Soiuza,* vol.1, p. 40.

45. For events in Cuba, see the memoirs of the first Soviet ambassador there: A. I. Alekseev, "Kuba posle pobedy revoliutsii," *Latinskaia Amerika,* no. 5 (1984), pp. 111, 119.

46. Braginsky in "O kharaktere i osobennostiiakh narodnoi demokratii v stranakh Vostoka," p. 85.

47. E. M. Zhukov, ibid., p. 86.

A number of scholars in the 1960s still insisted that the socialist and noncapitalist paths were identical,[48] but this created difficulties. The leaders of the new radical countries were denying that they were on the Soviet path. And to insist on the identity of the two might commit the Soviet Union to apply the socialist label to regimes that deviated too much, to intervene militarily if the revolution were overthrown, or to define the category so narrowly that it did not solve the problem of classifying the new regimes.

If the noncapitalist path were defined as a separate path, neither fully capitalist nor socialist, another problem arose. Virtually all the radicals were proclaiming that their revolution was a third path, an African form of socialism, or the like. To condone this would also be to legitimize third paths or national forms of socialism for Eastern Europe, precisely what the revisionists in Hungary, Poland, and Yugoslavia were demanding. Such a definition also raised more general questions. As one critic charged, any assertion that the noncapitalist path was "an independent path, still not socialist, but already not capitalist, that is, some golden mean between capitalism and socialism, must be recognized as . . . contradicting the Marxist dialectic."[49]

Most scholars with official connections and with a sense of the various political land mines treated noncapitalist development as "transitional."[50] This solved some political problems, but it left a nasty question unanswered. If it was transitional from feudalism to either capitalism or socialism, then evolution from it to capitalism was progressive, even if not the most progressive of the two alternatives. Yet no one wanted to say that, and the overthrow of radical regimes in Mali and Ghana in 1965 and 1966, respectively, was, in fact, treated as a big step backwards. If noncapitalist development were transitional to socialism, however, one was back with the original dilemmas of identifying it as a socialist path, although a nontraditional one. In the words of one critic, "not proletarian and not petty bourgeois, but 'transitional.' That is not an answer, but a retreat from

48. A. K. Bochagov, "O teoreticheskikh osnovakh nekapitalisticheskogo puti razvitiia," *Narody Azii i Afriki,* no. 4 (1966), pp. 59–66.

49. Iu. G. Sumbatian in "O nekapitalisticheskom puti razvitiia (obzor materialov, postupivshikh v redaktsiiu)," *Narody Azii i Afriki,* no. 2 (1969), p. 57.

50. A. Sobolev, "Natsional'naia demokratia—put' k sotsial'nomu progressu," *Problemy mira i sotsializma,* no. 2 (1963), pp. 43–45; and V. Tiagunenko, "Aktual'nye voprosy nekapitalisticheskogo puti razvitiia," *MEiMO,* no. 10 (October 1964), pp. 14–15, 22, and no. 11 (November 1964), p. 25.

an answer, for, in reality, the question is not whether they are transitional or nontransitional, but what kind of transition they are undergoing."[51]

In practice, recognition of noncapitalist development was a way of acknowledging that some third world regimes were following a more radical policy than others—even relatively progressive ones such as India—but that they still were not communist by the traditional definition. Noncapitalist development was a tentative movement in the socialist direction, but unlike the definition in the Stalin era, it was reversible. Precise definitions of this path remained a subject of debate, but they always included an emphasis on the state sector of the economy, thoroughgoing agrarian reform, limitations on foreign investment, and a pro-Soviet foreign policy.

Because the very phrase "noncapitalist development" inevitably led to problems, it tended to be replaced in the second half of the 1960s and in the 1970s by the phrase "socialist orientation," especially by scholars of the Institute of Africa.[52] The phrase "state of national democracy" was increasingly replaced by the phrase "revolutionary democracy."[53] These concepts had much the same meanings as their predecessors and hence basically the same ambiguities and contradictions. However, "socialist orientation" was at least a static phrase and did not automatically raise the question of "development to what?" "Revolutionary democracy" was a phrase that Lenin had used for regimes such as Sun Yat-Sen's and implicitly was more cautious.

The primary questions about political development and revolutionary

51. N. A. Simoniia, "Po povodu monografii 'Klassy i klassovaia bor'ba v razvivaiush-chikhsia stranakh' (tom III)," *Narody Azii i Afriki*, no. 3 (1969), p. 53.

52. So far as can be judged, Gleb Starushenko originated this concept: "Many Africans do not accept the term 'noncapitalist path' in view of the fact that it is only a negative formula ('noncapitalist') and does not contain any indication that socialism is a positive final goal of the struggle. I think that the term 'countries of socialist orientation' is more appropriate to characterize countries that are developing along the noncapitalist path." See "Sotsial'nye sily i perspektivy 'tret'ego mira,'" *MEiMO*, no. 8 (August 1968), p. 89.

53. Karen Brutents popularized "revolutionary democracy"; see "O revoliutsionnoi demokratii," *MEiMO*, no. 3 (March 1968), pp. 15–28, and no. 4 (April 1968), pp. 24–35, but it was previously used in pessimistic ways; see Avakov and Stepanov, "Sotsial'nye problemy natsial'no-osvoboditel'nykh revoliutsii," pp. 52–53. "National democracy" seems to have been developed by Rostislav Ul'ianovsky. For a quietly testy article that a decade and a half later still championed this concept over the diffuse "revolutionary democracy" and that radicalized the definition of the latter, see R. A. Ul'ianovsky, "O natsional'noi i revolutsionnoi demokratii: puti evoliutsii," *Narody Azii i Afriki*, no. 2 (1984), esp. pp. 9, 12–13.

strategy in the 1960s concerned the likelihood of a real transition to socialism in the third world and particularly the likelihood of such a transition
under noncommunist intellectuals like Castro or army officers like Nasser
in Egypt and Ne Win in Burma. Implicitly, the questions concerned the
price that the Soviet Union should be willing to pay and the risks it should
be willing to run to support revolution abroad.

On these questions, three major lines of analysis or models gradually
emerged. The first suggested that the Cuban path of revolution was the
natural product of the historical dynamics of the time and would be repeated. This line attracted those with revolutionary optimism. Associated
first with Viktor Tiagunenko and Georgii Mirsky, third world theorists at
IMEMO, and Rostislav Ul'ianovsky, deputy director of the Institute of
Oriental Studies and then deputy head of the international department of
the Central Committee, it implied that the Soviet Union should bet on this
possibility.[54]

When the concept of a noncapitalist path of development was first
proposed, the outcome of the Cuban Revolution was not clear, and little
had happened in Egypt and nothing in Burma. Most of the leading theorists were cautious. Viktor Tiagunenko, for example, argued in early 1962
that some of the policies of Ghana, Guinea, and Mali were "not capitalist
measures," but he still defined the situation as only "the creation of conditions for a transition to a noncapitalist path of development."[55]

Soon, however, scholars associated with the first model were beginning
to speak of the radical regimes as already on a noncapitalist path. Georgii
Mirsky in particular was very optimistic about the future of the United
Arab Republic under Nasser, and he contended that in our epoch the
national liberation revolution "does not stop with bourgeois democratic
transformations."[56] Ul'ianovsky spoke about the "anticapitalist state sec-

---

54. Tiagunenko was head of IMEMO's department on political and social development
of the third world. When he died, he was eulogized as "one of the first in Soviet science to
begin to work out the theoretical bases of the conception of the noncapitalist path of
development. . . . He raised the question about the possibility and conditions of the growing
over of the national liberation revolution into the socialist [and] was the first to work out the
difference between the contemporary national liberation revolution and the bourgeois democratic revolution of the past." See G. I. Mirsky and V. V. Rymalov, "Pamiati V. L.
Tiagunenko," *Narody Azii i Afriki*, no. 5 (1975), p. 247.

55. "Tendentsii obshchestvennogo razvitiia osvobodivshikhsia stran v sovremennuiu
epokhu," *MEiMO*, no. 3 (March 1962), p. 32.

56. G. Mirsky and T. Pokataeva, "Klassy i klassovaia bor'ba v razvivaiushchikhsia stranakh (stat'ia vtoraia), *MEiMO*, no. 3 (March 1966), p. 57. Mirsky's optimism

tor" in these radical countries, while Tiagunenko referred to the "interlacing of the tasks of the national liberation revolutions with the tasks of the socialist revolutions" and to the national liberation movement as "a component part of the world socialist revolution."[57]

The logic of the position was straightforward. Scholars assumed that nationalism had produced political independence from colonial rule in the third world, and, as a dominant force, would not tolerate the kind of economic dependence or slow economic growth that seemed inherent in third world capitalist development. As third world leaders tried to reduce their dependence, as they tried to encourage rapid industrialization, they would, the authors of this model insisted, run into resistance from the West or from their own businessmen. The West would react strongly to any nationalization or strong economic controls, perhaps even trying to destabilize the country. Local businessmen would begin sending money abroad, thereby creating investment or balance of payments crises or both. In this respect, Castro's step-by-step movement to the left was taken as inevitable for any regime that would be strongly nationalistic, and the analogous set of steps by Nasser seemed to be confirmation.

Because this first model saw nationalism rather than class as the driving force of revolution, there was no reason to suppose that a communist party and workers had to lead it. Instead, intellectuals and urban white collar employees were seen as more likely—and certainly better placed—representatives of nationalism. Georgii Mirsky, however, emphasized the army as an instrument of transformation:

The army is the most contemporary institution of society. . . . By its very nature the army is connected with the foreign world. . . . The element of competition, of equality with the outside world is organically inherent to the army. . . . No one feels the backwardness of the state like an officer. . . . The recognition of the backwardness of his country contributes to the rise of nationalistic, patriotic feel-

---

was forcefully expressed in his "Tvorcheskii marksizm i problemy natsional'no-osvoboditel'nykh revoliutsii," *MEiMO*, no. 2 (February 1963), pp. 63–68. Two associates at IMEMO who knew him well criticized him for exaggerating the significance of the reforms in the United Arab Republic; see R. Avakov and L. Stepanov, "Sotsial'nye problemy natsional'no-osvoboditel'noi revoliutsii," pp. 50–51.

57. R. Ul'ianovsky, "Diskussii: sotsializm, kapitalizm, slaborazvitye strany," *MEiMO*, no. 4 (April 1964), pp. 119–20; and V. L. Tiagunenko, *Problemy sovremennykh natsional'no-osvoboditel'nykh revoliutsii* (Moscow: Nauka, 1969), pp. 15–17. That Tiagunenko's statement was not simply pro forma propaganda was indicated in the attacks by other leading scholars who thought that he was exaggerating the revolutionary potential of the third world.

ings, and induces him to struggle for the liquidation of foreign control, for a renewal of the socioeconomic structure of society—in the final analysis for its reconstruction.[58]

The second model for third world development was a continuation of the old argument that the bourgeoisie was inherently counterrevolutionary and that the Soviet Union should support local communist parties against them. Advocates of this model spoke in class rather than nationalist terms. For example, in 1963 Vladimir Kiselev condemned Mirsky for examining national liberation revolutions "in isolation from the mutual relations of classes, from the class nature of power and the state." In Kiselev's view, "the two basic classes of the bourgeois society—the proletariat and the local national bourgeoisie—have already formed or are forming in the majority of countries of Asia and Africa." Kiselev went on to argue that politics inevitably also corresponded to this class dichotomy. "The anti-people's tendencies in the policy of the national bourgeoisie are continuously being strengthened [and] . . . two basic tendencies in the national liberation movement [are emerging]: the proletariat, democratic, and the bourgeois, antidemocratic." The petty-bourgeois nationalists fared no better than the bourgeoisie in this analysis. Indeed, the former "reflect, first of all, the class interests of the bourgeoisie and often—this particularly manifested itself in the events in Iraq in the beginning of 1963—come out as an active force in the struggle against the toilers."[59]

This last sentence got Kiselev to the nub of the matter. Iraqi officials who basically fit Mirsky's model had vigorously suppressed the local communists; proponents of the second model were outraged and contemptuous of proponents of the first model for expecting anything different. Supporters of the second model sometimes professed optimism about the chance of a socialist revolution led by communists, however. Kiselev spoke of "the quick proletarization of the population" and asserted that "the young working class is the most important political force in the national liberation movement." He went on to say that the "proletariat of the colonies, despite its youth, is called upon to play the decisive role in the struggle against imperialism and domestic reaction."[60] In general, however, the number of those in the Khrushchev era who were pessimistic

58. *Armiia i politika v stranakh Azii i Afriki* (Moscow: Nauka, 1970), pp. 9–10. Virtually the same words are found in an earlier article; see Mirsky and Pokataeva, "Klassy i klassovaia bor'ba v razvivaiushchikhsia stranakh," pp. 65–67.

59. "Rabochii klass i natsional'no-osvoboditel'nye revoliutsii," pp. 94, 96–97.

60. Ibid., pp. 94, 95.

about the repetition of the Castro path but optimistic about a classic communist victory seems to have been relatively small. The proponents of the second model more frequently were aging and petulant defenders of old truths who were unwilling to think seriously about revolutionary prospects.

The third model for development was the major rival of the first. If the first model was associated with the foremost scholars at the Institute of World Economics and International Relations (IMEMO), the third was developed by the top scholars at the Institute of Oriental Studies. The most outspoken and polemical theorist in developing the model was Nodari Simoniia, head of a section and then of a department at the institute. Like the second model, the third also began with doubts about the revolutionary potential of the bourgeoisie, but it also doubted the chance for a socialist revolution.[61]

The essence of the first two models had been the argument that the force of nationalism, together with the inevitability of slow and dependent development under capitalism, meant that the national liberation movement had two phases, the second being a socialist one. As chapter 4 showed, Simoniia denied that capitalist development was inevitably deformed and dependent. Moreover, he argued that third world nationalism was far more ambivalent than the proponents of the first two models implied, that third world boundaries were irrational from an ethnic point of view, and that many people identified primarily with the tribe or other ethnic subunit rather than the nation as defined by geographical boundaries. As a result, he argued,

The national-colonial question has two aspects—the internal and external. Prior to the achievement of political independence, the external aspect—that is, the struggle for political, state sovereignty—subordinates the internal to itself and muffles its impact. . . . The struggle against colonialism was a factor that unified all the political forces within the existing territorial boundaries. . . . The achievement of political independence began swiftly to advance the internal national aspect of the problem to the forefront.[62]

61. Because of the similarity between the second and third models, it was not always easy to judge whether an author skeptical about the bourgeoisie as a revolutionary force was optimistic about a communist victory or pessimistic about revolution in general. Although there has been a tendency for Western scholars to think that the Institute of Oriental Studies adhered strongly to the second model, the major scholars were really developing the third one. See Eran, *Mezhdunarodniki*, pp. 165–214.

62. "Natsionalizm i politicheskaia bor'ba v osvobodivshikhsia stranakh (stat'ia I)," *MEiMO*, no. 1 (January 1972), p. 94.

Although the national liberation movement could grow into a socialist one, Simoniia saw that growth as a separate revolution rather than an "uncompleted revolution."[63] And that second, socialist revolution seemed an unlikely outcome, at least in those countries that had begun to industrialize seriously (in Soviet jargon, those that had started on the capitalist path).

The real issue was the typicality of the Russian Revolution. Those who saw a strong possibility that the capitalist revolution could "grow over" into the socialist had the Russian model in mind. For Simoniia, however, the situation in Asian and African countries was very different. He became increasingly open in his argument that the Russian Revolution was the product of specific historical circumstances, although in the process he aroused the strong opposition of conservative theorists.[64]

While scholars such as Tiagunenko and Mirsky thought that nationalism and economic dependence made third world bourgeois revolutions fundamentally different from their counterparts in Western Europe in the eighteenth and nineteenth centuries, Simoniia emphasized the similarities and denied that the former should be considered revolutions of a new type.[65] The corollary of this argument, at first not spoken too loudly, was that the third world political development would resemble that of Western Europe. Just as it would take at least two centuries before Western Europe could experience socialist revolutions, so it clearly would take decades at a minimum before third world countries could reach the economic level of Western Europe in the 1970s and could move beyond the level of support for communist parties found in Western Europe.

Another scholar, Vladimir Khoros, used a different analogy to describe radical revolutions in the third world. For Khoros, the regimes that were considered to be on the noncapitalist path (including Algeria and Burma), as well as a number that had not been so considered, were not part of the national liberation movement with a socialist phase but were really popu-

---

63. "O kharaktere natsional'no-osvoboditel'nykh revoliutsii," *Narody Azii i Afriki,* no. 6 (1966), pp. 16–17.

64. For Simoniia's arguments, see "Leninskaia ideia revoliutsionno-demokraticheskoi diktatury i nekapitalisticheskaia put' razvitiia," *Narody Azii i Afriki,* no. 2 (1968), pp. 6, 11, and *Strany Vostoka: puti razvitiia* (Moscow: Nauka, 1975).

For reactions from conservative theorists, see R. A. Ul'ianovsky, "O nekotorykh voprosakh marksistsko-leninskoi teorii revoliutsionnogo protsessa," *Novaia i noveishaia istoriia,* no. 4 (1976), pp. 61–87; and A. L. Borisov and N. B. Aleksandrov, "Obsuzhdenie knigi N. A. Simoniia, *Strany Vostoka: puti razvitiia,*" *Narody Azii i Afriki,* no. 3 (1977), pp. 54–65.

65. "O kharaktere natsional'no-osvoboditel'nykh revoliutsii," pp. 3–7, 13.

list. Their members were comparable to the nineteenth century Russian Narodniks whose protest against capitalism contained strong traditional elements. By choosing this label, Khoros was, of course, saying that these regimes were scarcely likely to evolve toward scientific socialism.[66]

Simoniia's treatment of the national liberation revolution as one limited to the achievement of political independence became increasingly widespread in the late 1970s and in the 1980s. Sometimes this was reflected simply in a tendency not to use "national liberation" in a contemporary noncolonial setting. Sometimes it reflected an effort to develop new schemes of analysis. Thus A. I. Sobolev, one of the older theorists, wrote of three stages of revolution—the national liberation, the national democratic (radical, but not yet socialist), and the socialist (into which the national democratic could grow over).[67]

## The Vanguard Party

With the overthrow of Ben Bella in Algeria, Kwame Nkrumah in Ghana, Modibo Keita in Mali, and Sukarno in Indonesia, as well as disappointments in Syria and Iraq, much of the optimism about an early repetition of Castro's evolution to socialism faded. Left-wing military revolutions in Peru, Sudan, and Dahomey in the 1960s and the early success of Salvador Allende kept the hopes alive, but the failure of three of these four and Egypt's shift to the right in the second half of the 1960s had a further dampening effect.

Those who remained optimistic about third world revolutionary prospects turned partly back toward Stalinist perceptions about revolution, with a merger of the first and second models. Communist parties still remained too weak in nearly all third world countries for any serious thought of their leading a revolution, although a revolution led by other

---

66. "Populizm ili narodnichestvo," *Aziia i Afrika segodnia*, no. 8 (August 1977), pp. 30–33; "O populistskikh techeniiakh v razvivaiushchikhsia stranakh," *Voprosy filosofii*, no. 1 (August 1978), pp. 108–20; "Politika i traditsiia v razvivaiushchikhsia stranakh," *Aziia i Afrika segodnia*, no. 1 (January 1981), pp. 28–31.

67. "Rol' proletariata osvobodivshikhsia stran v sotsial'nom progresse obshchestva" in G. Kim, ed., *Rabochee dvizhenie v razvivaiushchikhsia stranakh* (Moscow: Nauka, 1977), pp. 33–42. This view was supported in S. Agaev and I. Tatarovskaia, "Puti i etapy revoliutsionnogo protsessa v stranakh Azii i Afriki," *Aziia i Afrika segodnia*, no. 7 (July 1978), pp. 28–31.

forces, including the army, was still possible. Thus the optimists began to emphasize the need for an equivalent to the Communist party, "a political organization of a socialist vanguard"—which, if it could not lead the revolution, would follow soon after.[68] In a 1967 discussion, Viktor Tiagunenko summarized this new approach: "capitalism develops spontaneously. Movement on the noncapitalist path demands conscious and goal-directed action by the toilers. But for this, it is indispensable to have a political organization, united in its aspirations and capable of mobilizing the masses in the construction of a new society."[69]

No doubt in response to Soviet urging and in an effort to obtain Soviet financial aid, an increasing number of radical regimes organized "vanguard parties" in the mid-1970s, often at least partially on the Soviet model. This was particularly true of regimes in countries emerging from the Portuguese Empire. These parties frequently expressed adherence to the principles of "scientific socialism," and some called themselves Marxist-Leninist. A number labeled themselves "people's democracies," the phrase that had been applied to the East European regimes. But did this development represent more than a change in rhetoric? Had a new generation of leaders emerged in Africa who were more dedicated to socialist evolution and who were adopting techniques of rule that would prove more successful in achieving it? Or were they simply adopting new language in order to obtain aid from a Soviet Union that was beginning to wonder whether its previous expenditures were paying off?[70]

Views on this subject varied widely. Probably the most optimistic opinion, at least in the mid-1970s, was that of Petr Manchkha, then head of the African section of the Central Committee's international department. "The countries of socialist orientation," he said "are approximately at the

68. Mirsky and Pokataeva, "Klassy i klassovaia bor'ba v razvivaiushchikhsia stranakh," p. 59.

69. "Iubileinoe zasedanie Uchenogo soveta IMEMO, posviashchennoe 50-letiiu velikoi oktiabr'skoi sotsialisticheskoi revoliutsii,"*MEiMO,* no. 1 (January 1968), p. 133.

70. One of the documents captured during the U.S. invasion of Grenada was a report home from the Grenadan ambassador in Moscow, dated July 11, 1983. He noted that the Soviets said that Grenada was at the "national democratic, anti-imperialist stage of socialist orientation" and that "the USSR assigns a special place to these types of countries in its foreign policy." The ambassador then cautioned the Grenadan leaders that "therefore, whatever [our] internal debate, it is important that we continue to maintain our public assessment of our stage of development as the national democratic, anti-imperialist stage of socialist orientation." See Paul Seabury and Walter A. McDougall, eds., *The Grenada Papers* (ICS Press, 1984), p. 199.

beginning of a path similar to that which the peoples of the Khorezm and Bukhara People's Soviet Republic took [in Soviet central Asia immediately after the Bolshevik Revolution]. As is well known, Khorezm and Bukhara in a comparatively short time—the period of one generation—moved from being patriarchal and medieval societies to socialism, bypassing the stage of capitalism." Manchkha included Zambia, Uganda, and Sierra Leone as countries undertaking "important socioeconomic transformations based on socialist principles," although they still were not countries with full socialist orientations.[71]

Similarly, Vladimir Li, a long-time enthusiast of people's democracy as the only correct path for third world development, proclaimed that the 1970s were such a step forward from the 1950s and 1960s that there was no comparison; people's democracy had become "the chief political weapon in the struggle for the conduct of revolutionary transformation."[72] Georgii Mirsky, who had become pessimistic about the old type of socialist-orientation country, had a very different view about the new type. In a 1978 discussion in which he was strongly opposed by Simoniia and moderately by Aleksei Kiva, deputy editor of the journal *Asia and Africa Today,* Mirsky said, "States such as Angola, Mozambique, and Democratic Yemen, and in the future Ethiopia . . . have a tendency, with the aid and support of the socialist world, to approach the Vietnamese, or perhaps more probably, the Laotian variant of development in the future."[73] Three years later he still wrote of Ethiopia, Angola, and Mozambique as having "not simply an orientation toward socialism but the beginning of socialist development."[74]

Obviously those who saw real revolutionary potential in the countries with vanguard parties tended to speak of those parties in favorable terms. Veniamin Chirkin, a specialist on the third world political system, emphasized the similarities between the new revolutionary parties and orthodox

71. *V avangarde revoliutsionno-osvoboditel'noi bor'by v Afrike* (Moscow: Politizdat, 1975), pp. 46, 16.

72. "Sotsial'nye revoliutsii v afro-aziatskikh stranakh i nauchnyi sotsializm," pt. 1, *Aziia i Afrika segodnia,* no. 2 (February 1981), p. 8; and pt. 2, no. 3 (March 1981), p. 2. Also see note 3.

73. "Natsional'no-osvoboditel'noe dvizhenie: nekotorye voprosy differentsiatsii," *Aziia i Afrika segodnia,* no. 6 (June 1978), p. 31. By 1984 Kiva had become more pessimistic; see "Problemy razvitiia stran sotsialisticheskoi orientatsii," *Mezhdunarodnaia zhizn',* no. 11 (November 1984), pp. 38–46.

74. K. Maidanik and G. Mirsky, "Natsional'no osvoboditel'naia bor'ba: sovremennyi etap," *MEiMO,* no. 6 (June 1981), p. 26.

communist parties, while Nikolai Kosukhin, head of the section of ideology and political organizations of the Institute of Africa, suggested that the organizations of the left wing of the new revolutionary democratic regimes were taking on the functions of Marxist-Leninist parties.[75] The choice of Chirkin and Kosukhin to write the most sensitive political chapters of a major collective work from the Institute of Africa in effect identified the institute with their position. As a review noted, they asserted that "there is a qualitatively new stage in the development of the national democratic revolution. The contents of this stage are not examined, but obviously they have in mind the process of a growing of the national democratic revolution into a people's democratic one—that is, a revolution in the course of which the national (antiimperialist) and democratic (antitribal and antifeudal) tasks are decided under the leadership of the working class and its Marxist-Leninist vanguard."[76]

Other scholars have been much more cautious about the prospects of the new stage. The reviewers of the book called its arguments insufficiently convincing, while another scholar disagreed with Kosukhin's characterization of the political organization of left-wing revolutionary democracy.[77] Kiva agreed with Mirsky "that the development of countries that [Mirsky] refers to as 'the Angolan-Mozambique' type . . . is essentially different from the evolution of states that went on the path of social progress in the 1960s," but still, "like Nodari Aleksandrovich [Simoniia]," Kiva doubted "that the concept 'people's democratic revolution' should be applied [to them] in an unqualified manner."[78]

The most outspoken pessimists about the African states with a vanguard party were, as had been the case in the 1960s, leading theorists of the Institute of Oriental Studies. Such scholars as Simoniia continued to present their former views with respect to the new phenomena. When Mirsky referred to "the difference in principle between countries that are,

75. V. Chirkin, "Strany sotsialisticheskoi orientatsii: razvitie revoliutsionnykh partii," *Aziia i Afrika segodniia,* no. 8 (August 1981), pp. 4–5; and N. D. Kosukhin, *Formirovanie ideino-politicheskoi strategii v afrikanskikh stranakh sotsialisticheskoi orientatsii* (Moscow: Nauka, 1980), p. 55.

76. The book was An. A. Gromyko, ed., *Velikii Oktiabr' i Afrika* (Moscow: Nauka, 1980). The review by G. A. Usov and V. S. Iakovlev appeared in *Rabochii klass i sovremennyi mir,* no. 3 (1981), p. 170.

77. A. M. Model, review of Kosukhin, *Formirovanie ideino-politicheskoi strategii,* in *Narody Azii i Afriki,* no. 3 (1981), p. 200.

78. "Natsional'no-osvoboditel'noe dvizhenie: nekotorye voprosy differentsiatsii," p. 32.

relatively speaking, people's democratic and national democratic," Simoniia interrupted with the retort, "extremely relatively speaking." For Simoniia, people's democracy is "distinguished by the fact that the liberation struggle on the 'national' stage is already headed by a Marxist-Leninist party."[79] He had none of Mirsky's optimism about countries of the Angolan-Mozambique type.

Georgii Kim, who became the institute's first deputy director for political analysis in the late 1970s, emphasized "the contradictions and difficulties to which we should not close our eyes," particularly the scale of the problem of transformation in African countries that have a very low level of economic development and "an extraordinarily undeveloped social class structure of society." Kim called the vanguard parties "a coalition of nonproletarian revolutionary democratic forces," language that was disparaging of their revolutionary potential, and considered the evolution of revolutionary democracy into socialism as likely only through "the formation of a national proletariat and the growth of its class consciousness and political organization," something clearly in the distant future.[80] By 1984 Kim was reporting that "sometimes frankly pessimistic voices are raised that place under doubt the effectiveness and in the final analysis the viability of the theory and practice of socialist orientation."[81]

## The Special Case of Latin America

Latin American countries have presented special problems of analysis to the Soviet Union because most of them received their political independence long ago and because most of the large countries have a much higher level of economic development than those in Asia and Africa. Latin American political development in the 1940s and 1950s was one of the factors that must have led to Stalin's general pessimism about revolution, but as Soviet pessimism faded and scholars came to see the third world as diverse, it was natural for them to ask whether the economically more advanced Latin American nations would have a different near-term political development than those in Africa and Asia.

79. Ibid.

80. "Razvivaiushchiesia strany: usilenie sotsial'no-klassovoi differentsiatsii," *Aziia i Afrika segodnia,* no. 11 (1981), p. 8.

81. "Aktual'nye problemy natsional'no-osvoboditel'nogo dvizheniia," *Mezhdunarodnaia zhizn',* no. 8 (August 1984), p. 53.

Most of the leading development theorists were specialists on Asia and Africa, and their generalizations flowed from studying countries with recent colonial experience and a level of economic development well below Latin America's. The major Soviet scholarly journal about the outside world, *World Economics and International Relations,* carried a series of roundtable discussions in the mid-1960s on the nature of the third world, on its relationship to the West, and on the revolutionary forces within it. Nothing would have prevented the Latin Americanists from participating in these broader theoretical discussions, but in practice none did until 1968.[82] The surprise of Castro's conversion to Marxism-Leninism and the embarrassment of his subsequent espousal of guerrilla tactics in Latin America in preference to support for the traditional communist parties (a tactic that seemed more in line with Chinese ideas) may have restrained the Latin Americanists somewhat, but, of course, specialists on Asia and Africa also dominated the early theoretical work in the West.

In the late 1960s several factors changed this situation. First, a specialized journal devoted to Latin America was inaugurated in 1969, and a lively editor, Sergei Mikoian, was appointed to head it. Mikoian not only deliberately published articles with conflicting views but organized roundtable discussions on major issues and devoted dozens of pages to the published exchanges. Second, the establishment of a leftist military regime in Peru and the election of Salvador Allende in Chile raised urgent questions about the nature of the social forces in major Latin American countries, the potential for socialism there and the paths by which it could be achieved, and the speed with which revolutionary tactics should be pushed in the transition stage.

Just as scholars such as Simoniia recognized that preindustrial countries like Afghanistan and Ethiopia were fully capable of radical revolutions, so no Latin American specialist doubted that revolution was also possible in Haiti. The Latin American countries at the center of debate were those already beginning to industrialize in a significant manner, those that had reached the stage of "middle-level capitalism." Countries such as Argen-

---

82. These discussions are found in *MEiMO,* no. 3 (March 1962), pp. 20–49; no. 4 (April 1962), pp. 68–98; no. 5 (May 1962), pp. 85–108; no. 6 (June 1962), pp. 85–105; no. 4 (April 1964), pp. 116–31; no. 6 (June 1964), pp. 62–81; no. 8 (August 1965), pp. 86–103; no. 9 (September 1965), pp. 77–89; no. 10 (October 1965), pp. 105–19; no. 11 (November 1965), pp. 88–97; no. 12 (December 1965), pp. 113–22; no. 4 (April 1967), pp. 106–27; no. 5 (May 1967), pp. 93–108; no. 5 (May 1968), pp. 90–104; no. 8 (August 1968), pp. 82–96.

tina, Brazil, Chile, Costa Rica, and Mexico were approaching southern European levels of economic and political development.

The first real debates centered on Chile. The major optimist on its revolutionary development was Kiva Maidanik, IMEMO's leading specialist on Latin America. Maidanik believed Latin America had reached "middle-level capitalism," although in a distorted and dependent form. While in his view this stage of history was inherently revolutionary—as it had been in France in 1850, Russia in 1917, and Spain in 1935—he doubted the ability of the bourgeoisie or intermediate forces (the intelligentsia, the army, the petty bourgeoisie) to make any progress. He described Latin American representative government—where it existed—in negative terms and saw little future in any kind of reformism or populism.

In the majority of Latin American countries, particularly in the post-Cuban political situation, the government could not, as it had before, seek to strike a balance between the direct interests of the ruling social groups and the long-term goals of economic development, between the demands of the oligarchy and the new strata of the bourgeoisie, of foreign capital and "national prestige," of the middle strata and organized labor. It was obvious that the denial of any of these interests or demands would lead—directly or indirectly—to instability, to a sharp intensification of social and political strife. But to preserve the former course also became objectively impossible.[83]

Because Maidanik considered Latin America to be "experiencing a critical, objectively revolutionary phase of development," he saw any "lengthy alliance between revolutionaries and bourgeois reformism" as being "objectively impossible" and treated any real collaboration with reformism as a betrayal of the revolutionary struggle at a time it might succeed.[84] Later he stated that any alliance between the Popular Front and the Christian Democrats in the Allende period was covered by this generalization.[85]

When Allende was overthrown, Maidanik directed his first fire at a *New York Times* editorial that had said the coup was caused by the regime's decision to push beyond the original nationalization of foreign firms and its failure to try to win over the leftist Christian Democrats. Maidanik scoffed at such a cautious policy as understandable for "liberal

83. "Sotsial'no-politicheskii krizis v Latinskoi Amerike i perspektivy ego predoleniia," *MEiMO*, no. 7 (July 1973), p. 37.
84. "Sumerki liberal'nogo reformizma," *Latinskaia Amerika*, no. 5 (September–October 1970), pp. 59–60. See also his "Sotsial'no-politicheskii krizis," p. 29.
85. "Vokrug urokov Chili," *Latinskaia Amerika*, no. 5 (September–October 1974), pp. 119–21.

reformist circles" but scarcely appropriate for those who favored the goal of revolution. To slow down would have meant the demoralization of radical workers and would have set the stage for a possible return to power by the bourgeoisie and their parties. Acknowledging that continued revolution might have failed, he argued that winning over the middle strata and the army was impossible without abandoning the revolution and that the only hope was to go forward. The right time for more direct action, he suggested, was after the elections in the spring of 1973. He admitted that various mistakes had been made by the regime, but he spoke with sympathy of the problem of the revolutionary in the midst of flux and uncertainty and cautioned against facile second guessing.[86]

However, so far as can be judged from the journals, most leading Latin Americanists saw the tragedy not as the result of excessive caution by the revolutionary forces but as the result of excessive lack of caution. This position was advanced most forcefully by Evgenii Kosarev, deputy director of the Institute of Latin America, in an article in the same issue of *Latin America* as Maidanik's piece. (Such a juxtaposition of contrasting interpretations of a key event was very unusual, perhaps unprecedented, behavior for a Soviet journal devoted to the outside world.) Kosarev ripped into "revolutionary romanticism," into "the illusions, the chief consequence of which became an unbalanced acceleration of the process of transformation." He accused the Allende regime of violating its own campaign promises about respecting private property and argued that a sound and careful economic policy should have been the first priority.[87] Irina Zorina, a specialist on Chile at IMEMO, made a similar point about the deviations of Popular Unity from its program, but she went on to insist that there should have been "political compromises, collaboration, and alliances" with parties representing the peasants and the middle strata, that is, primarily the Christian Democrats.[88] In the late 1970s this position became strongly associated with those who talked about the Europeanization of Latin American politics.

These discussions were not simply an abstract exercise of historical analysis or prognosis. One of their primary purposes was to establish what the communist attitude toward this development should be. How impor-

86. Ibid., pp. 112–33.

87. "Ekonomika i mirnyi put' revoliutsii," *Latinskaia Amerika*, no. 5 (September–October 1974), pp. 92–100, esp. pp. 95, 96, 99–100.

88. I. Zorina and Iu. F. Kariakin, "Politicheskaia khronika chiliiskoi revoliutsii," pt. 2, *Rabochii klass i sovremennyi mir*, no. 5 (1974), p. 148.

tant was it for communists to attempt alliances with the moderate left to try to promote representative democracy and fight military dictatorships? During the 1970s the Soviet Union and Latin American communist parties were generally hostile to the new left, including guerrilla movements that operated in the countryside. In 1982 a critic wrote savagely about the "sad experience" of the Nicaraguan communists in failing to join with the Sandinistas and charged that "from the end of the 1960s the line [of the Salvadoran party] ceased to answer reality, which led to the rise of the 'new left.'"[89] Although this scholar was fervent in her support of the guerrilla movements, nearly all the establishment in Latin American studies favored broad coalitions in conditions of military dictatorship. A scholar who is apparently head of the Latin section of the Central Committee was sharply critical of those "representatives of Latin American 'revolutionaries' from the camp of the ultraleft [who think] that the task of completing the socialist revolution is already on the agenda in Latin America."[90] By this time the communists had begun to support the guerrilla movements in Central and South America, but they remained very cautious.

In practice, the old-line communist parties had often had cozy relations with military dictatorships, but in theory there had long been general agreement that the communists should join in common fronts with other forces to overthrow them. The crucial question for most of the Soviet Latin Americanists was the proper behavior of communists once a military dictatorship was overthrown. If, like Kiva Maidanik, one believed that Latin America was passing through a revolutionary phase, that representative democracy was "fictitious in a majority of cases" and "the bourgeoisie in the whole world—not only on the periphery—seeks forms of power that demobilize the masses and isolate the executive from any parliamen-

89. T. E. Vorozheikina, "Revoliutsionnye organizatsii Sal'vadora i narodnoe dvizhenie," *Latinskaia Amerika,* no. 7 (1982), pp. 24–26.

90. M. F. Gornov, "Latinskaia Amerika: usilenenie bor'by protiv imperializma i oligarkhii, za demokratiiu i sotsial'nyi progress," ibid., no. 7 (1982), p. 10. "Gornov" is clearly a pseudonym. In a book he coauthored he was identified as a "doctor of historical science," an advanced degree above the Ph.D., but he had no earlier books. The status accorded him and the subject matter of his book and article (both of which focused on communist parties) as well as his identical first and middle name—make it virtually certain that he is M. F. Kudachkin, head of the Latin America section of the Central Committee. For the reference to the advanced degree, see M. F. Gornov and V. G. Tkachenko, *Latinskaia Amerika: opyt narodnykh koalitsii i klassovaia bor'ba* (Moscow: Politizdat, 1981), p. 2.

tary or other control," then one had little reason (or possibility, without abandoning the revolution) for major collaboration with moderates to forestall the reestablishment of a military dictatorship in the future. "The growth of the fascist threat in no way means that there is a need for revolutionaries to adopt a strictly 'defensive' strategy, a strategic moderation in raising and deciding problems of social transition in order to defend the institutions of bourgeois democracy."[91]

Opponents began with the assumption that the enemy of the good is the best. They combined a pessimistic view of near-term revolutionary prospects with a belief that bourgeois representative democracy is far preferable to an authoritarian military regime. Boris Koval', who had been promoted to the deputy directorship of the Institute of the International Workers' Movement, insisted that the struggle for bourgeois democracy in a presocialist system would be the determining feature of Latin American politics for years and perhaps decades. He left no doubt about his opinion on the position of the communists in this struggle. Similarly, Anatolii Shul'govsky's criticism of the image of an "extraordinary" or "satellized" state that always resorted to open violence and terror for the benefit of American corporations was coupled with clear-cut advice on communist strategy. He praised the communists for participating in the struggle for democracy in Argentina and "for the rejection of the socioeconomic policy based on the postulates of the 'Chicago school,'" and he was explicit in calling for such a strategy in other types of political systems as well:

The importance of the Communists' working out an antiimperialist and antimonopoly strategy and tactics of struggle acquires even more significance when we are speaking not only about countries with authoritarian repressive regimes, but also about those states where 'representative democracy' exists. There too a process of concentration and centralization of capital is occurring and the local monopolistic groups of the bourgeoisie are strengthening their position, striving to subordinate the state to their interests. . . . However, the Communists are alien to fatalism in evaluating the perspectives of the struggle against the coming to power of the forces of extreme reaction. They warn against the mistaken nature of the thesis that fascist counterrevolution already rules the country in practice. . . . It is not accidental that the central place in the alternative programs and plans of the

---

91. "K probleme sovremennykh pravoavtoritarnykh rezh'imov," *Latinskaia Amerika,* no. 6 (November–December 1975), pp. 107–08. Also see his "Ot reformizma k gosudarstvenno-monopolisticheskoi modernizatsii," in "Khristianskaia demokratiia v politicheskoi sistemy stran Latinskoi Ameriki," ibid., no. 2 (March–April 1982), p. 43, and "Mezhdunarodnaia sotsial-demokratiia i Latinskaia Amerika," ibid., no. 4 (July–August 1978), pp. 106–14.

Communists and other left forces is occupied by the problem of a dialogue with parties and movements of the social-democratic type, with Christian Democracy, with the believing masses, with the part of the higher clergy that has a democratic mood, with representatives of patriotic tendencies in the ranks of the armed forces.[92]

The leading scholars on Latin America were specialists on the larger countries, and the debate centered on those that were becoming industrialized. Then at the end of the 1970s revolution took place in the far less advanced Central America. Soviet testimony is universal that officials and establishment scholars did not expect a Sandinista victory in Nicaragua and gave the movement no significant support. A relatively unknown scholar, Kiva Maidanik's best student, was later to write with absolute contempt about "some scholars of an office-bound [kabinetnyi] type" who lumped "the left radical miltary-political movements" together as "ultra-leftists, Trotskyists, and Maoists," and who "at a safe distance from the field of battle" placed the chief blame for the heavy defeats of the revolutionary movement in Latin America on these forces.[93]

Beginning in the late 1970s the more prorevolutionary elements among Soviet scholars came out strongly in favor of guerrilla action. In the first discussion of Nicaragua in the journal Latin America after the Sandinista revolt, Maidanik firmly asserted that the need to support new left forces was an important lesson of revolution.[94] The Latin Americanist who denounced office-bound colleagues made the same point. Others spoke in more general terms about the importance of breaking up the old army if a revolution was to be successful and about the advantage of a guerrilla victory in contrast to an election (for example, in Chile) in achieving this automatically.[95] The guerrilla background of the radical and successful revolutions in Angola and Mozambique contributed to this conclusion.

The contending forces in the debate remained much as before. While a radical claimed that "the victory of the Nicaraguan revolution forced many not only to reject approaches and stereotypes that existed earlier, but essentially to reexamine their relationship to [guerrilla] movements, their

92. "Gosudarstvo i bor'ba za demokratiiu," pp. 19, 20, 21.
93. Vorozheikina, "Revoliutsionnye organizatsii Sal'vadora i narodnoe dvizhenie," p. 23.
94. "Kliuchevoi vopros—edinstvo," Latinskaia Amerika, no. 2 (1980), p. 43.
95. I. S. Shatilo, "Slom burzhuaznykh i zarozhdenie proletarskikh vooruzhennykh sil," Voprosy filosofii, no. 2 (1983), p. 71.

theoretical opinions, strategy, and methods,"[96] scholars who had been associated with the thesis of the Europeanization of Latin America still seemed very skeptical about Central America, although they expressed the point only in asides or by implication. Shul'govsky wrote of "the specifics and even unique character of the concrete historical conditions" in the Nicaraguan revolution and noted "that in distinction from Nicaragua, the preservation of the dominant position of the Salvadoran oligarchy was facilitated by the circumstance that it did widen the sphere of its influence and did not limit itself to the traditional place for investing its capital—coffee plantations."[97] Koval' wrote with near contempt about "petty-bourgeois revolutionism" based on peasants and white collar forces,[98] and while he did not say so, it was difficult to forget that Central American guerrilla movements were, first of all, based on intellectuals and peasants. Their judgments about the democratization of the major Latin American countries remained unchanged in the first half of the 1980s.

Above all, many scholars clearly worried about the foreign policy prerequisites of a socialist revolution. A number of articles referred to the importance of Western European and Mexican support for the success of the Sandinista regime. The apparent head of the Latin American section of the Central Committee seemed hopeful that resentment over the American role in the Falkland crisis (no doubt, later he would have added Grenada) would lead to a continuation of such support for the Sandinistas.[99] When, however, another scholar mentioned that Mexico agreed with the United States about the desirability of a capitalist alternative but disagreed on the method, readers must have asked themselves, "If Nicaragua becomes another Cuba, will Mexico and Western Europe continue their support?"[100]

Clearly the advice of the optimists—in this case, the official, "Gornov"—to the Nicaraguans was to maintain the support of "the middle strata" (and, no doubt, the Mexicans and Western Europeans) by "a careful determination of the order and the speed of the social transforma-

96. Vorozheikina, "Revoliutsionnye organizatsii Sal'vadora i narodnoe dvizhenie," p. 23.

97. "Gosudarstvo i bor'ba za demokratiiu," pp. 12, 13.

98. "Rabochii klass i revoliutsionnost' narodnykh mass: opyt 70-kyh godov," esp. pp. 8–9.

99. Gornov, "Latinskaia Amerika," p. 22.

100. See M. A. Oborotova, "Vneshnepoliticheskie usloviia razvitiia revoliutsionnogo protsessa," Latinskaia Amerika, no. 7 (1982), p. 98.

tions, which should not infringe on the economic interests of these strata."
Yet, the "Marxist-Leninist parties should always be able to preserve their
own revolutionary face and preserve their chief goals," and they should
remember that "with a certain correlation of forces inside the country . . .
there is a possibility of a quick transition from one stage of the revolution
to the other, from the first to the second, from the lower to the higher." In
other words, the revolutionary left was advised to go slow in socioeconomic reforms until it had consolidated political power. Gornov's position
also entailed advice to the Soviet Union: "the creation [by Nicaragua] of
an economy independent from monopolistic capital implies the development of new foreign economic and political ties with all countries of the
world, including the socialist ones."[101] But that remains the crucial question in foreign policy debates—how many Cubas can or should the Soviet
Union afford? The question of the trade-off between revolution and national interest is discussed in chapter 8.

## The Role of Communist Parties and Revolutionary Strategy

The discussions of revolutionary strategy in the last two decades show
beyond all doubt that the days of the Comintern are over and the Soviet
Union is no longer directing the world communist movement according to
its preconceptions. Communist parties often split into pro-Soviet and pro-
Chinese groups, and within limits, the Soviet Union has had to be responsive to or tolerant of the views of local communists in order to retain their
loyalty. To go even further, it is actually striking how irrelevant communist parties have been to most of the revolutionary activity of the last
quarter of a century. From the Soviet perspective of the late 1950s, Castro
was a "bourgeois nationalist," with a very uneasy relationship to the
Cuban Communist party while he was a guerrilla in the mountains. At that
time the Soviets considered armies as instruments of the ruling class and
hence hardly a source of radical coups such as occurred in Burma or of
radical transformations such as took place in Egypt in the early 1960s. The
new left movements from the mid-1960s to the mid-1970s almost all
associated themselves with China more than the Soviet Union, and the
Soviet Union necessarily tended to be dubious about them. This skepti-

101. "Latinskaia Amerika," pp. 11, 10, 14.

cism carried over to the Sandinistas in Nicaragua, even after China largely withdrew from the competition for the leadership of the revolutionary movement.

The Soviet Union did support factions in guerrilla wars against the Portuguese in southern Africa and the British in Rhodesia, but the leaders of these groups adopted Marxist-Leninist language largely after they received Soviet support. Whether the revolutions will evolve in a more radical direction or will follow the path of the anticolonial revolutions of the late 1950s and early 1960s remains to be seen. And the one revolution most harmful to American interests—Khomeini's in Iran—was led by Islamic mullahs rather than the left. Of the three left-wing components—the Mojahedin, the Fedayen, and the Tudeh (Communist) party—the Tudeh was by far the least important.[102] With the exception of Vietnam, only the revolution in Afghanistan was led by a party that could be called communist—and that revolution seems to have been an unexpected response to events rather than a planned coup.

The situation in Western Europe was no better. The Italian Communist party remained important, but its evolution in a social-democratic direction was deeply worrying to any orthodox Soviet observer. The communist parties that had been strong and loyal—notably the French and the Finnish—declined perceptibly in influence, despite the worst economic difficulties in the West since the 1930s.

To a considerable extent, the modifications in revolutionary strategy discussed in this chapter were a response to the irrelevance of the communist parties. Notions that revolutionary democrats or armies could lead the revolution, that vanguard parties could be created after the seizure of power rather than before, or that major third world countries were on a capitalist path were all in one way or another based on an abandonment of important assumptions about traditional communists. Yet the Soviet Union officially continued to identify itself with foreign communist parties, which had awkward consequences. On one hand it tended to alarm moderates and to complicate its relations with third world governments that decided to suppress their local communists (a periodic problem with Iraq, for example). On the other hand the communists have actually not been effective revolutionary forces around the world, which meant that the

102. In elections for the Constituent Assembly, the Mojahedins received 300,000 votes, the Fedayens 100,000 and the Tudeh 47,000. In the parliamentary elections, the figures were 530,000, 220,000 and 54,000, respectively.

Soviet Union often was not supporting revolution until after it had occurred.

Developments in Iran and Central America brought this question to a
head in the late 1970s. The Iranian Revolution was complex, with radicals, moderates, and Islamic fundamentalists allied against the shah. The
communist Tudeh party was the weakest of the radical factions and also
the most conservative (or at least cautious). After Khomeini's return to
Iran, the Tudeh not only supported him but informed on other radicals and
facilitated their arrest. The Soviet Union supported the Tudeh and Khomeini, even refraining from press criticism of his handling of the hostage
situation or the excesses of his revolution.[103] The result was a disaster: the
Tudeh itself was eventually suppressed, Khomeini turned against the Soviet Union, and the relative Soviet silence about the hostage crisis contributed to the worsening of relations with the United States. In Central
America the most radical forces were again not the local communist parties but guerrillas in the countryside.

The events in Iran and Latin America led to a more general conclusion
that must have occurred to a number of people before but that, so far as I
have been able to discover, was not permitted to be made flatly in print
until 1984. Semen Agaev, a specialist on Iran who originally came from
Azerbaidzhan and who strongly favored Soviet support for revolution
abroad, flatly emphasized the negative consequences of Soviet direction of
revolution and came very close to implying the need to abolish communist
parties.

The Communist parties played an outstanding role in their time in spreading
Marxism-Leninism in the East. However, this cannot hide the fact that their very
rise in the 20s and 30s became possible because of the influence of the accelerating
action of the external factor [that is, the Soviet Union], and that this in turn always
created the potential for isolation from the domestic environment. . . . Some left
radicals are in a more favorable position since the stimulus of their political
activity is not an already assigned ideological position. . . . They are more closely
associated with the domestic environment.[104]

Agaev's article was infused with contempt for the Tudeh party and, by
implication, the Soviet policy that supported it. When he called for communist support of new left forces, he was talking about Soviet support.

103. For the evolution of the Soviet policy, see Muriel Atkin, "The Kremlin and
Khomeini," *Washington Quarterly,* vol. 4 (Spring 1981), pp. 50–57.
104. "Levyi radikalizm, revoliutsionnyi demokratizm, i nauchnyi sotsializm v stranakh
Vostoka," *Rabochii klass i sovremennyi mir,* no. 3 (1984), p. 146.

Indeed, since Agaev knew full well that the Mojahedin and the Fedayen had refused to cooperate with the Tudeh because of its pro-Soviet character, he was saying that the Soviet Union should change its policy in a way that removed the bases for such charges.

Agaev's conclusion was not, however, the only one that could be drawn from the events of the second half of the 1970s. In a more cautious way Iurii Krasin, deputy director of the Academy of Sciences, wrote about communism abroad in much the same terms as Agaev: "the communists in truth stirred up the whole world, opening a new historical epoch to a revolutionary path. Now the world is seething: the worldwide historical initiative of the communists awakened noncommunist progressive forces that now are capable of participating in the solution of cardinal problems of renovating the world."[105] But unlike Agaev, Krasin has been less interested in supporting revolutionary new forces than in supporting the more moderate new left (particularly the West German Greens, the peace movements, and the environmental movement). In the Central Committee journal *Kommunist* he praised such groups, emphasizing the need for "alliance" (*soiuz*) rather than "struggle" (*bor'ba*) and calling for a change in style of political action.[106] Elsewhere he rejected the notion that "proletarian internationalism" must be abandoned because of the narrowness of its class approach, but he did so on the grounds that the term could be very broad in its meaning. Finally, he noted that "left doctrinaires in their forecasts rely chiefly on the foreign factor" and said that the internal situation is more important.[107]

Perhaps Krasin's most radical formulation came in the distinction he made between ideology and politics: "If ideological struggle is the clash of principles, and, therefore, uncompromising, then in politics one has to take concrete conditions and possibilities into account." He quoted Lenin on the need for temporary compromise but implicitly went much further when he said that ideology itself was not an unchanging category. "In the close interrelationship of ideology and politics, the latter plays an exceptionally important role. One can say that political practice is the generator

105. "Sootnoshenie ideologii i politiki v revoliutsionnom dvizhenii," *MEiMO*, no. 5 (May 1984), p. 87.

106. Iu. Krasin and B. Leibzon, "Kommunisty i novye dvizheniia obshchestvennogo protesta," *Kommunist*, no. 5 (March 1984), p. 113.

107. "International'noe i natsional'noe v revoliutsionnom protsesse," *Rabochii klass i sovremennyi mir*, no. 3 (1984), pp. 4, 9.

of the development of ideology. Both the direction of the development of theoretical ideology and its basic contents depend on [politics]."[108]

Only a person such as Agaev taking a prorevolution position can get away with talking about communist parties that support Moscow as being counterproductive. A liberal or moderate who denied the importance of the leading role of communist parties abroad would raise far too many questions about his views on the role of the Communist party in the Soviet Union. And disbanding communist parties would also conflict with the institutional interests of the international department of the Central Committee. In a sense, the politically acceptable way to abolish the communist parties as an instrument of Soviet revolutionary strategy is to focus exclusively on their nonrevolutionary tasks.

The real question is whether the revolutionary caution that should have been engendered by the changing Soviet perceptions of economic reality and by the failure of revolution in industrializing third world countries has permanently affected Soviet commitment to revolution. Obviously the Soviet willingness to make significant economic and military commitments has been limited to very few places, and outside of Afghanistan the Soviet Union has been very cautious in the third world in recent years. Does this mean that we are entering a new era in Soviet behavior?

Although Iurii Krasin was engaged in policy advocacy when he emphasized the importance of politics in the relationship between politics and ideology, his formulation was certainly accurate in describing what has happened with respect to the third world. Changes in the ideology of revolutionary strategy have generally followed rather than preceded events. Often the Soviet Union is reacting to events and successful revolutionary movements that are totally unexpected.

From the American perspective, this basic pattern leads to two somewhat contradictory conclusions. First, of course, the history of the last quarter of a century warns us against any simplified notion that all the world's troubles are caused by and directed from Moscow. Second, however, when revolution does unexpectedly occur, the Soviet Union has proven very flexible in adapting doctrine in order to accept it, at least as long as its leaders have not been pro-Chinese. For example, the original inclination—still the inclination among some—was to treat Khomeini's revolution as "a people's antiimperialist revolution, as a result of which

108. "Sootnoshenie ideologii i politiki v revoliutsionnom dvizhenii," pp. 87, 85.

the despotic, pro-American regime of the shah was overthrown."[109] The "antiimperialist" (that is, anti-American) aspect of the Iranian Revolution was more important than its religious, anti-Soviet component.

Both points are crucial. To believe that the Soviet Union has the power to ensure social peace in the third world as the price of détente, even if it wanted to make such a deal, is an illusion. A revolution such as the one in Iran needs no outside weapons, a left-wing military coup needs no outside assistance, and guerrillas such as Castro's and the Sandinistas need few enough weapons that they can buy them with money received from a variety of radical sources. Indeed, the bulk of Soviet military assistance to radical regimes and movements is sold rather than given. Yet because the Soviet Union supports unexpected or unorthodox revolutions so readily when they are successful means that the evolution of Soviet ideology will not lead to the end of ideology. The Soviet Union has many reasons to support left-wing revolutions, and the United States needs to understand them clearly if it is to handle the Soviet challenge intelligently.

First, Soviet support for left-wing revolutions is a human rights question for almost all members of the Soviet foreign policy establishment. Even those Soviet scholars who say privately that the East must be sacrificed in order to improve relations with the West do so with regret. Just as the instinctive reaction of Americans was to applaud the Solidarity movement in Poland, so the instinctive feeling of Soviet citizens is to think that the Sandinista or El Salvadoran rebels have represented the cause of justice in their battles with right-wing regimes. The opinion has become widespread that some left-wing regimes are repulsive and that some military regimes that claim to be left wing are frauds. However, because revolutionary movements seldom show their uglier sides at the time of their seizure of power—indeed, they put forward their most idealistic face at such times—the Soviet Union has little inclination to reject a left-wing revolution at the stage when it is asked to make commitments.

Second, because the legitimization of a regime and its citizens' concept of human rights are closely intertwined, the existence of successful revolutions abroad and at least low-level Soviet support for them generally is politically beneficial for the Soviet regime at home. ("Excess" support is another matter; large-scale foreign aid or foreign military commitments are no more popular in the Soviet Union than in the United States.) It is

109. A. Grachev and N. Kosolapov, "Tekushchie problemy mirovoi politiki," *MEiMO*, no. 4 (April 1980), p. 121.

useful for Soviet leaders to be able to say that, as ideology predicts, the world is moving toward socialism. Even if third world revolutions deviate from the Soviet model, their economic backwardness means that these deviations pose none of the threats of Eurocommunism.

Finally, radical revolutions are usually anti-American, and the Soviet Union has favored them because they are likely to produce a pro-Soviet change in foreign policy orientation. Of course, the split with China and later with Somalia demonstrated that left-wing revolution is not always a long-term foreign policy gain for the Soviet Union, and countries such as India demonstrate that revolution is certainly not a prerequisite for good relations. Nevertheless, there are almost always short-term foreign policy advantages in a radical transformation. Soviet policymakers seeking simple rules to guide them in dealing with the welter of political regimes and movements have a natural tendency to go along with the short-term consideration. The treatment of Khomeini's revolution as one of natural liberation because of its anti-American content shows how far the tendency may be extended.

Given these attitudes, the United States can do nothing to end general Soviet support for left-wing revolutions. The Soviet Union can no more fail to praise the revolutionaries in Central America and give them low-level aid than the United States could fail to do the same for Solidarity. The options for the Soviet Union, as for the United States in Poland, come in the scale and type of aid and in its response if the revolution is threatened. To the extent that support of revolution is associated with foreign policy goals, the support can be affected by the foreign policy trade-offs that are involved. As will be discussed in chapter 8, some scholars have criticized the Soviet support of Khomeini, and a larger number have suggested that foreign goals can be achieved by a strategy less wedded to radical regimes. It is only through tolerating Soviet verbal support for revolutionary movements, striving to reduce their chances for succcess, and changing foreign policy calculations that the West will affect the extent of support for revolutionary movements in a significant manner.

# CHAPTER SEVEN

# Soviet Theory of International Relations and the Posture toward the West

FOREIGN POLICY options are by far the most difficult subject for a Soviet specialist on international relations to discuss in print. It is possible to state openly that the five-stage pattern of history once considered universal does not exist. Advice on the proper revolutionary strategy to follow in different parts of the world can also be offered in fairly explicit terms. Foreign policy, however, can only be discussed in indirect ways, and sometimes opposing arguments can be very difficult to distinguish from each other.

The special attitude toward open discussion of foreign policy originated in the first years of the Soviet regime. Domestic policy questions were debated rather freely in public, including at party congresses, but as early as the 1920s, foreign policy was treated much more gingerly. The policy to be followed at the Genoa conference had provoked considerable controversy among the Soviet leaders, and Foreign Minister Grigorii Chicherin had repeatedly tried to persuade Lenin and the Politburo to adopt a more flexible position on the key question of whether to recognize the foreign debts of the tsarist regime.[1] Yet, at the Eleventh Party Congress, Lenin blandly told the delegates, "Genoa poses no big problems. I don't remem-

---

1. See Aleksandr O. Chubar'ian, *V. I. Lenin i formirovanie sovetskoi vneshnei politiki* (Moscow: Nauka, 1972).

ber that any disagreements or arguments at all arose on this question either in the Central Committee or the party as a whole."[2]

This coverup produced criticism, but at the party congress held the next year, Stalin answered it bluntly:

> We are encircled by enemies. That is clear to all. The wolves who encircle us are not dozing. This is a moment when our enemies try to seize hold of every little crack in order to slip through and harm us. . . . In such a situation, is it possible to bring all questions of war and peace out onto the street? But to discuss a question at meetings of 20,000 [party] cells means to bring a question out onto the street. What would have happened to us if we let our preliminary work for the Genoa conference go onto the street beforehand? We would have failed with a crash. One ought to remember that in conditions when we are encircled by enemies, a sudden blow from our side, an unexpected maneuver, and speed can decide everything. What would have happened if instead of discussing our policy plans for the Lausanne conference in a tight circle of trusted people, we would have taken this work out onto the street and shown our cards? Our enemies would have taken all the pluses and minuses into account, would have wrecked our plans, and we would have left Lausanne in shame. What would happen to us if we brought discussions of war and peace, the most important of all important questions out onto the street, or, I repeat, put these questions before 20,000 cells to discuss? They would dispatch us at once.[3]

Stalin's attitude is still widespread. For instance, an innovative 1983 book on international relations included three chapters in a section on global power centers—one each on the United States, Western Europe, and Japan—and four chapters on regional power centers in Asia, the Near East, Africa, and Latin America. If a Westerner wrote such a book and did not include the Soviet Union either as a global power center or as a regional power center in Asia or the Near East, cries of outrage and offense would result. Yet this book's implicit dismissal of the Soviet Union as a power center was required because Soviet foreign policy cannot be analyzed directly in any sophisticated manner.[4]

Nevertheless, foreign policy is far more crucial than revolutionary strat-

---

2. "Politicheskii otchet tsentral'nogo komiteta RKP 27 marta," in V. I. Lenin, *Polnoe sobranie sochineniia* vol. 45 (Moscow: Politizdat, 1963), p. 70.

3. I. V. Stalin, *Sochineniia* (Moscow: Gospolitizdat, 1952), vol. 5, pp. 224–25.

4. See V. P. Lukin, *"Tsentry sily": kontseptsii i real'nost'* (Moscow: Mezhdunarodnye otnosheniia, 1983). In a discussion in 1985 the author was criticized for this by Aleksandr Bovin of *Izvestiia* and answered lamely that the Soviet Union was not power oriented. See A. E. Bovin and V. P. Lukin, " 'Tsentry sily'—doktrina i real'nost'," *Rabochii klass i sovremennyi mir,* no. 2 (1985), p. 81.

egy to most Soviet citizens, and despite the difficulties, scholars do try to discuss it. If they treat the United States as an inexorable, monolithic threat, for instance, it is not difficult to see that they are rejecting a policy based on the hope of accommodation. If they emphasize divisions within the capitalist world, they imply the possibility of taking advantage of these divisions. Various other techniques have already been mentioned or will be discussed later in this chapter.

But such tactics have their limitations. For the last quarter of a century it has been unchallengeable dogma that the Soviet Union should seek good relations with all countries, regardless of their political system. And while it is easy enough to indicate optimism or pessimism about the probabilities of achieving better relations with this or that country, scholars cannot deal with the difficult choices to be faced. To what extent and in what situations should the Soviet Union make concessions in order to improve relations? Should the Soviet Union allow its relations with a country to be affected if that country suppresses its local communists? How much foreign aid should be provided to promote revolution or to try to acquire allies or both? Ultimately, should the Soviet Union moderate its third world policy in hopes of improving relations with the West, that is, choose the West over the East, as the point is made colloquially?

These trade-offs are the most difficult subjects to discuss explicitly in the Soviet Union, regardless of whether the question is domestic or foreign policy. The party leadership is jealous of its right to balance competing goals and priorities. If Soviet scholars really want to suggest that support for revolution should be sacrificed for foreign policy goals, they are forced either to concentrate on foreign policy questions, perhaps implying a lower priority for revolution, or to downplay the likelihood of revolution, perhaps implying the need to pursue other goals. And while the relative emphasis in an article is easy enough to see, it can remain very unclear how far an author would be willing to go in making a trade-off.

The problem with debates about foreign policy vis-à-vis the third world is particularly difficult because for most Soviet officials, scholars, and citizens policy toward the third world has always been less important than policy toward the West. In part this situation resulted because the Soviet Union has been weak for most of its history and the threat came from the West. In part it resulted from the intimate relationship between foreign policy toward the West and domestic attitudes toward Western ideas and practices. As a young theorist charged in 1963, Stalin had used foreign relations to serve "an obvious political goal—to justify theoretically . . .

mass repression and severe infringements of socialist legality. In essence, Stalin often began from the proposition, as they say: if you live with wolves then you must act like a wolf. He considered that so long as the socialist state was encircled by imperialist states, then it had to use the same methods they did."[5] The same general relationship between foreign threat and internal repression often exists today, and it makes relations with the West particularly salient.

Finally, policy toward the third world has often essentially been part of policy toward the West. At first, there was the hope that the loss of colonies would undercut the Western economies. After 1927 Stalin generally applied his Western policy to the East, both in revolutionary tactics and state policy. With Khrushchev and Brezhnev, third world policy became more independent but was seen as part of the U.S.-Soviet competition. In recent years, as some of the Khrushchevean optimism has faded, even the most dovish analyst finds it very difficult to retreat from active involvement in the third world simply because the United States is actively involved. If the Soviet Union and the United States are equals, how can the Soviet Union refrain from behavior that the Americans seem to regard as inherent in the role of a superpower?

As a consequence, if we are to understand the Soviet debates about policy toward the third world and the view of international relations in which they fit, we first must look at the debates about international relations as a whole, and especially about the proper posture toward the West.


## The Traditional View of International Relations

Before the revolution, Lenin presented a stark view of the conflict between workers and capitalists and an equally stark view of the relationship of Western governments to the capitalist class. Clearly, capitalist governments would be implacably hostile to the new socialist government, an assumption that the allied intervention after World War I seemed to confirm. In 1919 he wrote, "We are living not only in a state, but in a system of states, and the existence of the Soviet Republic side by side with imperialist states for a long time is unthinkable. One or the other must triumph in the end. And before that end supervenes, a series of frightful

5. F. M. Burlatsky in "Kommunisty i demokratiia," *Problemy mira i sotsializma,* no. 7 (1963), pp. 67–68.

collisions between the Soviet Republic and the bourgeois states will be inevitable."[6]

When both the European revolution and the Western intervention proved unsuccessful, however, Soviet leaders had to explain why the Western governments had withdrawn their military forces, and they had to consider what theory had said was impossible—foreign relations between capitalist and socialist states. The explanation of Western withdrawal has been discussed in chapter 5. Approaches to relations with capitalist states came to be based on *Imperialism, the Highest Stage of Capitalism*, in which Lenin argued that colonies were so vital to the economic survival of capitalist states that they were ultimately driven to war to acquire more of them. He said that these "interimperialist contradictions" or conflicts made international bourgeois class solidarity difficult to achieve and thus gave the Soviet Union the opportunity to play one capitalist power off against another if it acted skillfully. As a result, Lenin urged diplomatic relations and foreign trade with the capitalist world and agreed to a treaty with Germany at Rapallo that involved secret military cooperation.

Yet Lenin's rationale for this policy did little to moderate the Soviet sense of danger in international relations. Basically, he was saying that only an economically dictated compulsion of Western countries to go to war gave the Soviet Union the possibility of diplomatic maneuver, and this gave little reason for long-term hope. As Stalin said in 1922, the international arena was still composed of "wolves who encircle us." It seemed unlikely that Russia would avoid involvement in a new world war.

Despite its ideological justification, the policy of playing one capitalist country off against another bore a strong resemblance to Russian diplomatic behavior of the nineteenth century. Lenin had, after all, lived fifteen years in Europe and had a sophistication about the world not shared by the insular Stalin. Had he lived several more decades (he was incapacitated at the age of fifty-two and died at fifty-three) Lenin might have pushed Soviet international relations in an increasingly traditional direction. Certainly many Soviet scholars in recent years have tried to make that point. At the time of Lenin's death, however, Soviet foreign policy remained dualistic. The Comintern continued to try to promote the overthrow of regimes with whom the Commissariat was conducting foreign policy. The importance of the Comintern was suggested by the fact that it was headed

6. "Otchet tsentral'nogo komiteta 18 marta," in Lenin, *Polnoe sobranie sochineniia*, vol. 38, p. 139.

by a Politburo member—to be sure, not the most distinguished and not even one who did it on a full-time basis—while the leader of the People's Commissariat of Foreign Affairs (as the present ministry was then called) was not even on the Central Committee, let alone the Politburo.

In 1920 Stalin publicly endorsed Lenin's foreign policy line: "Internal contradictions between imperialist groups and states . . . do exist and it is on them that the activities of the People's Commissariat of Foreign Affairs are based. . . . The reason for the existence of the People's Commissariat of Foreign Affairs is to take account of these contradictions, to base itself upon them, and to maneuver within the framework of these contradictions."[7] Stalin continued Lenin's policy of diplomatic relations in the 1920s, and he appointed Maxim Litvinov, the most Western-oriented of those high in the Soviet foreign policy establishment, as commissar of foreign affairs. Litvinov actively sought improved foreign relations around the world, and after 1934 the Soviet Union followed a collective security policy that even involved a military alliance with France.

Nevertheless, the language both of Stalin and his chief foreign policy adviser, Viacheslav Molotov, was strikingly different from Litvinov's—far more suspicious and ideological, even during the period of collective security. Stalin's refusal to allow German communists to cooperate with the social democrats against Hitler, despite the advice not only of Litvinov but also the chief Soviet representative to the Comintern, implied an assumption that as long as Germany had a capitalist system it really did not matter who was its political leader. The nonaggression pact with Hitler in 1939 showed both continued willingness to try to maneuver within imperialist contradictions and a continuing conviction that the "imperialists" were all alike. But if class considerations so determined foreign policy that a Hitler was really no different from any other capitalist and if class conflicts were absolutely irreconcilable, then this maneuvering scarcely rested on the nineteenth century notion of international relations as the adjustment and management of finite conflicts among great powers.

The attitude toward international relations implied in Stalin's 1928–34 Comintern policy and in his later statements was that a temporary respite could be achieved in a ferocious conflict, but the conflict could ultimately be ameliorated only by a change in social system. Even during the height of the Popular Front period, foreign communists continued to push this

7. "Doklad ob ocherednykh zadachakh partii v natsional'nom voprose," in Stalin, *Sochineniia*, vol. 5, p. 42.

long-term goal. The Spanish communists acted as if they might take over the republican government, while the French communists sometimes talked of socialist Premier Blum as an Aleksandr Kerensky who soon would and should be replaced by a French Lenin. Stalin left the indelible impression that "Russia was not so constituted as to be a very reliable or comfortable ally for any outside force, whether it was the Western allies or Nazi Germany at the height of its wartime success. The ultimate aims of Stalin's Russia were contrary to the wartime purposes of both of the great warring parties in the West."[8] As the failure of the collective security policy showed, it was a self-fulfilling attitude.

Soviet language during World War II abruptly altered to portray allies as peace-loving states arrayed against international aggressors. It expressed hopes for continued allied collaboration and a successful United Nations rather than a communist revolution. While this phraseology may well have been tactical and propagandistic, it did provide legitimacy for those who wanted to advocate a new policy of international relations. In private and even several times in print, Maxim Litvinov, now in the shadows, proposed a more limited security policy that might permit a better relationship with the West:

> The crux of the matter was not the desirability of an empire (that was now taken for granted) but rather the ways and means of its possible integration into an international order compatible with the Western nations. To Litvinov, Anglo-American support of any settlement his government would wish to enforce in east central Europe was indispensable for Russia's true security. Keenly aware of the depth of Western sympathy for his country's security needs, he was also convinced that such support could be obtained if only the limits of those needs were stated sensibly and clearly enough.[9]

Others made a similar point.[10] In August 1945 Petr Fedoseev, chief editor of the Central Committee journal *Bol'shevik,* criticized those who thought that "international relations develops completely independent of classes" but contended that "Leninism does not consider war inevitable, even in present conditions. War can be averted if the peace-loving nations

8. George F. Kennan, *Russia and the West under Lenin and Stalin* (Little, Brown, 1961), p. 347.

9. Vojtech Mastny, *Russia's Road to the Cold War: Diplomacy, Warfare, and the Politics of Communism, 1941–1945* (Columbia University Press, 1979), pp. 223–24. For Litvinov's public advocacy under the pseudonym of N. Malinin, see pp. 219, 231–32.

10. The debates in this period are analyzed by Jerry F. Hough, "Debates about the Postwar World," in Susan Linz, ed., *The Impact of World War II on the Soviet Union* (Totown, N.J.: Rowman and Allenheld, 1985).

act in concord." He argued that World War II was not like World War I, that it was not a continuation of the capitalists' policy of plundering colonies but Germany's attempt at world domination. His assertion that "goals pursued in the war determine the policy of these states after the war" seemed very reassuring about American aims, and his praise of Soviet foreign policy for being "flexible, farseeing, and effective" was, if not a prediction, surely at least intended as advice.[11]

Stalin would have none of it. We cannot be sure whether he wavered in his attitude toward international relations in the mid-1940s, but the evidence is against such a hypothesis. From 1943 onward, Litvinov repeatedly warned of the isolation and parochialism of the Soviet leaders and the likelihood of a deterioration in relations. Stalin himself privately asserted in April 1945, "Whoever occupies a territory also imposes on it his own social system. Everyone imposes his own system as far as his army can reach. It cannot be otherwise." He stated in a matter-of-fact manner that the Soviet Union and the West would "recover in fifteen or twenty years, and then we'll have another go at it."[12]

By early 1946 Stalin was publicly attributing World War II to the economic forces emphasized by Lenin in *Imperialism*. By late 1947 an extremely simplified bipolar view of international relations was being imposed, with "class" and foreign policy orientation almost completely equated. A country that had a capitalist or feudal socioeconomic system inevitably had a government dominated by the ruling economic class (in fact, by a narrow upper group within the ruling class). This group's feelings of hostility toward the proletariat and the socialist system were supposedly so great that class considerations prevailed over conflicts in national interest.

The language of Soviet analysis was overwhelmingly economic, or at least class-economic. Not only did the economic system determine foreign policy, but the goal of American foreign policy in particular was defined as maximum economic profit (in essence, this meant that political consid-

---

11. Petr Fedoseev, "Marksizm-Leninizm ob istokakhe i kharaktere voin," *Bol'shevik*, no. 16 (August 1945), pp. 32, 46, 51–54, 57. Although the issue was labeled "August," it was published with a two-month delay and signed to press on October 9th with Fedoseev as the journal's new chief editor.

12. Milovan Djilas, *Conversations with Stalin* (Harcourt, Brace, 1962), pp. 114–15. For a collection of Litvinov's statements and an analysis of them, see Vojtech Mastny, "The Cassandra in the Foreign Commissariat: Maxim Litvinov and the Cold War," *Foreign Affairs*, vol. 54 (January 1976), pp. 366–76.

erations did not or could not override the economic drives that Lenin had emphasized). There was, however, one heavily political element in the analysis. Rule by a communist party loyal to the Soviet Union was the litmus test for membership in the socialist camp. Yugoslavia, the most orthodox of Eastern European countries in its internal development, was read out of the camp for foreign policy insubordination. China, on the other hand, was admitted immediately after the communist revolution, even before any socialist steps had been taken, and no problems ensued when the Chinese communists decided to follow a path that entailed considerable collaboration with the Chinese bourgeoisie.

The result, as William Zimmerman noted, was to shift the focus of international relations from the nation-state to the economic system.[13] In Soviet jargon, foreign relations now centered on the camp, or rather the two camps—the imperialist one dominated by the United States and the socialist, peace-loving one headed by the Soviet Union. Just as there could be no neutrals in domestic class warfare, so there could be no neutrals in international relations. Even if a noncommunist third world country declared its neutrality, adopted an anti-American position, or moved to nationalize foreign oil, the action was only an illusion, a trick, or perhaps a temporary aberration. Any so-called neutral country was essentially a pro-American puppet if it had a capitalist economic system.

Yet, for all the simplicity in the two-camp view, one basic anomaly remained in Stalin's theory of international relations during his last years. Stalin refused to abandon Lenin's contention that wars among capitalist states were inevitable. A number of scholars argued in print and then privately in the framework of a 1951 discussion of a political science textbook being prepared, that Lenin's analysis was outdated.[14] Apparently they were supported by Politburo members.[15] Stalin, however, decisively

13. William Zimmerman, *Soviet Perspectives on International Relations, 1956–1967* (Princeton University Press, 1969), pp. 82–83.

14. One such scholar was Eugen Varga. See "O nedostatkakh i zadachakh nauchno-issledovatel'skoi raboty v oblasti ekonomiki," *Voprosy ekonomiki,* no. 9 (September 1948), p. 56. Also see his discussion in *Ocherki po problemam politekonomii kapitalizma* (Moscow: Politizdat, 1964), p. 68.

15. In his rejection of the argument, Stalin criticized "some comrades" who had proposed it, a formulation that often means other Politburo members. Indeed, at the Nineteenth Party Congress in 1952, Georgii Malenkov stated only that wars between capitalist countries "may" be inevitable. See the discussion in Merle Fainsod, *How Russia Is Ruled* (Harvard University Press, 1953), p. 287. Also see Robert C. Tucker, *The Soviet Political Mind* (Praeger, 1963), pp. 27–35.

rejected this argument in his last work, *Economic Problems of Socialism.* [16] But his view fit very uneasily with the two-camp doctrine. If the conflict between socialist and capitalist states was so significant that a country's economic system determined its foreign policy orientation, if the United States was so dominant in the capitalist camp, then why would capitalist countries go to war with each other? Or if conflicts between capitalist countries were so significant, why couldn't the Soviet Union play one country against another and even form temporary alliances with one or the other as it did in the 1930s? The apparent inconsistency was so great that one Western scholar contended that when Stalin reaffirmed Lenin's doctrine on war, "the old dictator relegated to the scrap heap the whole world-of-the-two camps principle." [17]

Nevertheless, it is surely wrong to say that Stalin was repudiating the two-camp doctrine in 1952. He may have been inconsistent, but his critics were being as inconsistent as he was. The same people who took a position favoring détente also argued that wars between capitalist states were no longer inevitable. In the past these scholars had always emphasized divisions within the capitalist world, deviations or "contradictions" both among capitalist countries and within them, and a number of those favoring détente continued to make the point by emphasizing conflicts between the United States and Great Britain. [18] Hence they had a reason to argue that Lenin was still right about the forces producing conflicts.

The fundamental reason for the apparent inconsistencies was almost surely that both sides were really talking about the probability of a war between the Soviet Union and the West. [19] After World War II Stalin repeatedly denied that war between the Soviet Union and the capitalist countries was inevitable, but this must have been a tactical position. [20]

---

16. I. V. Stalin, "Ekonomicheskie problemy sotsializma v SSSR," *Bol'shevik,* no. 18 (September 1952), pp. 17–20.

17. George Ginsburgs, "Neutrality and Neutralism and the Tactics of Soviet Diplomacy," *The American Slavic and East European Review,* vol. 19 (December 1960), p. 540.

18. See, for example, I. Lemin, "Obostrenie protivorechii i neizbezhnost' voin mezhdu kapitalisticheskimi stranami," *Voprosy ekonomiki,* no. 12 (December 1952), p. 45. This point is emphasized in Franklin Griffiths, "Images, Politics, and Learning in Soviet Behavior toward the United States" (Ph.D. dissertation, Columbia University, 1972), pp. 372–78.

19. This point was made in Herbert S. Dinerstein, *War and the Soviet Union* (Praeger, 1959), p. 66.

20. *Izvestiia,* September 24, 1946; and *Pravda,* January 23, 1947; May 18, 1948; January 31, 1949; and April 2, 1952.

Russia had been drawn into both World War I and World War II, and everyone assumed that the same would likely be true of World War III. The issue of the inevitability of war between capitalist states was really the issue of the extent to which the Soviet Union needed to be a garrison state.

### The Post-Stalin Thaw

Four days after Stalin's death, the obituary issue of the Central Committee journal *Kommunist* was signed to press. In it Eduard Burdzhalov, head of the party history department of the Higher Party School and reportedly a close consultant of Georgii Malenkov, wrote an extraordinary opening article that overtly praised Stalin extravagently while covertly repudiating many of his central ideas. The article made clear that the new leadership was planning a change in domestic policy and that it had a different view of international relations than Stalin had had.

Burdzhalov implicitly attacked the insistence on the binding nature of the objective laws of socialism, one of Stalin's stands at the end and one implying that domestic policy could not be changed. If Stalin's policy was determined by objective laws, how could it be challenged? Burdzhalov's attack was carried almost to the point of suggesting that Stalin had adopted a Menshevik position, for he recalled that in 1917 the Mensheviks had said that a socialist revolution could not be carried out because of subservience to the presumed law that capitalism must come after feudalism. Burdzhalov reaffirmed the doctrine of the inevitability of war and the complete unacceptability of noncommunist socialism and said nothing critical about Stalin's emphasis on "the objective laws of capitalism," a code phrase for the unchangeable nature of capitalism. But by implication an attack on the binding nature of the laws of socialism could be—and soon was—extended. The Stalin whom Burdzhalov was quoting had called Marxism "the enemy of any dogmatism" and had cautioned that "Marxism does not recognize unchanging conclusions and formulas that are obligatory for all epochs and periods."[21]

On the question of foreign policy tactics, Burdzhalov noted that Stalin had praised the Treaty of Brest-Litovsk with Germany in 1918 as a neces-

---

21. "Vydaiushchiisia trud I. V. Stalina o strategii i taktike Leninizma," *Kommunist*, no. 4 (March 1953), p. 34.

sary retreat to gain a breathing space, but the author mentioned Lenin and Leninism more than Stalin:

The tactics of Leninism do not exclude reforms, compromises, and agreements. Under certain conditions they are necessary. V. I. Lenin indicated that, in leading a long and complicated struggle against the bourgeoisie, it is unreasonable to refuse beforehand to maneuver, to take advantage of differences between enemies, or to make compromises with allies, even if they are temporary, unreliable, wavering, and conditional. . . . This is like climbing an uninvestigated and unclimbed mountain and refusing beforehand to make zigzags sometimes, to turn back sometimes, to change direction. . . . The tactics of Leninism have a flexible, maneuvering character.[22]

The discussion of theories of international relations that soon opened up dealt originally with the issue of relations with the West, for the two were essentially synonymous. To say that there was an irreconcilable hostility between socialism and capitalism was to say there was irreconcilable hostility between the Soviet Union and the West. Stalin's view of international relations had been coupled with a xenophobic attack on the West and Western ideas. The easiest way to move toward a new image of international relations was to suggest the possibility of a more relaxed relationship with the West.

A number of devices were used to advocate this more open relationship. At the very beginning Petr Fedoseev returned to the fray, asserting that praise of Russian achievements "does not mean that the Soviet people shut themselves off from the culture of foreign countries." He pointedly criticized "the monopolists [who] want to isolate the toilers of the USA completely from the outside world."[23] Those who wanted to broaden cooperation with noncommunist forces or simply to widen the range of toleration within the Soviet Union argued that the progressive revolutionaries of the nineteenth century had cooperated with more moderate forces.[24]

The major technique used to undermine the Stalinist image of international relations was to try to reduce the sense of implacable Western hostility. Some emphasized the divisions in the West, "the differences on relations with the USSR and other countries of the democratic camp,

22. Ibid., p. 41.
23. "Sotsializm i patriotizm," *Kommunist,* no. 9 (June, 1953), pp. 25, 27.
24. See, for example, M. V. Nechkina, "N. G. Chernyshevsky v bor'be za splochenie sil russkogo demokraticheskogo dvizheniia v gody revoliutsionnoi situatsii (1859–61)," *Voprosy istorii,* no. 7 (July 1953), pp. 58, 65–66; and F. M. Burlatsky, *Politicheskie vzgliady N. A. Dobroliubova* (Moscow: Gospolitizdat, 1954) pp. 46, 55, 62.

variations on the tempo and scale of armaments and the methods of conducting foreign policy."[25] Others focused more on divisions within the American ruling circles and even "the pressure of the people" or the "role of the masses."[26] The future director of the Institute of the USA and Canada, for instance, wrote that there was a "growing dependence of foreign policy on the masses, on public opinion . . . the masses in our day display a vital interest in foreign policy, and the imperialist government cannot fail to take their opinion into account to this or that extent."[27] Above all, everyone in favor of détente tried to reduce fear by suggesting that while the United States was aggressive, it often was not successful.[28] Increasingly they spoke of the change in "the correlation of forces between capitalism and socialism" as an explanation of why the United States was now less threatening.

Until Khrushchev repudiated the doctrine of the inevitability of war in 1956, no one could directly challenge it, but in 1953 two scholars attempted to do so indirectly. M. Gus, a publicist, argued that the law of inevitability might be "limited," "averted," or "paralyzed."[29] A more remarkable article, which appeared at almost the same time, was written by Georgii Aleksandrov, director of the Institute of Philosophy. Aleksandrov asserted that war was inevitable but strongly attacked "the bourgeois theory" that it was "eternal" (*vechnyi*). He contended that "aggressive circles . . . kindle war psychosis because they oppose an easing of international tension and they fear a reduction in the arms race." For this purpose, they utilized "servant-theoreticians" who worked out "a series of 'theories' designed to fool the people in order to throw them into the abyss of a new war." These aggressive theories essentially contained three proposi-

25. N. Inozemtsev in "Novaia kniga ob anglo-amerikanskikh otnosheniiakh," *Voprosy ekonomiki*, no. 10 (October 1955), p. 151.

26. V. Zorin, "Predstoiashchie vybory i vnutripoliticheskaia obstanovka v SShA," *Kommunist*, no. 8 (May 1954), pp. 87–92.

27. Iu. Arbatov, "K voprosu o roli narodnykh mass v mezhdunarodnykh otnosheniiakh," *Mezhdunarodnaia zhizn'*, no. 9 (September 1955), pp. 64, 67.

28. See, for example, N. Inozemtsev, "Amerikanskaia politika 's pozitsii sily' i Zapadnaia Evropa," *Kommunist*, no. 9 (June 1955), p. 74; and I. Glagolev, "Voennye bazy SShA—ugroza miru," *Voprosy ekonomiki*, no. 5 (May 1955), p. 120. Glagolev went so far as to downplay the danger from American bases abroad. "From a military point of view, American bases, in particular those located near the countries intended to be attacked, are extremely vulnerable. With contemporary military technology, it is possible to put an important base out of commission with only one blow."

29. "General'naia liniia sovetskoi vneshnei politiki," *Zvezda*, no. 11 (1953), pp. 108–10.

tions: "(1) A striving to prove the eternal nature of war and thus justify the preparation of a new world war by the American imperialists; (2) attempts to infer the inevitability and even necessity of a new world war from so-called 'global' policy; (3) arguments that war serves as a source of progress."[30]

Aleksandrov fervently attacked each of these propositions, but the most interesting thing about his argument was the way in which his language shifted from that which applied only to the West to that which might apply to the Soviet Union. "Eternal war" seemed very close to "inevitable war," and the first proposition he listed could have meant that the Soviet doctrine of inevitable war played into the hands of the American imperialists. In defining the proposition about global policy, he seemed almost to be talking about those who promoted world revolution: "The policy of violence and of preparation of aggressive war is even declared to be a struggle for 'democracy' and for the triumph of 'freedom.' . . . The 'global' nature of the world . . . demands the unification of social systems: once the world is 'global,' then the USA *should* take on the task of organizing it on the American (that is, police) model."[31] Soviet conservatives were, of course, saying very directly that a new world war would further progress and would lead to a final collapse of capitalism.

Aleksandrov also moved back and forth between talking about American monopolists and "industrialists" and "manufacturers of arms." All Soviet sources agree that he was very closely connected with Malenkov, and it is almost certain that he was attacking Soviet administrators of heavy industry, who were supporting Malenkov's opponents, as well as American industrialists. The servant-theoreticians he had in mind surely did not all live on the other side of the Atlantic. In 1955 when Malenkov fell, Aleksandrov was exiled to the Institute of Philosophy in Minsk, Belorussia, and was scornfully denounced in a number of different contexts.[32]

The position against détente was made in as many different ways as the one in favor of it and, in fact, often in mirror ways. Thus if the forces favoring détente talked about cooperation between radical revolutionaries and more moderate figures, the conservatives denied the possibility of

30. "Protiv ideologii voiny i agressii," *Kommunist,* no. 16 (November 1953), p. 78.
31. Ibid., p. 81.
32. For his biography, see *Bol'shaia sovetskaia entsiklopediia,* 3d ed. (Moscow: Izdatel'stvo Bol'shaia sovetskaia entsiklopediia, 1970).

such cooperation.[33] They also reiterated that Western governments were strictly subordinated to the monopolies, which was the legitimate way of saying that their policies were not subject to the significant influence by other forces, including, of course, the masses.[34] Above all, the opponents of détente emphasized the nature of the American military threat. This emphasis was present in all Soviet writing about the capitalist world, and those in favor of détente never denied the aggressive character of capitalist governments, but they did try to suggest that Soviet strength, the resistance of foreigners to American domination, and the influence of the masses reduced the danger of American attack. Their opponents simply emphasized the American military buildup, John Foster Dulles's statements about "liberation," and the ring of military bases around the Soviet Union. The rearmament of West Germany was accompanied by scare stories about the rebirth of Nazism and the desire to reunite Germany by force.

The new element in the conservative argument about the Western threat was an emphasis by the military on the importance of nuclear weapons and surprise attack.[35] Stalin had insisted that surprise attack could never determine the outcome of a war, and he had forbidden any public discussion of nuclear weapons, but in the fall of 1953 a lively debate opened in the Soviet military press on these issues. Although Westerners have treated this development in terms of its military significance—the movement toward modernizing doctrine and accepting the facts of nuclear war—and this unquestionably was its major component, it also had foreign policy significance. The military considered the Soviet leadership's emphasis on consumer goods and agriculture a major threat to its budget, and, if Aleksandrov really spoke for Malenkov in his impassioned attack on eternal war and manufacturers of arms, worse might be coming. Indeed, Malenkov himself asserted that nuclear war would destroy civilization, not just capitalism, and seemed thereby to suggest that it was so terrible that it could and should be avoided.

The military's emphasis on nuclear weapons and the dangers of surprise

33. M. Iovchuk, "N. G. Chernyshevsky—velikii russkii uchenyi i revoliutsioner," *Kommunist*, no. 11 (July 1953), p. 95; and see A. Kornienko, "Velikii russkii revoliutsioner i myslitel' (Chernyshevsky)," *Voprosy ekonomiki*, no. 7 (July 1953), p. 84.

34. See V. Kruzhkov, "V. I. Lenin—korifei revoliutsionnoi nauki," *Kommunist*, no. 1 (January 1954), p. 23.

35. See the discussion in Raymond L. Garthoff, *Soviet Strategy in the Nuclear Age* (Praeger, 1958), pp. 61–96.

attack were important arguments that the Soviet Union faced an enormous danger and that major expenditures were needed for strategic weapons. This point became particularly strong in the articles appearing in the civilian press. As General Nikolai Talensky, editor of the chief military theoretical journal, said, "The decisions taken by the Atlantic bloc about the preparation for atomic aggression in no way remain on paper. On the contrary, the practical preparation for an atomic attack on the peace-loving is well ahead of the formal decision. . . . Atomic weapons of many types have become a completely normal weapon in the armed forces of the USA. . . . By their very nature, atomic weapons strengthen the danger of military adventures.[36]

Civilian theorists underscored the American threat by emphasizing the "objective laws" of capitalism. One, for example, wrote, "there are 'theoreticians' who suppose . . . that the 'repeal' or 'destruction' of the objective laws of the development of society is possible. . . . This has nothing in common with Marxism-Leninism. . . . The objective laws of social development work spontaneously, with destructive force."[37] Strong support for the continued validity of "the law of the uneven development of capitalist countries" was a typical way of asserting that Lenin's analysis of imperialism was still correct, but often the argument became more explicit. One leading conservative called "completely absurd" the "assertions found in our literature that the action of objective economic laws of capitalism are 'paralyzed' in contemporary conditions as a result of the peace movement."[38]

## Khrushchev vs. Malenkov

At the Twentieth Party Congress, Nikita Khrushchev changed the terms of debate about international relations by declaring that "the Marxist-Leninist precept that wars are inevitable as long as imperialism exists" was no longer valid. It was a remarkable statement. Khrushchev completely blurred the issues of the inevitability of war among capitalist states

---

36. "Ob atomnom i obychnom oruzhii," *Literaturnaia gazeta,* February 1, 1955. This article was reprinted from *Mezhdunarodnaia zhizn',* no. 1 (January 1955), pp. 20–27.

37. Kruzhkov, "V. I. Lenin—korifei revoliutsionnoi nauki," p. 22.

38. M. T. Iovchuk, "Tvorcheskii kharakter marksistsko-leninskoi nauki," *Vestnik Akademii Nauk SSSR,* no. 3 (1954), p. 11.

(which, strictly speaking, was the only kind of war declared inevitable in the official doctrine) and of war between capitalist and socialist states (which Stalin himself had been officially saying was not inevitable).[39] Khrushchev's formulation suggested that Stalin's insistence on the inevitability of war between capitalist states had, indeed, been an elliptical way of talking about the inevitability of war for the Soviet Union. Furthermore, in his battle with Malenkov, Khrushchev had associated himself with the primacy of heavy industry and with the argument that nuclear war would destroy only capitalism. For him to denounce the doctrine of the inevitability of war so quickly, as well as to declare that different roads to socialism were possible, was a powerful indication that the major political forces in party leadership were moving away from the garrison mentality of the Stalin period.

There did, however, seem to be significant differences in the perspectives of Khrushchev and Malenkov. It is dangerous to judge a man by his subordinates, but Malenkov's choice of Aleksandrov and Burdzhalov suggests that he was ready at least to contemplate a real opening to the West, both in foreign policy and in receptivity to Western ideas at home. To suggest that Malenkov might have been another Alexander Dubček probably goes much too far, but one can well imagine him pushing a modernization that required much greater integration with the West than was to occur over the next three decades. Charles Bohlen, the American ambassador to Moscow, found him a "man with a more Western-oriented mind than other Soviet leaders. He at least seemed to perceive our position, and, while he did not agree with it, I felt he understood it."[40]

Khrushchev was less knowledgeable about the West. After 1949 when he became Central Committee secretary for personnel, he did receive the daily foreign information packet reserved for top officials,[41] but in his first meetings with Western leaders he gave no indication of sophistication. When he dined with the British Labour party leader in August 1954—over a year after Stalin's death—the British ambassador to Moscow reported that "the first impression was alarming. . . . He seemed impulsive and blundering, and startlingly ignorant of foreign affairs. Bevan tried to put

39. This point is discussed in Frederick S. Burin, "The Communist Doctrine of the Inevitability of War," *American Political Science Review*, vol. 57 (June 1963), pp. 343–48.

40. *Witness to History, 1929–1969* (W. W. Norton, 1973), p. 370.

41. Nikita S. Khrushchev, *Khrushchev Remembers*, Strobe Talbott, ed. (Little, Brown, 1970), p. 373.

some quite simple United Nations point to him and he totally failed to grasp it, in spite of expert interpreting, until it was explained to him in words of one syllable by Malenkov."[42] Bohlen said of Khrushchev that "there was no meeting point, no common language. Like trains on parallel tracks, we went right by each other."[43]

Khrushchev was an optimist. In domestic policy he always acted as if the correct form of organization—and he tried a new one every year—would prove a panacea. Early in the Korean War he advocated the use of Soviet troops,[44] and he and his supporters often asserted that the so-called antiparty group "underestimated the strength of the socialist system" in international relations and were "thoroughgoing capitalationists."[45] While Westerners usually assumed that Malenkov (the moderate) and Molotov (the dogmatist) shared nothing in common and were unfairly lumped together in criticisms of the antiparty group, it is quite possible that the two were united on this key point.

In foreign policy Khrushchev was told by his top economists that the West was about to enter a severe depression. He seemed to believe that the third world would, indeed, evolve in a pro-Soviet socialist direction if only the Soviet Union supported that evolution sufficiently. He concluded that everything was possible: he could brag about Soviet bombers and rockets and provoke Western restraint rather than a military buildup; he could confront the West in Berlin and the third world and still have peaceful coexistence.

## The Primacy of Economics or Politics?

Khrushchev's assumptions were hopelessly naive, but their contradictory nature opened the way to debate about international relations. Discussions about the third world, the West, and even Western foreign policy began very early in the post-Stalin period, but it was only in late 1956 and early 1957 that leading scholars specifically appealed for a major change in the way that international relations was studied. By 1963 Leonid

42. William Hayter, *The Kremlin and the Embassy* (Macmillan, 1966), p. 38.
43. Bohlen, *Witness to History,* p. 370.
44. *Khrushchev Remembers,* pp. 370–71.
45. E. M. Zhukov, "XXII s"ezd KPSS i zadachi sovetskikh istorikov," *Voprosy istorii,* no. 12 (December 1961), p. 4.

Il'ichev, secretary of the Central Committee for ideological questions, was speaking about the development of international relations theory and calling for a movement of it beyond a legalistic analysis of state behavior.[46]

There are many ways to conceptualize international relations, and American political science has often tended toward abstraction. In the second half of the 1960s, Soviet theorists became fascinated with the American literature and began to think of adopting this or that aspect of it,[47] but essentially Soviet international relations theory flowed out of the realities of foreign policy that scholars were seeking to influence both in print and in their classified work. Hence the developing theory had a more practical character than that found in American academic work.

Stalin's theory of international relations had focused on class and economics as the key categories, and it considered conflicts in international relations just as irreconcilable as the domestic struggle between classes in traditional Marxist-Leninist analysis. On a tactical basis, in the 1930s Soviet leaders often focused on the nation-state as the key unit, seeking to play one capitalist state off against the other. Perhaps stung by his experiences during these years, however, Stalin basically seemed to give up on his ability to conduct a successful divide-and-conquer policy after World War II.

It was against this background that the attempt to develop a new perspective on international relations emerged. Those who tried to modify the Stalinist orthodoxy strove first of all to displace class and economics from their position as the sole determiners of behavior. They instead emphasized the primacy or at least the importance of politics. There was a new emphasis on the multiplicity of factors in international relations—not simply nation-states dominated by their ruling classes but a variety of economic groupings, social forces, and political and bureaucratic officials. Definitions of international relations now recognized common interests and collaboration (not simply peaceful coexistence) as well as conflict, and they frequently treated conflict as less than total. There was also a return to the 1920s concept of conflicts among capitalist nation-states rather than total U.S. hegemony and a definition of foreign policy as the

---

46. Zimmerman, *Soviet Perspectives on International Relations, 1956–1967*, pp. 38–41, 62–63.

47. The trend began with an article on game theory in 1966. See G. Gerasimov, "Teoriia igr i mezhdunarodnye otnosheniia," *Mirovaia ekonomika i mezhdunarodnye otnosheniia*, no. 7 (July 1966), pp. 101–08.

attempt to take advantage of these conflicts to promote Soviet security and other interests.

The proponents of détente have continued to argue the primacy of politics. Scholars who focus on domestic politics in the United States have almost always supported détente, and the same is true of those emphasizing the theoretical importance of politics. For example, one of the strongest supporters, Fedor Burlatsky, coauthored a book on the sociology of international relations in 1974 that began with a paragraph virtually reversing the old orthodoxy: "One of the most noteworthy phenomena of social life in our time is the sharp increase in the role of politics. . . . Politics exerts influence on the development of economics, on the forms and distribution of material goods, on ideology, culture, morality, family, way of life, in a word, on all sides of society's life."[48]

Those whose theory of international relations centered on politics expressed that focus in many ways. The cautious simply insisted on the autonomy of the science of international relations as a relatively independent region of knowledge.[49] Others emphasized a systems analysis of international relations.[50] Increasingly, scholars began to speak of triangles, quadrangles, or even of Japan emerging as a "multiangle" participant (*mnogougol'nik*) in the Pacific.[51] The editor of *Kommunist* discussed the social nature of international relations, asserting that they "have their beginnings in contacts between clans, tribes, and so forth."[52] All of this language had one thing in common: it implied that international relations was not simply the product of class conflict and that differences in social

48. F. Burlatsky and A. Galkin, *Sotsiologiia. Politika. Mezhdunarodnye otnosheniia* (Moscow: Mezhdunarodnye otnosheniia, 1974), p. 5.

49. N. N. Inozemtsev, "XXVI s"ezd KPSS i razvitie nauki o mezhdunarodnykh otnosheniiakh," *Pravda*, September 22, 1981.

50. Burlatsky was one of those advocating such a focus. See Burlatsky and Galkin, *Sotsiologiia. Politika. Mezhdunarodnye otnosheniia*, pp. 240–47; and Burlatsky, "Nekotorye voprosy teorii mezhdunarodnykh otnoshenii," pp. 36–48. See also E. A. Pozdniakov, *Sistemnyi podkhod i mezhdunarodnye otnosheniia.* (Moscow: Nauka, 1976). A reviewer has asserted that Pozdniakov's book was the first to apply systems analysis to Soviet foreign policy; see V. Dadaian in *MEiMO*, no. 5 (May 1978), p. 154.

51. E. Primakov, "Osnovnye tendentsii razvitiia mezhdunarodnoi obstanovki v aziatsko-tikhookeanskom regione," *MEiMO*, no. 11 (November 1979), p. 52. For a very interesting discussion of triangles and the like in the Pacific, see A. A. Kokoshin, *O burzhuaznykh prognozakh razvitiia mezhdunarodnykh otnoshenii* (Moscow: Mezhdunarodnye otnosheniia, 1978), pp. 61–97.

52. R. Kosolapov, "Obshchestvennaia priroda mezhdunarodnykh otnoshenii," *MEiMO*, no. 7 (July 1979), pp. 63, 67.

systems were not the only and perhaps not even the major determinant of international behavior.

In one sense the language of triangles and quadrangles implied a return to Lenin's policy of playing one foreign power against another. Yet the discussion of China as one of the points in the geometry made it clear that people were not simply thinking of capitalist "contradictions" in the old sense of the term. Indeed, many went beyond the old thesis favoring détente, which emphasized the role of the masses, to talk about a multiplicity of forces in international relations. In 1983 Burlatsky emphasized the importance of a wide variety of political factors in international relations—the desire of the political elite to strengthen its own domestic power, ideological goals, psychological motives of the leaders, the influence of different pressure groups, and the struggle for power between the political, military, and economic elite. He ended with the assertion that "the erosion of political leadership in the sphere of international relations is one of the most dangerous phenomena in contemporary political life."[53]

The primacy of economics and class have continued to be reiterated by more conservative scholars, however, and the struggle between classes and between the Soviet Union and the United States remains of central concern to them. Everyone has acknowledged that détente does not mean the end of ideological struggle, but the conservatives have emphasized its intensity. In 1970 Nikolai Kapchenko of the conservative journal *International Life* conceded that "ideological struggle is not a military battle," but he insisted that "nevertheless, it is just as tense, and it demands a maximum mobilization of forces and resources."[54]

The relative importance of economics and politics has been debated on many levels and in many settings. In a single issue of a scholarly journal one reviewer criticized the structure of a book on Israel because "it scarcely is justifiable to examine economic problems after the political ones," while another criticized a history of American policy in China from 1898 to 1905 for exaggerating the influence of "those circles of the American monopolistic bourgeoisie who were interested in economic expansion. . . . It is necessary to devote more attention to the general foreign policy

53. "Nekotorye voprosy teorii mezhdunarodnykh otnoshenii," *Voprosy filosofii*, no. 9 (1983), pp. 44–48.
54. "Vneshniaia politika i ideologiia," *Mezhdunarodnaia zhizn'*, no. 10 (October 1970), p. 99.

and military-strategic interests of the United States."[55] The question even became the subject of a behind-the-scenes conflict when the Soviet constitution of 1977 was being drafted. Should the section on the Soviet political system or the section on the Soviet economic system come first in the document? (Those who advocated the primacy of the political system won.)

Of course, "politics" and "economics" are very generalized code words. While the relative emphasis given them tends to correlate strongly with foreign policy position, this is not always the case. On one hand a scholar can essentially believe in the primacy of politics but still have a Hobbesian view of political life. A scholar can also hoist on their own petards those who emphasize the role of the masses and other social forces on American foreign policy by arguing that the aggressive tendencies of American foreign policy flow not simply from President Reagan or the ruling circles but from the basic American political culture and conception of morality.[56] Moreover, emphasis upon the economic dependence of the third world often has now acquired a very different meaning than it used to have. When people were convinced that third world economic growth was incompatible with dependence and that anti-Western nationalism was the dominant force, analysis of economic dependency was associated with revolutionary optimism; today the opposite is frequently the case.

## Military Force in International Relations

During the 1960s Soviet scholars and officials became increasingly interested in the so-called realist school of international relations in the West. To the extent that this development focused their attention on political factors and state relations, it was associated with a movement away from the Stalinist view of international relations. Yet the American literature, especially the realist literature, was very ambivalent. It emphasized the importance of power and force in opposition to those who had talked about international law and morality, but it also usually focused on finite and adjustable conflicts of interest between nation-states in opposition to

---

55. See A. M. Diakov in *Narody Azii i Afriki,* no. 4 (1969), p. 198; and A. Muradian, "Sovetskie istoriki o tikhookeanskoi politike SShA," ibid., p. 170.
56. See the discussion on pp. 223–25 of this chapter.

those who thought in terms of ideological crusades. During the Vietnam War, theorists such as Hans Morgenthau tended to move from an emphasis on the first theme to an emphasis on the second. Discussions about the efficacy of military force tended to be replaced by discussions of multipolarity.

In the Soviet Union, too, the issue of military force was crucial. During the 1930s the Soviet Union had perforce concentrated on building a defensive army that could withstand an attack from Europe. In the immediate postwar era it was absorbed with catching up in the ability to produce atomic and hydrogen bombs. From 1955 to 1965 basic attention was given to the construction of rocket delivery systems for the new atomic weapons. As the intercontinental ballistic missile program began to move forward, however, the Soviet Union faced some necessary choices. Should the factors that led President Kennedy to enunciate a doctrine of flexible response and to build up conventional military strength lead the Soviet Union to follow a similar policy? Or did Vietnam suggest the bankruptcy of the Kennedy policy, particularly in the third world?

During the Khrushchev era the leadership vacillated on the key questions about nuclear war and deterrence. Khrushchev had used Georgii Malenkov's statements that nuclear war would end civilization on earth against him, but as premier, Khrushchev then began to speak of nuclear war in more and more apocalyptic terms, especially in response to the Chinese charge that the United States was a paper tiger. Nevertheless, his deemphasis on ground forces and his tendency to boast about nuclear retaliation gave a strongly nuclear cast to the Soviet official posture, and the limited number of delivery systems pushed the country toward considering a preemptive strike in a crisis. The Soviet military talked about the use of nuclear weapons in battlefield situations in a matter-of-fact way that could be chilling. Thus in frankly recognizing that war would feature "the application of a wide-area weapon on the field of battle," some writers called for training exercises that would accustom the soldiers to fear. They recalled that massive artillery salvos just before battles in World War II had given soldiers real confidence, and they saw an analogy in any future war: "Atomic weapons, skillfully applied by our command [at the beginning of a battle] can inspire a huge enthusiasm in our troops."[57]

57. I. Lipodaev, P. Galochkin, and A. Tarasov, "Revoliutsiia v voennom dele i nekotorye voprosy partiino-politicheskoi raboty," *Kommunist vooruzhennykh sil*, no. 19 (October 1964), p. 10.

In the mid-1960s a number of issues about the nature of war came to the fore. To a considerable extent they were fought out within the framework of a discussion of Lenin's (really Karl von Clausewitz's) description of war as "a continuation of policy [or politics] by violent means,"[58] but the single focus should not obscure the complexity of the issues being raised and their difference over time. Clausewitz's definition has a Delphic quality to it; as a leading Soviet military theorist, Colonel Evgenii Rybkin, noted in 1965, "the formula can acquire different meanings, depending on the interpretation of the concepts 'policy,' 'a continuation of policy,' and 'violence.' " Rybkin noted that the sentence can mean that war is the product of politics (that is, not the product of the arms race, of military decisions, or of economic systems), that war is to be evaluated as just or unjust on the basis of the policy that guides it, that politics determines military strategy ("the character of the political goal has a decisive influence on the conduct of war"), or that armed action is a legitimate way of advancing a country's political goals.[59] Small wonder that it was so much fun to argue whether this short sentence was valid.

In the mid-1940s conservatives had attacked the Clausewitz formulation (Lenin was naturally not mentioned) because he treated war as the result of a conscious decision by a political leader rather than as the inexorable product of the capitalist system:

War is state policy continued by other means, wrote Clausewitz. . . . [In this view] policy is built on the desires and opinions of the sovereign. . . . [These propositions] are a clear expression of an idealist interpretation of the concepts of the state and politics. . . . Lenin emphasized that politics and economics are indistinguishable from each other, that politics is the concentrated expression of economics. The roots of policy must be sought, he emphasized, in the economic position of the classes that head the state.[60]

It was an early way of saying that Hitler was not the cause of World War II.[61]

---

58. The Russian word "politika," like its German counterpart, can be translated as either "policy" or "politics."

59. "O sushchnosti mirovoi raketno-iadernoi voiny," *Kommunist vooruzhennykh sil,* no. 17 (September 1965), p. 53.

60. B. Antropov, "O Klauzevitse i ego uchenii o voine," *Bol'shevik,* no. 10 (May 1945), p. 39.

61. An answer to this article pointedly quoted the Lenin formulation (Clausewitz was not mentioned) and asserted that those who started World War II had different goals than were manifested in the origins of World War I. See Fedoseev, "Marksizm-leninizm ob istokakh i kharaktere voin," p. 46.

In a military discussion of 1953–55 a central issue was whether war had a single law. General Talensky argued for the existence of such a law—"victory in modern war is attained by the decisive defeat of the enemy in the course of the armed conflict"—and he denounced the view of the late Stalin period that "permanently operating factors" (a country's size, its industrial capacity, the morale of its population, the strength of its political system, and the like) were always decisive in war.[62] The criticism of the doctrine of permanent operating factors opened the way for a reappraisal of the importance of a surprise attack in the nuclear age, but Talensky's retention of the concept of a single law was, according to a later report, rejected by most participants in the debate.[63] It was thought wrong to speak of war only in terms of decisive defeat because "the political contents of war determine the character of the armed violence in it."[64] The limited war in Korea, together with the fear of thermonuclear war, undoubtedly had had an impact on thinking.

During the mid-1960s the issue with respect to Clausewitz's sentence was explicitly the influence of nuclear weapons on war. To some extent the question was a simple one: "Is it possible now to see general thermonuclear war as 'another' but still rational means of state policy?" The answer by Aleksandr Bovin and a number of others was equally simple: "It is impossible to find an argument to provide a goal that would justify the unleashing of a general rocket-atomic war."[65]

No one in the Soviet Union had a good word to say about nuclear war, but the military (and probably some civilian theorists as well) was concerned that an all-out denunciation of nuclear war would destroy the basis for deterring it. In this respect the Soviet Union faced (and still faces) the same problems that have bedeviled the United States. If the idea of nuclear war and of nuclear retaliation are rejected, how can continual retreat in the face of nuclear blackmail be avoided? How can the other side be deterred? As a Soviet general phrased it in a classified military journal, only when there is an acceptance of "the justice of the corresponding retribution against the aggressor . . . can [the] problem be posed and solved from the

62. Quoted in H. S. Dinerstein, *War and the Soviet Union: Nuclear Weapons and the Revolution in Soviet Military and Political Thinking* (Praeger, 1959), p. 39, and see p. 38.

63. E. Rybkin in *Kommunist vooruzhennykh sil*, no. 7 (April 1965), p. 86.

64. The actual phraseology is from a later book; see M. V. Popov, *Sushchnost' zakonov vooruzhennoi bor'by* (Moscow: Voennoe izdatel'stvo ministerstva oborony SSSR, 1964), p. 53.

65. "Politika Klassovaia sotsialisticheskaia," *Molodoi kommunist*, no. 4 (1974), p. 26.

view of defending the socialist homeland." *Only* in this way can it be solved, he emphasized. The problem for the military went further; its whole mission was, of course, to fight a war if necessary and to prepare troops for battle:

What if the possibility of a world nuclear war nonetheless becomes a hard reality and turns into actual war? . . . [If] the concept of 'military victory' is unacceptable and 'military strategy, the strategy of conducting war,' loses its significance . . . the armed forces of the socialist states at the present time, in principle, will not be able to set for themselves the goal of defeating imperialism. . . . Our military science should not even work out a strategy for the conduct of war. . . . The very call to raise the combat readiness of our armed forces and improve their capability to defeat any aggressor is senseless.[66]

To a considerable extent, however, the arguments of the mid-1960s were not limited to questions of a general nuclear war. If the Soviet Union were to think seriously about limited nuclear war instead of massive retaliation, if it were to seek the capacity to fight a war without recourse to nuclear weapons, there would be implications for which services would control nuclear weapons and for the level of appropriations allocated to conventional weapons. The interests of the different services were deeply involved in these decisions, and the issue was a very sensitive one because the Soviet ground forces had lost their traditional superior status to the strategic rocket forces in the early 1960s.

Thus the most prominent military theorist to argue that the essence of war had changed was Colonel Rybkin. Rybkin was scarcely a pacifist. In the 1970s he was to denounce civilians who attacked the very concept of nuclear war, and in 1965 he said that there is "nothing more dangerous, especially in military affairs," than the "ignorant" ideas (which by implication he attributed to the just-fallen Khrushchev) that "the objective advantages of our progressive system would automatically secure us quick successes."[67] Yet he argued that nuclear weapons significantly changed the essence of war. Surprise was more important at the beginning, and political control of war was much more difficult after it started.

66. K. Bochkarev, "The Question of the Sociological Aspect of the Struggle Against the Forces of Aggression and War," *Voennaia mysl'*, no. 9 (September 1968), p. 14. Quoted in Raymond L. Garthoff, "Mutual Deterrence and Strategic Arms Limitation in Soviet Policy," *International Security*, vol. 3 (Summer 1978), p. 120.

67. "O sushchnosti mirovoi raketno-iadernoi voiny," p. 56. Rybkin's views were apparently expressed more fully in a lecture he gave at the time. For references to the lecture and quotations from it, see I. Grudinin, "K voprosu o sushchnosti voiny," *Krasnaia zvezda*, July 21, 1966.

Many Westerners thought Rybkin was a "red hawk" and was advocating preemptive nuclear strikes as the basis of Soviet policy,[68] but his works in this period seem to have been misinterpreted. In saying that political leadership of war must be exercised primarily in peacetime because of the difficulty of control during war,[69] he surely was advocating the utmost civilian care to ensure that war did not start and almost surely was criticizing Khrushchev for taking such a chance in the Cuban missile crisis. In saying that nuclear war could get out of hand, he was warning against the notion of a neat, well-controlled use of battlefield nuclear weapons. He clearly did not want the generals to think of launching an atomic artillery attack at the beginning of battle just to inspire enthusiasm in the troops.

The meaning of Rybkin's insistence on the change in the essence of war was indicated, first of all, in the horrifying openness with which he spoke about a nuclear war's getting out of control. He would not have written in such a way if he had been trying to promote support for the use of nuclear weapons. Second, the meaning was confirmed in the conservative attacks upon him. Thus Colonel I. Grudinin, who saw the battlefield in traditional terms, criticized Rybkin in an outraged manner. Grudinin took pride in the balanced nature of his views (he spoke pompously of thesis, antithesis, and synthesis), but to a person who believed that nuclear weapons—even tactical nuclear weapons—were qualitatively different, his discussion of the qualifications on their use chilled rather than reassured:

It would be a mistake to think that every target should without fail be neutralized or destroyed only by powerful contemporary means. In the first place, it is not necessary. In the second place, it is too uneconomical. In the third place, it is not always possible because of the danger of hitting one's own troops. In the fourth place, the quantity of objectives and targets can exceed the number of atomic weapons allocated to them. Conventional artillery . . . will receive the task of neutralizing objectives of the opponent that it is inexpedient to strike with atomic weapons."[70]

It is probably best to see the Rybkin of the 1960s as the central ideologist for the change in military strategy and policy instituted early in the Brezhnev era. During these years a strong effort was made to expand conventional military forces and to build the capability of fighting a war

68. See, for example, Roman Kolkowicz, *The Red "Hawks" on the Rationality of Nuclear War*, memorandum RM-4899-PR (Rand Corp., March 1966).

69. "O sushchnosti mirovoi raketno-iadernoi voiny," pp. 54–55.

70. "O dialekticheskom otritsanii v voennom dele," *Kommunist vooruzhennykh sil*, no. 3 (February 1965), p. 54.

without recourse to nuclear weapons. The reconciliation with Germany can be seen as part of this strategy and the Rybkin argument as part of the effort within part of the military to rethink strategy.

No doubt many civilian theorists were satisfied with the effort to move away from reliance on nuclear weapons. Yet the major buildup of conventional forces by the Kennedy administration had been quickly followed by their use in Vietnam. Because of the development of a deep-water Soviet navy, because of rumors of leadership conflict in 1967 over the degree of Soviet involvement in the Middle East crisis, because of the large-scale border battles that began with China in 1969, and because the expansion of conventional forces in the Soviet Union and the United States was not being accompanied by any reassuring changes in the nuclear arsenals, the civilian proponents of détente could not be overjoyed.

In this framework, Soviet civilian analysts increasingly questioned whether the role of military force in international relations had undergone a fundamental change in the nuclear age. The most prominent of these was Georgii Arbatov, director of the Institute of the USA and Canada, which had been created in late 1967. In 1970 Arbatov dismissed nuclear war as impossible or at least impractical and noted that Americans had discovered in Vietnam that limited wars were also very difficult.

When the world was bipolar, when all the remaining processes were pushed into the background by the conflicts and struggles between the United States and the Soviet Union, which to many bourgeois investigators seemed simply like great powers and not countries that represented two systems, ideas about military force as the basis of policy seemed convincing to them. With the onset of the period when all the complicated social and political processes that are developing in the world came to the fore, the need for the present policy instead of a confrontation of force between individual states became obvious.[71]

By 1973 Arbatov took a more far-reaching position. He argued that Marx was right in saying militarism would "perish because of the dialectics of its own development," for in the modern world "military force has become all the more difficult to translate into political influence."[72] He also noted that "the more obvious the impotence of military force becomes in its way, the more evident is the impossibility of using it for political goals."[73]

---

71. "'Doktrina Niksona': deklaratsii i real'nost'," *SShA*, no. 2 (February 1971), p. 47.

72. "Vneshniaia politika SShA i nauchno-tekhnicheskaia revoliutsiia (okonchanie)," *SShA*, no. 10 (October 1973), p. 8.

73. "Tupiki politiki sily," *Problemy mira i sotsializma*, no. 2 (1974), p. 45.

In Arbatov's view the struggle between the Soviet Union and the United States would still continue, but political competition should essentially supplant military competition. He wrote about the great significance of nonmilitary forms of struggle—in economics, politics, ideology, and also, of course, in the scientific-technical sphere. In addition he looked upon the struggle of ideas in relatively benign terms as a struggle for world public opinion—"as an argument between world views . . . in forms and with methods that will not harm peaceful coexistence."[74]

Others also argued that the importance of military force in international relations was declining, but they combined this position with a much harsher view of the inevitable political struggle with the United States. For example, Henry Trofimenko, first a section head of the Institute of the International Workers' Movement and then a department head of the Institute of the USA and Canada, believed that "at the present time military power considerations are all the more being pushed into the background,"[75] but he criticized Arbatov for vagueness in talking about appeals to world public opinion, the existence of which he skeptically questioned. Trofimenko agreed with William Kintner that Washington gave too much attention to the military aspects of the struggle and underevaluated the political aspects. He seemed to think that the political struggle between the Soviet Union and the United States was as fierce as Kintner had said.[76]

Trofimenko in effect reversed Clausewitz's formula, asserting that "international politics is a continuation of war by other means."[77] He was critical of Marshall Shulman for pushing "his old idea of 'limited competition' between the USSR and the USA" because he saw "such theorizing in practice [as] directed at disorienting the public of capitalist countries." It also incorrectly described the "class antagonism between the two systems and between the two ideologies as conflict that is exclusively intergovernmental and foreign policy in character." Indeed, in speaking favorably about the flexibility that its naval program gave the United States, Trofi-

74. "Vneshniaia politika SShA i nauchno-tekhnicheskaia revoliutsiia (okonchanie)," pp. 10–11.

75. "Voprosy ukrepleniia mira i bezopasnosti v sovetsko-amerikanskikh otnosheniiakh," SShA, no. 9 (September 1974), p. 16.

76. See the book review in Mezhdunarodnaia zhizn', no. 3 (1971), p. 110; and "Nekotorye aspekty voenno-politicheskoi strategii SShA," SShA, no. 10 (October 1970), pp. 16–17.

77. "Nekotorye aspekty voenno-politicheskoi strategii SShA," SShA, no. 10 (1970), pp. 16–17.

menko seemed to be advocating a political competition that sometimes featured a judicious show of force.[78]

Few in the Soviet military were charmed by talk of the general decline in the importance of force in international relations. When this was the issue, they vigorously defended Clausewitz's formula and condemned any exaggeration of the role of politics and the means and methods of political struggle. Even Trofimenko's formulation that international politics is a continuation of war by other means was denounced: "With such antiscientific ideas . . . a correct opinion on the essence of politics or the essence of war is impossible."[79] The military was particularly worried that some who promoted détente might be saying—or could be read to be saying—that war had ceased to be a policy option of Western governments. Pavel Zhilin, director of the Institute of Military History, was direct in warning that talk about an era of the end of war was dangerous.[80] Together with Rybkin he acknowledged that "universal thermonuclear war had ceased to be a rational means to achieve a political goal for the imperialists" (and certainly for the Soviet Union), but the two men were even more insistent about the influence of militarism on the formation of U.S. foreign policy: "Militarism continues to exist as long as the social system that gave birth to it exists. . . . As long as the socioeconomic soil exists that gives rise to militarism, so the political tendencies capable of taking the risks of a military adventure will also be preserved."[81]

The military particularly did not want force to be considered so unimportant in international relations that defense expenditures could be cut. Zhilin and Rybkin pointed to Sputnik (and undoubtedly the rockets that propelled it) as the major element that had changed Western attitudes about war, and they argued that continued Soviet military strength was going to be necessary to control the West. "It would be incorrect to think that the present great successes in the realization of the Program of Peace will automatically secure the further dying out of militarism."[82]

78. See "Antikommunizm i vneshniaia politika imperializma," p. 75; and "Doktrina Niksona: deklaratsii i real'nost'," p. 32.

79. V. Sheliag and T. Kondrakov, "Leninskii analiz suschnosti voiny i nesostaiatel'nost' ego kritiki," *Kommunist vooruzhennykh sil,* no. 11 (June 1970), pp. 13, 15.

80. "Voennye aspekty razriadki napriazhennosti," *Mezhdunarodnaia zhizn',* no. 11 (November 1973), p. 34.

81. P. Zhilin and E. Rybkin, "Militarizm i sovremennye mezhdunarodnye otnosheniia," *Mezhdunarodnaia zhizn',* no. 9 (September 1973), p. 33.

82. Ibid., p. 37.

The importance of military force in international relations was not, of course, simply an issue that divided civilians and the military. Most American theorists who called themselves realists had emphasized the importance of power and force as determinants of foreign policy, at least before Vietnam had caused serious questioning. Some Soviet civilian theorists were also attracted to such tough-minded analysis. Anatolii Gromyko, son of the foreign minister, reported with no criticism that American scholars had begun to defend the thesis that military pressure or the threat of its application was acquiring greater significance in international relations. He asserted that "the policy of 'position of strength' is . . . a constant and, indeed, focal element of American foreign policy" and quoted Leonid Brezhnev to suggest that Soviet foreign policy must respond in kind: "We know that extremely aggressive circles often influence the formation of foreign policy of important capitalist states. In order to curb their activity, we need firmness, an unmasking of their intrigues and provocations, and a constant readiness to rebuff decisively their feeble impulse."[83] Arbatov, by contrast, quoted Brezhnev's statement that the West has been "required to adjust to new conditions."[84]

The debate about the relative importance of force in international relations heated up once more in the early 1980s as the United States increased its military spending. Soviet conservatives described this development in alarming terms. In 1983 General Chervov asserted on Soviet television that the United States was determined to "lead the world and arrange the world along American lines, solely on the basis of strength. . . . [The only] acceptable condition for relations with Moscow is the restoration, at any price, of . . . complete and undisputed military superiority over the Soviet Union. . . . [Its] one goal [is] to try to attain military superiority and then, by threatening the use of force, to dictate its wishes to other peoples and states."[85] Similarly, A. Slobodenko, a major general from the Academy of the General Staff, charged not only that American policy is "calculated to secure superiority over the USSR in the region of strategic arms and to receive the possibility of inflicting a destructive atomic blow on it,"

83. "Dilemmy amerikanskoi diplomatii," *SShA*, no. 6 (1970), p. 22.

84. "Amerikanskaia vneshniaia politika na poroge 70-kh godov, *SShA*, no. 1 (1970), p. 30.

85. Translated in "TV Program on Effects, U.S. Views of Nuclear War," Foreign Broadcast Information Service, *Daily Report: Soviet Union*, December 27, 1983, p. AA11. Chervov is head of the directorate of the General Staff, which handles arms control questions.

but that the policy has a real chance of success. "The location of American rockets in Europe essentially upsets the global strategic balance of forces in favor of the USA and gives it great advantages in inflicting a first nuclear strike." In talking about the American policy of seeking superiority, Slobodenko implied that additional financial resources were needed if the Soviets were to maintain the balance.[86]

The military was not, of course, of one mind about the nature of the threat. While Slobodenko was typical of a majority who wrote about the danger of a preemptive American strike, Marshal Nikolai Ogarkov, then head of the General Staff, publicly asserted in 1984 that any thought of an unanswerable first strike on the command and control systems was evidence of "military incompetence." He declared that "you do not have to be a military man or a scholar to understand that a further buildup of [nuclear weapons] is becoming senseless." For Ogarkov, it was the American technological advances in conventional and space weapons that posed the significant danger.[87] In 1981 he described the situation as being as dangerous as the 1930s and insisted that "it is necessary to bring the truth about the existing threat of a military danger to the Soviet people in a deeper and more well argued manner."[88]

Scholars and officials who favor détente have continued to warn that the importance of the military factor should not be exaggerated. "It is unrealistic," wrote Oleg Bykov, deputy director of the Institute of World Economics and International Relations (IMEMO), "even to raise the question of the achievement of military superiority at the present time."[89] Iurii Davydov, head of the section on American policy in Europe of the Institute of the USA and Canada, asserted that "reactionary politicians and ideologues in the West" were inclined to define the correlation of force only in terms of the military-strategic factor, but that "of course" they were far from right. "The former military superiority that Washington pines for so much is nothing more than an unrealizable illusion in contem-

86. "Mif o 'sovetskoi voennoi ugroze' kak obosnovanie popytok narushit' voenno-strategicheskoe ravnovesie v pol'zu imperializma," *Mezhdunarodnaia zhizn'*, no. 12 (1983), pp. 98, 101, 102.

87. Ogarkov made these statements in an interview in *Krasnaia zvezda*, May 9, 1984. After his removal, he repeated them virtually word for word in "Nemerknushchaia slava sovetskogo oruzhiia," *Kommunist vooruzhennykh sil*, no. 21 (November 1984), p. 26.

88. "Na strazhe mirnogo truda," *Kommunist*, no. 10 (July 1981), p. 91.

89. "Zakreplenie ravnovesiia ili stavka na prevoskhodstvo?" *MEiMO*, no. 11 (November 1981), p. 24.

porary conditions." Davydov contended that "the source of the huge power of the countries of socialism is their peace-loving foreign policy."[90] A generally conservative scholar (and son-in-law of Boris Ponomarev) wrote in *Izvestiia* that the Soviets were not frightened by the new American rockets.[91] Vladimir Lukin noted that American military spending has been far higher than that of the Japanese but that the "correlation of forces" between the two has become more favorable to Japan in the last decade.[92]

A number of leading figures in the foreign policy establishment have explicitly argued that conceptions of national security need fundamental rethinking and cannot be limited to narrow military considerations. In the words of Iurii Zhilin, leader of the group of consultants in the international department of the Central Committee, "Previously the idea of national security, with more or less justification, required calculations about who would emerge victorious in war. But such calculations are not applicable to a nuclear war. . . . In contemporary conditions, national security is connected in the most organic manner with international security—more than that, with global security."[93] The same point was made by a member of the editorial staff of *Kommunist:* "Realistic-thinking Western European politicians . . . say that in the atomic age there cannot be security in relation to somebody, but only joint security. And this means that in the formulation of a security policy directed at the prevention of war, it is necessary to proceed not only from one's own interests and needs, but also from those of what is called the other side."[94]

Others tried to reassure Soviet citizens in more general terms. For example, in December 1983, two days after General Chervov's alarmist presentation, Vadim Zagladin, first deputy head of the international department of the Central Committee, appeared on Soviet television and advanced a very different picture:

This question also is heard sometimes: have we not passed [a] bifurcation, has the world not started rolling down the slope leading in a dangerous direction? I

90. Iu. Davydov and L. Berzin, "Sootnoshenie sil na mezhdunarodnoi arene i ideologicheskaia bor'ba," *Mezhdunarodnaia zhizn'*, no. 11 (1983), pp. 70, 71, 72. The same point was made at length in V. Petrovsky, "Politiko-ideologicheskaia bor'ba vokrug problem razoruzheniia," *Mezhdunarodnaia zhizn'*, no. 12 (December 1983), pp. 91–97.

91. *Izvestiia*, July 9, 1984.

92. Bovin and Lukin, "Tsentry sily'—doktrina i real'nost'," p. 89.

93. "Bezopasnost' v iadernyi vek," *Rabochii klass i sovremennyi mir*, no. 2 (1984), p. 13.

94. V. Nekrasov, "Imperskie ustremleniia," *Pravda*, June 7, 1984.

personally do not think that this is the case. . . . There is no doubt that the dangerous brink that exists in principle somewhere has now come closer to us. . . . On the other hand . . . there is another tendency alongside this dangerous one, and one that cannot be escaped. If there is a crusade, a whipping up of tension, then there is something else too—the continuing and unrelenting activity of the forces that oppose the crusade."[95]

## International Relations: Conflict or Cooperation?

While virtually all Soviet scholars and officials have expressed the conviction that general nuclear war can and should be avoided, they have continued to discuss the extent to which the existence of nuclear weapons, the Soviet achievement of military parity, and the impact of public opinion in Western political systems have modified international relations. To what extent are relations between the Soviet Union and the major capitalist countries characterized by implacable conflict and to what extent can they accommodate cooperation and collaboration?

Of course, the debates that have already been discussed in this chapter also deal with this question. Implicitly if not logically the issue of conflict or cooperation lay behind the disputes about the role of force in international relations. Those who emphasized force may have been thinking in large part about the possibility of using military power for expansionist purposes, but their public discussion has almost exclusively been of the threat of U.S. use of force. While this claim may sometimes be manipulative and is not at all incompatible with the pursuit of an aggressive Soviet policy, it would be a mistake to doubt the sincerity of those expressing a sense of threat or to forget the degree to which it is a part of the discussion of conflict and cooperation. After all, Western ideas of democracy pose a real threat to communist control in Eastern Europe and perhaps even in the non-Russian republics of the Soviet Union. It is very easy for the ideological and military threat of the West to merge in the mind of a Russian conservative.

The issue of competition or cooperation has also been raised in more direct ways, increasingly so in the 1970s and 1980s. Earlier the question often took the form of the meaning of the principle of peaceful coexistence. Although with varying degrees of emphasis, Lenin and Stalin al-

95. "'Studio 9' on U.S. Policy, INF Countermeasures," in FBIS, *Daily Report: Soviet Union*, December 27, 1983, pp. CC9, CC11.

ways endorsed peaceful coexistence as indispensable in relations between countries with different systems. (The phrase was never applied to relations between countries with the same system). Even when war between capitalist countries was said to be inevitable, Soviet leaders insisted that the Soviet Union and capitalist countries should coexist without war until the Western working class finally overthrew the capitalist system.

Nevertheless, there are different kinds of peace. The word "coexistence" intrinsically has a very cold and narrow meaning both in Russian and English. In 1973 the head of the USA department of the Ministry of Foreign Affairs, Georgii Kornienko (writing under his pseudonym, K. M. Georgiev), coauthored an article that noted, "Eisenhower said, 'There is no alternative to peace.' This formulation is fairly limited in its content, implying the simple absence of war."[96] Kornienko was critical of Eisenhower's phrase, but there have in fact been many in the Soviet Union who have spoken of peaceful coexistence in these terms: it is "an objective necessity. . . . Either peaceful coexistence or global nuclear slaughter—there is no third alternative. The policy of peaceful coexistence solidifies the position of Communist parties and their connection with the masses and strengthens the confidence of the masses in the Communists."[97]

For others, however, the "peace" in peaceful coexistence had a broader meaning. Cold war was, after all, peace, and those who criticized it and praised "the spirit of Geneva" after Khrushchev's meeting with President Eisenhower and Prime Minister Harold Macmillan there in 1955 had an image of a possible and desirable relationship between the Soviet Union and the West that went beyond the mere absence of military hostilities. After Kornienko quoted Eisenhower he asserted that "it is still a long distance from this point of view to the principle of peaceful coexistence."[98] Writing in 1974, Aleksandr Bovin suggested that this conception of peaceful coexistence was a new one, but he still insisted on it and spelled out its cooperative aspects: "Peaceful coexistence in its contemporary understanding is not only the absence of a 'hot' war and not only an overcoming

96. K. M. Georgiev and M. O. Kolosov, "Sovetsko-amerikanskie otnosheniia na novom etape," *SShA*, no. 3 (March 1973), p. 14.

97. S. Lukonin, "Kharakter nashei epokhi i general'naia liniia mirovogo kommunisticheskogo dvizheniia," *SShA*, no. 21 (November 1964), p. 19. There have been people who have described it in quite manipulative terms: "Peaceful coexistence is a specific form of class struggle."

98. Georgiev and Kolosov, "Sovetsko-amerikanskie otnosheniia na novom etape," p. 14.

of the inertia of a cold war. It is the establishment of trust and mutual understanding between states. It is all-sided collaboration between them."[99]

In the early 1970s, the catchword of the new Brezhnev policy was "razriadka napriazhennosti" (relaxation of tension) or simply "razriadka." In its origins the word meant "the unloading of the charge from a weapon," and the first meaning listed for it in the major Russian-English dictionary is "unloading."[100] Clearly, by its nature this Soviet equivalent of the word "détente" inherently has a more cooperative meaning than "peaceful coexistence." Soviet scholars have no more been able to criticize the principle of razriadka publicly than they have peaceful coexistence. But there have been two implicit ways of discussing its real meaning: through the language used to describe international relations and through variations on the possibility of relaxation of tension.

The language of those skeptical about détente who see international relations in terms of conflict need not be described at length. It is the traditional language, an emphasis on the class character of foreign policy and "the principled character of Soviet foreign policy," a focus upon the centrality of the Soviet-American conflict, which is defined not in bipolar terms but as a struggle of "two diametrically opposing ideologies [that] intensifies."[101] Those who see international relations as more cooperative can sometimes say so openly. Thus V. Petrovsky, head of the international organizations department of the Ministry of Foreign Affairs, warned against "turning [the concept of] global conflict into an absolute. . . . The concept of international conflict as an eternal, root category or even essence of international relations . . . in whatever phraseology it is clothed, in practice ignores the objective fact of the constantly widening collaboration in politics, economics, and science and technology of states of different systems."[102]

Vadim Zagladin made the same point in taking a statement by Marx that conservatives often had cited and reversing its usual elliptical meaning.

99. "Politika klassovaia sotsialisticheskaia," p. 21.
100. See G. A. Trofimenko, "SSSR-SShA: mirnoe sosushchestvovanie kak norma vzaimootnoshenii," *SShA*, no. 2 (February 1974), p. 12; and A. I. Smirnitsky, ed., *Russko-angliiskii slovar'* (Moscow: Izdatel'stvo Sovetskaia entsiklopediia, 1969).
101. N. Kapchenko, "Strategiia mira v deistvii," *Mezhdunarodnaia zhizn'*, no. 9 (September 1976), p. 99.
102. "Dogmy konfrontatsii (Ob amerikanskikh kontseptsiiakh 'global'nogo konflikta,'" *MEiMO*, no. 2 (February 1980), pp. 21, 22.

Marx had said that "international relations are secondary and tertiary, in general derivative, transferred, and nonprimary relations," and this has repeatedly been used by those who wanted to emphasize the priority of economics and the class struggle over political factors. Zagladin quoted it but asserted that the dominant economic development was an internationalization of the world economy and that this required a new kind of international relations.[103]

The cooperative nature of international relations is most frequently raised implicitly in discussions of "the global problem," "the general human problem," "global interdependence," and the like. Writers emphasizing these phenomena almost always insist that general human problems exert a deep influence on international relations: "The fact that mankind has entered a phase of development when an increasing number of important problems of a political, economic, and scientific-technical character acquire a worldwide aspect and, directly or indirectly, completely or partially, touch the peoples of all or a majority of states provides evidence about the increased mutual connection and mutual dependence of different countries."[104] Discussions of global problems usually center on such issues as pollution, food supply, the energy crisis, and oceanic questions. However, one article on global problems and the future of the world economy, written by an official of the Central Committee apparatus, contained a three-page section on the discontinuation of the arms race as the necessary condition for solving economic problems.[105] On Moscow television in 1982, Georgii Arbatov pointed to yet another common interest: "Everybody is dependent on the stability of the international economic system and the international monetary system."[106]

Sometimes the necessity for cooperation is implied in the use of phraseology far removed from "irreconcilable class conflict" or "two camps." One scholar writes of the "human association" (*soobshchestvo*); a foreign ministry official asserts that "mankind continues to exist as a united whole"; a Central Committee official speaks on Soviet television of "we Europeans." An editorial writer for *Kommunist* states that "it is well

103. "Marksizm-leninizm o roli rabochego klassa i mezhdunarodnykh otnosheniiakh," *Rabochii klass i sovremennyi mir,* no. 4 (1984), pp. 16–17.

104. M. Maksimova, "Vsemirnoe khoziaistvo, nauchno-tekhnicheskaia revoliutsiia i mezhdunarodnye otnosheniia (chast' vtoraia)," *MEiMO,* no. 5 (May 1979), p. 25.

105. S. M. Men'shikov, "Global'nye problemy i budushchee mirovoi ekonomiki," *Voprosy filiosofii,* no. 4 (1983), pp. 113–15.

106. *"Studio 9,"* May 29, in FBIS, *Daily Report: Soviet Union,* June 1, 1982, p. CC6.

known that the history of the European peoples, be they on the east or west of the continent, is not subject to artificial division," and other scholars refer to "the two lines in the world politics—between the proponents of an aggressive policy and the advocates of the preservation and deepening of détente," without suggesting that these two lines coincided with the division between classes or even between the two systems.[107]

In delineating these competing images of international relations as stark class conflict and as a combination of conflict and a growing degree of cooperation, I have, of course, grouped scholars who have differences in their views. Arbatov of the Institute of the USA and Canada, whose articles deal almost exclusively with the United States, has usually written more cautiously in the last five years than Petrovsky of the Ministry of Foreign Affairs, who deals with the international scene as a whole. In addition, many people clearly occupy positions in between. For example, V. Mshvenieradze, deputy director of the Institute of Philosophy, subtly suggested some chance of change in the West and warned against either exaggerating the possibilities of détente or giving up on it if it were not perfect. Yet his article also contained some chilling statements. "Being based on force, imperialism recognizes only force," he asserted. "V. I. Lenin warned, 'The more we win, the more the capitalist exploiters will learn to unite and move to more decisive attacks against us!' "[108]

A second important nuance in the Soviet discussion of conflict and cooperation centers on the countries with whom cooperation is possible. In a bipolar world the real question is whether cooperation is possible with the other superpower, and traditionally the analysis of the threat posed by the United States has been a way of discussing the degree of cooperation that is possible in international relations. In a number of cases this continues to be true. All Soviet scholars and officials hold a very negative view of the Reagan administration, no doubt sincerely so, but those suggesting that the possibility of cooperation still exists argue that U.S. policy

107. See V. N. Shevchenko, "K kharakteristike dialektiki sovremennoi epokhi (chast' pervaia)," *Filosofskie nauki*, no. 5 (1981), p. 23; V. Petrovsky, "Kontseptsiia vzaimozavisimosti v strategii SShA," *MEiMO*, no. 9 (September 1977), p. 71; V. Kobysh in "'Studio 9' on U.S. Policy, INF Countermeasures," in FBIS, *Daily Report: Soviet Union*, December 27, 1983, p. CC10; and D. Tomashevsky and V. Lukov, "Radi zhizni na zemli," *MEiMO*, no. 2 (February 1983), p. 10.

108. "Politika razriadki i krizis burzhuaznoi politologii," *MEiMO*, no. 2 (1981), pp. 110, 112, 120, 121. He was identified as deputy director of the institute in *Voprosy filosofii*, no. 6 (1983), p. 146.

is not permanent. For example, Aleksandr Bovin, who was quoted previously calling for a broad definition of peaceful coexistence and for a renunciation of thermonuclear war, tried to reassure the Soviet reader in 1983 when the Euromissiles were deployed. "[There is] a cyclical character to the evolution of Soviet-American relations, an alternation between periods of détente and periods of confrontation. . . . These ups and downs of the political temperature reflect the confrontation between different factions and groups within the U.S. ruling class." He added that "Sooner or later the combined effort of all the factors [working against Reagan's policy] will lead to a new alignment of political forces within the United States. That is when a new, fifth period will begin in the development of Soviet-U.S. relations."[109] In 1985 Bovin stated explicitly that the world would become far less bipolar by the end of the century, but he warned, "the more poles, the more difficult it is to hold the system in equilibrium."[110]

Similarly on October 6th, 1984, the most important Soviet television talk show, "Studio 9," carried a discussion of the prospects for a Reagan second term in the light of his softer rhetoric toward the Soviet Union. General Chervov emphasized that Reagan had not changed and that the military danger "not only is not decreasing, but is growing." Valerian Zorin, the show's host and a long-time supporter of détente,[111] asserted that there are "specialists who say . . . that it is an unquestionable fact that in the field of foreign policy the last four years were surprisingly unsuccessful for Washington [and] who speak about the aspirations of some circles in Washington to draw some conclusions from the failure of the past term." Zorin associated himself with this position.[112]

If the kind of harsh statements about the United States uttered by the Soviet military are coupled with equally harsh statements about Western Europe and its subordination to the United States (and they usually are), then clearly little room exists for cooperation in international relations. However, among a number of analysts, primarily civilians, a strong anti-Americanism is combined with a much more favorable attitude toward Western Europe and Japan. This implies the possibility of international

---

109. "50 let—chto dal'she?" *Izvestiia,* November 16, 1983.
110. Bovin and Lukin, '"Tsentry sily'—doktrina i real'nost'," pp. 80, 86.
111. See the discussion on p. 196 of this chapter.
112. The quotations from "Studio 9" are in FBIS, *Daily Report: Soviet Union,* October 9, 1984, pp. CC2–CC9.

relations in which cooperation with some of the major countries is not only possible but indispensable.

For example, Lev Tolkunov, the editor of *Izvestiia* under Andropov, not only damned President Reagan in December 1983 but also gave considerable attention to a book by Richard Nixon. "The theme of the book . . . is that not détente, not negotiations with the USSR, but force and only force, the growth of military might, and control of strategically important regions of the earth should lie at the base of the foreign policy of the USA. The global conflict between the USSR and the USA, which began at once after the end of the Second World War, is in the opinion of the ex-president, a third world war." Tolkunov's charge that "the present president thinks in an analagous way" was not nearly as disturbing to the reader as the idea that the one president associated with détente also thought in such terms. Nevertheless, Tolkunov ended his article with a fervent appeal for détente as the only possible foreign policy.[113] During early 1984 when *Pravda* was beginning an anti-German campaign and emphasizing the dangers of Euromissiles, *Izvestiia* was emphasizing economic conflicts in the West and the possibility of good relations with Western Europe.

Aleksandr Iakovlev, appointed director of IMEMO in September 1983, pushed such a position even more clearly. In the first article he published after becoming director, he took direct aim at scholars such as Bovin and Arbatov: "Some politicians and public figures with a certain complacency are inclined to consider this an accidental moment in history, a moment of an irrational character, attributing it to the personal characteristics of President Reagan. It is indisputable that the current American president exerts an extremely destructive influence on the international situation. . . . But R. Reagan at the same time is carrying out a social task [*sotsial'nyi zakaz*]."[114] In Iakovlev's view, Reagan is not all that different from his predecessors. "It is a rare American president who has not spoken about the claims of the USA to 'world dominion.' Truman, Eisenhower, Kennedy, Nixon, as well as presidents before them and after them—they all loved to talk about the 'divine' mission of this country and its 'special responsibility.'" The list of presidents was a sobering one for the Soviet

---

113. "Ideologicheskaia bor'ba i mirnoe sosushchestvovanie na sovremennom etape," *Mezhdunarodnaia zhizn'*, no. 12 (December 1983), pp. 75–76, 78, 81.

114. "Zakusivshie udila," *Izvestiia*, October 7, 1983. For a similar line of argument, see the interview with him in *Komsomol'skaia pravda*, December 25, 1983.

reader. Kennedy has been idealized in the Soviet media, Nixon launched détente, and immediately before Truman was Roosevelt, a leader almost in the pantheon.

Iakovlev insisted that one must not only look at Reagan's policy, but at the American response to it. "Why are there so many people who are so indifferent to the militarization of the country, to the creation of the nightmare of universal terror, to the threats by their leaders to destroy other countries, to appeals of maniacs for nuclear war? . . . There can be only one answer . . . the deep amorality built on a convulsive worship of success, on gain for some and suffering of those doomed to failure," "the messianic idea of ownership of the world that is characteristic of the American social fabric," "the cult of power," "the feeling of superiority and omnipotence." These, Iakovlev contended, are part of American political culture, and he went out of his way to say that the messianic concept is believed in "let us say directly, not only by the ruling elite of society, but not a small part of those Americans on whom rained pieces of the pies baked by wars. They often sincerely believe that 'barbarians' in other lands need American tutelage, education, political institutions—in a word, the American order."[115]

Especially coming from the only important foreign policy appointee of the first year that Andropov was in power, the article was not very heartening to Americans. If the American people are as bad as their ruling circles are said to be, it is hard to see where change for the better was to come from, at least in the United States. Indeed, a decade earlier, Iakovlev, then first deputy head of the propaganda department of the Central Committee, had written an article criticizing Russian chauvinism and had immediately been appointed ambassador to Canada (a post he held until his appointment to IMEMO). His pessimism about Soviet-American relations and the possibility of a calm adjustment of national interests may have been even more deeply rooted than the 1983 article indicated.

When Iakovlev turned to other parts of the world, however, he painted a far less gloomy picture. He wrote of a "relative leveling in the strength of the three centers of power: the USA, Western Europe, and Japan," and he argued that "in the historically foreseeable future the centrifugal tendency in the capitalist world will grow." He put special emphasis on Japan by stating that it has assumed first place in many technologies, has become

115. Ibid.

"a world economic state," and has supplanted the United States as "the symbol of youth and dynamism in the Western world."[116] He surely was hinting not only at the desirability of basing policy more on cooperation with Western Europe and Japan but also of instituting an economic reform that would open the Soviet Union more to Japanese technology. Because Iakovlev has risen to become one of Gorbachev's chief advisers, his views are very important to understanding the thrust of current policy.

The subtleties of the debates about Europe and the posture to take toward the United States are the subjects of other studies.[117] It is enough to note here than a nontraditional image of international relations with the West can come in many forms. Although Iakovlev's position has similarities with the old view of taking advantage of capitalist contradictions, it takes on very different overtones when it is combined with a belief in the internationalization of the world economy that Zagladin explicitly adopts and that Iakovlev surely shares. When taken in conjunction with the type of opinions about the world economy cited in chapter 4 from Ivan D. Ivanov, Iakovlev's deputy director at IMEMO, this viewpoint can imply a strong attack on the protectionism in the Soviet economy, with radical implications for Soviet foreign policy. It also, as shall be discussed in the next chapter, can provide the basis for a fundamental attack on the basic foreign policy posture that the Soviet Union has taken in the third world.

116. "Imperializm: sopernichestvo i protivorechiia," *Pravda*, March 23, 1984.
117. See Jerry F. Hough, "Soviet Perspectives on European Security, International Security," *International Journal*, no. 1 (Winter 1984–85), pp. 20–41, for a preliminary statement from what will be a multiyear project.

CHAPTER EIGHT

# Relations with the Third World

USUALLY WE think of foreign relations in government-to-government terms, but Soviet foreign relations have always been much broader. Thus after 1919 when the Soviet Union began to establish diplomatic relations, the really interesting issues concerned the policy to be followed toward noncommunist but anti-Western movements in the colonies, as well as the analogous movements under Kemal Ataturk in Turkey and Chiang Kai-shek in China (see chapter 6).

Soviet relations with Turkey and China, for instance, could be complex. The Soviet Union maintained formal diplomatic relations with the pro-Western regimes in Constantinople and Peking and conducted correct—even friendly—relations with them. It also had an informal working relationship with the Manchurian warlord who had de facto control of the territory through which ran the Chinese eastern railroad to Vladisvostok. At the same time the Soviet Union also provided substantial military assistance to Ataturk and Chiang Kai-shek who were trying to overthrow the official governments, and, of course, it attempted to direct the activities of the local communists through the Communist International (Comintern). In China, in particular, the Soviet Union helped organize Chiang Kai-shek's party, the Kuomintang, and it ordered the Chinese communists to participate in it.

With the defeat of this policy in 1927–28 the Soviet Union in practice adopted a semi-isolationist policy toward the third world—reasonably friendly but passive governmental relations,[1] often coupled with hard-line

---

1. For a memoir containing a picture of the friendly relations between the Soviet Union and Iran, including a personal friendship between the ambassador's son and the future shah, see N. G. Pal'gunov, *Tridtsat' let vospominaniia zhurnalista i diplomata* (Moscow: Politizdat, 1964), pp. 61–62.

226

directives to the Communist party. Only after World War II, as the colonial empires in Asia began to break up, did the Soviet Union really have important decisions to make. As had been the case in the 1930s, it was happy to establish diplomatic relations with any new country, but the important policy question was the quality of the relationship and the price to pay for it. Should the Soviet Union strive to develop economic ties, especially by providing aid and credit? Should it provide military assistance? Should it instruct foreign communists to support neutralist or pro-Soviet "bourgeois" governments even if this meant the sacrifice of revolutionary goals?

In the early postwar period the focus of attention was India. If any colony were to achieve some foreign policy independence, it should be India and, as discussed in chapter 5, a number of leading scholars asserted that it would, in fact, be able to do so. Vladimir Balabushevich, the leading Soviet Indologist, stated, "the Indian representatives can now take a more independent position in the organization of the United Nations."[2] After 1949 Stalin did not permit this idea to be expressed publicly, but it has been reported that three of the leading orientalists—Balabushevich, Aleksei D'iakov, and Ivan Reisner—continued behind the scenes to advocate a more flexible policy toward the third world.[3]

Stalin rejected such flexibility. In the first place, he believed that the third world bourgeoisie would evolve in a pro-Western direction, as had Turkey under Ataturk and China under Chiang Kai-shek. Because India remained part of the British Commonwealth, retained top British military officers, and accepted foreign investment, Stalin did not think it could be truly independent, even though it proclaimed its neutrality and criticized U.S. policy in Korea. Its independence also seemed unlikely to him because the capitalist countries would inevitably be driven to war with each other out of an absolute economic need to exploit colonies, and they were scarcely likely to permit third world countries to exercise any independence.

In practical terms Soviet policy toward the third world in the late Stalin period tended to be isolationist. Trade remained at extremely low levels.[4] No military aid was given to a radical new regime in Guatemala (nor were arms sold to it), and neither the Soviet government nor the Iranian Com-

2. "India posle razdela," *Mirovaia ekonomika i mirovaia politika*, no. 12 (1947), p. 49.
3. This point was made by L. I. Reisner of the Institute of Oriental Studies of the USSR Academy of Sciences in private conversation.
4. See Joseph Berliner, *Soviet Economic Aid* (Praeger, 1958), pp. 81–87.

munist party gave any support to Prime Minister Mossadegh when he nationalized the British Petroleum Company. In fact, the communists led demonstrations that added to the chaos and that provided one of the impetuses for a military coup.

## The Breakup of the Old Orthodoxies

The disenchantment of scholars with Stalin's policy could have had several causes and results. By the end of his life, Stalin had retreated from pressure on Berlin and was concentrating his real foreign policy (to the extent that it existed) in the West on support for communist-front peace movements critical of the United States and NATO.[5] He would not cooperate with independent peace forces and certainly not with Western governments in any meaningful way. A scholar's desire to abandon the general isolationalist, even zenophobic, posture and increase contact with the outside world could lead to an appeal for better relations with former colonies as part of the call for an opening to the West and cooperative relations with the United States and Western Europe.

By contrast, unhappiness with Stalin's image of the dependent character of the third world capitalist countries could arise from the fact that it led to their de facto abandonment to the United States. Such critics wanted the Soviet Union to function as a more active great power, selling arms to Guatemala, trying to use Nasser as a proxy, and cooperating with any country that resisted having Western military bases. A rejection of the old orthodoxy could therefore imply a more competitive relationship with the United States in the third world rather than a more cooperative one.

For this reason, any attack on the old views had potentially ambiguous implications for foreign policy. The ambiguity was heightened because Nikita Khrushchev himself seemed fundamentally ambiguous about relations with the third world. He seemed genuinely to want improved relations with the West, but he also seemed to be genuinely optimistic about the course of developments in the third world, and he certainly wanted to compete with the United States in those countries. This dualistic policy made it especially difficult for participants in the debates to clarify their intentions.

5. See Marshall D. Shulman, *Stalin's Policy Reappraised* (Harvard University Press, 1963), pp. 7–12.

In 1953 the Soviet Union shipped arms to Guatemala, but at the same time, Georgii Malenkov began to speak in more favorable terms of third world leaders such as India's Jawaharlal Nehru. Within a year the official evaluation of the "bourgeois nationalist" leaders had changed. In 1955 Khrushchev sent his personal representative to negotiate an arms agreement with Egypt, and together with the new premier, Nikolai Bulganin, undertook a ceremonial visit to South and Southeast Asia. The Soviet Union began providing major foreign aid to the third world, including construction of a steel mill in India and the Aswan Dam in Egypt. In 1956 the doctrine of the inevitability of war between capitalist states was repudiated, including, of course, its basic analysis of the function of colonies.

Those who favored good relations with bourgeois third world regimes found it easy to do so simply by praising Khrushchev's policy. One of the leading young scholars, Georgii Mirsky, explicitly asserted that a country's foreign policy was not necessarily linked with its internal system: "The example of the United Arab Republic shows how a country, the internal development of which is extremely contradictory, conducts a consistently anti-imperialist foreign policy. Such a policy unquestionably flows from the national interests of the country and is produced by deep internal reasons, but it also reflects the influence of the general atmosphere in the world."[6] Similarly, it was very easy to support Khrushchev's foreign aid policy by hailing socialist generosity.

At the more esoteric level, the supporters of good relations with "bourgeois" third world countries employed a number of devices already discussed in the last chapter. Thus in the 1954 *Kommunist* attack on a book about Latin America, the authors of the review insisted that Latin America is not a uniform whole. They contended that there were differences from country to country and in particular that the degree and form of dependence upon the United States varied substantially. "The time has passed when Wall Street inspired and carried out the overthrow of governments in Latin America without obstacle."[7] They asserted that the bourgeoisie in Latin America, let alone the petty bourgeoisie and the intelligentsia, were not united in their point of view and that many were opposed to the United States and to American corporations.

6. R. M. Avakov and G. I. Mirsky, "Desiat' let antiimperialisticheskoi bor'by egipetskogo naroda (1952–1962)," *Narody Azii i Afriki,* no. 4 (1962), p. 50.

7. V. Ermolaev, S. Semenov, and A. Sivolobov, "Ser'eznye oshibki v knige o rabochem dvizhenii v Latinskoi Amerike," *Kommunist,* no. 7 (May 1954), pp. 119–23.

Supporters of this position defined the nationalist bourgeoisie broadly and described it favorably. They emphasized the importance of domestic political struggles inside third world countries.[8] They argued that Western Europe and Japan were challenging the position of American capitalism in the third world, thereby implying more maneuvering room for developing countries. They mentioned divisions within the United States itself, suggesting that America might not be wholehearted in its determination to dominate the third world.[9] They insisted on the importance of political rather than economic factors in American policy toward Vietnam.[10]

The critics were in a much more difficult position, for they were opposing Soviet foreign policy—and they were opposing it on an issue that was at the heart of the conflict with China. Indeed, they may well have been advocating higher priority for relations with China, even if relations with the "bourgeois nationalists" had to be sacrificed for this purpose. Evgenii Zhukov, the highest-level political scholar who seemed skeptical of the new line, ceased publishing on the third world altogether from 1960 to 1963, and this must have been related in some way to the heightening conflict with China.[11] In this situation the conservatives tried to repeat the old analyses as best they could—that the United States was dominant and led by a desire for profit, the third world bourgeoisie was united and dedicated to narrow class interests, and so forth.[12] They also probably made their points through discussions of revolutionary strategy and praise for local communist parties, for the latter was a reasonably safe position.

The important debates about foreign policy toward the third world in the 1950s and 1960s were in fact probably not those that focused on foreign policy as such but those that overtly dealt with economic development and revolutionary strategy and that have already been discussed in previous chapters. Certainly, the scholars who suggested the need to rely on local communist parties rather than other forces for revolution cannot

8. B. Abdurazakov's review of V. P. Nikhamin, *Ocherki vneshnei politiki Indii, 1947–1957 gg.*, in *Narody Azii i Afriki*, no. 1 (1961), p. 188.

9. G. L. Bondarevsky's review of M. A. Grechev, *Kolonial'naia politika SShA posle vtoroi mirovoi voiny*, in *Problemy vostokovedeniia*, no. 6 (1959), p. 179.

10. See Georgii Mirsky's statement that "what the Americans are doing in Vietnam is not so much a drive for profits, as a defense of their political interests," in "Metropolii bez kolonii," *Mirovaia ekonomika i mezhdunarodnye otnosheniia*, no. 10 (October 1965), p. 107. (Hereafter *MEiMO*.)

11. For Zhukov's views, see chapter 6, p. 149. For a complete list of his publications see "Spisok osnovykh rabot akademika Zhukova," *Narody Azii i Afriki*, no. 6 (1967), p. 154.

12. See the books criticized in book reviews cited in footnotes 8 and 9.

have been happy about Soviet legitimization of the Nehrus and the Su-karnos, let alone providing military and economic assistance to them.

Those presenting the nontraditional positions on revolutionary strategy may also have often been making a foreign policy argument. Thus the first serious criticism of the old orthodoxies at the time of the Guatemalan crisis may simply have implied that radical noncommunist regimes such as that in Guatemala had a chance to evolve to the left and that they should be supported as representing an alternative route to socialism. Yet, the criti-cisms could also be read as appeals to foreign communists to subordinate revolutionary goals to the foreign policy struggle against the United States. Once the Guatemalan regime was overthrown, this argument became the natural one (at least until the success of Castro in the early 1960s).

The optimistic argument of the 1960s that Castro's evolution was the natural one in the third world was clearly congruent with Khrushchev's foreign policy. It suggested that the suppression of communists by men such as Nasser was relatively irrelevant in a country's revolutionary devel-opment and that Soviet support of such leaders promoted revolution rather than sacrificed it (as the Chinese had charged). It strongly advocated an active Soviet foreign economic policy toward the third world. Indeed, optimistic endorsement of the Cuban path of revolution may sometimes have been nothing more than a cynical justification for an activist foreign policy. Those who wanted the Soviet Union to compete vigorously with President Kennedy's activism and the Alliance for Progress could find it productive to claim that this furthered world revolution even if they did not believe it themselves.

In the 1970s, when scholars such as Georgii Mirsky and Viktor Tiagunenko emphasized the crucial importance of the political leadership or, later, of a vanguard party and worried about the long-term impact of bureaucracies and markets on revolutionary evolution, they could have been making a distinction between radical regimes (in fact, regimes be-coming progressively more radical) and moderate ones. It is possible that they thought the Soviet Union should bet on the radicals rather than on moderate regimes such as that in India. Those who were beginning to suggest that major third world countries were on a capitalist path not strikingly different from the one taken by Western Europe offered no reason for the Soviet Union to invest heavily in radical regimes. By the 1980s some of the proponents of this position were explicitly asserting that the natural Soviet allies were capitalist countries such as India. Because the Institute of Oriental Studies, the prominent center of pessimism about third world revolutionary prospects, had long tended to be dominated by specialists on India, perhaps from the beginning they had an intention of advancing Soviet-Indian relations as a model for future Soviet foreign policy strategy.

## Dependence and Independence

As has been seen, the issue of dependence and independence with respect to the third world has had a checkered history in the Soviet Union. Stalin essentially argued that a third world capitalist country would inevitably be dependent both in its economic development and in its foreign policy. For most of the Khrushchev era, scholars generally retained the Stalinist position on economic development but suggested that third world capitalist contries might be capable of an independent foreign policy. Independent, however, meant "anti-imperialist" or "pro-Soviet," not a policy of treating the superpowers evenhandedly. It was still taken for granted that a radical regime was more likely to have a pro-Soviet foreign policy, and it was widely assumed that problems of economic dependence made the nationalistic third world especially subject to radical revolution.

By the second half of the 1960s a number of these assumptions were being challenged by events. The defection of China and Albania and many of the most radical elements in the world communist movement from the Soviet orbit of influence shattered the belief that radical evolution abroad inevitably meant a pro-Soviet foreign policy. Conservative coups in countries such as Ghana and Indonesia destroyed any belief that nationalism made left-wing evolution of radical regimes irreversible. In addition, third world countries themselves often showed an independence in foreign policy that had little relationship to the East-West confrontation. The war between India and Pakistan, ended through Premier Aleksei Kosygin's mediation in Tashkent in January 1966, illuminated a problem and suggested a possible foreign policy role for the Soviet Union that did not fit well with Stalin's or even Khrushchev's theories.

The most important questions about the dependence of the third world countries on the industrial countries were raised by the oil crisis of 1973 and the accompanying dramatic increase in the price of petroleum and other commodities. Did this demonstrate, as some scholars insisted, "the growing dependence of industrial states on developing ones" rather than the reverse?[13] Or was Viktor Tiagunenko, a leading exponent of dependency theory, right in arguing that the oil crisis actually increased the dependency of most of the third world countries because they were petroleum importers and had to come to the West for loans to purchase it?[14]

Even in retrospect it is often not clear which question was being raised in an article about dependency. Sometimes the issue was whether third world countries were capable of sustained and healthy economic growth without a socialist revolution. Sometimes it was a very practical issue for the Soviet Union as an exporter of petroleum and other commodities: what would happen to commodity prices and what assumptions about foreign currency receipts should the planners be making for the future as they formulated five-year plans? Sometimes the issue was one of foreign policy: how independent could capitalist third world countries be in their foreign policies and how much opportunity and danger did this present to the Soviet Union?

At a minimum the oil crisis shattered any simplistic notions of foreign policy dependency as fully as it did such notions about the impossibility of growth by capitalist countries in the third world. It was, after all, the conservative and pro-American governments of Iran and Saudi Arabia that took the lead in the OPEC actions. One could no longer say in any serious way that conservative regimes—even military allies of the United States—could never show independence of U.S. foreign policy. The probability of such independence might be low, but the possibility still existed. Evgenii Primakov, the most interesting and influential scholar clearly writing about foreign policy when he discussed dependence, coined the phrase "asymmetrical character of mutual dependence" to describe North-South relations,[15] and it was difficult to avoid such an image, at least for the major third world countries.

In addition, Soviet scholars began to recognize the possibility of independent third world activity that did not fit into the old "metropolis-periphery" debates or, to phrase it differently, into a view of foreign policy as primarily concerned with East-West relations. This possibility emerged in a controversial suggestion in the military literature that the classification

13. R. Andreasian, "Resursy razvivaiushchikhsia stran i kapitalizm," *MEiMO*, no. 9 (September 1976), p. 144.

14. "Vyvoz kapitala iz razvivaiushchikhsia stran," *MEiMO*, no. 3 (March 1975), p. 95.

15. "Zakon neravnomernosti razvitiia i istoricheskie syd'by osvobodivshikhsia stran," *MEiMO*, no. 12 (December 1980), p. 38.

of types of war be modified. Traditionally, Soviet military analysis had listed four types of war, but only one—the war of national liberation—was really relevant to the third world. In 1968, however, two military officers, K. Stepanov and E. Rybkin, argued that there was another type relevant to the third world, a war "between countries that are equal in their relations." "Suffice it to cite such cases as the Indo-Pakistani military conflicts over Kashmir (1947–48 and 1965), the Arab-Israeli wars, the military conflict between Yemen and Saudi Arabia, the Moroccan aggression in Algeria (1963), the military conflict between Ethiopia and Somalia (1964), and others."[16] Gradually this position became more widely accepted within the military.

Innovative civilian scholars focused more of their discussion on economic and political development, but increasingly there were those who began to treat third world countries as independent actors with their own local and regional interests vis-à-vis each other. In Africa, for example, regional differences traditionally had been interpreted as the result of attempts by colonial powers to divide and conquer. Articles now appeared that formally repudiated this position. Nodari Simoniia, whose views have been discussed in previous chapters, pointed to the internal ethnic composition of countries with a socialist orientation as a significant factor in explaining the diversity in their foreign policies. Those countries that were ethnically homogeneous—Egypt, Somalia, Syria, and Yemen—were said to be more active in interstate relations, while those that were ethnically diverse were usually less active.[17] The article left no reason to suspect that countries without a socialist orientation would be any less diverse.

The most alarming analyses of third world independence were those suggesting that countries not only followed independent goals but did so in a way that could involve the superpowers against their better interests. The scholar most explicit in expressing this view was Vitalii Zhurkin, deputy director of the Institute of the USA and Canada. In 1970 Zhurkin took a relaxed view about most third world conflicts. "As a rule, the various territorial, ethnic, and other conflicts, of which there are indeed not a few in the developing countries, remain events of local significance if the

16. "The Nature and Types of Wars in the Modern Era," *Voyennaya mysl'*, no. 2 (February 1968), p. 79. Quoted in Mark N. Katz, *The Third World in Soviet Military Thought* (Johns Hopkins University Press, 1982), p. 47.

17. N. Simoniia, "Natsional'nyi vopros v stranakh sotsialisticheskoi orientatsii," *MEiMO*, no. 7 (September 1983), pp. 107–08.

imperialist states do not interfere in them."[18] However, the possibility of
such intervention and the dangers posed by it struck him as great, and
there was little in his analysis that might not apply to Soviet intervention as
well. In a book Zhurkin coedited with Evgenii Primakov in 1972, he
spelled out his concerns about "the presence of an uncontrolled element—
the independent actions of medium or small powers. . . . At the present
time international political crises quickly (almost instantly) acquire a universal character and directly or indirectly drag in all the most important
states and military coalitions. . . . The harm is not limited to . . . threat of
war. [Conflicts] lead to a strengthening of international tensions [and] can
for a long time exacerbate relations between great powers."[19]

## The Probabilities and Correlates of Independence

International relations involve relations with many individual countries
in changing circumstances. Every specialist in the Soviet Union knew in
the early 1980s that capitalist India had good relations with the Soviet
Union, that Zaire sometimes served as an American proxy, and that Ethiopia was a strong Soviet ally. It was also clear that many countries had
ambivalent policies. "Why," a Soviet scholar asked rhetorically, "did we
not see Olympic participants from Argentina but received grain from this
country?"[20] Any generalization that precluded the possibility of any such a
development was obviously wrong.

Moreover, any American or Soviet who thinks seriously about foreign
policy will have to agree with Soviet scholar A. A. Matlina (who strongly
believed that Latin American countries have relative autonomy in making
their foreign policies[21]) that "insofar as economic factors play a dominant
role in the final analysis, countries that are economically dependent sooner
or later come before a barrier that will limit (or already are limiting) their
foreign policy independence."[22] The same economic barriers ultimately

18. "SShA i mezhdunarodno-politicheskie krizisy," *SShA*, no. 12 (1970), p. 15.
19. *Mezhdunarodnye konflikty* (Moscow: Mezdunarodnye otnosheniia, 1972), p. 20.
20. K. L. Maidanik in "Latinskaia Amerika: vneshniaia politika i ekonomicheskaia
zavisimost'," *Latinskaia Amerika*, no. 8 (1981), p. 75.
21. See the contribution of A. A. Matlina, "Latinskaia Amerika: vneshniaia politika i
economicheskaia zavisimost'," *Latinskaia Amerika*, no. 8 (1981), pp. 68–72. Her article,
"Vneshniaia politika: samostoiatel'nost' v usloviiakh ekonomicheskoi zavisimostii,"
*Latinskaia Amerika*, no. 6 (1980), pp. 76–92, served as the stimulus for the discussion.
22. "Latinskaia Amerika: vneshniaia politika i ekonomicheskaia zavisimost'," p. 71.

stand before all powers, including superpowers, of course, and other military, population, and psychological barriers also exist.

These subtleties and variations in international relations are recognized by all the participants in the Soviet debates. They provide a framework within which the debates take place, but important differences in emphasis exist with respect to the tendencies of development and the opportunities open to the Soviet Union.

One general view is best represented by the recent articles of Karen Brutents, deputy head of the international department of the Central Committee, whose relative pessimism toward the revolutionary movement was discussed in chapter 6. Brutents thinks that it is wrong to speak of third world countries as becoming like those in Europe. In his view they still occupy a "dependent and exploited position in the world capitalist economy," and their "objective commonality of position . . . defines their relation to imperialism."[23] He believes that "despite the differentiation among them, they ought to be characterized on the whole as anti-imperialist and anti-neocolonial, capable of limiting the influence of imperialism." Indeed, he sees Reagan's efforts to exercise control as increasing conflicts between the United States and the third world.[24]

A second point of view treats economic dependence not as a source of resentment but as a factor that, in the words of Lev Klochkovsky, "places sufficiently harsh limits on autonomy, [which] limits the possibility of conducting an independent foreign policy."[25] Klochkovsky still sees a fair amount of independence in the foreign policies of some countries, but other scholars with this general point of view put greater emphasis on "the field of dependence" in which these countries are caught, or even on independence as a tactical step they take in unimportant conflicts to create an illusion for domestic public opinion or "to disorient world public opinion."[26] This perspective is implied in specific analyses of events even more than it is presented in sophisticated theoretical discussions—for example, in the statements of those who see Israel simply as an American puppet or Sadat's visit to Jerusalem as something orchestrated by the United States.

23. "Osvobodivshiesia strany v nachale 80-kh godov," *Kommunist*, no. 3 (February 1984), p. 105; and "Dvizhenie neprisoedineniia v sovremennom mire," *MEiMO*, no. 5 (May 1984), p. 33.

24. "Osvobodivshiesia strany v nachale 80-kh godov," pp. 102–03, 106, 108.

25. *MEiMO*, no. 9 (1981), p. 50.

26. For "field of dependence," see K. L. Maidanik in "Latinskaia Amerika i vneshniaia politika i ekonomicheskaia zavisimost'," *Latinskaia Amerika*, no. 8 (1981), p. 73; and for "tactical," see V. P. Totskii in ibid, pp. 55, 60, 70.

If the emphasis on the limitations imposed by economic dependence is linked with the traditional view about the connection between dependence and capitalist development—and it is a natural link in the Soviet Union—then the logical conclusion is that foreign policy independence is correlated with the internal economic system. Thus in 1981 Anatolii Glinkin, the leading foreign policy specialist of the Institute of Latin America, insisted that Latin American countries have become much more independent in their foreign policy, but he still quoted Marx's characterization of international relations as "secondary and tertiary—in general, derivative, transferred, nonprimary production relations" and asserted that this characterization has "exceptional relevance in contemporary conditions."[27] Glinkin argued that the foreign policies of Latin American countries varied with their domestic socioeconomic and political systems. He divided the area into six groups: countries that are socialist or people's democracies; countries where significant socioeconomic transformations have taken place in recent years; reformist capitalist countries with stable, bourgeois democracies; modernizing capitalist countries with military dictatorships associated with multinational corporations; young Caribbean states that have become independent in the second half of the twentieth century; and backward countries with slow evolution of their traditional structures.[28] The order of the groups was meant to proceed from most friendly to most hostile in their foreign relations posture toward the Soviet Union.

A third view emphasizes the military-political factor more than the economic, but it and the second point of view tend to come to similar conclusions about major third world capitalist countries. This argument was expressed most starkly in 1982 by Evgenii Primakov, director of the Institute of Oriental Studies. Primakov explicitly broke with economic analyses to emphasize the importance of political-military factors in writing about the position of Western Europe and Japan vis-à-vis the United States, but he did so to make the point of their dependence on the United States: "the growth of the economic potential [of Western Europe and Japan] was not accompanied by the loss of the dominant positions of the U.S. in the military-political region, which permit it to preserve its position of hegemony in the capitalist subsystem of international relations, and, as a rule, to impose its approaches on questions of principle on other

27. A. N. Glinkin in *Latinskaia Amerika*, no. 8 (1981), pp. 43, 52–53.
28. Ibid., pp. 52–53. Glinkin was head of the interstate relations department of the institute. See B. S. Bolov, "Tsentr sovetskoi latinoamerikanistiki," *MEiMO*, no. 4 (1981), p. 106.

capitalist states."[29] Primakov extended this analysis to the third world, concluding that "the tendency to polycentrism in the capitalist world creates few real opportunities for political maneuvering by developing countries to defend their national interests." Then he went further to speak about the creation of " 'minicenters of force' among the developing countries, special kinds of 'subimperialist foci [*ochagy*].' " Primakov also warned that despite the continued existence of contradictions within developed capitalist states, many minicenters have themselves "turned into base points [*opornye punkty*] for the policy of imperialism."[30]

A fourth point of view shared the optimism of the first about the possibility of independent third world action, but paradoxically it was associated with those who began from opposing assumptions. If Brutents emphasized the commonalities in the third world because of its dependent and exploited position, the supporters of the fourth point of view argued that the major third world countries had the potentiality for foreign policy independence precisely because they were well on the capitalist path and were developing fairly strong and complex economies. Thus one of the most forthright spokesmen for this position, Nodari Simoniia, criticized "the illusions about a 'community' on a pancontinental, panracial, and panreligious basis" that he saw disappearing very rapidly. While asserting that it was "still early to speak about the full overcoming of 'third world' moods and ideas in the developing countries themselves," he saw the Colombo conference of nonaligned countries as evidence of "distinct centrifugal tendencies."[31]

Simoniia did not attribute differentiation in third world foreign policy dependence to domestic ideological orientation. Indeed, when he wrote in early 1983 about the "relative independence of foreign policy from the internal orientation of social development toward a formation," he left no doubt that he really meant what he said.[32] As may be remembered, Simoniia had argued that the countries undergoing serious industrialization were firmly on a capitalist path similar to that of Western Europe in the nineteenth century. However, he saw no reason for the Soviet Union to be concerned from a foreign policy point of view. As a general rule in

29. "Osvobodivshiesia strany v mezhdunarodnykh otnosheniiakh," *MEiMO*, no. 5 (May 1982), p. 22.

30. Ibid., p. 19.

31. "Natsional'no-osvoboditel'noe dvizhenie: nekotorye voprosy differentsiatsii," *Aziia i Afrika segodnia*, no. 6 (June 1978), p. 35.

32. "Natsional'no-gosudarstvennaia konsolidatsiia i politicheskaia differentsiatsiia razvivaiushchikhsia stran Vostoka," *MEiMO*, no. 1 (January 1983), p. 94.

countries where "the internal market has progressed far enough and serves as the chief base of the national capitalist substructure [*uklad*], one characteristically finds an independent foreign policy and an active positive role in the nonaligned movement (India and others)." He saw pro-Western foreign policies predominating only where there were many colonial remnants—specialization on raw materials production, ties of African countries with the European Community, and so forth.[33]

Few other scholars have analyzed the foreign policy consequences of capitalistic development in such sweeping terms as Simoniia, but a number did make analyses that pointed in the same direction. Glinkin's 1981 categorization of Latin American countries by the level of their foreign policy independence placed modernizing capitalist countries with military dictatorships and ties to multinational corporations rather low on the list of independent nations. This category prominently included Brazil and Argentina at the time, and a substantial number of the Latin Americanists were unhappy with the suggestion.[34] Often they explicitly linked growing foreign policy independence with the growing economic strength of these countries (and also Mexico) and even with their development of "state-monopoly capitalism," that is, the kind of capitalism found in the West.[35]

A fifth point of view, which strongly overlapped with the fourth, pointed to the same countries as being independent, but it emphasized a different reason. With a few exceptions such as Singapore, those countries that are well on the capitalist path tend to be fairly populous states with large domestic markets. Because of their size, population, and aggregate industrial output, they can become fairly significant regional military powers. Those who give greater emphasis to national interests and national power than to stage of economic development as such, who speak in terms of "triangles," "quadrangles," and so forth, were inclined to assign countries such as Brazil, Argentina, and Mexico greater weight for this reason.

Thus in a 1980 article, Vladimir Lukin explicitly discussed "power centers" in Latin America in terms of multipolarity and the criteria of national power developed by Hans Morgenthau. He quoted Zbigniew Brzezinski to the effect that Brazil had a better chance of becoming a

33. Ibid.

34. See P. P. Iakovlev, "Latinskaia Amerika: vneshniaia politika i ekonomicheskaia zavisimost'," *Latinskaia Amerika*, no. 9 (1981), p. 57.

35. M. L. Chumakova, "Meksika: neft' i vneshniaia politika," *Latinskaia Amerika*, no. 2 (1983), p. 36.

superpower than Japan and Robert Alexander to the effect that Brazil would be one of the world's great powers by the end of the century. Already it had moved from alignment with the United States, had distanced itself from it, and had moved closer to Western Europe and Japan. Mexico, in his view, had also become a regional power.[36] In a 1983 book, *"Power Centers": Conceptions and Reality,* Lukin included the Latin American article as one of the chapters but analyzed other regions in similar terms. He explicitly criticized Primakov for seeing third world power centers as U.S. proxies.[37]

A common thread in a number of these analyses is their implicit questions about the foreign policy value to the Soviet Union of the left-wing regimes in preindustrial societies, except in providing widely scattered naval bases. Simoniia has had serious doubts about the domestic policy of regimes such as Sukarno's that were radical in their rhetoric but that essentially destroyed their countries' economies. He expressed doubts about their foreign policies as well. As noted above, in the early 1970s he saw these countries as following differentiated policies, and in 1983 he was scathing in charging that "interference in conflicts (say, between Arab and non-Arab states) on the basis of national-ethnic 'solidarity' can introduce right-nationalist and reactionary-chauvinist elements in the foreign policy course of this or that country that claims [*pretenduiushchii*] to have a progressive orientation."[38]

The irritation with some third world countries that was shown in this last statement is not limited to Simoniia; it is increasingly manifested in the work of a number of leading scholars. Of course, third world claims that the Soviet Union is included in the rich North and has an obligation to transfer wealth to the poor South has produced general outrage. One of the deputy directors of IMEMO was scornful in his reference to the "politicized interpretation of 'wealth' and 'poverty' of states" that issue from "developing countries with their transitory, multistructural systems that inevitably give rise to amorphousness and variability in their ideology."[39] The thought that third world countries might default on Soviet loans as

---

36. "Konseptsiia 'tsentrov sily' i Latinskaia Amerika," *Latinskaia Amerika,* no. 8 (1980), pp. 5–19.

37. *"Tsentry sily": konseptsii i real'nost'* (Moscow: Mezhdunarodnye otnosheniia, 1983), pp. 18–19.

38. "Natsional'no-gosudarstvennaia konsolidatsiia i politicheskaia differentsiatsiia razvivaiushchikhsia stran Vostoka," p. 94.

39. I. Ivanov, "Kontseptsiia 'bednykh' i 'bogatykh' stran: istoki, sushchnost', napravlennost'," *MEiMO,* no. 1 (January 1983), p. 29.

well as Western ones provoked the normal reaction of any banker, even among fairly traditional scholars.[40] And, of course, there were hints of a view familiar in the United States as well—that the third world might be using the superpowers more than the reverse. Lev Klochkovsky asserted that "often the ruling circles of some developing states (particularly those where the predominant influence belongs to the elite, exploiting classes) try to use collaboration with the socialist countries not so much for an improvement of the economy of their country as to have a means of pressure on the West."[41] Klochkovsky, many readers undoubtedly noticed, said "particularly" where exploiting classes were in power, not "only" in such cases.

## Analysis of American Policy

Before the age of détente, American policy in the third world was to some extent an irrelevant consideration for the Soviet leadership. Obviously the United States was a great power that was going to try to promote its interests in the third world. It could use military force, as actions in Korea, Guatemala, and Lebanon demonstrated, but its success was going to depend on the relative effectiveness of different economic systems and the nature of the sociopolitical forces in the third world. If poor economic performance of nonsocialist countries and anti-Western nationalism were to be the dominant facts of life in the third world, the United States was ultimately not going to be able to do much to prevent the process of revolutionary change. If Western investment was going to be critical and private property instincts were going to develop among third world peoples, the United States would be in an extremely strong position as long as it followed an intelligent economic policy.

With the development of détente and the possibility of some Soviet-American cooperation, however, new questions arose. Did competition in the third world come into conflict with Soviet-American strategic and economic cooperation, and if so, should the competition be muted? If the Soviet Union unilaterally retreated from third world competition for the sake of economic gain, would this not make it open to blackmail on any

40. M. Volkov, "Vneshnii dolg stran Azii i Afriki," *Aziia i Afrika segodnia,* no. 1 (1983), p. 31.
41. *Latinskaia Amerika,* no. 3 (1983), p. 139.

other political issue and perhaps even call into question its will to use its nuclear deterrent? Finally, were there situations within the third world itself on which the Soviet Union and the United States should and could cooperate?

During the height of the Vietnam War, it was difficult to talk of cooperation with the United States, but as the war began to wind down, the situation changed. The "Guam doctrine" was enunciated in 1969 and the "Nixon doctrine" in 1970, while U.S. military doctrine was changed to call for the capability of fighting one and one-half wars instead of the previously announced two and one-half. President Nixon talked about an overextension of American commitments, about the need to rely on allies, and so forth. Was this a real change in attitude? If so, did the American defeat in Vietnam create the conditions for a major Soviet advance in the third world, or did it provide a desirable opportunity for a mutual reduction of Soviet-American involvement in the area?

No Soviet scholar concluded that the United States was suddenly abandoning all involvement in the third world—as, indeed, it was not. However, a range of views was expressed on the question. In a published discussion of the Nixon doctrine, Vitalii Zhurkin, deputy director of the Institute of the USA and Canada asserted that "the 'Nixon doctrine' introduced some—even fairly significant—new elements in the policy of the USA in international conflicts and crisis situations," and Iurii Davydov, another scholar of the institute, saw the administration moving toward "a more differentiated, flexible approach."[42] A more cautious position suggested that the number of questions on which the United States was willing to negotiate was extremely limited.[43] Anatolii Gromyko was more skeptical, asserting that relying on allies simply meant that Nixon intended to use proxies and that Israel (whose role in the Middle East Gromyko described in the darkest of terms) was the ideal model that Nixon had in mind.[44] Those statements came from a roundtable discussion at which Georgii Arbatov was present, and because he attacked Gromyko's position, politeness put limits on what could be said. In independent articles scholars could describe the new doctrine as "diplomatic camouflage" or as evidence of growing attention to "the disinformation of opinion."[45]

42. V. V. Zhurkin in " 'Doktrina Niksona': deklaratsii i real'nost' (diskussiia v Institute SShA AN SSSR)," *SShA*, no. 2 (1971), pp. 39, 22.

43. N. N. Arkad'ev, ibid., p. 24.

44. Ibid., p. 44. Arbatov's attack on this view followed immediately.

45. The first statement is by a scholar at IMEMO, O. Bykov, in "O nekotorykh

Until the expression of hope for cooperation with the United States in the third world became extremely difficult with the deterioration of relations in the 1980s, the published statements on U.S. policy continued to cover a wide range of views. Those making statements about relentless ideological struggle between the Soviet Union and the United States obviously expected such struggle to be particularly irreconcilable in the third world. Those who thought that cooperation or at least a moderation in competition was possible were obviously disheartened by the impact on détente of events in peripheral countries such as Angola and Ethiopia, but these events convinced them even more deeply that cooperation was necessary.

Not surprisingly, the skeptical view of U.S. policy was strengthened the most in the 1970s. It was extremely difficult for a Soviet scholar to hint that American anger over Soviet policy in Africa was a justified response to a foolish Soviet policy, and the closest any could come was probably a generalized criticism of the arms race in the third world. In private, most Soviet scholars seemed genuinely to believe that Cuban involvement in Angola was a fully justified response to prior covert American and South African intervention and that support for Ethiopia was a necessary response to the invasion by Somalia. (The earlier large-scale Soviet armament of Somalia is another matter.) Many wrote that the United States was deliberately using pretexts in the third world in order to undermine détente.[46]

Because no scholar was able to describe American policy in the third world as a whole in favorable terms, the more relevant discussions concerned American policy in specific areas. Of course, the policy was always criticized, but the ways of describing it varied and implied different American driving motivations and different probabilities for successful diplomatic action.

The Middle East—the one region in the third world of vital interest for both powers—provides an excellent example of the techniques used to convey varying images of U.S. policy. Israel is always treated as follow-

---

chertakh vneshnepoliticheskoi strategii SShA," *MEiMO*, no. 4 (April 1971), p. 62. Like Gromyko, Bykov thought that Israel was "the ideal embodiment of the principles of the 'Guam doctrine' " (p. 60). The second statement is from G. A. Trofimenko, "Nekotorye aspekty voenno-politicheskoi strategii SShA," *SShA*, no. 10 (1970), p. 19.

46. V. Kortunov, "Leninskaia politika mirnogo sosushchestvovaniia i klassovaia bor'ba," *Mezhdunarodnaia zhizn'*, no. 4 (1979), pp. 90–100.

ing an unjustified and aggressive policy. The United States is condemned both for its cooperation with Israel and for its own military involvement in the Persian Gulf. But, if read closely, articles analyze American policy and motivations in very different ways. At one extreme some of the conservative scholars almost see an international Zionist conspiracy that controls the United States and Israel and drives both to inexorable expansionism: "The interests of the USA and international Zionism are practically indivisible in general, but in the Near East in particular. Leaders of this most reactionary movement are shareholders of the most important banks and trusts. Some of them proclaim Zionism as an independent political force in the contemporary world, even a 'third great power' after the USA and the Soviet Union."[47]

For a much larger number of conservatives, the United States is simply determined to dominate the Middle East militarily, primarily as part of a strategic plan to encircle the Soviet Union. Even before President Reagan's election, such an author could write about "the militaristic psychosis of the Pentagon and the White House" toward the region.[48] In this view, Israel is an American "subcontractor," a proxy that America uses.[49] The United States is seen as the instigator of anything unpleasant: the Sadat visit to Jerusalem was planned and coordinated by Washington, and the 1982 Israeli invasion of Lebanon was thoroughly planned by Washington and Tel Aviv.[50] "Tel Aviv fulfills the role of a shock force of American imperialism. . . . The troops of the USA were sent [to Lebanon] in order, in connection with Israel, to turn it into a military platform of American imperialism."[51] Such analyses not only give the reader little reason to hope for an agreement in the Middle East, but they also create a sense of relentless threat on the southern border of the Soviet Union that is as intense as that which the most conservative Americans create in their analysis of Soviet involvement in Central America.

47. I. Beliaev, "Sily soprotivleniia agressora rastut," *MEiMO*, no. 5 (1970), p. 74.

48. L. Medvedko, "Blizhnii i Srednii Vostok v strategii imperializma," *MEiMO*, no. 11 (November 1980), p. 53.

49. See Medvedko, *K vostoku i zapadu ot Suetsa*, p. 270; and V. Viktorov, "Ekspansionistskaia politika SShA na Blizhnem Vostoke," *Mezhdunarodnaia zhizn'*, no. 5 (1983), pp. 87–96.

50. See Medvedko, *K vostoku i zapadu ot Suetsa*, p. 273; and Viktorov, "Ekspansionistskaia politika SShA na Blizhnem Vostoke," p. 92.

51. A. Osipov, "Antiarabskoe 'strategicheskoe sotrudnichestvo,'" *Mezhdunarodnaia zhizn'*, no. 12 (1983), p. 65.

Other authors occupy a more middle position. They seem not to have much hope for an improvement in Soviet-American relations in the Middle East, but for them the Middle East is not to be explained simply in terms of American domination. In this view Israel is more than an American proxy; it often initiates aggression, which the United States then supports and protects or simply permits.[52] American goals are seen as more complex (and less threatening to the Soviet Union) than a mere determination to strengthen its strategic position on the Soviet border. These goals can include a desire to divide the Arab world, to prevent radical revolution in the Middle East, and to guarantee access to petroleum.[53] The head of the Near East department of the Institute of the USA and Canada, who generally seems pessimistic about American motives toward the Middle East, believes that local factors play "not a little role" in the arms race there, and he criticizes the thesis that the United States orchestrated the Sadat visit to Jerusalem beforehand.[54]

A third group of Middle East specialists is more optimistic about the possibility of some regulation of the conflict. Given the flow of events in the Middle East, even the most optimistic realist either in the Soviet Union or the United States frequently must feel deep despair, but some scholars such as Evgenii Primakov write much more frequently about the need for Soviet-American agreements on the Middle East than about relentless American expansionism, and at times they suggest the possibility for agreement is real.[55] These scholars seem dubious about an exclusive Soviet reliance on radical states in the Middle East and are certainly dubious about Arab tactics. In a chapter titled "Israeli Leaders' Utilization of Extremist Appeals against the State of Israel," Primakov asserted that the Arabs were making a major mistake to question the existence of the state of Israel and implied that this mistake may have been a significant factor in the failure of Arab policy in the Middle East.[56] Although he could never

52. O. Kovtunovich and V. Nosenko, "Blizhnevostochnaia problema i strategiia amerikanskogo imperializma," *Mezhdunarodnaia zhizn'*, no. 7 (1980), p. 33.

53. Ibid.

54. A. Kislov, "Avantiurizm Pentagona na Blizhnem Vostoke," *Mezhdunarodnaia zhizn'*, no. 3 (1983), p. 106; and A. K. Kislov, book review, in *SShA*, no. 8 (August 1981), p. 112.

55. E. Primakov, " 'Sbalansirovannyi kurs' na Blizhnem Vostoke ili staraia politika inymi sredstvami," *MEiMO*, no. 12 (December 1976), pp. 38–51.

56. *Anatomy of the Middle East Conflict* (Moscow: Nauka, 1979), pp. 114–38.

discuss such a point explicitly, this line of analysis certainly implies far more sympathy with Yasser Arafat than with Syrian PLO rebels if the Soviets had to choose.

The most striking statement about the Middle East was Simoniia's previously quoted complaint about the "right-nationalist and reactionary-chauvinist elements" that can be introduced into the foreign policy of a "country that claims to have a progressive orientation" by "interference in conflict (say, between Arab and non-Arab states) on the basis of national-ethnic 'solidarity.'" One imagines that Simoniia had in mind the war between Iran and Iraq (which is strongly condemned in the Soviet Union), but the phraseology allowed the mind to wander.

If proponents of the hard-line Soviet position depict the United States as a unified force pursuing strategic-military goals, then their opponents assert that "domestic political considerations weigh heavily in the formulation and exercise of American policy in the region."[57] They refer to the Israeli lobby as one of the major pressures on American policy. As long as they do not paint a picture of an all-powerful Zionist conspiracy, they can imply that other political forces, certainly including the oil companies, might be able to overcome this lobby.[58]

U.S. and Western European policy in southern Africa is also described in a variety of ways. One group that tends to be associated most strongly with the Institute of Africa has a skeptical view of Western policy there and gives little reason to hope that anything the Soviet Union might do or propose could have any impact. Evgenii Tarabrin, a leading foreign policy specialist of the institute, has insisted that U.S. policy in the region constitutes a definite system. While the United States might try to maneuver between South Africa and black African countries, he argues, ultimately it bases its policy on South Africa and will not change. Tarabrin acknowledges some policy differences among Western countries, but he emphasizes more their similarities.[59] Anatolii Gromyko's analysis has, if any-

57. Ibid., p. 163.

58. Primakov always writes in these terms. For an early statement of the position that also saw less than unanimous support for Israel by American Jews, see G. Mirsky in "Zionizm—orudie reaktsii i imperializma," *MEiMO*, no. 3 (March 1973), p. 129. Also see R. M. Rogov, "Amerikanskaia evreiskaia obshchina i Izrael," *SShA*, no. 8 (1979), pp. 57–69; and R. V. Borisov, *SShA: Blizhnevostochnaia politika v 70-e gody* (Moscow: Nauka, 1982), pp. 42–48.

59. E. Tarabrin, "Afrika v global'noi strategii imperializma," *MEiMO*, no. 2 (February 1982), pp. 30, 32.

thing, been more pessimistic, placing great emphasis upon the West's strategic dependence on the minerals of southern Africa.[60]

Another group of scholars paints a more nuanced picture and implies that under certain circumstances policy might change substantially. Viktor Kremeniuk of the Institute of the USA and Canada has argued that because of various factors, including Western investment, not only is the third world dependent on the United States, but to some extent the reverse is also true, a factor that restrains U.S. freedom of action.

Without denying the necessity of strengthening the position of the USA in countries possessing valuable natural resources, many American politicians and representatives of the scientific community recognize that the economic and social stability of the developed capitalist states now in ever greater degree depends on the actions and positions of the developing countries. . . . These countries can exert growing pressure on the developed capitalist states to achieve their goals.[61]

When Kremeniuk turned directly to a discussion of southern Africa in 1982, he combined his harsh analysis of existing U.S. policy with suggestions that it might change. He quoted the *Washington Post* to the effect that a number of major corporations that had supported Reagan's candidacy opposed his policy in Angola. He indicated that the differences between the United States and Western Europe on South Africa were real by noting the British, French, West German, and Canadian criticism of the American veto of the Security Council resolution condemning South African aggression against Angola in August 1981. And, above all, he quoted with approval the opinion of "the realistic thinking Americans and Western Europeans" about "the necessity of avoiding conflicts that would bring the superpowers or their allies into confrontation and grow into regional or wider wars."[62]

The feeling that the United States might be motivated by concerns other than a desire to control and exploit was expressed even more strongly by M. L. Vishnevsky. He explained that the United States was strengthening its relations with South Africa out of a feeling of despair among American ruling circles and out of the conviction that the situation in southern Africa

60. *Konflikt na Iuge Afriki* (Moscow: Mysl', 1979), pp. 29–60.
61. "Razvivaiushchiesia strany i SShA: usilenie protivoborstva," *SShA*, no. 2 (February 1981), pp. 8–9, 10.
62. "Sovetsko-amerikanskie otnosheniia i nekotorye problemy osvobodivshikhsia gosudarstv," *SShA*, no. 6 (June 1982), p. 17.

was the result of Soviet initiatives. "The international support of the USSR, Cuba, and other socialist countries of the struggle of African peoples against imperialism and neocolonialism was examined and is examined in Washington in a geopolitical framework."[63] Vishnevsky mentioned the American proposal of a solution of the Namibian problem in exchange for a Cuban pullout, and because he did not ridicule the offer, the reader was left with the thought that it might be a serious one.

## Soviet Policy Options

In the first half of the 1970s, scholars took several basic positions on the proper Soviet response in the third world. One was essentially a human rights response from a Marxist perspective. Many who emphasized the importance of ideological struggle often left the strong impression that they believed such struggle not only inevitable but desirable. For those scholars "the contemporary national liberation movement ought to be considered an inalienable part of the world social [socialist] revolution,"[64] but it was a movement that faced powerful opposition from the Western powers. As a result, "no serious transformation is possible in countries with underdeveloped social and economic structures without collaboration with the socialist states." The national liberation movement could overcome its problems "only with mutual ties with the international workers' movement that fulfills the mission of the proletarian vanguard in relationship to the national liberation movement."[65]

People adopting this line could never criticize the Soviet Union directly, but they could insist on what they thought the nature of the Soviet duty to be. "Struggle for military détente," one said, "should be in no case understood as a refusal . . . of socialist countries to support the national liberation struggle of the toilers of exploited countries."[66] After emphasizing the

63. "Sgovor Vashington-Pretoriia," *SShA*, no. 10 (October 1981), p. 57.

64. Iu. N. Gavrilov, in "Teoriia i praktika nekapitalisticheskogo puti razvitiia," *Mezhdunarodnaia zhizn'*, no. 10 (1970), p. 23.

65. Vl. Li, "Mesto sovremennogo natsional'no-osvoboditel'nogo dvizheniia v anti-imperialisticheskoi bor'be," *Mezhdunarodnaia zhizn'*, no. 11 (1971), p. 103. For Li's views on revolution, see chapter 6, p. 167.

66. P. Zhilin, "Voennye aspekty razriadki napriazhennosti," *Mezhdunarodnaia zhizn'*, no. 11 (1973), p. 33.

importance of understanding foreign policy from a class position, another scholar pointedly reminded readers that "the Soviet Union gave material help to Turkey and Afghanistan in the difficult years [of the civil war and the early 1920s] in the midst of devastation and a complicated international situation."[67] The clear implication was that if it could be done then, a richer Soviet Union in the 1970s had no excuse. Americans often cite such statements as evidence of Soviet duplicity about détente; more often, the statements are demands by conservatives that the Soviet Union not retreat and implicit complaints that it is retreating.

The central issue about support of revolutionary regimes in Latin America and Africa has usually been one of money. To what extent should the Soviet Union provide enough aid to compensate a radical country for formal and informal Western boycotts? In overall terms the Soviet Union clearly cannot afford to substitute for Western investment in the third world, but in individual countries such as Nicaragua, Ethiopia, and Grenada (but not India) the costs are well within Soviet capabilities. Many of the statements of the conservative Soviet writers about ideological struggle should be read in that context.

This point is also discussed within the framework of the revolutionary prospects of the vanguard parties. Thus Arkadii Kaufman, who sees the national liberation revolution in a new stage and who expresses optimism about new states where the party is led by Marxist-Leninist techniques, emphasizes the importance of the fact that "the Soviet Union, together with other brotherly countries, provides assistance in strengthening the defense capability of liberated countries when they make such requests." In asserting that the new regimes "rely in their struggle for independence and freedom on the powerful military-political and economic possibilities of world socialism," he implies that he strongly favored this policy, even in cases of "internal counterrevolution" in Angola and Ethiopia.[68] Those who consider the new regimes ideologically unstable and unreliable do not make such statements. They cannot raise directly the question of whether the Soviet investment in Egypt or Ghana was worth it, but they—and their readers—must have the parallel in mind.

67. A. Kiva, "Rol' molodykh natsional'nykh gosudarstv v mezhdunarodnye otnoshe-niia," *Mezhdunarodnaia zhizn'*, no. 2 (1973), p. 99.
68. "XXVI s'ezd Kommunisticheskoi partii Sovetskogo Soiuza i nekotorye problemy natsional'no-osvoboditel'noi revoliutsii," *Rabochii klass i sovremennyi mir*, no. 3 (May-June, 1981), p. 33.

In other cases the issue is more complex. For example, the Soviet Union bought grain from Argentina at a time when the latter had death squads and supported U.S. covert action in Nicaragua. The Soviet press never mentioned Argentina's internal repression and even ignored its economic connections with Israel when discussing Israel's role in Latin America.[69] The Soviet press is generally also silent about defects in left-wing, pro-Soviet dictatorships. Some scholars have begun to criticize these regimes in general human rights terms, however, and some of the general discussion of democratization in the third world is likely to be as much a criticism of Soviet support for left-wing dictatorships as it is advocacy of revolutionary strategy.

In Iran, Soviet policy was peculiarly vulnerable to criticism because the Soviet Union not only abandoned principle and morality but did so with what seemed very naive hopes about foreign policy gains. The Tudeh party cooperated with Khomeini, even to the extent of informing on other revolutionaries when he was repressing them. Especially after the seizure of American hostages, the Soviet press (even that in Moslem Central Asia) virtually ended all criticism of the distasteful aspects of Khomeini's Iran. This policy was apparently based on the hope that the clerics would have to rely on the Tudeh for administration of the country or that Iran would support Soviet foreign policy.

This treatment of Khomeini enraged two disparate groups among Soviet intellectuals—most of those dedicated to détente with the United States and many of the strongest supporters of revolution for human rights reasons.[70] The 1984 denunciation of the Tudeh (and by implication, the Soviet) position by Semen Agaev and his endorsement of noncommunist radicals has already been discussed in chapter 6. A strange 1983 article in *Literaturnaia gazeta* by Rostislav Ul'ianovsky seems to have had a similar thrust. (Indeed, it was a condensation of a preface written for a book by Agaev.) The article combined a severe attack on Khomeini's despotism with a bizarre criticism of President Carter for his immoral support *(sic)* of Khomeini. The article was entitled "Immoralism in Foreign Policy," and

---

69. Theodore H. Friedgut, "Soviet Anti-Zionism and Antisemitism—Another Cycle," *Soviet Jewish Affairs,* vol. 14 (February 1984), p. 7.

70. A. Bovin, *Mir semidesiatykh: politcheskie ocherki* (Moscow: *Izvestiia,* 1980), pp. 291–93.

it made sense only if it was an attack on the immoralism of Soviet support for the Iranian leader.[71]

A second Soviet policy position has also emphasized support for left-wing movements and regimes but for other than human rights reasons. Westerners have often said that the Soviet Union supports revolution abroad because it validates the ideology and thereby contributes to the legitimacy of the system at home. Although this argument has obvious limits (people in both the Soviet Union and the United States are happy with victories abroad but dislike paying for them with casualties and heavy economic aid), it can be found in the Soviet media. One writer, for example, quoted Lenin as saying "we consider it our duty *and our interest* [to support national liberation movements], for otherwise socialism in Europe will be unstable." This writer asserted that "successes of foreign policy . . . create important international conditions for the strengthening of the socialist order."[72]

More usually, the pragmatic reasons suggested for supporting revolutions center on their direct foreign policy implications. Obviously countries such as Angola, Ethiopia, and Nicaragua tend to support the Soviet Union in international forums such as the United Nations, and some are willing to pay a fairly high price for such support. Anatolii Glinkin's insistence that general foreign policy orientation in Latin American countries is associated with the character of the domestic regime clearly points to the conclusion that the Soviet Union should be interested in the character of domestic regimes, although Glinkin himself seems to be a cautious man. Sometimes specialists are extremely straightforward in expressing this opinion. Writing in 1980 about "neo-Islamism," another scholar stated bluntly, "This process has an anti-imperialist direction and, therefore, is progressive in its essence. Its progressive character does not change if the struggle is led under religious slogans because of the peculiarities of this or that country. Consequently the Soviet Union decisively

71. "Moral'nye printsipy v politike i politika v oblasti morali," in S. L. Agaev, ed., *Iranskaia revoliutsia SShA: mezhdunarodnaia besopastnost'* (Moscow: Nauka, 1984), pp. 7–8.

72. M. Mnatsakanian, "Internatsionalizm leninskoi vneshnei politiki SSSR i natsional'no-osvoboditel'noe dvizhenie," *Aziia i Afrika segodnia*, no. 4 (1984), p. 2. The italics are Lenin's.

supports the revolution in Iran."[73] (He then cited a statement by Brezhnev that actually was far more ambiguous than he suggested.)

Support of left-wing movements for foreign policy reasons can also have a narrower military justification. Large countries such as China and India can be sensitive about foreign military bases, but smaller countries are frequently a different matter. If a regime will ally itself with the Soviet Union militarily and use proper-sounding language so as not to confuse Soviet soldiers, some in the Soviet military appear to worry very little about the reality of its domestic policy. This attitude came out most clearly in a review by Colonel E. Dolgopolov of a book by Georgii Mirsky. Mirsky has consistently been optimistic about the possibilities of the most left-wing, noncommunist regimes of the time, but he has had a clear perception of their blemishes and, at least since 1966, of the factors that might lead them to evolve in a rightward direction. When his 1976 book on the military in the third world suggested that all military regimes had some common features, including some negative ones, Dolgopolov, was outraged at this "objectivism." In his view, left-wing, pro-Soviet military regimes must be treated as qualitatively different from the others.[74]

Such an attitude may reflect simpleminded ideological conviction, but this is not likely to be the case for prominent officials and theorists. Soviet generals treat Africa as an important strategic region and express concern about American bases in and around the Horn of Africa.[75] Clearly they are little worried about human rights in Ethiopia and Somalia if the Soviet Union can be guaranteed a foothold in one of them. Another military-political reason for supporting left-wing movements was recently given by Dolgopolov, who argued that "it is wrong to underestimate the danger of local wars that are led and planned by the USA and other imperialist powers," because of the psychological impact of Western victories. While Dolgopolov did not speak about tests of will or credibility of Soviet commitments, he used a functionally equivalent argument. Local wars that are not resisted, he warned, "create in imperialist circles an illusion of everything's being permitted in the use of war. . . . It is necessary to watch the

73. Medvedko, *K vostoku i zapadu ot Suetsa*, p. 318.

74. Y. Dolgopolov's review of G. Mirsky, *'Tretii mir': obshchestvo, vlast', armiia* (Moscow: Nauka, 1976) in *Kommunist vooruzhennykh sil*, no. 21 (November 1976), pp. 90–92. This is discussed in Katz, *The Third World in Soviet Military Thought*, p. 104.

75. L. Kuzin, "Afrika v agressivnykh planakh imperializma," *Zarubezhnoe voennoe obozrenie*, no. 6 (1984), pp. 16–17.

intrigues of the enemies of peace and social progress vigilantly and to be constantly ready to repel them."[76]

A third position with respect to Soviet policy in the third world has emphasized the dangers of an East-West crisis arising in the area. Some scholars have feared that third world conflicts might draw in the superpowers against their better interests and almost against their will. The policy implication of this analysis is obvious, and it is not surprising that it has been associated with a number of the scholars of the Institute of the USA and Canada who have been most concerned with managing the overall Soviet-American relationship—notably Vitalii Zhurkin, Andrei Kokoshin, Vladimir Lukin, and Viktor Kremeniuk.

A closely associated view can be found among some scholars who specialize more narrowly on third world issues. These specialists seem to be involved in an effort to redefine the conception of the kind of international relations that the Soviet Union should be valuing and trying to develop. Traditionally the Soviets have defined an independent foreign policy as one that is overwhelmingly pro-Soviet or at least anti-Western. Those who now talk about the independence of Brazil and Mexico or who like Simoniia speak positively about the foreign policy consequences of capitalist development in the major countries obviously do not expect such countries to become Soviet satellites.

Those who emphasize relations with moderate regional powers rather than radical (and generally smaller) ones may simply be saying that the Soviet Union should be competing more vigorously with the United States in relations with these powers. Implicitly, however, the argument often contains an image of international relations in which superpower relations with other countries are inevitably ambiguous and in which the superpowers are striving for limited gains. India, Iran under the shah, Nigeria, and Mexico—and Western European powers as well—can have reasonably good relations with both superpowers, with neither of the latter really hoping for or seeking a fundamental realignment.

From this perspective, a relaxation of Soviet policy that permits the development of better relations with Egypt, Saudi Arabia, Kenya, and Brazil may be more valuable than a strident one emphasizing ideological struggle that orients the Soviet Union toward expensive radicals in less

76. "Lokal'nye voiny v voennoi politike imperializma," *Zarubezhnoe voennoe obozrenie*, no. 1 (1984), p. 14.

significant countries. Such a position is, to some extent, a part of the general viewpoint that emphasizes the more cooperative possibilities in international relations.

It is, of course, easy to say that third world conflicts should be prevented from escalating into superpower crises—and, indeed, difficult to make the opposite case. The real question is what types of accommodation should a country seek, what types of self-restraint should it exercise in order to reduce the possibilities of a conflict? Analysis of American flexibility in southern Africa, which was discussed in the previous chapter, for instance, has hinted at the possibility that Cubans might be withdrawn from Angola in exchange for an agreement. Those Latin Americanists who fervently praise the Contadora efforts and the peace-loving Soviet policy in Latin America seem to be putting their priority on a peaceful settlement rather than radical transformation.[77] The most interesting question is whether the many scholars who emphasize the disastrous economic consequences of the third world arms race are actually criticizing the Soviet policy of arms sales, but this question is so sensitive that one can only guess.[78]

The fourth position, the most ambivalent and probably the most important in the Soviet policymaking machinery, advocates a combination of competition and cooperation in the third world, a management of the relationship. To use Soviet jargon, "the Soviet Union categorically speaks out against the exportation of revolution," but "the Soviet Union [also] speaks out in the most decisive manner against the exportation of counterrevolution."[79]

The most prominent spokesman for this view is Evgenii Primakov, the new director of IMEMO. Primakov has suggested the possibility of regulating conflicts in the Middle East. He has also advocated "the necessity of the political regulation of international conflicts," "prophylactic measures [profilaktika] against armed conflicts," and "rejection of attempts at one-sided management of conflict situations."[80] On the other hand, Primakov began as an optimist about the evolution of Nasser's Egypt to social-

77. P. P. Iakovlev, "Dva kursa v mirovoi politike i Latinskaia Amerika," *Latinskaia Amerika,* no. 3 (1984), pp. 5–16.

78. For a recent such article, see N. Simoniia, "Gonka vooruzhenii i razvivaiushchiesia strany," *Aziia i Afrika segodnia,* no. 1 (1984), pp. 2–5.

79. E. Primakov "Osvobodivshiesia strany v mezhdunarodnykh otnosheniiakh," p. 22.

80. Ibid., pp. 22, 23.

ism and the inability of the United States to control the Arab national liberation movements.[81] He continued to show moderate hope for radical regimes, including, at first, Khomeini's. He specifically criticized "the mistaken evaluation of the state sector in countries of socialist orientation as completely state-capitalist in nature"[82]—the pessimistic evaluation made by some in his institute.

Because Primakov was relatively pessimistic about the independence of medium-sized power centers, he could be read as taking a position similar to Glinkin's on the relationship of domestic regime and foreign policy. However, as the 1970s gave way to the 1980s, Primakov wrote a growing number of articles that essentially used the language of geopolitics. He spoke of "triangles," "poles," and "equilibrium between two systems"[83] and described U.S. policy as one of " 'balancing' between 'centers of force' with the goal of isolating the USSR." He tried to straddle the line between those who saw the third world in terms of dependence and nondependence by coining the phrase " 'asymmetrical' character of mutual dependence."[84]

In short, the Primakov image of international relations in the third world seems similar to that of such representatives of the "realist school" as Hans Morgenthau. Primakov emphasizes the importance of military-strategic factors and takes a struggle for power for granted (although he could not use the phrase in print), but he thinks that the superpowers should manage their conflicts in ways that do not give small powers the ability to drag them into dangerous situations. If the United States is not willing to cooperate, Primakov seems willing to engage in fierce competition. His contention that "the dominant positions [of the United States] in the military-political region . . . permits it to preserve its position of hegemony in the capitalist subsystem of international relations" certainly suggests that the use of Soviet and proxy troops as well as arms supply

81. " 'Doktrina eizenhausera'—tsep' neudach," *Sovremennyi Vostok* no. 1 (1958), p. 19. As late as 1970 he asserted that "the revolutionary process in the Arab world continues to develop both in breadth and in depth." See "Blizhnevostochnaia politika SShA: istoki, perspektivy," *SShA,* no. 9 (1970), p. 13.

82. "Strany sotsialisticheskoi orientatsii: trudnyi, no real'nyi perekhod k sotsializmu," *MEiMO,* no. 7 (July 1981), p. 11.

83. "Osvobodivshiesia strany v mezhdunarodnykh otnosheniiakh," p. 16.

84. "Zakon neravnomernosti razvitiia i istoricheskie syd'by osvobodivshikhsia stran," *MEiMO,* no. 12 (December 1980), p. 38.

could and should be important for consolidating the Soviet position in the third world, at least in those countries that have chosen the path of socialist orientation. Others have been even more explicit about the positive values of a Soviet military presence in certain third world situations.[85]

A number of scholars clearly are much more dubious than Primakov about the utility and significance of the military factor, but still seem willing to engage in political competition. Those who downplayed the importance or even possibility of changing the military balance may have been thinking primarily about the nuclear balance, but as their analysis became more general or referred to conventional weapons, it clearly was the third world that they had in mind. Similarly, those who were arguing the most strongly about the importance of the internationalization of the economy and the resulting economic dependence of the third world on the West generally were exhibiting little faith that military assistance would right the balance, but at least some who have emphasized the independence of countries like India and Brazil believe that the Soviet Union should be engaged in a vigorous competition for them.

Of course, the problem with a policy of both cooperation and competition is that it is easy to emphasize the competitive aspect, especially when the question is whether to exercise restraint in order to promote cooperation in the future. When pro-Soviet forces seek support, it is not easy to turn them aside. When the possibility of a victory arises, it is not easy to forgo. One should not be surprised, therefore, that in the debates on Iran, Primakov seems to have been one who was pushing the pro-Khomeini line for foreign policy reasons.

## Conclusion

It is easy enough to see differences in perspectives in the Soviet Union on foreign policy options. The important question—and the one most difficult to answer—is the extent to which major specialists on East-West relations really get involved in the foreign policy issues of the third world and the extent to which the impact of these issues on East-West relations is

85. See A. M. Dudin in V. M. Kulish, ed., *Voennaia sila i mezhdunarodnye otnosheniia: Voennye aspekty vneshnepoliticheskikh kontseptsii SShA* (Moscow: Mezhdunarodnye otnosheniia, 1972), pp. 136–39; and A. K. Kislov, "SShA i Sredizemnomor'e: novye real'nosti," *SShA,* no. 4 (1972), p. 35.

part of scholarly advice. That is, the USA department of the Ministry of Foreign Affairs has a section on bilateral Soviet-American relations and one on multilateral relations (Soviet-American relations in third world areas). Do scholars become involved in multilateral issues as well?

In some cases the structure of the institutes encourages some involvement. The Institute of the USA and Canada, for example, has long had sections on American policy in the Far East and in the Near East respectively; IMEMO had a top Middle East specialist while Primakov was deputy director. Anatolii Gromyko, the director of the Institute of Africa, certainly has had broader-gauge involvement, both because of his relationship with his father and his own experience as an Americanist.

Nevertheless, an outsider's impression is that the Soviet debates and expertise are much more compartmentalized than they should be. A department on American policies in the third world was created in the Institute of the USA and Canada at the end of the 1970s, but when events in Africa and then Latin America were having a devastating impact on Soviet-American relations, the institute did not have a serious specialist on these issues. It is difficult to believe that Arbatov would have left himself without staff support if he were being consulted on these questions. In fact, the institute's department on the Middle East is responsible for studying American policy in the Middle East, and it is unclear that it participates that much or, indeed, has deep knowledge of the actual options in Middle East settlements.

Similarly, IMEMO has had a surprisingly random quality to its inner expertise on multilateral international relations. It has virtually no one on international relations in Latin America, and its specialist on African international relations seems to focus on inter-African relations rather than ones with East-West overtones. Once Primakov left, no one really filled his place as a Middle East specialist. Both the Institute of Oriental Studies and the Institute of Africa have had professional governmental officials as deputy directors for international relations, apparently testimony to a judgment that their own specialists on international relations were not broad enough for these responsibilities. Indeed, the outsider's impression is that, leaving aside their respective directors, the two institutes are much stronger in their studies of political and economic development than international relations. It is a serious shortcoming that may explain some of the difficulties the Soviet Union has had in its third world foreign policy.

CHAPTER NINE

# Conclusion

SOVIET scholarly institutes and Soviet perceptions of the outside world have become the subject of rising interest in the United States over the last twenty years. This interest has resulted from the increase in the number and size of such institutes, from growing American recognition of the changes and the diversity of perceptions in the Soviet Union, and from greater access to the institute scholars.

The questions that American scholars ask about the institutes and the publications of their scholars, however, are not always the ones most relevant to policymakers. Scholars ask whether the institutes have power and access because they want to know whether they are talking with men of high status. They ask whether the scholars speak and write honestly or whether they are mere propagandists. (Americans generally ignore the probability that the role of a Soviet scholar in the written domestic debates may be quite different from that in official settings abroad when he is representing his country.) Americans also ask whether Soviet scholars have overcome their old misperceptions, usually implicitly assuming that American perceptions are the correct ones by which Soviets are to be judged. Finally, they fail to ask what policy difference a change in Soviet perceptions actually makes.

It is necessary for Americans to go further and to raise other questions. First, do the ideas and debates found in the scholarly literature reflect those that are relevant in the policymaking process, and do the debates give clues about the evolution of the thinking of policymakers in that process? On a large number of issues—the stages of history, the relationship of government and classes, the role of tradition or culture in history, the relative weight of political and economic factors in foreign policy, and so forth—Soviet scholars of the generation now in their fifties or younger

258

generally take less "dogmatic" positions than scholars of the Brezhnev generation. Is this reflected in the leadership as well, and is it possible that as the older generation passes from the political scene, more realistic and pragmatic views and policies are likely to emerge?

A second set of questions focuses on the relationship of American policy and policy options to Soviet perceptions and policy choices. Are there policies and postures that the U.S. government might take that would lead Soviet policy to evolve in a less dangerous direction? At the simplest level, will a conciliatory American policy strengthen the more pragmatic elements in the Soviet foreign policy establishment and leadership, or will a hard-line and confrontational American policy strengthen such forces by allowing them to argue that Soviet adventurism is dangerous? Would a more complex set of U.S. policies be more productive? Finally, does the very existence of the debates suggest a complexity in the Soviet policy process that demands different American responses and sensitivities than would a Soviet policy directed by a single leader or group with firm goals?

### Ideology and the Soviet Debates

The existence of the debates described in this book and the way in which they have evolved are important facts in themselves. By their existence they have implications that have not been absorbed in the American understanding of the Soviet Union.

First, of course, the debates require many assumptions about the relationship between ideology and Soviet foreign policy to be modified. Few policymakers retain the most simplified notions of some Soviet foreign policy master plan permanently put in place by Lenin, but assumptions derived from the totalitarian model continue to dominate the thinking of many nonspecialists, officials and rank and file alike. Some are so much the prisoner of the model that they compare the foreign policies of the cautious Brezhnev and Chernenko to those of Hitler merely because the Soviet Union and Nazi Germany have both been labeled totalitarian. Many more retain the notion that the Soviet Union has some simple drive to dominate the world that flows from a definable ideology accepted throughout the leadership and the foreign policy establishment.

For anyone with such a belief, this book should have been a revelation. The debates obviously demonstrate that all Soviet communists do not think alike, because all or virtually all of the persons cited in this book are members of the Communist party. Moreover, the disputes have not been on trivial matters but on the most fundamental issues of ideology and of revolutionary strategy and foreign policy.

Consider the subjects of debate discussed in this book. The question of whether there is a natural and inevitable evolution from a primitive-communal stage of history to a slaveholding stage to feudalism to capitalism was considered by Stalin—and by Westerners—to be a fundamental tenet of Marxist-Leninist ideology. To talk about a single precapitalist type of society in which the state is more powerful than the owners of the means of production, as scholars now often do, is to present a view of historical evolution and the driving forces of history that is far from simpleminded economic determinism. The same is true of an insistence that all developing countries are passing through a long transition in which there is no dominant class and in which, therefore, government does not represent an owning class.

Or what is one to say about the argument—now very widely accepted among Soviet economists—that countries with "capitalist-oriented" economies in the third world have a natural tendency to grow more rapidly than countries with a "socialist orientation" because well-rounded development seems to be dependent on foreign investment and integration into the world market? A quarter of a century ago, let alone in the Stalin period, it was just as widely accepted that integration into the capitalist world economy doomed a third world country to slow, deformed growth and that foreign investment exploited a local economy.

Assumptions about the engines of revolutionary change have also undergone profound transformation. From the belief that violent revolution by a communist party was the only way to socialism and that such revolutions were the normal path of development in newly industrialized countries, the largest group of scholars came to speak of "bourgeois nationalists" such as Fidel Castro or the army as the natural agents of revolution. By 1985, as has been seen, some of those most dedicated to revolution have begun to argue that communist parties directed from Moscow are actually counterproductive. They have instead been advocating support for "spontaneous," "new left" revolutionary movements. Indeed, paradoxically, the position that the socialist revolution must be led by a communist party based on the proletariat has come to be the way of expressing the greatest pessimism about the prospects for revolution in the third world. It is a way of saying that revolution is not possible until the third world becomes industrialized—perhaps even more industrialized than today's Western Europe.

On foreign relations a whole range of views has been expressed. International relations have been conceptualized as essentially conflictual or essentially cooperative, with a number of intermediate positions. These relations have been seen as deriving from class conflict, which implies implacable hostility between the Soviet Union and the West, or from the need to regulate interrelationships among different ethnic communities, which tends to imply the possibility of good relations with the West. The third world can be described as an area where major Soviet gains can be made, where the Soviet Union has the duty to support revolutions even if they are costly, or where conflicts with the United States should be avoided.

Most interesting of all, a number of analysts have begun to suggest that, because revolutions are occurring only in the dwindling number of preindustrial societies and that Marx was right in arguing that feudalism (or traditional society) is naturally followed by capitalism, the Soviet Union is wrong to emphasize relations with radical regimes so strongly. They contend that the Soviet Union should follow the model of its relationship with India and concentrate on geopolitically based relationships with large, moderate countries.

As we try to understand the driving forces of the debates, we must recognize that Iurii Krasin was right in the statement quoted in chapter 6: "In the close interrelationship of ideology and politics, the latter plays an exceptionally important role. One can say that political practice . . . is the generator of the development of ideology. Both the direction of the development of theoretical ideology and its basic contents depend on [politics]."

Soviet "ideological" assumptions have not been rigid; they have repeatedly been affected by events. Castro's evolution to Marxism-Leninism and the radical army coups of the early 1960s led to the recognition that forces that Marx and Lenin had considered anticommunist could, in fact, lead a radical revolution. Patterns of third world economic growth demonstrated the possibility of major growth under capitalism and the difficulty of achieving it in countries of "socialist orientation" without major petroleum reserves. Pessimism about the success of revolutions in third world countries well on the path of industrialization flowed from observation rather than from deductive analysis, while greater optimism about the more backward countries also reflected experience. The success of the Sandinistas in Nicaragua tilted the balance of opinion toward those scholars who thought that guerrilla war should be promoted, while the success of OPEC weakened the positions of those who thought capitalist third world countries inevitably followed the West in foreign policy. If

Americans insist that Soviet ideology is monolithic and unaffected by events, they are being far more ideological than their Soviet counterparts.


## Scholarly Debates and Soviet Policy

As Westerners have begun to notice the published Soviet scholarly debates in recent years, the question that has aroused the most controversy has been their relationship, if any, to the policy process. The word "academic" has two meanings in English—"scholarly" and "irrelevant." Are the academic debates in the Soviet Union academic in the second sense as well, or are they debates that we should be studying and taking very seriously if we want to understand Soviet policy?

One of the reasons for the controversy on this question in the United States is that the question really needs to be subdivided. The first subquestion is whether Soviet scholars have direct influence on Soviet decisionmakers. Certainly we should have no illusion about high policymakers eagerly awaiting the latest issue of a scholarly journal so that they can read the newest idea. A number of middle-level officials, especially in the Central Committee apparatus, sit on the editorial boards of journals and do attend scholarly conferences, and they are subject to such influence, but the behavior of high officials was undoubtedly well summarized in a warning purportedly made by the deputy director of a Soviet institute to his subordinates: "Those who write don't decide; those who decide don't read." He was warning about the need to be brief, and a great many American specialists would vigorously nod their heads in recognition and agreement about a universal phenomenon.

Nevertheless, Soviet scholars, especially the ones who have been quoted in this book, are not limited to academic publication. The institutes produce classified analyses for the various decisionmaking bodies—analyses that range from brief informational memorandums to formal prognoses of the future with policy advice attached. Moreover, the most prominent Soviet scholars are often drawn into the interagency committees (*komissiia*) that review policy, write speeches or ideological documents, and even draft policy options for Politburo consideration.[1]

---

1. This is true not only now but also in the 1950s and 1960s. See Igor S. Glagolev, *Post-Andropov Kremlin Strategy* (Washington, D.C.: Association for Cooperation of Democratic Countries, 1984), pp. 22–83. Despite the title, the first part of this book is Glagolev's story of his years in the Soviet Union; he was the highest ranking scholar to have emigrated.

Of the two forms of classified work, the participation in the committees is likely to be the more important. Individual documents can have a direct influence on policymakers that is unlikely for a journal article, but on the whole the impact of even this work should not be exaggerated. The just-quoted statement about the reading habits of decisionmakers referred to the preparation of a classified memorandum. The existence of a large number of Soviet scholars adds more paper to the flood already crossing the desk of an overburdened official and thereby reduces the chance that any one piece will be read.[2] It is small wonder that individual scholars bemoan their personal lack of influence.

The interagency committees can be a different matter. Policymaking is always essentially an oral process. Meetings, committees, conferences, talks, briefings, and conversations at parties are the major means of communication in Washington, D.C., and other capitals such as Moscow are no different. The interagency committees are created on an ad hoc basis, and they include representatives from powerful institutions—the Ministry of Foreign Affairs, the Central Committee apparatus, the KGB, and (if military issues are involved) the Ministry of Defense. On specialized issues, representatives of relevant domestic ministries (for example, the Ministry of Fisheries) are also included. The scholars do not represent a powerful institution, but once a committee has been constituted, the influence of individual members will depend on their individual skills and personalities as well as on the posts they hold. In such a setting scholars obviously have sometimes had an influence on specific questions, but these are precisely the people who know that a passion for anonymity is crucial for continued influence and who do not talk to Westerners about their experience.

On the whole, however, it would be wrong to emphasize the direct influence of scholars on policy, except in relatively atypical cases. The greatest direct influence of scholars is likely to be informal and to be felt in the interpretation of events. When some development occurs abroad, the leading scholars are going to be asked their opinion on the telephone, if not formally. How do they explain the Khomeini revolution, how seriously do they think President Reagan is about space negotiations, what prospects do they see for the Salvadoran rebels, who do they think bombed the American embassy in Lebanon? Their analysis may conceivably become the

2. See Nora Beloff, "Escape from Boredom: A Defector's Story," *The Atlantic* (November, 1976), p. 45.

accepted one, but in any case they are part of the process by which these judgments are made.

The formulation of the Soviet reaction to current developments is, however, the type of question on which operational officials in the Ministry of Foreign Affairs and in the Central Committee apparatus have the greatest natural advantages. The scholars are seldom drawn in to this kind of policymaking, and less frequently do they have an impact on the day-to-day decisions of these institutions.

The second question that needs to be addressed with respect to the relationship of the scholars and Soviet policy is that of indirect influence, especially over the long term. Whether it is recognized or not, the target of published work in any country is not the major decisionmakers, but those who have contact with decisionmakers in conversations or conferences— or those who have contact with those who have contact with decisionmakers. Indeed, even within a specialized scholarly community in any country, the amount of general reading that is done is surprisingly low, and one of the first purposes of writing is to gain enough legitimacy to be more generally read and to be invited to the settings where oral communication takes place. Ultimately its purpose is to achieve the legitimacy that will produce invitations to the oral settings closer to the inner circle of decisionmaking.[3]

Debate and policy analysis is, therefore, to be understood in horizontal terms (within a community) rather than vertical (from the individual to upper decisionmaker). Thousands of people are involved in the percolation and the serious discussion of ideas, and each is part of an elaborate network that not only has links in many institutions and localities but that also extends backward in time. Individual influence within this network is always ambiguous and ill defined. Even if seminal figures can be identified, they themselves are products of prior influences, and they can have no impact except to the extent that others take up their ideas and propagate them. The sheer number of people involved tends to guarantee that none will have enormous individual influence.

Consequently, although Soviet scholars have had an accurate sense of the limits on their individual influence, the politics of persuasion must be

3. The insights of Paul Lazarfeld and his associates about a "two-step flow of communication" and those of David Easton about the aggregation of demands are relevant in this respect. See David Easton, *A Systems Analysis of Political Life* (New York: John Wiley and Sons, 1965), pp. 86–96.

understood in different terms. After all, the individual voter in the United States never has any personal impact on the election of a president, and from the point of view of pure individual rationality, he or she should not take the effort to vote.[4] Yet, the paradox of collective action is that even when it is irrational for each individual to participate because of the impossibility of influencing the outcome, the collective action may have a determining influence if it does, in fact, take place. All the votes pooled together in a presidential election are of decisive importance. Similarly, the gradual changes of perception within a foreign policy establishment, produced in extremely subtle ways, can also have major effects, even if individual members of the establishment are right in thinking that their individual voice is not significant.

The debates that have been the subject of this book have essentially been aimed beyond day-to-day policy disputes. Even the serious newspaper articles that try to affect current perceptions usually are written with a broader establishment in mind and with the intention of influencing a general mood—reducing or intensifying a sense of tension, promoting a sense of optimism or pessimism about the course of revolution abroad, and so forth. The main purpose of the scholarly articles or books (other, of course, than the need to publish if one is not to perish) is to influence the thinking of the scholarly intermediaries, to legitimize oneself as an intermediary, and to try to change the categories of thinking and analysis in a way that may have a long-term impact on policy. The fact that the Soviet Union has an official ideology and that the debates must take place through the medium of ideological categories makes this latter activity peculiarly important in the Soviet framework.

The influence of this aspect of the debates can occur through a gradual change in mood and perception (the acceptance of the necessity of Western investment in third world countries, for instance, or the growing pessimism about revolution in industrialized third world countries), through changes in the people chosen as advisers by Soviet policymakers, and through shaping the views of the next generation of leaders.

John Maynard Keynes once remarked that the "practical-minded" man who has no use for economists is always the prisoner of some defunct economist, and the point has general applicability. Many of the influences

---

4. Mancur Olson, *The Logic of Collective Action* (Cambridge, Massachusetts: Harvard University Press, 1965).

on the present are found in the past. Perhaps they are events and debates that took place when the officials were young adults.[5] Perhaps they took place more recently, when younger officials were frustrated by what they saw as the inflexible response of old leaders to new developments. For example, the new Soviet leaders introduced major changes into Soviet foreign policy in 1953, but these changes did not emerge full-blown out of the heads of the new Zeuses. Rather, they had been shaped by the discussions—to be sure, at that time mostly behind the scenes—that had been taking place before 1953. If significant changes in policy take place now that Chernenko has departed, the same will also be true of them.

This possibility of a delayed impact of debates on policy is particularly important to keep in mind at the present time. The top foreign posts in the Soviet Union have been occupied by men with incredible tenure. Andrei Gromyko, minister of foreign affairs, headed the American desk in the Foreign Ministry in 1939 and was minister from 1957 to 1985. The United States had nine secretaries of state in that period. Boris Ponomarev, head of the international department of the Central Committee, worked in the Comintern beginning in 1935 and has headed the international department since 1955. Dmitrii Ustinov, the minister of defense, was named one of four defense industry ministers in 1941, was in charge of the Soviet rocket program after the war, and became the top defense industry administrator in the early 1960s, before dying in 1984. The minister of foreign trade, Nikolai Patolichev, was in his post from 1958 to 1985. Andrei Aleksandrov-Agentov served as chief foreign policy assistant for Brezhnev, Andropov, and Chernenko.

In the United States it is said that a secretary of state often burns out after five years or so and in any case becomes so identified with old policies that he loses flexibility. Because the Soviet policy team was so stable for so long, those who have been advocating different approaches have faced enormous obstacles. This was particularly true in the last years of Brezhnev's life because the ailing general secretary did not want any major foreign policy change of any type. In these circumstances the scholarly debates were really aimed at the successor generation in the hopes that younger men would be more receptive to new approaches. Mikhail Gorbachev's quick replacement of Gromyko suggests that these hopes will be

5. See Ernest R. May, *Lessons of the Past: The Use and Misuse of History in American Foreign Policy* (Oxford University Press, 1973), especially pp. 7–18.

realized and that arguments that seemed to have little impact on policy will prove in the long run to have been more effective than they seemed at the time.

The third question about the relationship of Soviet scholars to policy is not one of influence at all. Rather, it is whether the debates that we can observe are somewhat like the shadows on the wall of Plato's cave: a reflection—sometimes very diffuse and hazy, sometimes much sharper— of the real policy debates going at the highest level of the party and the state.

Although great care must be taken in interpreting the shadows we see and although the play of the shadows must be examined over a long time, there are many reasons to believe that the debates tell us a good deal about what is occurring behind the scenes. At a minimum they show that the Soviet leaders are often of divided minds about basic foreign policy questions. If Soviet leaders knew what they wanted, they would not permit the kind of debates that they do. It is one thing to encourage a detailed study of new phenomena; it is something very different to permit a published discussion on whether the Sandinistas in Nicaragua should push their revolution toward the comprehensive socialism of a Cuba.

In fact, one surely can go further. The classified work done by Soviet scholars has a crucial implication that frequently is overlooked in the West. Career success for a scholar—that is, promotion to such administrative posts in the institutes as section head, department head, deputy director, and director, and even more so into the Central Committee apparatus—depends less on a scholar's ability to conduct individual research than on his ability to produce and organize classified analyses and to function as an effective committee member. Most of the scholars frequently cited in this book have, in fact, risen to administrative posts. When they have written publicly, they have been aware of the policy options under consideration at higher levels, and they have known the ways the issues are formulated. If they have been ambitious, they have wanted to use their published work to promote their privately expressed positions (or, if they are younger, to demonstrate their capacity to handle relevant issues in a sophisticated manner). They have wanted to identify themselves with issues and lines of analysis that will mark them for promotion.

When we see, therefore, a consensus developing among the scholars, it is highly probable that some functional equivalent is being duplicated among relevant policymakers. If a powerful Politburo figure holds a view, let alone a Politburo majority, some major policy intellectuals would find it personally profitable to identify themselves with it simply in order to obtain a patron. The same thing may be true on domestic issues. It is inconceivable that the majority of Soviet economists on the third world would have openly spoken so contemptuously about the efficacy of the Soviet model in producing growth there had they not had a strong sense that this was safe—that the coming generation of leaders was planning major economic reforms and would not punish them. Even when divisions continue among scholars, an examination of which scholars are promoted and which demoted can be revealing about the direction of thinking at higher levels, because higher officials ultimately determine these promotions.

As a consequence, the evolution of the debates that we have seen demonstrates something important about the nature of Soviet foreign policy. In particular, to say that the Soviet Union is bent on dominating the world misses the point of the changes in Soviet thinking. Obviously the Soviet Union, like every power, is trying to protect the internal and external security of its political regime while also trying to increase its power and influence. Sometimes it does support changes in foreign political systems and leaders; it normally does establish good relations with governments that are hostile to its adversaries; it does try to gain influence and forward military bases at the same time that it earns foreign currency with its arms sales. Such behavior does not, however, make the Soviet Union unique. What is crucial is the means that a country uses to achieve its goals and the degree to which it is willing to pay costs and incur risks to do so.

The distinctive characteristic of the Soviet Union in the past was the assumptions of its leaders about the relationship of national security and revolution abroad. Stalin seemed to think near-term Soviet successes in the third world were unlikely; but he also seemed to believe deeply that communist governments would be friendly or even subservient, while noncommunist governments would in the long run inevitably be hostile. For a leader with this perspective, a policy of promoting worldwide revolution was the only intelligent policy, even for the most defensive of reasons. Today all such assumptions have dissolved. A Soviet leader might dismiss the apostacy of Yugoslavia as an aberration, but he could not do so after China, Cambodia, and Albania had also gone their own ways, or after the very mixed Soviet relationship with the leaders of North Korea and Romania and the difficulties of developing popular support for communist regimes in Eastern Europe. There simply is no reason for any sane Russian to think that a communist regime outside the reach of Soviet military power will necessarily be subservient or, given the experience of Polish, Hungarian, or Romanian governments, that even one within the reach of Soviet military power will be completely so.

The radical third world regimes have been even less stable in their orientations, with Mozambique only the latest example of significant deviation. The Soviet Union has thus come to accept far more limited goals in the third world than traditional Western views have suggested. The growing sense of pessimism about third world developments means that willingness to take chances or to make expensive commitments is correspondingly reduced, at least if the United States does not turn the developments into tests of will.

## American Policy and Soviet Debates

We are, of course, interested in Soviet published debates not only in order to try to understand the thinking of those making policy. U.S. policy is one of the phenomena about which Soviet officials and scholars are thinking and debating, and it is something to which they must react. Presumably, different policies will produce different conclusions and reactions. The practical question that arises for Americans is what can the United States do that will influence Soviet perceptions and debates in the direction that will promote a more reasonable Soviet policy?

This question needs to be answered with great caution. First, of course, Soviet analysts can interpret a given American policy in very diverse ways, depending upon their prior perspectives and policy views. As has been seen, some Soviet scholars drew the lesson from the outcome of the Vietnam war that the Americans would use less force in the future and that stronger Soviet support of national liberation movements was desirable; some assumed that little would change in U.S. policy; still others believed that Vietnam showed that all outside military force (presumably including the Soviet) had limited efficacy in the third world and that the Soviet Union and the United States should cooperate in avoiding conflicts. One suspects that if the United States had won in Vietnam, the first group of people would have concluded that force was useful and that the Soviet Union should develop its own ability to project it into the third world, while the third group would have preached the need for more accommodation because of the ability of the United States to crush national liberation movements.

Second, people in the Soviet Union with a given policy position have the need to use somewhat contradictory arguments. A Soviet scholar or official who is seeking to moderate Soviet policy must be able to say that the United States can be dangerous, for otherwise it is hard to say that the Soviet Union has something to fear in an aggressive action. Yet such a person must also be able to say that there is something to gain through accommodation, that the United States is willing to compromise and make agreements. Similarly, the advocate of a more aggressive Soviet policy must argue that the United States is too hostile for meaningful negotiation, but that it will not react too strongly to more assertive Soviet actions.

For these reasons no simple American strategy will affect Soviet thinking in a desired direction from an American point of view. Certainly it would be a major mistake for the United States unilaterally to moderate its competition with the Soviet Union in the third world simply in an attempt to demonstrate its peaceful intentions. (A quid pro quo such as a mutual end of support for covert action in specific cases or cooperation to achieve a common aim is another matter.) All students of the psychology of international relations have emphasized the strong tendency for every nation to see its own policy in benign terms and to assume wrongly that its opponent must see it that way as well, and a number of scholars have proposed various techniques to try to break through this vicious circle—notably, gestures to demonstrate nonaggressive intentions.[6] In practice, however, it is not a trivial accomplishment to do something effective in such matters, even in the best of circumstances.

The basic problem is that almost every nation's policy is somewhat ill defined and ambiguous. Every major power is expansionist *and* opportunistic *and* defensive. Every nation is trying to expand its influence, to strengthen the internal and external security of its political regime, and to achieve some historically defined national interests. These goals are often mutually contradictory, and unless a leader is peculiarly single-minded, any country's policy will be marked by the inconsistencies implicit in the different goals. Consequently, it is easy to find plenty of evidence to support any thesis about any country's behavior and next to impossible to disprove any thesis that is not wildly extreme. The processes of selective

---

6. The classic statement is found in Charles E. Osgood, *An Alternative to War and Surrender* (Urbana: University of Illinois Press, 1962), pp. 85–134. For a recent statement, see Ralph K. White. *Fearful Warriors* (Free Press, 1984) pp. 87–106.

perception are particularly seductive on this issue precisely because there is real behavior that corresponds to any preconceptions.

In these circumstances, deliberate behavior that is intended to modify a suspicious adversary's perceptions will usually look like trickery unless the gestures are so sweeping that they will harm a country's interests if they are unsuccessful. In the last five years, the Soviet Union has made a number of small, conciliatory gestures in Europe, including troop reductions, but they have had no impact in the United States because Americans rightly believe that they do not fundamentally change the Soviet military position.

Indeed, as Robert Jervis has emphasized, accommodating gestures may be totally counterproductive if the opponent is really aggressive. Such an opponent may interpret accommodation as weakness and may become convinced that further aggression is possible.[7] Recognition of this possibility makes accommodating gestures difficult to offer from a domestic political point of view. As long as there is controversy about the adversary's motives—and this is inevitable—any gestures will be interpreted by hard-liners at home as disastrous signs of weakness. The gestures themselves will result in the significant expenditure of political capital unless they are quickly reciprocated, but reciprocal gestures are already a matter of negotiation and in another category altogether.

Reducing the opponent's sense of threat in the third world is much more difficult than in the nuclear realm. Because of the unimportance of minor variations in the nuclear balance, each side can afford major unanswered concessions without really endangering its safety, and gestures that reassure the adversary that the danger of a first strike has been lessened may significantly weaken the forces of hysteria on the other side. In the third world, however, both the Soviet Union and the United States really are expansionist in the sense that each is trying to expand its influence vis-à-vis the other. There is every danger that accommodation in the third world for its own sake would be perceived as weakness and would be counterproductive.

On the other hand, a policy of thoroughgoing confrontation is also counterproductive. Confrontation can be useful in reminding both the Soviet Union and its supporters that there are limits to what it can do. Indeed, confrontation can strengthen the hand of those in the Soviet Union

---

7. Robert Jervis, *Perception and Misperception in International Politics* (Princeton University Press, 1976).

who urge greater restraint. Yet, confrontation for its own sake, confrontation that does not have specific goals, can degenerate into mindless bullying. Bullying can be temporarily effective, but it builds up resentments and counteraction when one is in a vulnerable position. In addition, a constantly bullying type of confrontation throws away the opportunity to make important gains. One must be willing at some point to back away from the confrontation and sign an agreement or nothing is accomplished unless it proves possible to destroy the adversary altogether. Such a hope in the Soviet case—or even in cases such as Nicaragua—seems utopian.

Two factors increase the inadvisability of a thoroughly confrontational policy by the United States. First, the United States has seldom, in fact, been willing to use enough force to destroy the adversary. As a result, it has applied too little force to be successful, but enough to permit the hard-liners in a hostile regime to identify themselves with local nationalism and even achieve a heroic victory over the American colossus. This was true of the Western intervention in the Russian Civil War and of the American-backed Bay of Pigs operation in Cuba. Nicaragua seems a repetition of these sad cases.

Second, the trend in the Soviet debates discussed in this book suggests that the Soviet leaders would find it in their interest to pull back from their commitment to radical movements. The United States has never really assimilated a major lesson of the Cuban missile crisis—namely, that if an adversary wants to retreat, he should be given a face-saving avenue to do so. Instead, in its relations with the Soviet Union in the third world, the United States tackles Soviet allies frontally, and it gloats about its victories. It even proclaims the impossible goal of excluding the Soviet Union from the Middle East, which is directly on the Soviet southern border.

As discussed in the previous chapter, the one clear-cut interest that the Soviet Union has in the third world is to maintain its credibility as a great power. It is inconceivable that the Soviet Union can make even small retreats under open public pressure that humiliates it. It is inconceivable that the Soviet Union can abandon allies under pressure unless the pressure is an unstoppable invasion, as in the case of Grenada. If the Soviet Union began to make threatening statements about Turkey, the United States would be forced to send more military aid, if only as a gesture. The Soviet Union is in the same position when the United States talks threateningly about Cuba or organizes forces of counterrevolutionaries against Nicaragua. The United States complains about the untoward Soviet military shipments in these areas, but the latter are more a response to American threats than a cause of them.

To strengthen the hands of the moderates in the Soviet Union, the United States must follow a very sophisticated policy that avoids either unilateral accommodation or all-out confrontation. It must understand that conflicts of interest are endemic to international relations and that a super-power such as the Soviet Union is never going to withdraw from the pursuit of its interests in the third world. Above all, the Soviet Union will never be able to avoid verbal and small-scale economic or military support for a pro-Soviet and radical regime any more than the United States will be able to avoid giving support to movements such as Solidarity.

These are givens. The United States must decide how to react to them and how to deal with them effectively. Or, rather, it must decide how to deal with them most effectively, given the costs that it is willing to pay. It was clearly in American interests to have a stable, Christian government in Lebanon, but President Reagan was surely correct in his judgment that this interest was not strong enough to justify the price that would have been required to achieve it.

The same calculus must be made by the Soviet Union as well, and if the American goal is to moderate Soviet behavior, the United States must learn to affect the cost-benefit ratio for the Soviet Union in a skillful manner. This point is generally understood in the United States, but the costs and benefits to be affected are often thought of in rather simplistic terms. In the 1970s many in the United States hoped—or at least professed to hope—that the desire of the Soviet Union for arms control agreements and trade with the United States could be used to provide the benefits to encourage a more moderate Soviet third world policy. The costs, other than a denial of trade and arms control agreements, have usually been seen in more military terms: military intervention to prevent Soviet gains, as well as threats of military action, actual covert actions, and economic threats against Soviet allies in order to force the Soviet Union to expand its expenditures for arms and economic aid to these countries.

To the extent that the hidden agenda of those advocating a linkage of trade and arms control with Soviet third world behavior was really to destroy détente by setting impossible conditions for it, the strategy was a success. If accepted on its own terms, however, the policy of linkage was essentially a failure; the costs and benefits for the Soviet Union in trade and arms control were not high enough to moderate its third world policy.

In the future, linkage is likely to be even more unsuccessful. Brezhnev and Gromyko seemed genuinely to want agreements with the United States—even substantially meaningless agreements—simply to obtain symbolic recognition of equality with the United States. The new leadership seems less insecure in this respect and less willing to pay a price for agreements with the United States for their own sake.

If the United States is going to impose costs for Soviet third world actions, it will have to do so in the third world itself—as, indeed, it basically had to do in the 1970s in areas such as Afghanistan. The only "sanction" that really mattered in Afghanistan was the aid to the rebels. The United States should not, however, think that the threat of military intervention in the third world has much impact on Soviet political support of radical movements. After all, the United States lost the Vietnam War, and it failed to intervene militarily in Iran, Lebanon, Nicaragua, and elsewhere. When it sent forces only against tiny Grenada while it was unwilling to do so against small Nicaragua, the action only dramatized the limited character of the threat. It is only direct military action by the Soviet Union and its allies against neighbors that is likely to stimulate a corresponding response.

Similarly, the imposition of costs on the Soviet Union through forcing it to assume economic burdens to support its allies also creates a great dilemma for the United States. As the debates described in this book demonstrate, the sharp reduction in Soviet optimism about revolution in the third world was really caused by internal third world developments and by the working of Western (and Far Eastern) economic institutions and mechanisms. Those cautioning their leaders to moderate their hopes (and, by implication, their activism) in the third world have said, first, that Marx was right: the collapse of "feudalism" is accompanied by (in fact, generally caused by) the rise of classes that want more or less capitalist institutions because they benefit from them. In this view even the state sector is staffed by people who naturally become "bureaucratic bourgeoisie," at least if they have a private sector into which to funnel their money. Second, those counseling Soviet moderation have been arguing that the availability of Western capital, the access to the world market, and the transfer of technology through multinational corporations have been highly beneficial for growth and that third world leaders tend to moderate their radicalism in order not to frighten off foreign investors and lenders.

When the United States tries to increase the costs for the Soviet Union by imposing sanctions on its allies, it faces the paradox that it is interfering with Western mechanisms, both outside investment and the domestic market, that have been the most powerful U.S. tools in winning the third world. For example, a confrontational U.S. attitude toward Cuba has virtually forced the Soviet Union to spend large sums of money to support that country. Yet, twenty-five years of boycott have meant that the economic forces that moved many radical regimes of the 1960s to the center have not had the chance to work in Cuba. Clearly, the policy followed has not moderated either Soviet policy in Cuba or Cuban support for the Soviet Union. One cannot be certain whether a different policy would have led to a different evolution of policy in Cuba or whether it simply would have lessened Soviet costs, but the burden of proof is on those who think the American policy was effective.

As the United States tries to affect the Soviet cost-benefit calculus and to strengthen those calling for a more moderate Soviet policy, it should be more optimistic about the natural forces at work in the world. The American government should try to rely on them more rather than take on the burden—and costs—of acting unilaterally. For example, economic sanctions are usually not necessary. If a country is behaving in a radical way, if it is curtailing the private sector, if it is threatening nationalization, private corporations and banks will avoid it for normal economic reasons. In various ways the government can informally affect the risk analysis of the private sector (both in discouraging investment or in encouraging it in a country such as Mozambique that begins to move away from the Soviet Union). But informal action in conjunction with the natural working of the market permits a much more calibrated response—and much easier change of policy on both sides—than formal governmental action.

Similarly, in the geopolitical realm, costs need not be imposed by the United States alone. It is the Afghanistan rebels who are really making the invasion extremely costly for the Soviet Union. It is France and Egypt that are playing the major deterrent role against Libya in Africa. It is the fear of Soviet expansionism on the part of a number of independent governments around the border of the USSR that has resulted in its encirclement by hostile powers. If Nicaragua begins to pose a real threat, Mexican opinion will change, and Mexican power will be exercised—indeed, economically, it is already being exercised.

In fact, Americans tend to forget all the basic tenets of international relations theory when they think of the Soviet Union in the third world. They assume that a Soviet success will have a "domino" effect on neighboring countries. International relations theory, however, has always suggested that an expansion of one country's power produces the tendency for other countries to unite against it to right the balance of power.[8] The Soviet victory in Vietnam naturally led Southeast Asian countries except in Indochina to draw more toward the United States. An American victory in Vietnam might well have had the opposite effect.

Evgenii Primakov, it may be remembered, pessimistically argued that polycentrism in the capitalist world did not lead to major centers of opposition to the United States but to "the creation of 'mini-centers' of force among the developing countries, special kinds of 'subimperialist' bases . . . base points of the policy of imperialism."[9] One only wishes that Primakov were always right, and certainly the United States should strive to ensure that he is. A country that tries to exercise power too publicly and alone is a country that periodically will be entrapped at an airport in Beirut. The USSR has been wiser—and more effective in the use of power—by acting in Lebanon through Syria, and the United States too needs to learn to act less visibly and in conjunction with other countries.

There are two realms in which direct governmental action is important in strengthening the hand of moderating forces in the Soviet Union. The first is in being firm that direct military action by the Soviet Union will be answered. The large-scale military aid to Afghanistan rebels was appropriate, and Soviet action against countries in which the United States has an important interest (for example, Turkey and those of the Persian Gulf) should be resisted by American military forces. There should also be no doubt about the American response—and there surely is no doubt—if Nicaragua were to use its military force against a neighboring country.

The second realm in which direct governmental involvement is necessary is in giving Soviet moderates the ability to argue that cooperation with the United States is sometimes possible. This is, of course, absolutely vital in the case of cooperation to avoid a direct Soviet-American military confrontation. In this respect, American policy under all American presidents, including President Reagan, has actually been quite good, and the same can be said of Soviet policy. Each side has been very restrained where truly important interests of the other are involved, even in the Middle East where important interests of the two countries overlap.

Since World War II, for example, Afghanistan has been conceded to be in the Soviet sphere of influence, and the country has little direct importance to the West. The Soviet invasion was not, therefore, a grave threat to

8. Stephen M. Walt, "Alliance Formation and the Balance of World Power," *International Security*, vol. 9 (Spring 1985), pp. 3–43.

9. See chapter 8, pp. 237–38, 254–55.

the United States or even a significant change in the regional balance of power, and direct American military involvement would have been fraught with danger. Everyone understands that a Soviet invasion of Iran would be a very different matter and almost surely would result in a very different American response.

By the same token, the Soviet Union has never given the slightest sign that it would think of defending Grenada or Nicaragua with its own military forces against an American invasion. Everyone understands that an American invasion of Cuba would be a much more serious challenge to the Soviet Union. While a Soviet response in Cuba cannot be predicted with certainty, the possibility of some drastic action has to be taken into account by American policymakers, and surely it has been.

In more ambiguous cases both sides have also made careful distinctions. The Korean and the Vietnam wars were fought by implicit rules that minimized the danger of Soviet-American confrontation. In the Middle East in the 1960s and 1970s, the Soviet Union would not support Egyptian attacks against Israel, and, somewhat surprisingly, it did not insist on Egyptian control of both banks of the Suez Canal even though the canal was a vital link between European Russia and Soviet Far East ports. Nevertheless, the Soviet Union made clear that it would defend Cairo itself and actually used its own planes and pilots at the time of the 1970 Israeli air attacks. Israel backed off. In the 1973 war when Cairo was threatened, Henry Kissinger flew to Moscow and issued an ultimatum to Israel from there.

In recent years the Soviet deputy minister of foreign affairs with senior responsibility for the United States has also handled relations with the Middle East, almost surely a step deliberately designed to prevent policy toward the Middle East from leading to a confrontation with the United States. The Soviet Union has been very cautious in the Lebanese civil war, even when Israeli shells damaged the Soviet embassy in Beirut. As earlier with Egypt, the Soviet Union refused to provide any guarantees for Syrian actions abroad but indicated a determination to defend Damascus. It installed powerful antiaircraft rockets in Syria, manned with its own officers, both to make this point and to ensure that Syria could not use the rockets in a way that might draw the Soviet Union into the conflict against its will. The United States for its part has not challenged Syria directly, let alone the Soviet rockets.

In the Persian Gulf, Soviet specialists correctly understand that a direct Soviet military thrust could easily provoke nuclear war, and the Soviet

Union has taken care not to become too deeply involved in the Iranian-Iraqi war. Indeed, it has continually called for an end to that war. The United States too has been extremely careful in this war, and its allies have not provided aid or arms sales that would permit either side to achieve a victory.

While both the Soviet Union and the United States have handled the potentially dangerous situations well thus far, neither should forget that this has not happened automatically. Disaster has been avoided precisely because both sides have been careful. With the death of old Soviet leaders and now the removal of Andrei Gromyko as Soviet foreign minister, and with a major generational change likely in the United States in a few years, it is possible that new leaders, quite unknowingly, will not retain all of the implicit assumptions about "rules of the game" of the older generation. New leaders may not react in the same way that old ones have.

The greater dangers probably do not arise with respect to well-recognized crisis points such as the Arab-Israeli conflict; they arise in other areas where general rules have tacitly been adopted but never clearly defined or emotionally accepted. In Africa, for example, low-level military intervention by allies of the superpowers has come to be more or less tolerated by both sides. Cuba and Libya play roles that are congruent with Soviet interests, while France, Zaire, and several other countries perform similar roles for the United States. Clearly, however, U.S. toleration of the Cuban role is grudging at best, and the level of permissible intervention by proxies is very ill defined. In Angola in the mid-1970s, each side genuinely thought that the other exceeded the acceptable level of military intervention in a competitive situation, and there is no reason to assume that such disagreements will not arise again.

The most serious problems arise from the lack of clearly defined rules regarding military assistance in areas close to the other's border. Perhaps it would be more accurate to say that clear rules have been defined by the United States and tolerated by the Soviet Union but never really accepted by it. Even though Managua is 1,000 miles from American shores, the United States considers Central America within its inviolable sphere of influence, but it denies the legitimacy of any Soviet influence in the Middle East, which is geographically closer to the Soviet Union. The United States believes that it can sponsor military action against Nicaragua for its involvement in the El Salvadoran revolution, but that the Soviet Union will not engage in analogous action against the areas in Pakistan from which American-financed rebels enter Afghanistan. Unless these rules are clarified to the satisfaction of both, they will produce a major crisis sometime in the future, for they are inherently unstable.

In addition to cooperation in avoiding military conflict, moderating forces in the Soviet Union should also be encouraged to fight for positive cooperation with the United States to promote common interests. Americans have had a tendency to believe that the United States and the Soviet Union have few interests in common other than preventing a nuclear war. In fact, however, they cooperate in many ways: they allocate radio frequencies, develop rules on whale hunting, use satellites to locate each other's downed pilots, and so forth. Most recently, agreement has been reached on channels of communication about airplanes that stray into Soviet airspace so that a repetition of the shooting down of the Korean airliner can be avoided. The question for Americans and Soviets is not *whether* Soviet-American cooperation occurs, but the nature of the activities on which the two should cooperate.

More substantial cooperation in the third world is difficult. Spheres of influence are impossible to establish because of the instability of the third world and the lack of superpower control over events. The Soviet Union could not control the domestic policy of the Marxist regime in Afghanistan before it invaded, even though the Carter administration was doing little to destabilize the situation. The United States could not persuade or compel the shah of Iran to do what it thought necessary. The Soviet Union gave almost no support to Sandinista rebels in Nicaragua before they came to power, and Somoza refused to make the reforms the United States thought necessary.

The United States and the Soviet Union have little ability to enforce spheres of influence in such circumstances. When Egypt wanted to move from the Soviet side to the American in the 1970s, a sphere of influence agreement would have required the United States to reject the offer. Obviously, this would have been politically and psychologically inconceivable. By the same token, when Ethiopia and Nicaragua wanted to move in the opposite direction in the second half of the 1970s, it would have been equally inconceivable for the Soviet Union to refuse. The level of aid and support that the superpowers give can, of course, be varied, but if the United States wants limits on this aid, it must understand that such limits would apply to the very large aid it provided Egypt as well as that the Soviet Union provided Ethiopia.

For all the problems, however, there are still many ways in which the United States and the Soviet Union may gain from cooperation in the third world. Both are threatened by Islamic fundamentalism, the Soviet Union perhaps more than the United States. For this reason, neither wants Iran to win its war with Iraq or radical Shi'ites to win in Lebanon. The Soviet mediation of the war between India and Pakistan in 1965 served American as well as Soviet interests; a Syrian-imposed order in Lebanon that kept both the Palestinians and the radical Shi'ites under control could have the same character.

The list of possible types of cooperation could become much longer, depending on how the United States and the Soviet Union define their interests. As has been seen, Georgii Arbatov has asserted on Soviet television that "everybody is dependent on the stability of the international economic system and international monetary system." Most Soviet scholars insist that the Soviet Union wants stability on its borders in the Middle East. In the Philippines, the Soviet Union has mixed interests: a radical revolution might deprive the United States of bases (unless the latter maintained them as it does Guantánamo on Cuba), but it would also frighten Japan in a way that would stimulate Japanese rearmament. Soviet interests in Cuba and Central America are minimal, as are American interests in Afghanistan, and some reciprocal restraint is at least conceivable.

In addition, the perception of the degree of Soviet-American hostility can affect third parties. Neither the United States nor the Soviet Union can be happy with the tendency of small countries to play the Soviet-American conflict for their own purposes. Neither can be happy when a third country can inflict harm on it, knowing that the other superpower will be supportive. Is it so certain that Iran would not have held American hostages for so long if Khomeini had the perception that the Soviet Union and the United States were cooperating and that the Soviet Union was strongly opposed to the hostage-taking? Was the tacit Soviet-American cooperation in Lebanon and the strong Soviet denunciation of the taking of the TWA hostages one of the factors that contributed to a relatively speedy resolution of that crisis? These are difficult questions to answer, but the assumption that Soviet and American cooperation is possible is one that should be fostered. Overt cooperation often is counterproductive, but informal cooperation or even parallel activity can be quite effective, and the Soviet Union should be encouraged to think in these terms.

## Learning from the Soviet Debates

When told that I have been working on a book on Soviet debates about the third world, scholars have often asked whether Soviet work on the third world would be interesting to American specialists in the area. It is a difficult question to answer unless one is a specialist on the American

literature. Certainly many of the ideas of a man such as Nodari Simoniia
seem fresh to many American specialists when told of them, but only a
specialist can judge whether the difficulties of the Marxist jargon and the
limitations imposed by the censorship make the expenditure of time to
read much of Soviet literature worthwhile.[10]

For the reader who, like the author, is not a specialist on the third world
or who is professionally interested only in specialized questions or regions, however, the contents of the Soviet debates are well worth assimilating and pondering. Paradoxically, the old Stalinist orthodoxy that has
been almost universally abandoned in the Soviet Union still retains a
strong hold in the United States, and especially among conservatives.
Some of the most basic insights of the Soviet specialists need to be absorbed into the American body politic.

Recall the Stalin orthodoxy. It insisted that the socialist revolution was
the natural wave of the future in the third world—and at a much earlier
stage of industrialization than in the West—because nationalism would
drive third world politics in this direction. The instrument of revolution
could only be a party organized on Marxist-Leninist principles and accepting Marxism-Leninism as defined in the Soviet Union. Once such a party
won, it would set out on a path that inexorably took it to Soviet-style
socialism. Such a communist regime would, of course, be a faithful Soviet
ally in foreign policy.

Now most Soviet scholars recognize that radical revolutions have been
occurring only in preindustrial societies and that the large third world
countries seem on a long-term capitalist path. They point to the enormous
attraction of Western investment and loans as a major cause of this, for
business people and banks will not put their money in countries where it is
at risk because of radicalism. After Somalia, few Soviet scholars assume
that a third world leader's profession of allegiance to Marxism-Leninism
or "scientific socialism" should necessarily be taken at face value, and
they know that most "vanguard parties" are pale copies of real communist
parties and sometimes are paper organizations. No one believes that radical revolutions inevitably proceed toward Soviet socialism. Indeed, most
Soviet scholars are so eager for major reform of the Soviet economic
system that they do not even advise third world countries to adopt it. After

10. Generally the best Soviet work is not available in Western languages. However,
many of Simoniia's recent ideas are found in his *Destiny of Capitalism in the Orient*
(Moscow: Progress Publishers, 1985); and the journal *Latinskaia Amerika* is translated in a
Spanish-language edition, *America Latina*. It would be interesting to hear from specialists
whether they find such sources useful.

China—and Yugoslavia and Albania and Pol Pot in Kampuchea and even Eastern Europe to a considerable extent—certainly no one thinks that a communist regime will always remain a Soviet ally.

What all Soviet scholars now emphasize is the complexity of the third world. They recognize that religion, ethnic ties, and cultural factors can be as important as—or more important than—economic class in driving politics. The nationalism they now emphasize is not an anti-Westernism that pushes the third world toward the Soviet Union but ethnic nationalism inside a country or the kind of nationalism shown in the Iran-Iraq war that leads countries in directions that neither superpower desires. Terms like "regional centers of power" are entering the Soviet discussions.

There is little in this analysis that will astonish Western third world specialists. They may even be inclined to speak smugly of the disappearance—at last—of ideological blinders in the Soviet Union, although, if the truth be known, both Soviet and Western views have evolved enormously in the last quarter of a century under the pressure of events. But how different this analysis is from that which drives American policy and colors the thinking of a large part of the American public!

Consider the official American doctrine on Central America. It is taken for granted that a Nicaraguan party calling itself Marxist-Leninist is, indeed, inexorably on the Soviet path. (The same assumption was made about Maurice Bishop in Grenada until he was overthrown because of his movement to the center and his attempt—coldly rebuffed—to improve relations with the United States.) The notion is not entertained that the Nicaraguan revolution may be a virulent populist one like the Mexican and that, whatever its name, it might evolve—and be induced to evolve—in the direction of the Mexican one-party system. Instead, the multiparty system of the United States is seen as the only acceptable alternative to a Soviet-type system.

No attention is given to individual differences from country to country in Central America, either in their stage of economic development or in their admission of the majority ethnic group to political power. Instead, it is assumed that a revolution in undeveloped Nicaragua, in which a tiny white minority was dominating the mestizo majority, could easily spread to industrializing Mexico, in which the mestizos were long ago drawn into the ruling party.

Indeed, the thought that Mexico might be a real center of power—the natural great power in Central America—seems quite absent from the

American dialogue about the area. Yet Mexico is a country with 79 million people (the number in Germany or Japan in 1939), and has the industrial base to be a major power. The Contadora process is in a very real sense a way of giving Mexico responsibility for Central America and allowing (and helping) it to tame the Sandinista revolution, but it is never discussed in these terms. The Contadora process thus becomes the "soft" alternative rather than the hard-nosed geopolitical solution that it really is.

Least of all does the United States have the sense that domestic policy can be separated from foreign policy in a socialist regime. Americans seem extremely afraid that the Soviet Union could "Finlandize" solidly capitalist countries in Western Europe (that is, make their foreign policy accommodating without changing their domestic system), but they have no sense that they might Finlandize a Nicaragua, let alone a Cuba. Americans have little of the sense of Soviet scholars about the power of Western investment and the multinational corporation and their ability eventually to moderate a Central American revolution after negotiations (and the threat of force) moderate its foreign policy.

The United States has been extraordinarily slow in abandoning the set of perceptions that underlay the Stalinist orthodoxy, and Central America provides only the most visible example. (The United States fought a ten-year war in Vietnam without either hawks or doves realizing that the revolution was directed against the ethnic Chinese middle class in Vietnamese cities as much as against the West.) The United States has also been extraordinarily slow in thinking through its growing realization that the costs of military intervention in the third world almost always outweigh the benefits. It no longer is willing to fight in Lebanon and Nicaragua—and rightly so—but it builds a huge navy that has little other purpose. It has not comprehended that military expenditures that produce high interest rates undercut the American national security in the third world far more than the Soviet Union does.

## Gorbachev and the Future

It is vital that these outdated assumptions be rethought. Many Americans have the comfortable feeling that the Soviet Union is in an irreversible decline. Would that it be so. The selection of the young Mikhail Gorbachev as general secretary and the unprecedented urgency of his demands for economic reforms suggests, however, that the Soviet leadership is determined to reverse the decline. Gorbachev, who will only be sixty-nine years of age in the year 2000, surely has the hope of ushering in the new century in triumph.

For Gorbachev to do so, very fundamental changes are necessary. Nothing seems as anachronistic as the American fear of 1960 that the Soviet Union might become a technological equal. In fact, the Soviet Union has fallen further behind the West in the computer age and also behind Japan and even advanced third world countries such as South Korea, Taiwan, and Mexico. The Soviet technological lag has many devastating consequences. It lies behind the lack of appeal of the Soviet economic system in the third world. It threatens to erode the Soviet military position further as the world's armies begin the transition to computerized conventional weapons. And, of course, if the American space defense initiative and the Chinese modernization were actually to succeed, the results would be disastrous unless the Soviet Union were able to modernize as well. If the Soviet population gains the sense that the Soviet system dooms Russia to second-class status, the regime will become as unstable as the Polish regime because it will have lost its crucial identification with Russian nationalism.

The Soviet economists who have been discussed in this book have a very clear and strong belief about what is necessary to promote economic growth and technological advance in a developing country. They are convinced that an attack on protectionism and integration into the world economy is vital. They have seen the results produced in East Asia when governments have created conditions to force manufacturers to export technology. If the United States has not assimilated the implications of developments in the third world, there is every danger that Gorbachev has. One of his closest advisers has been Aleksandr Iakovlev, the former director of IMEMO, who has been quoted in these pages and who has been making the case for reform and a change in foreign policy.

At a minimum, Gorbachev has been told—indeed, he has not had to be told—the Brezhnev policy of trying to rely on imported technology with which Soviet manufacturers do not have to compete has essentially been a failure. He has been told that the Soviet Union needs to follow the third world in having greater integration into the world economy and that the strategy causing the least drastic reforms in the planning mechanism is the East Asian one of encouraging exports. He has been told—and told correctly—that only if Soviet industry is compelled to export technology will it be compelled to produce goods of a sophistication, quality, and efficient cost that meet world standards for the domestic market as well.

A Soviet integration into the world market has enormous implications for foreign policy. It will require a far greater integration of Russia into world civilization—an opening of Russia to the outside world—for only in that way will Soviet businessmen and salesmen have the necessary feel for the foreign market and how to operate in it. The problem is not only one of opening to the West. The Soviet Union should be exporting technology to the Middle East and using its own Moslem population as sales personnel. This would require them to have a feel for Middle East culture and practices.

In many respects, an evolution of the Soviet Union in the direction of accepting the international order and becoming an increasingly "normal" power in international relations is to be welcomed. However, the most logical way of pushing such a monumental change through against the opposition of Soviet conservatives is to emphasize its necessity for defense reasons against the United States, to play down the attempt to focus relations on the United States, and to open to the West by focusing on Western Europe, Japan, and the major third world countries.

An expert strategy will be directed first at the third world. A country with inferior technology must compete with low costs, and that will produce dumping charges in the West. A moderate third world policy would open many more congenial markets. Already the Soviet Union is foregoing support of communist rebels in the Philippines and is courting Marcos (Gorbachev met Mrs. Marcos at Chernenko's funeral and awarded President Marcos a medal). It has also established diplomatic relations with Oman and is engaged in sports diplomacy with Saudi Arabia.

Such a multipolar policy would not always be comforting for the United States. A Soviet Union that gave back the disputed islands to Japan and opened its markets to Japanese investment would have an important impact on geopolitical realities in the Pacific. A Soviet Union that (correctly) concluded that it does not even have an interest in a military victory in Western Europe because a communist Italy, a communist France, let alone a united communist Germany, would be a greater political threat than capitalist countries in Europe since they might make changes in military posture that would really shake the American-European alliance. A Soviet Union that relied less on small radical states and played geopolitical international relations with the major "capitalist" third world countries might effectively support an Argentina in a Falklands war or cooperate more vigorously with India against a Pakistan that harbors Afghan rebels.

With such a multipolar policy and an increasing openness to the outside world, the Soviet Union would really leave the postwar period as we have known it. The United States too would have to leave the postwar era if it were to compete effectively. It will not be easy. At a time when Ronald Reagan was already in his late twenties, the United States was essentially a regional power, with its president trying in vain to involve the country in international politics to restrain German aggression. Then, as in World War I and in the postwar period as well, the appeal that was used to break the United States out of its isolationism was the need to enlist in a struggle of good against evil.

As a consequence, the American elite and the American public have gained little of the perspective on international relations that is acquired in a long history of involvement with countries that are equals. They have never really accepted that conflict in international relations is inevitable, that other countries' pursuit of their interests is normal and should not lead to moral outrage. The ambiguities of combining cooperation and conflict that were implied in détente (which always was a much more limited concept than the friendship of entente) was simply not tolerable in the politics of the 1970s.

Since the United States has been winning the competition with the Soviet Union, it has had little reason to change its approach. If, however, the Soviet Union becomes a "normal" power and a more effective actor in international relations, the United States too will have to become a more "normal" participant in the international system as well. In no area will this be more difficult than in the third world because of the multifaceted nature of the competition and the instability of the countries in it. If we can move beyond the lack of confidence embodied in our pre-Vietnam and post-Vietnam syndromes, if we can accept the complexities and ambiguities of the third world already understood by scholars both in the Soviet Union and the United States, if we can come to understand the strength of the economic cards in our own hands, there is no reason that we cannot compete as effectively in the post-postwar era as in the postwar one.

# Index

Afghanistan, 2, 24, 276–77
Africa: five-stage model of historical development applied to, 43, 46; military intervention by superpower allies, 278; proletariat in, 154; southern Africa, U.S. policies re, 246–48; vanguard parties in, 166–67
Agaev, Semen, 179–80, 250
Agrarian reforms, 155–56
Aleksandrov, Georgii, 196–97
Aleksandrov-Agentov, Andrei, 266
Alexander, Robert, 240
Algeria, 4, 5
Allende, Salvador, 25, 137, 171–72
Andreev, Igor, 48
Andropov, Yuri, 16
Arbatov, Georgii, 114–15, 211–12, 214, 220, 221, 242, 280
Argentina, 97, 250
Asia: five-stage model of historical development applied to, 40–41; national liberation movements in, 149
Asiatic mode of production, 40–41; domestic implications of, 46–47; interpretations of, 47–48; reemergence of, 45–46; rejection of, 48; in the third world, 135
Association of Political Science, 122
Asymmetrical character of mutual dependence, 233, 255
Ataturk, Kemal, 113, 143, 145, 226

Balabushevich, Vladimir, 112, 113, 118, 152, 227
Bechin, A. I., 72–73
Bernstein, Eduard, 105
Bevan, Aneurin, 200
Biafran secession, 146

Bishop, Maurice, 282
Bohlen, Charles, 200, 201
Bonapartist states, 135–36
Bourgeois democracies, 119–20, 137–39, 174–75
Bourgeoisie, definition of, 118
Bourgeois nationalists, 144, 145, 147–48, 229–30; definitions of, 152–53
Bourgeois nationalization, 109–10
Bourgeois state: Lenin's analysis of, 105–06. *See also* Western political systems
Bovin, Aleksandr, 208, 218, 222
Brazil, 239–40
Brest-Litovsk, Treaty of, 194
Brezhnev, Leonid I., 15–16, 187, 214
Brown, Archie, 125
Brutents, Karen, 236
Brzezinski, Zbigniew, 239
Bukhara, 167
Bulganin, Nikolai, 229
Burdzhalov, Eduard, 194
Bureaucratic bourgeoisie, 132–33
Burlatsky, Fedor, 61–62, 120, 121, 123, 203, 204
Business cycles, Soviet interpretation of, 72–73
Bykov, Oleg, 215

Capitalism: depression, prediction of, 72–74, 77; in five-stage model of historical development, 43; "general crisis" in, 74; growth in, Soviet explanation for, 72–74; in multistructural society, 57–58; objective laws of, 199; in third world, Soviet acceptance of need for, 100–01; third world economic

287